A HISTORY
OF THE
ANGLO-SAXONS

I. DRINKING-HORN FROM TAPLOW ON THE THAMES

A HISTORY
OF THE
ANGLO-SAXONS

By

R. H. HODGKIN

THIRD EDITION

VOL. I

OXFORD UNIVERSITY PRESS
LONDON: GEOFFREY CUMBERLEGE
1952

Oxford University Press, Amen House, London E.C. 4

GLASGOW NEW YORK TORONTO MELBOURNE WELLINGTON
BOMBAY CALCUTTA MADRAS CAPE TOWN

Geoffrey Cumberlege, Publisher to the University

First edition 1935
Second edition 1940

Reprinted photographically in Great Britain in 1952
by LOWE & BRYDONE, PRINTERS, LTD., LONDON, from
corrected sheets of the first edition

PREFACE TO THIRD EDITION

SINCE June 1939, when the second edition of this book was published, archaeological finds have added much to our knowledge of the period with which it deals. Of these, by far the most important is that of the ship-burial at Sutton Hoo in September 1939. Had I been in better health, and living within reach of libraries, I should have incorporated a description of these finds into this edition of my history, and endeavoured to bring the text up to date.

As things are, I have been most fortunate in obtaining the help and advice of Mr. R. L. S. Bruce-Mitford, who has not only supplied an Appendix on the Sutton Hoo excavation but has also suggested small changes in the text, which it has been possible to incorporate and which help to bring it more into line with recent work.

R. H. H.

1951

PREFACE TO THE SECOND EDITION

I HAVE endeavoured to bring this second edition up to date, and to correct mistakes noticed in the first edition. Some changes which I should have liked to make have been impracticable owing to the photographic process used in reproducing the book; but the notes of the first volume have been entirely reset. The changes are naturally most numerous in the earlier chapters, since these deal with the darkest period. Here the views of Professor R. G. Collingwood and Mr. J. N. L. Myres, in their book *Roman Britain and the Saxon Settlements*, published in 1936, are especially noteworthy. For example, on the interesting question when exactly the Romans left Britain, Professor Collingwood has changed his opinion and has argued that the Romans, after the withdrawal of their main army by Constantine III, sent over new levies which about 417 for a few years reoccupied the south-east of our island.* Strong support for this theory has also come from Mr. C. H. V. Sutherland, who has examined the coin evidence in a valuable work *The Coinage and Currency of Roman Britain*. In my text I have called attention to other attractive speculations with which Professor Collingwood entertains his readers, such as his theory that 'Arthur was in effect the *Comes Britanniarum*'.

Mr. Myres's story of the Settlement, I am glad to say, does not differ fundamentally from that which is given in the following pages. Being both an archaeologist and an historian he is well equipped for writing in due time an authoritative treatise on this perplexing subject. The studies of Saxon pottery which he has contributed to learned periodicals now give the discussion a firmer foundation. One of the new ideas offered us by Mr. Myres is a theory that the name 'Northumbrians' was passed into circulation by Bede, and that the original name for them, the 'Humbrenses' (Mr. Myres always keeps it in this Latin form), covered the settlers in Lindsey and the Trent valley as

* See below, p. 55.

well as those north of the Humber. He may be right about the name, but his argument that Mercia was 'a dependent offspring of the Humbrenses' leaves me unconvinced. When Nennius said that Penda 'first separated the kingdom of the Mercians from the kingdom of the Northerners', he was presumably thinking only of Mercia's escape from temporary conquest. It was a confused way to put it, but Nennius was a confused writer.

With reference to another point of Mr. Myres',* I see that my own views about Cerdic's invasion were not made sufficiently clear. Since it has not been possible to remedy this in the text, I must explain here why in my opinion the dearth of place-names of an early type in Wiltshire and Hampshire is no more fatal to a belief in the general story of the Chronicle than is the dearth of archaeological evidence. The reason why Cerdic's war bands left few or no traces of their existence in the place-names of southern England is, I think, the fact that they remained a fighting force and did not become farmers like the invaders to the east of them. I conceive that there was a long phase when they lived chiefly on the tribute or spoil of the Britons—'a phase when they were hill-dwellers before they . . . settled down to plough the heavy soil of the valleys'.† I certainly did not mean to suggest that the war bands of Cerdic were 'the main mass of the West Saxon people'; but if they were only, as Mr. Myres says,‡ 'a single family and its retainers', how could they have defeated a king of Kent?

In the four years since my book was published, the study of these early centuries has been advanced by other works besides those of Professor Collingwood and Mr. Myres. Perhaps the most notable of them is Mr. T. D. Kendrick's *Survey of Anglo-Saxon Art*. This has shown me that I had left gaps in my references to that subject. In order to call attention to the chief of these and to illustrate how Mr. Kendrick has enriched our

* Op. cit., p. 401.

† Cf. below, pp. 131–2 and 135; also the introduction to *The Place-Names of Wiltshire*, vol. xvi of the English Place-Name Society, a volume published since this preface was written. ‡ Op. cit., p. 399. Cf. p. 402.

knowledge of Saxon art, I have, with his and Messrs. Methuen's permission, reproduced in this edition his Plate of the shaft at Codford St. Peter, a sculpture which he assigns to the reign of Ethelwulf. I have also accepted his dates for the crosses. Though these dates are admittedly tentative, they must be treated with respect, since in arriving at them he has related the ornamentation of the crosses to that of the illuminated manuscripts.

Mention should also be made of the Ordnance Survey Map of England in the Dark Ages. After comparing my sketch-maps with it I have made such corrections as I could. Since the maps which were printed with colour could not well be altered, I have called attention in my notes to the chief changes which I should have liked to make.

Lastly, I offer my thanks to those to whom I am indebted for corrections made in this edition. Foremost among these are Professor F. P. Magoun, the Rev. Father P. Grosjean, and the Rev. E. C. Ratcliff. Apologies for things left undone must accompany thanks. For example, Professor Magoun has pressed me to substitute 'The Old English Annals' for the familiar but inaccurate descriptions which I use—'the Chronicle', 'the Saxon Chronicle', &c. This is one of the changes which, though desirable, have not been practicable.

PREFACE

DURING the last thirty years, while important advances have been made in the study of Anglo-Saxon history, there has, I think, been some loss of general interest in the subject. The Victorians turned with zest to the Saxon period because Stubbs, Freeman, and Green showed them there the dawn of English democracy. Now, however, the colour has faded; and democracy, both the primitive and the modern varieties of it, has lost its glamour. It is left to the Germans to idealize the virtues—but not the liberties—of our Nordic ancestors. In this island it too often happens that our history is made to start only at the conquest of England by the Norman-French, and that our Germanic ancestors, the Æthelberhts, the Ælfgifus, and the rest, are regarded as uncouth, like their names. But even if we have no wish to seek our ideals or our politics in the Dark Ages, the Anglo-Saxon dawn should never be a subject of indifference to us. That is a general excuse for this book; a special one is that the Anglo-Saxon period of English History more than any other needs to be retold. During the last decades old views—especially those about the Saxon conquest of Britain—have been challenged. Mr. E. T. Leeds and others, 'drawing their conclusions from the more perfected methods of archaeology', have argued that the early annals of the Saxon Chronicle are incredible. Important work has also been done in other directions. Professor Chadwick has offered us new interpretations of the constitutional data. Armies of philologists, both here and abroad, have joined battle over the problems of Old English literature. Other valuable work has been done on the place-names, the charters, and the art of the Anglo-Saxons. There has been a definite strengthening of knowledge all along the line. In the following pages I attempt to adjust the new views and the old.

I have kept in my mind the needs of students, including students of the Old English language, who wish to understand the background of its literature. At the same time I hope there may be other readers ready to endure the more arid tracts of pre-Norman history in order to learn what may now be believed about the beginnings of our Germanic forefathers, our monarchy, our Church, our literature, and our art.

I have focused on the great men and the big subjects—the Conquest, the Conversion, the results of the Conversion, the success of the Southerners in the struggle for supremacy, the Viking invasions, the life and beliefs of the people. My choice of the great men has necessarily been determined by the fullness of our information about them. It is fortunate that the layman whom it is possible to know most intimately was also, it seems, the greatest of all—King Alfred. He must be the centre in any picture of Saxon times. Accordingly the story of England before the Norman Conquest divides into two parts. The first leads up to Alfred, and this is contained in the present volumes: the second follows the influence of Alfred and that of the Danes who during his reign made their home in England, and this I hope to narrate in a sequel.

There are features of the book which need defence. My readers will, I trust, agree that the dearth of written authorities is reason enough for making the fullest use of illustrations. At the same time I must confess that my illustrations vary greatly in evidential value. The modern 'reconstructions' are sometimes open to criticism. There is still much difference of opinion about some of the objects illustrated; for instance, the Lindisfarne Gospels. Others, like the drawings of the Utrecht Psalter, which can now be analysed with some certainty, are composite productions, in which features derived from different centuries are blended. The maps also unavoidably contain more guess-work than I like. I have tried to give guidance on many of these points in my notes.

Something must also be said about the plan of the book. My experience in teaching this early history has shown me that beginners are often baffled by the strange names. I have therefore deliberately abstained from crowding my pages with the record of kings and others who can never be much more than names. This policy may have led me to do less than justice to certain parts of the subject, such as the history of Mercia, but some of the gaps thus left are filled in the genealogical and chronological tables at the end of Vol. II. I have written at some length because I believe that students thrive best when they are not brought up on too condensed a historical diet.

Throughout the book, alike in my figures, my maps, and my text, I have acted on the principle that an approximation to the truth is better than a complete blank. This principle is far-reaching; but I fear that it will not cover all my statements on the highly controversial subjects which thrust themselves forward in this period. Since a general historian, who has to assemble the parts made by specialists, is obliged to cut and shape those parts before they can be made to fit, it is, I fear, inevitable that he should make mistakes. And apart from the fallibility of the human worker, it has also to be admitted that Saxon archaeology has not yet attained to a high degree of scientific security. In so far as the following pages rest on its dicta, or what I have taken to be such, they must be regarded as nothing more than an interim report.

ACKNOWLEDGEMENTS

One great difficulty of a synthesis is that of acknowledging fully indebtedness to other works without over-weighting the text with an apparatus of notes. The references at the end of each volume will, I hope, sufficiently indicate the books which I have used; but I must here acknowledge more generally my debt to the works of the late Professor G. Baldwin Brown, of Edinburgh; to Professor H. M. Chadwick, of Cambridge; and to Professor F. M. Stenton, of Reading. There are others who have kindly helped me by their advice as well as by their writings; and among these I must specially mention Mr. E. T. Leeds, Keeper of the Ashmolean Museum; Mr. T. D. Kendrick, of the British

Museum; Dr. R. E. M. Wheeler, Keeper of the London Museum; Professor Roeder, of Göttingen; and Professor R. G. Collingwood, of Pembroke College, Oxford. In view of the uncertainties of the subject I need scarcely add that some at any rate of them will think that I have erred in what I have written about the Saxon Conquest.

The list of those who have been good enough to answer my questions on all kinds of points is a long one. It includes: Miss M. V. Taylor, Miss M. H. Longhurst, the Provost of University College, London (Dr. Allen Mawer), Dr. E. C. Curwen, Mr. T. C. Lethbridge, Mr. J. P. Bushe-Fox, Mr. R. G. de Beer, Dr. Gudmund Hatt, and Dr. Hans Kjær, of the National Museum, Copenhagen. Those whom I have pestered in an attempt to make my maps reproduce as far as possible the natural features of the Dark Ages are the following: Major Gordon Fowler, Dr. Gordon Ward, Mr. R. Rainbird Clarke, Mr. C. E. Stevens, Dr. H. Schütte of the Landesverein Oldenburg für Heimat-kunde und Heimatschutz, and Dr. H. Hesmer of the Forstliche Hochschule, Eberswalde. My questions to the last two were about the coastline and the forest conditions of North Germany in the fifth century; and I much regret that I was unable to follow up the information which they gave me, so that my map of North Germany is still not all that I could wish. To this list I must add the name of Dr. G. B. Grundy, Fellow of Corpus Christi College, Oxford, who kindly copied for my map of the Athelney campaign his own map of trackways indicated by Saxon charters; and also the name of Mr. O. G. S. Crawford, of the Ordnance Survey. It has been unfortunate for me that the projected Ordnance Survey map of Anglo-Saxon England has not appeared before this book goes to press. When it does appear, it will, of course, be the standard map which should be used by all students of the Saxon period; and I can only hope that my own maps will be found roughly to agree with it.

I am under obligations of a different kind to the many authors and publishers and others who by their kind permission have enabled me to make this book well illustrated. My thanks, even when unexpressed, must be read into my List of Figures. In this preface it is right that I should thank Miss E. D. Brinton, Mr. E. W. Oldham, and the members of the Staff of the Clarendon Press who have made drawings for the book; Mr. C. D. Waterhouse, of the British Museum, on whose sketches most of my coloured plates are based; and others who have helped me to obtain photographs and the like, namely: Miss M. P. Ramsay, of the Fine Art Department of Edinburgh University; Dr. C. Rothmann, of the Schleswig-Holsteinisches Museum, Kiel; Mr. H. St. George Grey, Curator of the Somerset County Museum; Mr. Norman Cook, of the Maidstone Museum; Mr. C. W. Pugh, of the Devizes Museum; the Rev. E. C. Ratcliff, of Queen's College, Oxford; and Mr. J. E. Hodgkin, of Darlington.

In the next place I must thank the publishers who have allowed me to quote from their publications: Messrs. G. Bell & Sons, the Cambridge University Press, Messrs. Chatto & Windus, Messrs. J. M. Dent & Sons, Messrs. Longmans, Green & Co., and the Society for the Promotion of Christian Knowledge. My obligations to the authors I have acknowledged in my notes.

Finally, I am deeply indebted to Mr. C. L. Wrenn, who devoted part of his summer holiday in 1932 to reading and criticizing this book in manuscript; and of those who have given me the greatest help of all there is no need to say anything in public.

R. H. H.

April 1935

CONTENTS

VOLUME I

VOLUME II

LIST OF PLATES

VOL. I

The passage is as follows:

In illo tempore Saxones invalescebant in multitudine et crescebant in Brittannia. Mortuo autem Hengisto Octha filius eius transivit de sinistrali parte Brittanniae ad regnum Cantorum et de ipso orti sunt reges Cantorum. Tunc Arthur pugnabat contra illos in illis diebus cum regibus Brittonum, sed ipse dux erat bellorum. Primum bellum fuit in ostium fluminis quod dicitur Glein. Secundum et tertium et quartum et quintum super aliud flumen, quod dicitur Dubglas et est in regione Linnuis. Sextum bellum super flumen, quod vocatur Bassas. Septimum fuit bellum in silva Celidonis, id est Cat Coit Celidon. Octavum fuit bellum in castello Guinnion, in quo Arthur portavit imaginem sanctae Mariae perpetuae virginis super humeros suos et pagani versi sunt in fugam in illo die et cedes magna fuit super illos per virtutem domini nostri Iesu Christi et per virtutem sanctae Mariae virginis genitricis eius. Nonum bellum gestum est in urbe Legionis. Decimum gessit bellum in litore fluminis, quod vocatur Tribruit. Undecimum factum est bellum in monte, qui dicitur Agned. Duodecimum fuit bellum in Monte Badonis, in quo corruerunt in uno die nongenti sexaginta viri de uno impetu Arthur: [et nemo prostravit eos nisi ipse solus, et in omnibus bellis victor extitit].

VOL. II

MONOCHROME PLATES
which were in colour in first and second editions

VOL. I

VOL. II

is Early Christian. Top right, ring of Ethelswith, daughter of Ethelwulf, wife of Burhred, King of Mercia; inscribed (inside) +EAÐELSVIÐ REGÞA. The animal on the bezel is intended to be an Agnus Dei.

Centre, Dowgate Hill brooch with enamel figure. Its workmanship is better than that of the Alfred Jewel, and is probably of the tenth century. Below, the Alfred Jewel. Legend round the side: +AELFRED MEC HEHT GEWYRCAN (Alfred ordered me to be made). Almost every aspect of the jewel is a subject of controversy: its purpose, the signification of the enamelled figure, of the engraving on the back, and of the monster's head. Cf. J. Earle, *The Alfred Jewel*. From a drawing by Mr. C. O. Waterhouse. The Alfred Jewel is in the Ashmolean Museum, Oxford. The others in British Museum . . . *Facing page* 671

LIST OF TEXT FIGURES

(† = Headpiece or Tailpiece)

VOL. I

VOL. II

LIST OF MAPS

VOL. I

I

THE ANGLES AND SAXONS IN GERMANY

DRIFT TOWARDS THE WEST

THE subject of this book is the history of the Angles and Saxons from the time when they are first mentioned among the German tribes. We shall be following the main stream in the rise of the English, that which gave them their name, their speech, and their fundamental institutions; but in doing so we shall obtain some ideas about the course of other tributaries to our nation, Celtic, Roman, Danish, and Norwegian.

If we seek out the original England of the continental Angles, we must go to the district of Angel,* in the Cimbric, that is the Danish, peninsula. Whatever its original extent, Angel is now only a small district, a part of Schleswig. It is no bigger

HEADPIECE.—Destruction of a German village by Roman soldiers. From the Column of Marcus Aurelius at Rome. Reconstructed.

* Spelt in German *Angeln*.

than an average English county, stretching for some forty miles along the Baltic coast between the Flensburg fiord and the Schlei. In this old 'England' there is still much to make those of us who belong to the new England of Britain feel at home. Not only do the faces of the men and women constantly remind us of types to be seen in the Anglian districts of our island, but by some chance the appearance of the land itself, with its irregular fields and hedgerows and undulating well-timbered country, is also what we should call typically English.

The emigrants to Britain preserved, at least from the time of Bede, a continuous tradition that their forefathers dwelt in these lands before they came to Britain. The passage in Bede's history in which this is stated as a fact must ever remain the starting-point for investigation into the continental homes of our race:[1]

'Those who came over were of the three most powerful nations in Germany—Saxons, Angles, and Jutes. From the Jutes are descended the people of Kent and of the Isle of Wight and those in the province of the West Saxons who are to this day called Jutes, seated opposite to the Isle of Wight. From the Saxons, that is, from that region which is now called Old Saxony, came the East Saxons, the South Saxons, and the West Saxons. From the Angles, that is, from that country which is called Angul* and which is said from that time to the present day to have remained deserted (between the provinces of the Jutes and the Saxons) are descended the East Angles, the Midland Angles, the Mercians, all the race of the Northumbrians . . . and the other nations of the Angles.'

No passage in Bede has evoked more controversy. One recent writer[2] has argued that Bede's statements are unreliable since they were 'in a great measure founded only on conclusions drawn from similarities of names'. We are told that Bede blundered both when he implied that the Jutes came from Jutland, and also when he asserted that the Angles came from the district of Angul.

* Latin *Angulus*.

In the present chapter our chief object will be to test and supplement Bede's statement about the Angles and Saxons, leaving on one side the problem who were the Jutes until we come to the Jutish settlement in Kent. We shall try to supplement Bede in two directions. In the first place we shall seek for information on questions such as what were the relations between the tribes along the Germanic seaboard; what was the determining cause that brought these Germans to Britain; and by what stages and by what routes they were drawn towards our island. Afterwards we shall try to find out what these 'barbarians' were like; how they were armed, how clothed, and what were their gods.

The chief contributions to these subjects in recent years have come from archaeologists, and it is on archaeology that we shall have to place our hopes of learning more about these matters than has usually been told us in text-books. But before we can understand the bearing of the archaeological evidence we must, as a preliminary, set out some of the fragmentary and confusing information which comes to us from Greek and Latin writers.

Let us then begin with Tacitus' well-known division of the 'Germans' (really the West Germans only) into three groups, and with the identification of the group called the Ingaevones as that which comprised the tribes spread out along the coast of the North Sea, the tribes which spoke the Germanic dialects commonly described as 'Anglo-Frisian'. About the position of some of these tribes at the end of the first century of our era when Tacitus wrote his *Germania* there is no serious doubt. The Frisians were the inhabitants of modern Friesland, and the Chauci, praised by Tacitus as 'the noblest of the German race', were on the coast between the Ems and the Elbe.

It is unfortunate that the position of the tribes among whom the Anglii are enumerated is not made clear beyond dispute. Tacitus mentions the Lombards as situated apparently on the lower Elbe. 'Next come the Reudigni, Aviones, Anglii, Varini, Eudoses [and others]. . . . They are fenced in by rivers and forests. None of these tribes have any noteworthy features except their common worship of Nerthus, who is the same as Mother Earth.' Tacitus describes the island of the ocean, where is the sacred grove of the cult, and ends with the remark that 'this branch of the Suevi stretches into the remoter regions of Germany'. But what was the principle on which Tacitus was

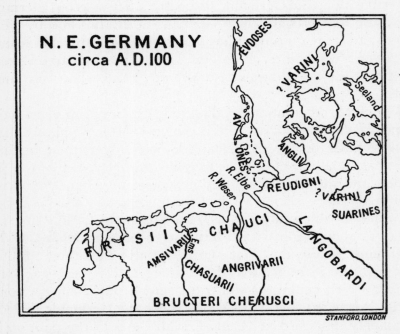

N. E. GERMANY
circa A.D. 100

EVDOSES
? VARINI
Seeland
AVIONES
ANGLII
R. Elbe
R. Weser
REUDIGNI
? VARINI
SUARINES
F R I S I I
CHAUCI
LANGOBARDI
AMSIVARII
Ems
CHASUARII
ANGRIVARII
BRUCTERI CHERUSCI

STANFORD, LONDON

enumerating these tribes? Was he working from south to north? If we accept this, the most reasonable assumption,[3] we must look for the Reudigni beyond, that is to the north of, the Elbe, and then for the Aviones, the Anglii and the Eudoses (? Jutes) up the Cimbric peninsula.

But the Saxons? For the first mention of these we must go to Ptolemy, who, writing about the middle of the second century, places them 'on the neck of the Cimbric peninsula', that is presumably in Holstein. The great puzzle is to know how to explain the failure of Tacitus to mention the Saxons. Shall we by a simple equation say that they are the Reudigni and some of their neighbours? If so, the name 'Saxons' even from the first was a group-name for an alliance of tribes—a group-name like that of the Franks (the spearmen) and that of the Alemans (the men of all kinds), great Germanic confederacies which

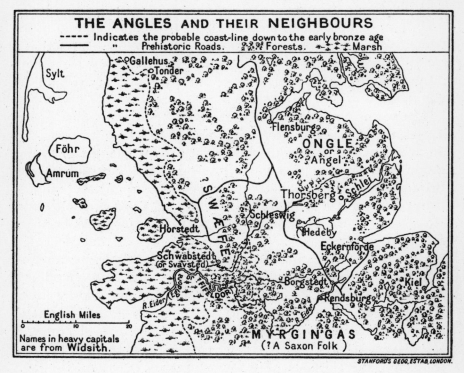

THE ANGLES AND THEIR NEIGHBOURS

Names in heavy capitals are from Widsith.

appear in the second century, the one on the lower, the other on the upper, Rhine. It is natural to suppose that this group-name like the others had a meaning; and scholars are fairly well agreed that the Saxons were so called because they were the users of the *seax* or *sahs*, a short one-handled sword.

The map above indicates what seems to have been the position of the Angles and their neighbours three centuries after Tacitus. It shows how in prehistoric times the settlements of the Angles, though mainly on the middle of the peninsula and

round the inlet from the Baltic called the Schlei, were within
easy reach of good harbours giving access to the North Sea,
so long as the marshland of the lower Eider was navigable
for light craft. On the strength of a place-name it is suggested[4]
that the next-door neighbours of the Angles, that is the people
who lived on the western seaboard, were called the Swæfe,
and that it was the union of these two small communities
which gave the Angles their 'window to the west'. A reference
to this union is made in *Widsith*, one of the earliest extant poems
in the English language; and to this we shall return later in
the chapter.

The point to notice is that the Angles, though hemmed in on
a narrow peninsula and forced by nature to take to the sea, had
an excellent position, with one good harbour facing east to the
Baltic and another facing west towards the North Sea and
Britain. The Eider, which lay between them and the Saxons,
being a navigable river, must have brought the two folks into
close connexion. They were bound to be either great enemies
or allies.

How exactly it came about that the two peoples became so
intimately linked to one another that in our own island the
Angles were called Saxons by strangers and the Saxons were
content to call themselves Angles and to speak of their language
as English can never be explained by any records of history.*
Of written records indeed there are scarcely any. If we try
to sketch the outlines of what happened between the time
of Tacitus and the migration to Britain, we have to give our
attention to the theories of the archaeologists, and to these we
must now turn.

In the study of primitive peoples scientific archaeology has
of course to depend mainly on the evidence provided by their
burial customs. Now the peoples of northern Germany at the
time of the migration to Britain, and for many centuries before
that, had as a rule followed the custom of cremating their dead.

* See below, pp. 157–61.

They had placed the ashes and what was left of the brooches and buckles which had fastened the clothes of the dead body when it was placed on the fire, in an urn, either an elaborately ornamented urn made for the purpose, or else any cooking-pot

FIG. 1. Typical Saxon and Anglian urns of the first and second centuries (according to Plettke). *Above.* From Bornhöved, Holstein. ¼. *Below.* From Nottfeld, Schleswig. ¼.

which might be handy. Since the fashions in urns, and to a less extent in brooches also, varied from region to region and changed like any other fashion, it may be possible with their evidence to fix the distribution of a tribe and to follow its movements. The most interesting attempt as yet published to detect in this way the distribution and the expansion of our Anglo-Saxon ancestors is that made by A. Plettke, a young German who was killed in the Great War. Plettke claimed that the type of urn to be identified as that of the Anglo-Saxon section of the Ingaevones is one found during the first two centuries of our era in the cemeteries of west Holstein and southern Schleswig. Two cremation urns from this district assigned to this period are shown in Fig. 1. The type is differentiated both by its shape and by its ornamentation with 'hatched triangles'.

Now the fact that the Angles and Saxons in their original homes resembled one another in their funeral fashions is certainly significant, especially in view of the contrasts between their urns and those of their neighbours: the handled urns of the Lombards to the south, and the few and poorly ornamented urns of the Chauci across the Elbe.

A story can be extracted from the changes—or what Plettke takes to be the changes—occurring in the urn-fields during the next centuries. While those of the Angles in Schleswig and those of the Saxons in west Holstein seem for the most part to have been used continuously down to about A.D. 500, the great Lombardic cemeteries near the lower Elbe came to an end about A.D. 200. These folk who buried their dead in the handled urns disappear. What had happened? Presumably they had packed their families and scanty goods into their wagons and, driving their herds before them, had set off on their long wanderings seeking—who knows?—richer lands, the spoil of the south, a place in the sun. At any rate the Lombards passed away. Their old neighbours, the Saxons, remained on the neck of the Cimbric peninsula. For some hundreds of years after the Lombards had vanished from the scene these Saxons continued to plough the lands of north Germany.

The changes to be detected west of the Elbe in the lands of the Chauci concern us more closely. Here, says Plettke, none of the earlier cemeteries are continued into the period of the later Roman Empire, but all the cemeteries of that period seem to begin about A.D. 200. Moreover, the characteristic urns of these new cemeteries are similar to those of west Holstein.

PLATE 1

Early fourth century—one type

Later fourth century—narrower in
the mouth and more spherical

From about 400—many are stamped

During the fifth century bosses and moulded feet come into fashion

SOME SAXON URNS OF THE FOURTH AND FIFTH CENTURIES ($\frac{1}{4}$)

(*After* PLETTKE)

PLATE 2

A and *B*. Oldendorf-Weissenmoor, near Stade; window urn. ⅜

C. Wester-Wanna; spout-handled urn.
About ¼

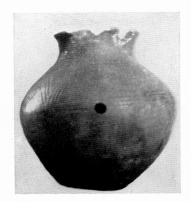

D. Wester-Wanna; holed urn.
About ⅐

PECULIAR URNS FROM THE ELBE-WESER REGION

The conclusion which he draws is obvious. The Chauci—
or most of them—had migrated, and the Saxons, having overrun the lands about Hamburg formerly possessed by the Lombards, had drifted still farther west to take the place of the
Chauci, or absorb what was left of them. On the spits of higher

FIG. 2. Issendorf, near Stade; Saxon urn, *c*. 450.
The boar on the lid is the only excavated sculpture
of the early Saxons.

ground which lie between the marshes of the Elbe and those
of the Weser the Saxons seem to have found a promised land.
The soil was light and easily worked. There were open spaces
free from the endless trees which made so much of the interior
of Germany hard to colonize. In this region between the Elbe
and the Weser the Saxons increased and multiplied. We know
of no less than sixty urn-fields, many of them very large—that
at Wester-wanna, the only one which has been completely
excavated, yielding no less than four thousand urns.

It is still impossible to say with any finality whether those

North Germans who were packed so closely on the cultivable land between the Elbe and the Weser were composed mainly of descendants of the Chauci, the tribe once belauded by Tacitus, or whether they were, as Plettke and others have argued, immigrant Saxons from beyond the Elbe.[5]

Whatever view we take about the origin of the so-called 'Saxons' who were so thickly strewn in the lands between the Elbe and the Weser, one fact indicated by their cemeteries need not be questioned. These lands clearly did not give enough elbow-room for so prolific a people. Crowded out from this district, their overflow can be traced farther to the west. The lands between the Weser and the Ems, though barren or swampy, have some traces of them.[6] But west of the Ems, that is in Frisia, their urns and brooches reappear in some numbers.

Such are some of the conclusions drawn by Plettke from the cemeteries of north Germany. Once more we must protest that these conclusions are quoted here not because they are to be received as a sure and ascertained truth, but because they illustrate the kind of story which may finally emerge from the testing fire of controversy.

In recent years some important contributions to the subject have been made by the German archaeologist F. Roeder. He has studied with exemplary thoroughness the development and distribution first of one type of urn or brooch then of another, bringing within his survey both the cemeteries of the continental Saxons and those of the migrants to Britain. The reader will find in the illustrations specimens of the peculiar vessels and of certain brooches which appear on the Continent and then reappear in Britain: the pots with perforated handles,* strange vessels called 'window urns', which have pieces of glass let into them; and even more mysterious 'holed urns', that is urns with holes deliberately made in them.[7] The map on page 33 shows

---

* This statement must be modified in so far as it is now proved (cf. Roeder, *Neue Funde*, 24 ff.) that the only English example—from Great Addington—has Scandinavian rather than Saxon affinities.

the distribution of other significant objects, and it provides one of the best arguments which help to fix definitely the home of the men who invaded the eastern Midlands of Britain.

FIG. 3. Nydam Moor, north of Flensburg fiord; archetype of the cruciform brooch. ½.

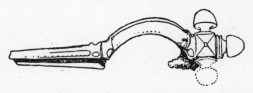

FIG. 4. Tolkwade, Schleswig. Cruciform brooch. The lower end has no trace of an animal's head as in examples found in England. ¾.

FIG. 5. Perlberg, near Stade. A 'round' brooch (of the 'saucer' variety) with spiral design. ½.

In the past it has been very difficult to relate the brooches of the continental Saxons with those of the invaders of Britain, owing to the fact that well-preserved brooches were hardly ever found in their cremation urns.[8] Now, however, this gap in our knowledge is being filled by the fortunate discovery of one or two 'mixed' cemeteries,[9] that is cemeteries in which the Saxons can be seen passing, as in Britain, from the older custom of cremating their dead to the new custom of burying them unburnt with their ornaments and weapons of war. The types of brooch which appear on both sides of the North Sea, and are most useful in helping us to trace the migration of our Germanic ancestors, are the following: the 'cruciform' brooch, the 'round' brooch (in two

Fig. 6. Urn of Saxon type from a Frisian terp.   Fig. 7. Rijnsburg, near a mouth of the Rhine; urn (?) of Saxon type.

varieties), the 'Luton' type, and the 'equal-armed' brooch (see Figs. 3, 4, 5, 8, 9, 28).

All these grave-goods help us to pick up the tracks of our ancestors as they moved westwards towards Britain. As we have seen, the traces are most numerous and unequivocal along the north German coast. They appear sparsely west of the Weser. They become numerous again in Frisia, especially in the district between the mouth of the Ems and the Zuyder Zee. Here the Anglo-Saxons found a half-way house—or let us rather say a stepping-stone—of so strange a kind that we may well pause to observe it.

It seems that about the first century B.C. the sea began to break through the rampart of sand-dunes which had previously protected this low-lying coast. The inundations in course of time became so bad that the unhappy Frisians had to choose between deserting their homes or constructing mounds (*terpen*) from clay and sods and reedy manure on which, during the

FIG. 8. Dösemoor, north of Stade, equal-armed brooch. Roeder's date, *c.* 500.
(Slightly enlarged.)

FIG. 9. Nesse, near Geestemünder, equal-armed brooch. Roeder's date, *c.* 500.
(Slightly enlarged.)

high tides, they could find safety for themselves and their belong-ings. No existence could well have been more miserable than theirs in this corner of the Continent opposite our own shores. So at any rate it appeared to Pliny the Elder.[10]

'With immense tidal flow the Ocean floods over the land twice in every twenty-four hours, spreads its waters wide, and raises Nature's eternal question, whether these regions are to be regarded as belonging to the land or to the sea. Here the wretched inhabitants dwell upon high mounds, as it were platforms constructed by men's hands above the level of the highest tides. Thus when the waters cover everything around, they are like sailors on board a ship; but are more like ship-wrecked men when the sea retires, and around their huts they pursue the fish receding with the tide. . . . They dig the peat up with their hands and dry it, more in the wind than in the sun, and then with it cook their food and warm their bodies benumbed by the north wind. Their only drink is rain water, which they collect in holes dug at the entrance of their huts. And yet these tribes, were they to be conquered by the Romans to-day, would call it slavery!'

The fact that the migrant Anglo-Saxons found lodging on the terp mounds, and perhaps for a time dominated all this sea-swept corner of the Continent, is attested by the discovery of many 'Saxon' cremation urns buried in the mounds beside the inhumed skeletons of the Frisians, and also of cruciform and 'round' brooches.

If, therefore, we try to construct a map* to show the routes by which the Teutonic invaders found their way to Britain, the route by Frisia is the first and most obvious one which we must mark.

In what direction they set their course when they rowed away from the terps of Frisia is more open to question. Many of them no doubt turned to the south, either down the coast or inland by the waterways which could conduct their boats through still waters to the Rhine. But others may have waited for calm summer weather and then pointed their bows due west and

* See map facing p. 9.

made out into the open sea with a view to striking the Wash
and the rivers of the Wash which could bring them without
fear of molestation into the heart of Britain. It was only a
hundred and thirty miles of open sea—less than the distance
which was regularly crossed by traders from Ireland or western
Britain to Gaul.

We have said that many ships of the Saxons would turn from
the Zuyder Zee by inland waterways to the Rhine mouths. This
brings us to what we may consider the second route to Britain.
Let us call it the Rhine ferry—the ferry running, needless to say,
down the coast to the narrow straits so as to gain the shortest
crossing of open sea. What is not obvious is whether the Saxon
invaders had access to the Rhine also by an overland route
through the heart of north Germany, and whether they remained
settled about the lower Rhine for some time before they crossed
to our island. These are points about which archaeology supplies a little evidence. There is no series of cemeteries in southern
Hanover and Münster corresponding to that which can be traced
along the north coast of Germany. Those lands were indeed
mostly forest and moor. They did not attract colonists. Dutch
archaeologists, however, claim[11] that urn-burials of the Saxon
kind are found in some eastern districts of Holland—in Drenthe
and the Veluwe—and again in one or two cemeteries near the
mouths of the Rhine, notably at Rijnsburg (Fig. 7). But these
urns are few, and this evidence is clearly not sufficient in itself
to lay any solid foundation for the theory that the Teutonic
invaders of Britain, or a section of them, had occupied lands
about the lower Rhine before they crossed the sea.

But the theory has won adherents on grounds other than
archaeological. Most notable among these is J. Hoops, who,
in a learned work on the trees and plants of ancient Germany,[12]
built up an argument that while certain Old English words,
derived from Latin, such as *pipor* (pepper), *mynet* (money, from
moneta), might have been imported through the ordinary intercourse of trade, and while others such as *cāsere* (Caesar), *pīl* (a

pointed stick, from *pilum*), were no doubt carried home by Angles
and Saxons who had served in imperial armies, there are yet
others which cannot be so explained. For instance, the English
resemble the Frisians and Dutch in calling the seventh day of
the week Saturday,* other Germanic peoples speak of *Sams-
tag*. The only explanation, according to Hoops, is that Angles
and Saxons must have picked up the expression before they conquered Britain, when bands of them were for a time settled somewhere near the lower Rhine. So also the Old English *cleofa* (a
chamber) and *miltestre* (a loose woman, from Latin *meretrix*): these
too, it is said, must have been learned by our migrant ancestors
when they were in contact with Latin-speaking peoples in the
Low Countries before they crossed the Channel and conquered
Britain. This theory has not won general favour. A distinguished
French historian has called attention to its 'extreme fragility'.[13]
Is it not rash, he says, to assert that the words enumerated by
Hoops must have been transferred into the English language
before A.D. 600? Why should not the English and Dutch have
borrowed them independently of one another?

The philological foundation of the theory being weak like the
archaeological, an attempt has been made to obtain support
from a famous sentence in Adam of Bremen's twelfth-century
chronicle which says that the Saxons were at first settled about
the Rhine before a part of them came into Britain and drove out
the Romans.† But this corrupt passage in a work written some
six centuries after the event is scarcely calculated to add much
solidity to the theory. Such strength as it still possesses is derived
from arguments about the origin of the Jutes and from occasional
mentions of the doings of 'the Saxons' by writers who lived
within the Roman Empire. To these passages we must now
turn, postponing the Jutish problem till our Chapter III.[14]

How incomplete is the information about the Saxons to be

* OE. *Sæterdæg.*
† I. c. 3: 'Igitur Saxones primo circa Renum sedes habebant, (et vocati sunt Angli)
quorum pars inde veniens in Brittanniam, Romanos ab illa insula depulit.'

obtained from the Roman world is at once brought home to us
by the fact that after Ptolemy's statement that the Saxons were
to be found 'on the neck of the Cimbric peninsula', we have to
wait for more than a hundred years before we again hear of
them. Then about A.D. 286 they are mentioned along with the
Franks, first as pirates who infest the coasts of Gaul and later
as allies of Carausius, the Roman admiral who revolted and
established himself as emperor in Britain. In the course of this
long interval covering the end of the first century and the
greater part of the second, most of the changes which we have
already traced from the archaeological evidence had taken place.
The Chauci had been absorbed or displaced. The Frisians had
been overcome. Men of Germanic stock who called themselves
'Saxons' (they may have been mere confederates of the Saxons
of the Elbe lands) had become a power on the lower Rhine.
In the fourth century these Saxons of the west trod on the heels
of the Salian Franks as the latter moved step by step into Gaul.
Zosimus, the Byzantine, could read into the story the idea that
the Saxons were pushing the Franks forward from behind. When
the government of Roman Gaul crumbled in the first decades
of the fifth century and Rome finally gave up the attempt to
control the waters of the Rhine mouths, this way to the sea was
completely opened to the Saxons. Accordingly while the Franks,
now confining their operations to the land, were occupied in
building up a kingdom in the north-east of Gaul with a capital
at Tournai, the Saxon marauders were left free to establish
themselves at various points on the Gallic coast, settling now,
if not earlier, in the villages round Boulogne (names of which
still betray their Saxon origin by the ending -*thun* or -*tun*),[15] and
establishing themselves also in the Bessin round Bayeux and
near the mouth of the Loire.

Though no consecutive story can be built up from the occasional references to the Saxons in the writings of the later Empire,
enough is said to justify us in showing on our map the Saxon
confederation reaching almost up to the lower Rhine, and in

shading the Boulonnais and the Bessin as nests of the Saxons on the northern shores of Gaul.

This completes our sketch of the westward drift of the Saxons, the drift which had been going on for some three centuries before it brought them to the settlement of Britain. We have already noted at least two possible bases from which their ships could sail to our island: one the most northerly in the *terpen* of Frisia; the other somewhere about the lower Rhine. Now, from the written authorities and the place-names, we have found traces of a third possible base, namely these nests of Saxons on the coast of Gaul.

Of the three the situation on the Rhine is in every way the most obscure. We do not know for certain where exactly it was, nor how large, nor whether it should be thought of as a populous settlement or as a merely temporary post. We do not know who these hypothetical folk were—whether Saxons from the Elbe or men of neighbouring tribes such as Jutes, Angles, and Chauci, passing under the name of Saxons. Common sense suggests to us that the Rhine-Meuse-Scheldt mouths opposite the Thames must have been the taking-off place for many of the invaders of Britain. But so far we have had no good proof of its existence; it remains no more than x, the unknown quantity in the problem.

For the present it will be sufficient if in thinking of the three possible bases we understand how different the invaders might be who came from these different quarters. The Saxons who had been established in the advanced posts of Gaul may have learned something of the ways either of the Franks or of the provincials around them. They were probably federates like the Franks and the other barbarians who had established themselves on Gallic soil; and it is possible that they contributed the Saxon levies who fought on the imperial side in the army of Aëtius against Attila's Huns.[16]

The 'Saxons' of the Rhine, if they existed, may also have been changed by long contact with the Franks. They also may have grown unlike their kinsmen in the homelands, those who were

PLATE 3

Details, doubtless mythological, from the upper sections of the horn

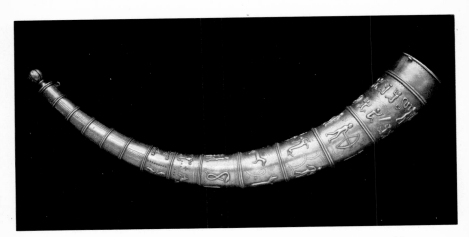

Replica of golden horn, found at Gallehus, near if not within
the ancient Angel

It is not certainly of Anglian workmanship

PLATE 4

German chiefs in council, a moot of a free people
From the column of Marcus Aurelius

still living in old-fashioned ways by the North Sea or the Baltic. This is not an empty conjecture. We seem to trace some differences of this kind reflected in their burial customs. Re-examine the evidence: in the Elbe-Weser country, cremation urns crowded together by the thousand in numerous cemeteries; in the terps of Frisia, similar finds, but few of them; on the lower Rhine, finds still fewer and less characteristic; but in Gaul, though Saxons must have died there in their thousands, not a single Saxon burial-place has been discovered.

This question of the character of the Saxons cannot be dismissed in a paragraph. We must now take it up and devote to it a new section of the present chapter.

CHARACTER AND BELIEFS

The fullest description which has come down to us of the Saxon pirates was written by Sidonius, a Gallo-Roman noble who flourished in the latter half of the fifth century. He was writing to a friend who, he had heard, was at the moment combining the duties of a sailor and a soldier, 'looking out for the curved longboats of the Saxons'.[17]

'When you see the rowers of that nation,' he says, 'you may at once make up your mind that every one of them is an arch-pirate; with such wonderful unanimity do all at once command, obey, teach, and learn their one chosen business of brigandage. For this reason I ought to warn you to be more than ever on your guard in this warfare. Your enemy is the most ferocious of all enemies. Unexpectedly he attacks, when expected he escapes, he despises those who seek to block his path, he overthrows those who are off their guard, he always succeeds in cutting off the enemy whom he follows, while he never fails when he desires to effect his own escape. Moreover, to these men a shipwreck is capital practice rather than an object of terror. The dangers of the deep are to them, not casual acquaintances, but intimate friends, for since a tempest throws the invaded off their guard, and prevents the invaders from being descried from afar, they hail with joy the crash of waves on the rocks which gives them their best chance of escaping from other enemies than the elements.

'Then again, before they raise the deep-biting anchor from the hostile soil, and set sail from the continent for their own country, their custom is to collect the crowd of their prisoners together, by a mockery of equity to make them cast lots which of them shall undergo the iniquitous sentence of death, and then at the moment of departure to abandon every tenth captive to the slow agony of a watery end, a practice which is the more lamentable because it arises from a superstitious notion that they will thus ensure for themselves a safe return.'

Sidonius, repeating the hearsay about an enemy, gives us a vivid but evidently an exaggerated picture of the Saxons. To obtain truer notions about them, we must leave these, the advanced bands of the Saxon marauders, and, studying the Angles and Saxons in their continental homes, see if we can find any answers to the questions: What they were really like? How did they live? How was it they came to give up their old homes and to venture forth into strange lands across the North Sea?

In the first place, what did they look like? Roman sculptors carved representations of German barbarians on their monuments. On the column of Marcus Aurelius at Rome they are portrayed clothed in shirts to the knee, cloaks buckled on the right shoulder, and long trousers to the ankle. Look, for instance, at the scene on page 1 where Roman soldiers burn a German village. The German men (*Marcomanni*) with arms upraised beg for mercy as their huts are burned. The Roman soldiers slay the village folk with the sword and the spear, they burn their huts, and the German mother, with long hair falling over her shoulders, hurries away from the scene of the destruction of her home and the slaughter of her kinsmen, pulling her young son by the arm—a fitting introduction to the later invasion of the Roman Empire by the Germans. On another relief (Pl. 4) of the same column, German chiefs are represented sitting in an assembly; again it is a memorable scene, the moot of a free people.

The bust in Berlin (Pl. 5) was for long said to illustrate how a primitive German man wore his hair. Now, however, it is

PLATE 5

Bust of a German woman
British Museum

An idealized German. Bust of the eighteenth century
Königl. Museum, Berlin

PLATE 6

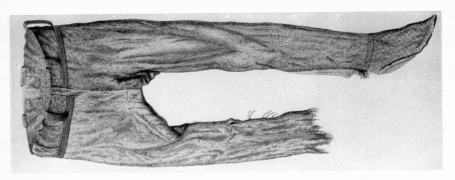

C. Trousers from Thorsberg

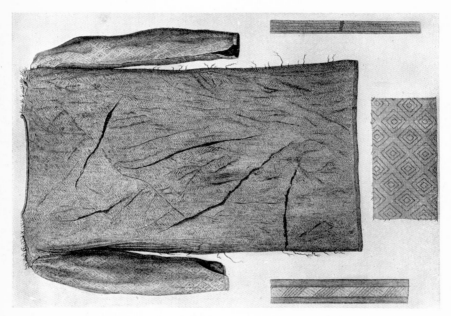

B. Tunic or shirt found at Thorsberg

All in the Kiel Museum

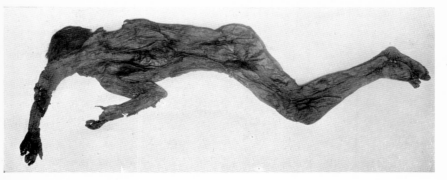

A. The Damendorfer man

certain that it is only a 'fake' of the eighteenth century.[18] The
bust in the British Museum (also on Pl. 5) has a pedigree and
some claim to illustrate the Roman idea of a German woman;
but there is no certainty about her race and the bust has been
much mended. Such works of art cannot well be produced
to support the statements of Tacitus about the nobility of the
Germans. They are not evidence for the existence of a Teutonic
type in general; still less for a Saxon type in particular.

And what we want to see is not a Nordic man or German
in the abstract, but if possible an Angle or Saxon of the time of
the invasion. Such a one may be found in the museum at Kiel
(Pl. 6A), no idealized portrait in marble, but the veritable
man himself, preserved for some fifteen centuries beneath the
heather of Damendorf in Schleswig—preserved, or rather pickled,
in the peat of the moor; his flesh, his skin, his long fair hair
(dyed red by the peat), and his clothes—all are there; but by
some strange chemical action of the peat, his bones have disappeared, and the weight of the earth above him has pressed his
body till it is little more than a silhouette. There lying in the
peat he was found in the year 1900, his left arm stretched out
and his head resting on it as if in sleep. Whatever beauty he
may once have had could no longer be discerned in his wrinkled
skin, his gaping mouth, and his tangled hair. More interesting
than the man himself are his clothes. Spread out over his naked
body was found a large woollen cloak almost two yards square,
and at his feet, wrapped up in his trousers, were his shoes, his
puttees, and his belt. These and similar finds elsewhere (Pl. 6B
and c) not only tell us how our Anglian forefathers were dressed,
but they give a good idea of the daily work and the skill of
their womenfolk.[18a] One could weave a diamond pattern into
the cloth for a tunic. Another, to give her man protection
against the storms and rains of a northern winter, sewed a
covering of hides on to his cloak. Thus did the women of the
Anglo-Saxon tribes spend their days: spinsters, weavers, sewers,
producing clothes for their families while their menfolk were

ploughing in the fields or were out on the war-path with spear and bow.

Now it so happens that the peat moors in the neighbourhood of Angel have yielded their richest harvest of finds from the period preceding that of the migration to Britain. Those which concern us most immediately are the finds at Nydam, north of

FIG. 10. The Nydam boat.

the Flensburg fiord. There parts of three ships—three 'keels' we may call them if we use the old Germanic word—were dug out; but only one of them, a ship made of oak, was sufficiently preserved to be repaired—the long ship which is now to be seen in Kiel Museum. Since the Anglo-Saxons presumably crossed over to Britain in somewhat similar vessels, the Nydam boat and the things found with it are worth our attention. The boat is very long (77 feet) and very narrow (less than 11 feet) and very low amidships (Fig. 10)—so long and so low and so narrow that it almost recalls a modern racing 'eight ' or a Pacific canoe. It had provision for fourteen oars on either side. When propelled by its twenty-eight oars it must have been fast, fast enough to elude the clumsier Roman galleys. It is generally said that it possessed among other merits notable buoyancy and elasticity. The way in which its builders obtained these results is interesting.

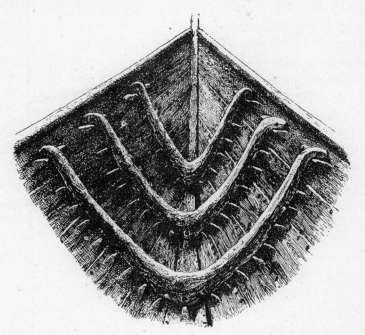

FIG. 11. Prow of Nydam boat, to show construction.

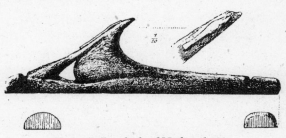

FIG. 12. Rowlock of Nydam boat.

The vessel was clinker built and the five oak planks on each side were held together by large iron rivets fastened on the inside with washers or nuts, but these side-planks were not nailed on to the main framework: they were tied to the ribs by ropes made of bast.

The arrangement of the rowlocks exhibits a somewhat similar mixture of ingenuity and primitive experiment. They also were tied on to the gunwale by ropes, and the oar was passed through another rope attached to the rowlock to keep it in its place. The rowlock itself with its sloping form is said to be stronger than our ordinary double rowlock. On the other hand the boat had obvious defects: owing to the form of the rowlock it could only be rowed in one direction; since it could not be backed with any force and could only be steered by a large paddle over the stern, its manœuvring capacity was slight. Moreover,[19] its keel was weak. It could not carry a mast or sail. Its stability was so poor that heavy ballast was necessary to keep it steady. This would accordingly make it harder to propel than the later Viking ships.

The experience of crossing the North Sea in it must have been unpleasant in the extreme. The waves must have constantly broken over its low sides; and the soaked passengers—some forty persons all told might have been packed into the vessel—must have been kept at work with endless baling.

At the bottom of the Nydam peat moor, mixed up with the fragments of boats, were exhumed quantities of weapons and miscellaneous articles which give some idea of what it must have meant to be attacked by the men who rowed these long ships from the Elbe lands to Britain. Of their swords we need say little because they were largely imports of barbarian-Roman make from the Rhine lands, such as could no longer be bought in the time of the Saxon invasions. Spears were evidently the commonest weapons of the marauders. More than five hundred spear-heads were found in the deposit. The shafts were mostly made of ash, and varied from eight to ten feet in length. Formidable weapons these, almost like the pikes of the seventeenth century. There were also spears of other kinds, some to be used as missiles and some for hunting purposes. Such spear-heads

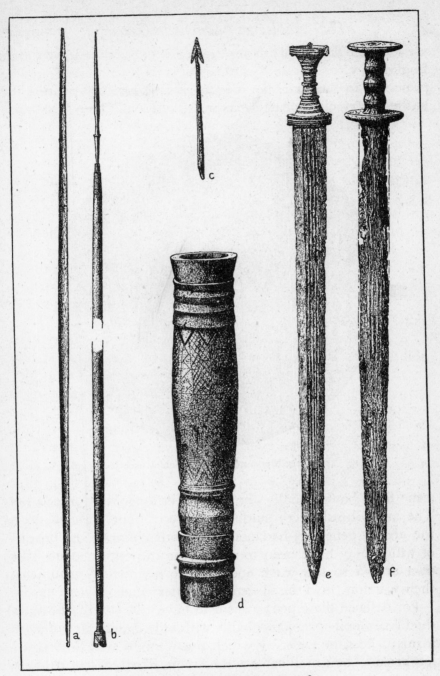

FIG. 13. Nydam Moor, weapons, &c.:
(a) bow, about 5 ft. long; (b) spear, 10 ft. long; (c) arrow;
(d) wooden quiver; (e), (f) imported swords.

are found in numbers among the bones of the invaders in their English graves. But at Nydam we also find what could only be preserved in the peat, the long bows and arrows to which the battle poetry of the Anglo-Saxons so often alludes. At Nydam

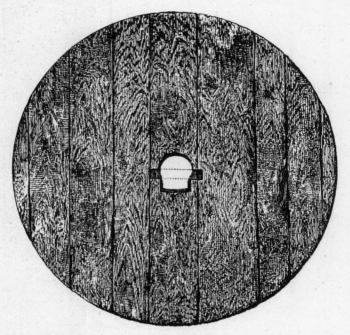

FIG. 14. Thorsberg Moor, north of the Schlei: wooden shield. $\frac{1}{12}$.

some forty bows, usually about five feet long, were discovered. The arrow-heads were made of iron and bone. The shafts of the arrows generally had notches or other marks, the purpose of which may have been to enable the owners to collect their own arrows so that each could prove his own prowess when their warriors 'held the place of slaughter' after a fight.

For defence these people seem to have trusted only to round shields of wood covered probably with hide, having in the centre a raised boss, or *umbo*, by which the weapon was held in the left hand. Their mail-coats and helmets, like their finest swords,

seem to have been imported from the Rhine lands. The supply
of such luxuries failed in the fifth century, and few even of the
Anglian and Saxon chiefs, when they landed on the shores of
Britain, can have been equipped with a shining helmet or byrnie.

So far we have been studying all that is external about our Germanic forefathers—their brooches, their clothes, their weapons,
their ships. Is there any way by which we can discover something more important than these buried belongings of theirs?
Can we penetrate beneath the surface and see how their minds
worked?

Now without doubt even the material objects excavated from
their graves should throw some light on the ideas of these men,
if only we could read them aright. It is just here that difficulties
become most acute.

For instance, if we try to understand why it was that the men
were buried in the bogs, and why the ships and all the para-
phernalia with the ships were sunk at Nydam, what are we told
by the experts? At one time it was said[20] that when these things
were deposited there was at Nydam a lake, evidently a sacred
lake; and that into it the men of that age had cast their most
precious belongings; that the motive at work had been the religious motive of sacrifice, for holes had been cut in the boats,
the swords had been bent, the spear-shafts had been broken.
And if this were true, the character of the gods who had been
propitiated by such orgies of destruction might be guessed, and
the character of the men who made their gods in their own
image. And noting these things we might remember that the
periodic rites of Nerthus—rites in which our Anglian ancestors
participated—were concluded with the cleansing of the car of
the goddess in a lake by slaves who were instantly swallowed
up in its waters. This sacrificial view of the deposits in the
peat has been succeeded by many others.[21] One theory explains
them as dumps of worn-out things collected at the end of a
campaign. Another holds that they were depots of war-booty,

'hidden treasure to which men meant to return'. Yet another interprets them by the primitive belief known as animism. The things themselves were thought to have souls, and to set their souls free for a dead owner they must be bent or broken, i.e. they must be 'killed'.

On the whole a quasi-religious motive seems to be the most adequate explanation. It is a useful reminder of the childlike ideas which from remote ages had been working in the minds of these Germanic tribes, and which were still so powerfully operative that they impelled men to destroy, to sacrifice, those things which they valued most.

Our clearest information about the religion of the Ingaevonic tribes, including the ancestors of the Angles and Saxons, is a famous description given by Tacitus of the worship of 'Nerthus, that is Mother Earth': of the sacred grove on the island where is the sanctuary of the goddess, and the sacred car which no one except the priest of the goddess may touch; of the procession of the car through the villages, the peace and festivity which reign wherever the goddess goes, and the cleansing in the secret lake, ending with a sacrifice of the slaves which the deposits in the Nydam Moor have just recalled to us. It is now usual[22] to recognize in the Nerthus cult of the Ingaevonic tribes some influence from oriental religion—'vegetation rites' which may have drifted in the Bronze Age along with the rites of the over-sexed Cybele down the trade route from the Black Sea to the Baltic. In historic times the cult passed from the Danish islands to the Swedes, where the place of Nerthus was taken by the god Frey, the son of Njorth, that is of Nerthus. The Scandinavian traditions tell of a war between the Njorth-Frey family ('the Vanir') and the family of Odin ('the Anses'). Here we have a true reminiscence of the rivalry between the competing cults which no doubt caused a great stir among the Angles and Saxons in the centuries preceding their migration. It was a struggle between the cult of Mother Earth on the one hand— bountiful Mother Earth, with her gods who gave peace and who blessed agriculture with plentiful increase—and on the other hand the heroic gods, the gods of war who gave victory.

Woden himself was the chief god of the warriors at the time of the migration because, in the early centuries of our era when the worship of Christ was advancing from Palestine to Britain, the worship of Woden, coming probably from the Rhine lands, was spreading both east and north. Woden, it seems, was driving out Thunor, the Thunderer, the weather-god beloved by the common people, much as Thunor coming at an earlier age from the west had driven out Tig (the god of our English Tuesday), the oldest of the great gods, so old indeed that by the fifth century he had faded into the background of men's minds. It was the kingly families who looked to Woden. From him they traced their descent. His character varied. Originally, it is said, a wind-god, a god of the homeless dead, followed through the air by the Wild Hunt of disembodied spirits; lord of life and of death; lord of fighting and inspirer of battle fury—Woden appealed in a variety of ways to the kingly dynasties and the aristocrats. In all probability he was now becoming, as in Scandinavia, the master of potent spells. He could arm men with the mysteries of the Futhorc, the new runic alphabet. Thus it was easy for him to dethrone his rivals among the gods, Tiw and Thunor and the peaceful prolific Vanir gods.

Lastly, let us seek an approach to the minds of our Germanic ancestors by the way of literature. Probably the oldest poem in English, the oldest at any rate in parts, is *Widsith*. It takes its name from the far-travelling minstrel to whom the poem is attributed. Though Widsith, the nominal author, can be no more than the creation of some later poet's fancy, and though parts of the poem cannot have been composed much before the end of the sixth century, the latest editor[23] thinks that other parts may have been 'brought to England by late migrants from Schleswig', and be thus authentic ideas of the invaders.

We must not expect to get much from the poem, for it is little

more than a 'Who's Who' for the Heroic Age, a catalogue of
the kings and heroes whose deeds stirred the imaginations of
the Germanic peoples in the age when there was an Empire to
be sacked and kingdoms to be won. Even a catalogue like that,
however, is something for which we may be thankful. This is
how it begins:

'Widsith spake, unlocked his store of words, he who of all men had
wandered through most tribes and peoples throughout the earth: oft in
hall had he received the lovely treasure. . . .

'He began then to speak many words: "Of many men have I heard
ruling over the nations. Every chieftain must live virtuously (one lord
after another, ruling his land), he who desires his throne to flourish.

' "Of these was Hwala for a time the best, and Alexander most mighty
of all the race of men, and flourished most of those of whom I have heard
tell throughout the world. Attila* ruled the Huns. Ermanaric† the
Goths . . . Caesar‡ ruled the Greeks, and Caelic the Finns" ' . . . and
so on.

Widsith himself, the reputed author of the poem, is said to
be a minstrel who set out from 'Angel in the East', that is the
continental home of the Angles, and he is represented as the
one who of all men had wandered through most tribes and
peoples throughout the earth. He enumerates in all sixty-nine
tribes and tribal heroes. Those which he knows best are the
tribes and heroes of the northern seas. In the myths of northern
tradition Baltic chiefs assume heroic proportions. Kings and
tribes are mentioned who never appeared above the horizon of
the southern Roman world.

Among the crowd of obscure northern heroes mentioned by
Widsith there is one who concerns us directly. Recent writers[24]
have given Offa of Angel his proper place at the head of English
history as the first king of the English who is something more
than a mere name. What Widsith tells us is that in those days
when 'Offa ruled Angel; Alewih the Danes, he was the boldest
of all these men, yet did he not in his deeds surpass Offa. But

* *Aetla.*   † *Eormanric.*   ‡ *Casere*—the Eastern Emperor.

Offa gained, first of men, by arms, the greatest of kingdoms whilst yet a boy; no one of his age [did] greater deeds of valour in battle with his single sword; he drew the boundary against the Myrgingas at Fifeldor.* Engle and Swæfe held it afterwards as Offa struck it out.'

Now the interesting thing about Offa of Angel is that traditions about him continued to flourish both among the English in Britain and among the Danes, who in appropriating the province of Angel took over some of its Anglian folk-lore. The Danish version which emerges in the twelfth century in the History of Saxo portrays Offa† as a prince of great stature who in early youth was considered to be dull and silent and useless in all affairs, and whose true worth was only revealed to the Angles. For it was then agreed that the fate of the kingdom should be decided by a duel between Offa and the son of the aggressor. These were the circumstances under which a duel was fought on an island of the river Eider—the duel in which Offa 'whilst yet a boy . . . with his single sword drew the boundary' for the Angles, when the kingdom of his father, an old man, was attacked by the king of the Myrgings from the south of the Eider.

Since there are eight steps in the Mercian genealogy (vol. ii, p. 719) between Penda (? 626–55) and his ancestor Offa, we may calculate that the incident which gave birth to these traditions probably occurred about the end of the fourth century; and we may accept as highly probable the conjecture that Offa of Angel was remembered because his reign had been in fact unusually successful. Thus at a time when the Roman power in the west was beginning to crumble, when the Saxon raiders were an increasing menace in Britain and Gaul, the Angles of Schleswig were enjoying the rule of a strong king.

This introductory chapter is already long enough; yet the picture of the Angles and Saxons on the Continent before their migration is lamentably incomplete. Some of the blanks which

---

* The river Eider (but cf. Siebs, 65). For the Swæfe see above, p. 6.   † Spelt Uffo.

have been left are inevitable; some will be in part filled up when we learn about the emigrant peoples in their new colonies; others may be made good by the reader in his own mind from the evidence which has already been given.

The deficiency which is perhaps most likely to give a wrong impression is the omission so far of any description of the wild nature surrounding these Germanic tribes—the vast stretches of forest and marsh and heath which hemmed them in and did so much to form their characters. This is one of the subjects about which little is here said because the conditions will be much the same when the emigrants reappear in Britain. The forests and heaths of Britain will be less extensive, but the struggle of the farmer with forest and moorland will continue with little change or abatement.

For a like reason little has been said about the agriculture of the Angles and Saxons, though this rather than the chase or cattle-raising must have been the pursuit which filled the day of most men from morning till night. At this point it must suffice to say that in Britain the skill of Anglo-Saxons in plough-ing the heavy clay lands of the river valleys will be an all-important factor in their successful advance.

Again, little has been said about many points made familiar by the sketch of Tacitus. In his own day the common charac-teristics which he ascribed to scores of different 'German' tribes can have been but half-truths. By the fifth century they were necessarily something less. The lazy life in which sleeping and feasting alternated with fighting and hunting may still have existed in some war-bands of chiefs or kings at the time of the migration as in the time of Tacitus; but it was clearly not the normal life of the farming folk who made the villages of England and laid out their open fields.

The evidence which has been already produced will, on con-sideration, supply answers to many of the questions which rise in the mind when we try to picture the society of our forefathers by the Elbe and the Eider.

What arts did they possess? We must remember their runes. We must remember their cremation urns with ornamental lines and stamps and bosses. Above all we must remember their brooches. The 'round' and the 'equal-armed' brooches (Figs. 5, 8, 9) are good examples of what is called 'chip-carving' or

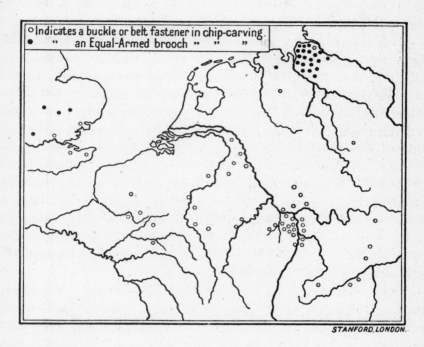

○ Indicates a buckle or belt fastener in chip-carving.
●   ,,   an Equal-Armed brooch ,,   ,,   ,,

STANFORD, LONDON.

Kerbschnitt technique. This was the last fashion in metal-work to gain sway in the Western Empire before the Empire was inundated by barbarians in the fifth century. The map, showing the distribution of certain objects made in this style in western Europe, indicates that the chief home, perhaps the factory, of the chip-carving craftsmen was the region of the middle Rhine. That was a region where 'barbarian' influences were strong, and it may well be that the influence of German woodcraft is reflected in the designs of this chip-carving. It is true that in the art-motives and in the technique there is much borrowing from Roman-provincial work both of the Rhine lands and of north-east Gaul. This is the important point, for here we see the contrast between the Germans who invaded Britain and the Germans of Tacitus—the contrast between a people almost untouched by Roman influences and a people who for many generations had received, along with goods manufactured in the Roman Rhineland, some infusion of Roman culture.[24a]

With regard to the political institutions of our Anglian fore-fathers—the subject on which Victorian writers became most eloquent—we must for the time being be content with the one fact gleaned in *Widsith*, namely, that the dynasty of Offa of Angel had its roots in the past. The genealogy which was carried to Britain and traced the Mercian kings back to and beyond Offa showed that the monarchy was no recent experiment among the Angles. *Widsith* gives us something more than the mere name of an early 'English' king. The poem illustrates the political spirit of these primitive people, showing how the devotion of the community or the tribe gathered round the heroic deeds of chief or king. It reminds us that all the security and the success of the tribe depended on the valour of its fighting men and pre-eminently on that of the leader.

There is more ground for doubt about the antiquity of the monarchy among the Saxons. A famous sentence of Bede which says that 'the old Saxons have not a king but many chiefs each set over his own tribe' certainly suggests that the conglomerate of tribal communities calling themselves Saxons had been less unified in a common obedience than the Franks and other new confederate groups of the Germanic world.

We need not discuss here how the German tribal system worked, since the migration of the Angles and Saxons over sea could not be a migration by tribes. The crews who manned the longboats may have been animated by a strong sense of equality bred on the fields of northern Germany, but the success of their enterprise, whether on sea or on land, depended primarily on the skill of the leader and the discipline of the followers. The spirit which permeates *Widsith* was no later invention. It was an essential to success in the age of the migration.

One last question remains: What were the motives which impelled these peoples to leave their former homes and risk everything in a long voyage to Britain?

Remembering that the invaders may have come from regions as widely sundered as is the north coast of Gaul from the Jutish peninsula and that they probably continued to come for more than a century, we shall see that many different causes must have been at work. For example, some of the Saxons in Gaul may have been squeezed out by the advance of the Franks, but this would chiefly be towards the end of the fifth century. Then some fifty years later the northward expansion of Frankish power may have moved any Saxons still camped about the Rhine mouths and have closed that route to the emigrants. Some writers, observing that the first Saxon settlement in Britain coincided roughly with the climax of the Hunnish power in western Europe, have argued that 'panic-stricken tribesmen—English, Saxons, Jutes and others—took to their ships and fled overseas'[25] in order to escape from Attila. But this is a mere guess; and it seems to exaggerate the terror caused by Attila in north Germany and the suddenness of the migration. It may well be doubted whether the migration was ever such a mass movement as Bede[26] implied. When Bede spoke of the old home of the Angles being still a desert in his day, he may not have realized how much of it was then rendered uninhabitable by nature.[27]

There is, however, no need to seek further for motives. In the fifth century the Germanic nations were on the move. The unrest in the souls of men is reflected even in Widsith's scanty catalogue of the nations and their great men. The stories of Ermanaric the Goth, of Gundahari the Burgundian, and many of the other heroes, known and unknown, to which he alludes, had no doubt stirred the minds of Germans even when they lived in remote wastes near the shores of the Baltic. They had helped to bring home to them the truth that the Empire was crumbling, that the old defences were broken down, that the way was open to those who had followers ready to risk death in the hope of winning gold or land. And apart from the tales of the minstrels, the ordinary talk of the shipping folk along the north German coast must have kept rumours circulating about the events in Gaul and Britain: rumours of the outposts of Saxon adventurers thrust forward to the Rhine lands, to the Loire; rumours of world-shaking events such as the advance of the Germanic peoples into Gaul; then finally of the lodgements effected by Jutish or Saxon adventurers in Britain. When these rumours reached the villages crowded on the narrow spits of habitable land by the Weser and Elbe, the minds of men along the over-populated seaboard must have been seized with a new contagion. For long it may have been a fever which only attacked the young and the adventurous, like one of the gold manias which in modern times have driven descendants of the Anglo-Saxons to the Rand or Klondike. In the end the epidemic clearly became less virulent but more universal, a land-hunger which drove whole families, sometimes whole communities, to make the great resolve, to take the step which required much more faith than is needed for a colonist in our modern mechanical days, to pack their stores and weapons on one of their long narrow ships and to adventure into the unknown world. In this phase the motive force of the migration was a land-hunger like that which has carried men of Anglo-Saxon stock as migrants round the globe.

Redditor lucis aeternae.

II

THE END OF ROMAN BRITAIN[1]

THE UNDERWORLD OF ROMAN BRITAIN

THE chief aim of this chapter is to throw such light as there is upon the condition of Roman Britain in the middle of the fifth century. At the outset we have to admit that we are facing a dark tract of history which can never —not even with the help of archaeology—be made clear; all that can be done is to approach the unknown through the known, to get as near as we can and then to conjecture the state of Britain in the fifth century from what we have seen of it in the preceding period, when it was still an integral part of the Western Empire.

The civilization of Roman Britain—the 'known' which is to be our starting-point—need be represented in this book only by a 'reconstruction' of Roman London (Pl. 7 A) which may serve to remind those whose imaginations are not stirred by objects in museum cases, of the majesty and wealth of the Roman world—the majesty which for long awed the barbarians and the wealth which in the end attracted them. There is also no need

HEADPIECE.—Gold medallion celebrating the relief of London, A.D. 296, by Constantius Chlorus. ¼.

to describe the Romanized superstructure of society during the first centuries of the Roman occupation—the three strongholds of Roman culture: first, the military garrison and the lesser army of civil servants; secondly, the Romanized communities of the towns; and thirdly, the Romanized country gentlemen who inhabited the larger villas of the countryside. These need not detain us, since they had little connexion with the Saxons. In this history we shall be more concerned with the offspring of the underworld of Roman Britain, the descendants of the serfs living in the outhouses of the villas along with the animals, or of the natives whose primitive round huts were clustered in villages and homesteads on the outskirts of civilized society. They are the people who in the long run were to come into chief contact with the Saxons and who, whether as enemies or subjects, were to influence them through the succeeding centuries. The future of Celtic Britain was to be determined by these backward communities of the country districts rather than by the more civilized inhabitants of the towns and villas; and it is therefore these that we should study. Though our knowledge of the native settlements is still far from complete, we can see their varying gradations of Romanization in different regions. At the top of the scale we may place the farms excavated in Cranborne Chase, headed by Woodcuts. Here the usages of civilized society had made some headway. A building has walls in colour-painted plaster and a paving of shale. The inhabitants bought such goods as they could afford in the Roman towns—their furniture, their glass, their spoons, their jewellery, their tools. They could write with iron *styli* in the Roman manner. In some ways they were worse than barbarians; for example, they buried their dead in ash-pits without order or decency.

Next in the scale of superficial civilization we may place other upland settlements on the open hills of southern Britain. The plans of their habitations and fields have been recently revealed to us by air photography (Pl. 8). Their culture and habits

PLATE 7

A. Roman London—reconstructed

From a drawing by the late Mr. A. Forestier

B. Roman soldiers

From the column of Marcus Aurelius

PLATE 8

Air-photograph of Celtic Fields, near Kingston, Dorset

There are faint indications of habitations near the top. The double line (right centre) is a lane leading to the fields. The fields were here separated by stone walls and within them may be seen the ancient 'lands', two or three yards wide

are well illustrated by the excavations of a homestead at Lowbury Hill on the Berkshire Downs above Moulsford, where

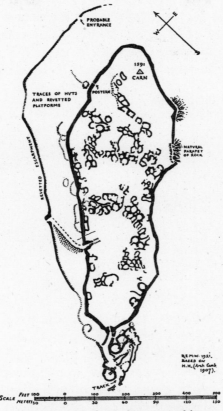

FIG. 15. Tre'r Ceiri, Carnarvonshire.
Note the circular and oblong hut-sites within the dry-wall
enclosure. Outside this enclosure the hill falls away steeply
on all sides and on the SE. is precipitous.

the jewellery and pottery found had enough likeness to the
things excavated in Silchester to make the archaeologist picture
the Celtic inhabitants 'going down to Silchester from time to
time to do their marketing and see life'.[2]

The identification of other British settlements is now being
pursued by archaeologists all over the country. They are found

not only on the chalk hills but on gravel patches in the valleys
and wherever in those days there was open ground with a dry,
easily worked soil.

In the native settlements in the hill country of western Britain,
where towns and villas were few or non-existent, the tinge of
Romanization naturally becomes faintest. Thus in the north-
west, while there were some places behind the frontier forts

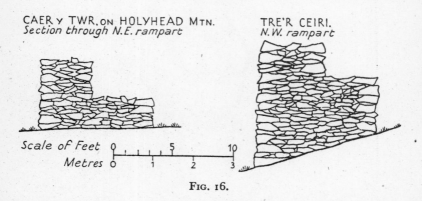

FIG. 16.

where the Britons could dedicate altars in the Roman manner,
in the ordinary villages the natives only bought from Roman
traders a few pots and tools and ornaments. In the hills of Wales
there were bank-defended villages which tell much the same
story. There too were larger and more strongly fortified hill-
top towns, the rough stone walls of which seem to reproduce
features of Roman engineering such as the parapet walk (Fig. 16).
In the south-western peninsula we pass from a few luxurious
Romanized villas in Somerset to farmsteads of a humble type,
and to upland settlements like that on Ham Hill, where the semi-
barbarous peasantry lived in huts and pit dwellings. Then,
penetrating farther into the peninsula, we come to hill-top villages
on Dartmoor and in Cornwall which have yielded few or no
traces of Roman culture. Homes such as these were the strongholds of the Celtic race and the Celtic spirit. Here the more
civilized fugitives from the east would find some kind of shelter.

Here too they could soon forget their Latin and lose the habits of Romanized life.

Thus excavation is constantly giving us new glimpses of the more primitive communities of Roman Britain—those which,

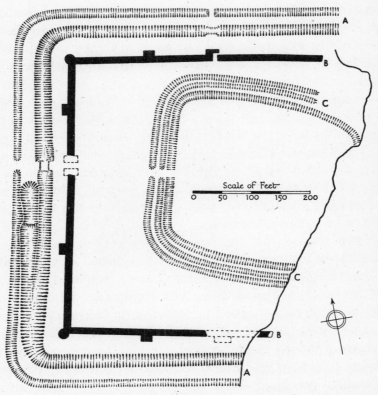

FIG. 17. Plan of Richborough, showing earlier (CC) and later (BB, AA) forts.

partly owing to their poverty and the small temptation they offered to the spoiler, and partly owing to their hills, were able to escape the first waves of invasion: islands in the deluge, where remnants fleeing from the cities and the lowlands could find a refuge in the evil days, and where Romano-Britons could grow into Welshmen.

THE LATER DEFENCES OF ROMAN BRITAIN

When exactly was it that the evil days did come? When did
the Golden Age of Roman Britain end? About this there is room
for difference of opinion. So far as it is a question of the Saxons'
advent, the answer is that they began to molest the island some
time in the latter half of the third century. Before that the
houses of the well-to-do could be built in happy security beside
the shore of the Channel. After 250 the imperial authorities
began to construct defences along the coast. The first sign that
all was not well was the making of a fort at Richborough,* where
no military works had been needed since the days when the
army of Claudius on its first landing protected itself against
a hostile Britain. The new fort (cc on Fig. 17) began as a small
affair, defended by three ditches and covering less than two
acres, but the fact of its construction suggests that the Saxons
were already finding their way as enemies to the Shore which
came to be called after them.

Written records for the later history of Roman Britain are
few; and the Saxon raiders are not mentioned in them till the
last quarter of the third century; then, it is said, they were
repelled by the imperial fleet, but Carausius, the commander
of the fleet, was encouraged by his 'victoria Germanica' to usurp
the rule within the island, and for seven years (286–93) the
Emperor of Britain, with his fleet commanding the narrow seas,
was able to defy all the land forces of the Continent. (Pl. 43, 1.)

It is these two phenomena, so closely inter-related—the Saxon
raids and the revolt of the Roman fleet—which explain the
developments of the following century, the last century of Roman
rule in our island.

When Constantius Chlorus re-established the authority of the
Empire in Britain in 296–7 and in 305–6, he organized as
part of the permanent defences of Roman Britain the chain of
massive forts along the coast between the Wash and Southampton

* Rutupiae.

Water, some of which had perhaps been begun in the disorders of the preceding period.[3]

For the scheme of defence of Roman Britain in its last phase we have to consult the government handbook called the *Notitia Dignitatum*. The edition of this book which has come down to us seems to date from about 428. Whether it in truth gives the dispositions of that age or those of the fourth century is a disputed point. With this caution, we may gather from the *Notitia* that the garrison which had to protect Britain in the period when the Saxons became a menace was disposed as follows.

(1) The command in the north was given to a 'Duke of the Britains'.* Under him were the Sixth Legion, 'Victrix', based as of old on York, and a number of auxiliary troops. (2) The commander-in-chief of the new south-eastern forts was the 'Count of the Saxon Shore'.† The centre of the defence was at Richborough, to which fortress the Second Legion, 'Augusta', had been wholly or partly removed from the borders of Wales. At the eight other forts were stationed auxiliary units, each with an establishment of five hundred or one thousand men. Then (3), at any rate in the last phase of Roman rule, there was in reserve somewhere—we do not know where—a field army, a mobile striking force under a 'Count of the Britains'.‡

The disposition of the Roman army in Britain described in the *Notitia* and the ruins of the fortresses of the Saxon Shore rising from the meadows of our south-east coast, both speak to us with equal emphasis of the serious view of the Saxon menace taken by the imperial government during the last phase of Roman Britain. The walls of these forts of the Saxon Shore are more imposing at the present day than the ruined foundations of the Roman forts in northern Britain. No quarrying of post-Roman times has been able to destroy the concrete core of their

---

* *Vir spectabilis Dux Britanniarum* ('Britains' in the plural because there were now five provinces within the 'Diocese' of Britain).

† *Vir spectabilis Comes Litoris Saxonici per Britanniam.*

‡ *Vir spectabilis Comes Britanniarum.*

walls. The modern excavations at Richborough and at Pevensey (Pls. 9, 10) are enabling the present generation to see these fortresses with a new understanding. Their walls, rising in places to a height of twenty-five feet, their ditches, their bastions—such things as these show how the Romans in this latest period were thrown upon the defensive. In name and in appearance the *castella* of the Saxon Shore were coming to resemble the castles of the Middle Ages. But while the medieval castles were well adapted to protect a local magnate from the attacks of his neigh-bours, the forts of the Saxon Shore were not so well devised to meet the raids of volatile sea-raiders. We seem to see in them a scheme stamped with the mentality of generals accustomed to the land warfare of the continental Empire and obsessed with a theory about a new artillery defence. It looks like the scheme of men who did not sufficiently understand that the main pro-tection of an island must be with ships rather than walls, even the highest, the solidest, the most impregnable walls. None the less, it must be confessed that at present we do not know enough about the Channel fleet of the Romans in the fourth century to condemn their High Command for stupidity. The positions of the Saxon Shore forts, placed at what were in those days the harbours of that coast, and the fact that their walls were extended to the sea, suggest that they were planned for the protection of shipping. We do know that among the Romans' ships were certain forty-oared camouflaged vessels used as scouts.[3a]

It is possible to claim a high strategic value for the forts. Thus it is argued:[4] 'These forts which formed a strong coastal defence and were also probably supply bases for the fleet, must have done much to minimize the raids, as, although the Saxons might have penetrated inland between them, the fear must always have been present that their retreat would be cut off by the garrisons, and their ships destroyed by the patrolling Roman galleys.'

Enough has been said to show that we have here a good example of the perennial controversy about the relative value of

PLATE 9

Richborough—an air-photograph
Royal Air Force Official. Crown copyright reserved

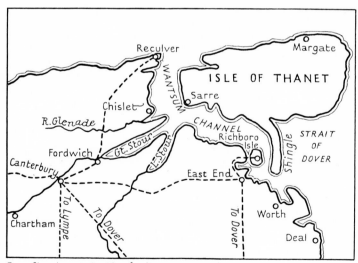

From Chartham to Deal is 16¾ miles

N.E. Kent—probable waterways of the Roman period
To show the importance of Richborough as a port

PLATE 10

Richborough. North wall of the Saxon Shore Fort

By permission of the Controller of H.M. Stationery Office

mobile forces and fixed defences in warfare. But until the spade turns up more substantial evidence that a strong Roman fleet was based on the harbours of the Saxon Shore, we may continue to suspect that the Romans, with their massive concrete walls, were acting like children who attempt to keep out an incoming tide with a dam of stones; efforts may be made to fill in the gaps, but they are doomed to fail. Indications that the rulers of Roman Britain in the fourth century experienced something of this kind may be found in the existence of other fortifications along the Saxon Shore supplementary to those enumerated in the *Notitia*. There was, for instance, Walton Castle (now covered by the sea), near Felixstowe, and at the western end of the Shore there have been discovered traces of a fort at Carisbrooke, which in the Middle Ages was used as a foundation for the castle. A fort at Cardiff occupied down to 375, or later, shows that some attempt was made to extend the system even to the west coast. In Lincolnshire, walls of the new type at Caistor and at Horn-castle illustrate a modification in which inland fortifications were used to supplement, or to take the place of, shore defences. Even a posting station like Margidunum on the Fosse Way was given its strong walls.

Significant additions were also made to the defences of London and of York. At London the river wall was probably built about the same time as the forts on the Saxon Shore, and was evidently intended to protect the city from Saxon attack by river. Bastions also were built on to the walls on the landward sides. At York the river wall was constructed about 300, and some fifty years later magnificent corner bastions were added, one of which, the Multangular Tower (Pl. 68), topped with medieval work, may be seen in the Museum Gardens. Then, when peace had been permanently dispelled by great barbarian inroads about 360, further attempts were made to strengthen the defences of northern Britain. Small stations were built at intervals of about ten miles along the coast of Yorkshire and elsewhere. Those of which the clearest traces remain extend from Huntcliff to Filey.

Being placed at the top of the cliffs, they were not intended like the forts of the Saxon Shore to protect shipping. All that their small garrisons could do was to watch for the approach of an enemy from the sea and then to signal a warning which could be brought back to the base fort at Malton and so to the head-quarters at York.

FIG. 18. Restored view of north corner of Roman fort at Malton.

What is most extraordinary about the disposition of the Roman army detailed in the *Notitia* is the fact that, apart from some garrisons posted in the extreme north-west to guard the flank of the great Tyne–Solway Wall, there is an almost complete absence of regular troops in the west of Britain. This official record of the imperial army assigned no units to any station in the west of the island between the Ribble and Southampton Water. Here the *Notitia* does not tally with the discovery of the Roman fort at Cardiff, or with the evidence that Segontium (Carnarvon) was repaired and re-garrisoned about 364. How-

ever, it is indubitable that towards the end of the Roman
rule there was no adequate defence of western Britain by the
imperial troops.

What is the explanation of this strange gap in the British
defences? To answer this we are thrown back on mere conjecture. We may say that the scheme revealed in the *Notitia* was
planned before the danger from the Irish had been brought
home to the government, and that the later Emperors, being
too much occupied with dangers nearer home to do more than
tinker at the old plan, failed to recast it thoroughly and readjust
it to the new situation. Or we may say[5] that the defence of the
western uplands was informally handed over by the Romans to
the friendly natives; in other words, that the tribes of Wales and
of the south-western peninsula were left to their own devices
because they were, as has been seen, too little Romanized and
their hills too barren to justify the organization of an Irish
Shore with a network of costly forts like those on the south-
eastern coast. But the root of the matter no doubt was this:
the Empire was suffering from a shortage of men, or rather of
the money to pay for them. It was one thing to see that the
west of the island needed systematic defence, and it was quite
a different matter to find the wherewithal. What was of primary
importance was that the communications between Britain and
the Continent should be kept open and that the corn-land and
sheep-walks of the eastern half of the island should be protected.
Thus did the military policy of the later Empire accentuate the
contrast between the two sides of Britain: that contrast between
the more civilized lowlands and the wilder hill country which
had its origin in remote geological ages.

However we explain the contrast between the Roman defences
on the east and the west of the island, there can be no question
that the incomplete, lop-sided disposition of the troops did as a
matter of fact expose the country to its enemies. In one way or
another, by peaceful infiltration or by violent conquest, a tribe
like the Irish Desi from county Waterford was able to settle in

Pembrokeshire; and the extent of the Irish penetration of the west is marked by the finds of stones with Ogham inscriptions in the Irish manner—incised probably about the fifth century.

THE LAST PERIOD OF ROMAN RULE (360–(?)410)

The beginning of the end of Roman rule may be placed about 360. The preceding period had in general been one of peace and of some prosperity. British corn and cloth had been exported; Britain like the rest of the Empire had benefited from the reforms of Diocletian (284–305) and Constantine (306–37). Its civil government had been separated from the military, and had been reorganized into five provinces. Christianity had been introduced as the official religion. The first half of the fourth century has accordingly been described by Haverfield[6] as 'the zenith of ancient history in Britain'. Nowadays our attention is more drawn to the shadows in the picture; to the sense of insecurity in the hearts of men, revealed by the new forts on the coast and the new walls round inland towns. Recent excavation has also supplied evidence that even from the beginning of the fourth century—or earlier—there was a decline of prosperity in the towns. When buildings in Viroconium (Wroxeter) were burnt about 300 they were not rebuilt. The pavements of Verulamium (St. Albans) when injured were rudely patched up with clay. In the fourth century the arts were less cultivated than in earlier times. Fewer inscriptions were set up. The builders who added bastions to the walls of London used ruins of neighbouring houses, including their columns and sculptures, as material. These houses were presumably derelict, because London, like other towns, was on the decline. The kernel of inhabited houses had shrunk within the shell of its walls.[7] Our best experts are now agreed that the town had been overbuilt. The imperial government had, like Peter the Great, been in too great a hurry to civilize its barbarians. Accordingly in the fourth century, even before the troublous times, the towns were becoming depopulated and impoverished. Then about 360 the troubles began,

PLATE 11

An Elk fight, an amusement in the Roman
Empire, *c.* A.D. 400–450

PLATE 12

A. Reconstruction of the temple-settlement, Lydney

B. Minimissimi, minute sub-Roman coins. From Lydney. $\frac{1}{2}$

C. Bronze Dog from the Temple of Nodens at Lydney. $\frac{1}{1}$

and first one and then another part of the Roman superstructure crumbled: first the villas of the well-to-do landowners, next the civil service and the army, lastly the towns. The years from 360 to 367 were a crescendo of ravage. In 360 the Picts from north Britain and the Scots from Ireland broke into the province and harried the lands near the frontier. By 364 the Saxons and other barbarians had joined in and were taking their share of the spoil of the province. Then in 367 the Count of the Saxon Shore was slain by the enemy and the Duke of the northern army was surprised and overwhelmed. London and the other towns were cut off and threatened by the wandering bands of plunderers. Theodosius, the imperial general who was sent to restore order, had to wait for reinforcements before he could advance from Richborough to London. In the following year the situation was restored by him. The enemy were punished and their wandering bands expelled; the discipline and morale of the garrisons were re-established. Outwardly the military situation was restored, but the old social order was wrecked and the prestige of the Empire was dangerously shaken.

The importance of the devastation caused in these years has recently been emphasized by R. G. Collingwood. He has argued[8] that 'Roman Britain, by 367, had all her eggs in one basket'— the villa; and that the coin finds prove that the disaster was fatal to most of the villas, as centres of civilized life. This view of the ruination caused by the raids of 360–7 is now generally credited, though it is admitted that there were many exceptions up and down the country, especially in Kent, Somerset, and the Cambridge region, and it is probable[9] that many villa owners saved themselves, though not their villas, by fleeing to the towns.

An illuminating sidelight has been cast on one spot in Roman Britain in this latest age after the beginning of the troubles, and it is a reminder that the shadows must not be made too black. Recent excavations at the Temple of Nodens at Lydney, a temple placed on a hill by the Severn, nine miles north of Chepstow,[10] have shown that soon after 364–7, elaborate Roman buildings

were constructed within a prehistoric earthwork: large bath-
ing establishments, a row of shops (or priests' rooms), and a large
guest house for visitors to the shrine. The masonry is solid;
floors are tessellated: there is no sign here that the civilization
of the Severn valley had been destroyed. Nor is there any sign
that Christianity had long been the official religion of the
Empire. The priests of Nodens, evidently a Celtic divinity,
found that the healing powers ascribed to the god were profitable.
Of the 8,000 Roman coins which have been recovered from the
neighbourhood most were of the fourth century. We see then
that even towards the close of this century life could in places
still be lived on much the same peaceful lines as of old, and
that in the Severn valley men were still able to bring themselves and their families to enjoy the luxury of a 'cure' in the
quiet of the Lydney woods. Soon, however, events occurred
across the seas which turned the order of Britain, as of all the
civilized world, into irretrievable confusion.

On the death of the Emperor Theodosius in 395 the Empire
was cut into two; thenceforth the two halves of it went their
different ways to ruin. Honorius, to whom was bequeathed the
rule of the Western Provinces, was a child, and remained till
his death in 423 childish in mind (Pl. 13 A), without wisdom
or capacity, a breeder of pigeons. Yet the dangers now threatening the Western Empire were so great that only the highest
qualities of foresight and leadership could have saved the State.
Germans had gained the chief positions in the government; German troops had become the backbone of the Roman army;
Germans hesitating between service and spoliation were both
within and outside the Empire—within its borders Alaric the
Goth was already beginning to see the truth that the Empire
could not withstand those determined to seek kingdoms for themselves; outside, wild bands of Alans, Vandals, and Sueves were
massed beyond the Rhine like the besiegers of a city, restlessly
waiting an opportunity to assault Gaul and to sack it. In the
north, Franks were pushing persistently from Toxandria into the

valleys of the Scheldt and the Lys, ever planting their villages farther into the heart of Belgic Gaul, and thus threatening the line of communication between Britain and the Continent. And behind the Franks there came, as we have seen, the Saxons —Saxons pressing on their heels in the forest lands of western Germany; Saxons packed in long boats, exploring the waterways of the Low Countries and looking to the sea and to the sea-coasts of Britain and Gaul for their fortunes.

FIG. 19. A Pict.

FIG. 20. A Scot.

The generation which had the ill fate to be born in the latter half of the fourth century was to see the civilized world end in catastrophe. Everything was going wrong at the same moment, and for that reason the troubles were becoming unmanageable. The Empire was sick, not only in its head but in every one of its members; and the Saxons, though they were still a nuisance to those who lived near the sea (as they had been for well over a century) were one of the lesser evils of the age.

So far as the Roman provinces of Britain were concerned, the danger which threatened civilization came from nearer home. It was raiding bands of Picts from the north who brought fire and slaughter to the country round York and then penetrated to the heart of Britain. It was the men of Ireland (then called 'Scots') who destroyed the civilization of the west and carried off thousands of peaceful Britons to sell them as slaves.

This was the general situation. And in such a world three well-known incidents by ill luck combined to denude the island of its regular garrison and sever its effective connexion with the central government.

First, in 383, Maximus (Pl. 43, 2), who held a high command in Britain, revolted and led a considerable part of the British garrison across the narrow seas to Gaul to assert his claim to the imperial diadem. It was the selfish act of an adventurer, and its effect on Britain was to expose the north to the barbarians. Coins found in the forts of the Roman Wall go down to the year 383, but after that only minims are well attested.*[11a] For a few years Honorius allowed the military prestige of the Empire to be restored by Stilicho, a man of Vandal origin, who had climbed to the position of commander-in-chief. Thanks to Stilicho, wrote a court poet of the age,[11] Britannia need no longer fear the Scot and the Pict, nor keep watch along all her coasts dreading the coming of the Saxons with every change of wind. But he spoke too soon. For (this is the second incident of the three) in 401, when Alaric and his Visigoths advanced against Italy, Stilicho did not hesitate to withdraw another 'legion' (perhaps no more than a thousand men) from Britain.

Then, thirdly, in 407, the Roman troops in Britain, revolting against the incapacity of Honorius, set up successively three usurpers, of whom the last, Constantine, followed a course outwardly not unlike that of Maximus in 383. Constantine was no sooner hailed as Caesar in Britain than he transported his army to Gaul, and the troops withdrawn never returned.

The event of 407 which had stirred the troops of Britain to this feverish insubordination was the terrible irruption of Vandals, Sueves, and Alans into Gaul. In midwinter they had crossed the Rhine. Gaul had then become a stormy sea of barbarians, or rather one vast, smoking, funeral pyre.* Britain seemed to be cut off from the imperial government. In this

* *Uno fumavit Gallia tota rogo.* S. Orientius, in Migne, *P.L.* lxi, col. 995.

PLATE 13

The Emperor Honorius and his
wife, a daughter of Stilicho the
Vandal (his commander-in-chief)

A plundered Roman flagon of silver.
From the Traprain hoard. About $\frac{1}{3}$

PLATE 14

Air-photograph of Cissbury, Sussex, a disused fort reoccupied about the fourth century

crisis, Constantine and the troops who followed him to the Continent may have dreamed that in Gaul they would defeat the enemies of the State, or they may have been thinking less of the State and more of themselves, their own fortunes, and their own pay in a dissolving world.

In 407 the situation of the Roman army in Britain may well have seemed desperate. Britain was raked by barbarians attacking from three sides. Some signs of the barbarities which

FIG. 21. Silver ring buried with a horde of coins near Wilton, about A.D. 400. The device is found on coins with the legend, *Concordia militum*.

made the Pictish or the Saxon invasions a terrible reality have been found. For instance, in the Yorkshire coastguard station at Huntcliff, when the fort was stormed about the year 400, the defenders were slain and their bodies, together with those of their women and children, were tossed into a well. At Caistor by Norwich a house has been excavated which was inhabited till about 400 and was then burnt with thirty-six persons, presumably refugees, inside it. It was probably about this same time—about the turn of the century—that Niall of the Nine Hostages, the first High King of Ireland known to history, overran the west of Britain, and in a merciless raid Patrick, the son of a British decurion, and 'many thousands' of other captives were carried off to slavery.

The end of the connected story of Roman Britain—such as it is—is contained in two passages referring to the year 410. One from a contemporary Gallic chronicle says briefly[12] that 'the multitude of the enemy so prevailed, that the strength of the Romans was extremely diminished. The provinces of Britain were laid waste by an incursion of the Saxons.' This disaster is placed in the chronicle side by side with the devastation of Gaul by Vandals and Alans and the sufferings of Rome, 'the head of the world'. The strength of the Romans in Britain passed away in the same year that Rome itself endured the three days' sack at the hands of Alaric and his Visigoths.

The other passage is contained in some ambiguous sentences of Zosimus:[13]

'. . . The barbarians from beyond the Rhine [i.e. the Saxons] ravaging everything at pleasure compelled both the inhabitants of the British Isle and some of the peoples of Gaul to secede from the Empire of the Romans and to live independent of them, no longer obeying the Roman laws. The people of Britain, therefore, taking up arms, and braving every danger, freed their cities from the invading barbarians. And the whole of Armorica, and other provinces of Gaul, imitating the Britons, liberated themselves in like manner, expelling the Roman officials and setting up a civil polity according to their own inclination.

'This secession of Britain and of Gallic peoples took place during the time of Constantine's usurpation, the barbarians rising up in consequence of his neglect of the government. . . .

'Honorius moreover having written letters to the cities in Britain urging them to look to their own safety . . . lived at ease.'

The value and real meaning of this passage is one of the puzzles of history, but if, as is probable, Zosimus, who lived in the latter half of the fifth century, drew his information from an earlier writer (Olympiodorus), we may give weight to the statements that the people of Britain now took up arms; that they fought well; and that the local rulers in 'the cities'*—some of them old centres of cantonal administration—sundered from the central government by the force of circumstances and the waves of barbarism which now flowed between Italy and Britain, found that in practice they were left to shift for themselves.

THE SUB-ROMAN PERIOD (*c.* 410–*c.* 450)

And so we pass to the age of the greatest darkness: it is so dark that neither the date of its beginning nor of its end can be fixed

---

* e.g. Exeter, Dorchester, Winchester, Chichester, Canterbury, Silchester, Caerwent, Colchester, Caistor by Norwich, Leicester, Wroxeter.

with certainty, and in calling it 'sub-Roman' we are simply confessing our ignorance of its positive characteristics.

We can say vaguely that while Roman Britain in the previous generation had lost most of its civilized villas, now in this sub-Roman period it had to struggle on without the main body of the Roman garrison and without the unifying authority of the bureaucracy appointed by the Emperor. In spite of the catastrophes which at this time destroyed so much of the old order, the change now as elsewhere in history came gradually.

Just how far the circumstances of Roman Britain were changed about 410 is still a subject of controversy. Bury, the historian of the later Roman Empire, whose opinions must carry great weight, has argued that the *Notitia Dignitatum* gives something like the real distribution of the Roman troops in the period 428–37, and that 'the true date of the Roman abandonment of Britain [is] A.D. 442'.[14] Bury's view was at first condemned as it was thought to be contrary to the evidence of the coins. This last was held to point decisively to the abandonment of the Wall by its garrison about 383, and to the abandonment of most of Britain even before 410. The coins which have come to light at Richborough in recent years number more than sixty thousand. The examination of the first finds has shown that the great bulk of them, where they could be identified, were minted in the last thirty-five years of the fourth century and a considerable number about A.D. 400. R. G. Collingwood, once a chief critic of Bury, has come round to a view not unlike Bury's. Impressed by an argument that officials like the Count of Britain are later than 409, he holds that the Britain of the *Notitia* in general is later. His change of view has also been caused by a reconsideration of the coin evidence. The difficulty in interpreting this arises from the fact that the continental bronze and silver mints which had supplied the pay for the troops in Britain were closed about the end of the fourth century, and that consequently the coins of Honorius and of Arcadius (his brother and colleague in the

East) remained in circulation as no other imperial coins had done before them.

At present all that can be said is that while the argument from the coins is sufficient to discredit the *Notitia*'s garrison of the Wall, it is not sufficient to prove a complete negative. Regions on the Continent can be pointed out, such as Noricum

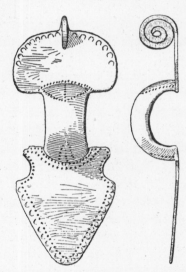

FIG. 22. Lydney; brooch excavated in 1928–9, assigned to the post-Roman period. ¼.

Ripense and parts of Normandy,[15] where the coin finds ceased as in Britain though the authority of the Emperors survived down to the middle of the fifth century. We must still hesitate before we assert that no Roman troops whatever, no cadre of the former garrison supplemented it may be with reinforcements from the Continent, lingered on in Richborough and the south-eastern parts of the island long after 410.

In other directions also the results of the troubles of the early fifth century are often exaggerated. When Honorius sent his rescript to the cities of Britain urging them to look after their own safety, he was taking a sensible step which may have given

Britain a fairly satisfactory government for some decades. The presumed condition of affairs has been summed up by R. G. Collingwood in the following words:*

'What the cities lacked was a co-ordinating power; they must therefore have run on more or less parallel but unconnected lines, always in danger of getting to cross-purposes, and also in danger of becoming the tools of ambitious men bitten by a desire for local greatness. They continued also to raise and employ local militia: but these forces, adequate for a defence of town walls against casual barbarian raids, would be useless for a campaign and therefore unable to drive an enemy out of a countryside.'

Archaeology unfortunately can do little to fill in the gaps in our knowledge of the sub-Roman period. The Romano-British provincials, engrossed by the immediate necessities of their existence, seem to have used up their old belongings, or if they made new things they must have made them out of perishable materials like wood and leather. None the less, even for the fifth century the spade has supplied some data, few but significant. At Silchester and elsewhere a town gateway has been found half blocked up with masonry; an entrance built in the Golden Age could be dangerously wide in days when the *pax Romana* was ending. At Lydney, by the Severn, men thought it necessary to strengthen a prehistoric rampart. In the southern downlands disused earthworks like Cissbury (Pl. 14) and Yarnbury were reoccupied, doubtless by refugees, some time towards the end of the Roman period. In the north a rude fort like 'the Castles' near Hamsterley in County Durham may tell a similar tale, since it is built on a Roman plan, though with stones neither squared nor cemented.

Two other finds in this necessarily disconnected list are specially interesting. One is a memorial stone with an Ogham inscription, excavated at Silchester, which shows that the Irish, either as friends or foes, penetrated into the heart of southern Britain. The other is the hoard of spoil carried off about the

* Privately communicated.

beginning of the fifth century from a Roman province (probably Gaul) and buried on the top of Traprain Law, the hill which is a well-known landmark in the country south of the Forth. The beautiful silver flagons and dishes (Pls. 13 B and 15), now in the Museum at Edinburgh, were evidently loot from a church and from the mansion of some wealthy landowner. Since many of them had been hacked in two, it is conjectured that two bands had co-operated in the raid and had then divided the spoil equally. Thereafter one band, being surprised in their lair on the hill, buried their treasure in haste, and were overtaken by death before any of them could return and recover the hoard. In these battered silver vessels we see the process by which the beautiful things of the Roman world were carried off to be melted down and converted into jewellery for the barbarians.

External ravage was accompanied by internal decay. It is now possible to study the latter in the coins (some of them scarcely deserve that name) found at Richborough and Lydney. These show the makeshifts used by the people of Britain when, isolated from Roman mints, they had to produce a currency of their own.[15a] Sometimes they minted small barbarous copies of genuine Roman coins in base metal, sometimes they used minims or minimissimi, the smallest coins ever produced in this island. Since they are so small that fifty of them can be placed side by side on a halfpenny (Pl. 12 B), we need not wonder that they have rarely been noticed by previous excavators. Now, however, they are our best illustration of the poverty and degradation which overtook the deserted provincials. The sub-Romans could attempt to repeat on their barbarous imitations the inscriptions of happier times—'Victoria'; 'Gloria Romanorum'; 'Fel[ix] Temp[orum] Reparatio'.[15b] But these were mere parrot-cries. The figure of Mars was so badly copied that it became a woman: in another series a female figure with arms outstretched was copied till in time it became a Saxon cross.

Are these miserable substitutes for a coinage a fair measure of the degradation to which the Romano-Britons succumbed in

PLATE 15

A view of Traprain Law

The treasure as found

the fifth century? Archaeologists are beginning to identify jewellery which shows a survival of British craftsmanship in the fifth century. E. T. Leeds assigns to it certain Romanizing penannular and disc brooches. T. D. Kendrick claims for it even the finest 'Kentish' brooches and other objects with enamel or Celtic curvilinear art, found in Anglo-Saxon graves, especially the enamelled plaques of numerous hanging bowls.[15c] But on the other hand the clumsy masonry of the sub-Roman period, the barbarous patchings of tessellated pavements, the mud floors, the resort to earthworks of the primitive type, the lettering and grammar of the tombstones and the minims—all these tell a convincing story of rapid demoralization.

Having obtained from the archaeologists some information, however fragmentary, about the sub-Roman period, we have next to fall back upon the few references to it in literature.

Nennius,* the Welsh antiquary of the early ninth century, who did his best to be the historian of the Britons, relates, in one of the more reliable sections of his book,[16] a tradition that Cunedda, son of Eternus and grandson of Paternus, came towards the end of the fourth century† with his eight sons from the north, that is, from the region called Manaw Gododin, near the Firth of Forth, and expelled the Irish from Gwynedd and other parts of Wales, defeating them so utterly that never again did they try to settle there. The Britons among the hills of Wales were thus reanimated; they obtained a vigorous dynasty, tinged with Roman civilization but essentially Celtic in thought and language. This story illustrates the complexity of the situation in Britain about the time of the great catastrophe. There was no simple straightforward conflict between provincials and barbarian invaders. A chieftain with a Roman pedigree could come

---

* I retain the name by which he has been known in the past, though R. Thurneysen (in *Zeitsch. f. Celtische Philologie*, xx (1933), 97–138) argues that the name should be read as Nemnius or Nemnivus.

† i.e. '146 years before Maelgwn reigned'. Maelgwn died in 547.

from beyond the pale of the Empire. When he settled in Wales, those whom he drove out were not Britons but Irish, who had for some indeterminable period been in possession of this region.

For the rest, British sources are too untrustworthy to be of much help in disentangling fact from fiction. Even Gildas (of whom as of Nennius we shall have more to say in the next chapter), though he ought to have possessed some traditions of value about the sub-Roman period since he lived in the middle of the sixth century, allows his main story to be discredited by a schoolboy howler about the Roman Wall. A few details remain which carry conviction. Gildas tells us of 'civil wars' which broke out among the Romano-Britons, and civil wars were surely inevitable where competing cities and individuals were left stranded without a central government. He refers to an appeal made to Aëtius in his third consulship; and Aëtius at any rate was an historical figure, a commander who for thirty years was the mainstay of Roman power in the West and whose third consulship is known to have occurred in the year 446.

If we discard the narrative of Gildas as improbable (and there is almost general agreement that it is necessary to do so for the first half of the fifth century, but not, be it noted, for the second half) we surrender the hope of obtaining any sort of connected history for the sub-Roman period. What remains? We have two contemporary writings which throw some light on the general condition of the country in the fifth century; and we have certain contradictory statements about the date of the first submergence of Britain—or of part of it—by the Saxons. The two books which help us to understand the former, the more important, subject are the *Life of St. Germanus* and the writings of St. Patrick.

The *Life of St. Germanus* is no better than the ordinary run of hagiography in its accumulation of miracles, but we do at any rate know that it must have been written before 490 (probably about 480), and that the author, Constantius, a priest of Lyons,

PLATE 16

Portrait from diptych, now identified as Stilicho, at
one time supposed to be Aetius

PLATE 17

VERULAMIUM : "LONDON GATE". SUGGESTED RECONSTRUCTION BY P. M. ANDREWS, A.R.I.B.A.

Reconstruction of the Gate through which St. Germanus probably entered Verulam

(? already falling into ruin by the 6th century)

had opportunities of learning about Britain at first or second hand, since he was a friend of Sidonius, who was in his turn a friend of Lupus, a companion of Germanus on the journey to Britain.[17] The *Life* tells us that Germanus, archbishop of Auxerre, paid two visits to Britain with the purpose of stamping out in the island the heretical views concerning free-will propagated throughout the Empire by Pelagius, a man of British* birth. On his visit in 429 Germanus showed the Britons that he was an old soldier as well as a saint. He held a council in which the damnable heresies of Pelagius were denounced. He accompanied the clergy attending the council to the tomb of St. Alban the Martyr, and he then taught the Britons how to defeat a combined army of Picts and Saxons by shouting 'Alleluiah' three times as they closed with the enemy. At first sight the alliance between Pictish-speaking Highlanders and German-speaking Saxons seems so great an improbability that it is reasonable to see in it one of the author's imaginative touches intended to enhance the fame of the saint, a victory over two peoples being more miraculous than a victory over one. He would regard the change as a laudable improvement of the story, quite in keeping with the principles of hagiography. Another explanation, however, is possible. There is, it is asserted,† archaeological evidence for the view that Saxons were entering the eastern Midlands for some time before 429. These, being hard pressed, might conceivably call to their aid Pictish pirates—and we have the authority of Gildas for thinking that the Pictish raiders came by sea rather than by land. Such bands might well cause fear among the militia of London and of Verulam, unused to fighting in the open. The skirmish between the Christian and the heathen might occur in the hills of the Chiltern escarpment. The 'Alleluiah' shout may have been intended to beat the Germans at their own game, the battle shout—a custom as old as the time of Tacitus. These are possibilities rather than probabilities; and when we are told that the 'Alleluiah' was re-echoed by the rocks

* Or Irish.   † See below, p. 116.

of the surrounding mountains we recognize the easy rhetoric of a hagiographer.

But whatever view we take of the Alleluiah victory of St. Germanus, we need not doubt that his *Life* contains a residuum which may reasonably be accepted. We have the significant points: that a Gallic archbishop could cross to Britain as a matter of course and co-operate with the clergy of Britain; and that south-eastern Britain was still a land where Romano-Britons lived their old life even though they were vexed by invaders as well as by Pelagian heresy.

About 447 or somewhat earlier Germanus returned to Britain, but he was then an old man and his second visit supplied fewer incidents to the biographer. The saint on landing was welcomed by a certain Elafius, the leading man of the district. Britain still does not appear to be submerged by barbarians. But what is most remarkable of all is that at the time when the *Life* of the saint was composed—say about 480—the author could still think of Britain as a wealthy island,* and boast that the pure doctrine taught by Germanus was still preserved in those parts. Even in the last quarter of the fifth century the encroachment of the Saxons had not become so flagrant that it was necessary for a Roman provincial to observe that the Britons, in spite of their orthodoxy, were no longer in possession of Britain. The *Life of St. Germanus* thus supplies some local colour which we cannot afford to disregard, even when we admit that it comes from an alien author writing about fifty years after the chief event which he describes.

More satisfactory and more vivid are the short writings of St. Patrick, the only Briton of the sub-Roman period whose words take us straight to the heart of the man and near to the spirit of the age. We have the *Confession* in which he pours out a wandering but a glowing defence of his career:[18]

'I, Patrick the sinner, am the most illiterate and the least of all the faithful, and contemptible in the eyes of very many. My father was

* *opulentissima insula* (c. 18).

Calpurnius, a deacon, one of the sons of Potitus, a presbyter, who belonged to the village of [?] Bannavem Taberniae. Now he had a small villa* hard by, where I was taken captive.

'I was then about sixteen years of age. I knew not the true God; and I went into captivity to Ireland with many thousands of persons, according to our deserts, because we departed away from God, and kept not His commandments, and were not obedient to our priests, who used to admonish us for our salvation.'

The raid which carried off Patricius, the well-born Romano-Briton, to Ireland, and which, as we have seen, probably occurred about 400, helps, like the Traprain hoard, to bring home to us what really happened in the interminable wars which distressed the wretched inhabitants of our island decade after decade from 360 onwards. A boy of sixteen driven off to slavery with 'many thousands' of others, sold and set to tend swine in a remote part of Ireland—that may stand for the fate of untold numbers of Romano-Britons. The matter-of-fact way in which St. Patrick speaks of his misfortune is also typical of the times. The raid is accepted as a matter of course: it is simply one of the punishments with which God is admonishing His people for their own good. Misfortune is fostering religion.

Let us quote once more from the *Confession*:

'Now after I came to Ireland, tending flocks was my daily occupation; and constantly I used to pray in the day-time. Love of God and the fear of Him increased more and more; and faith grew and the spirit was moved, so that in one day [I would say] as many as a hundred prayers, and at night nearly as many, so that I used to stay even in the woods and on the mountain [to this end]. And before daybreak I used to be roused to prayer, in snow, in frost, in rain; and I felt no hurt. . . . And there verily one night I heard in my sleep a voice saying to me, "Thou fastest to good purpose, thou who art soon to go to thy fatherland". And again after a very short time I heard the answer [of God] saying to me, "Lo, thy ship is ready". And it was not near at hand, but was distant, perhaps, two hundred miles.'

The story which follows, of his escape on the heathen trading-

* *villulam.*

ship (probably to Gaul), of his wanderings with the crew for twenty-eight days, through country devastated so that it was little better than a desert: all this need not detain us, though the story itself illustrates the curious juxtaposition of civilization and barbarism which marks this age—here merchants who trade in Irish sporting-dogs, there a countryside so wasted that travellers may almost die of hunger.

Other allusions in St. Patrick's writings also help us to conceive the conditions of the sub-Roman period. For instance, when he speaks of his return to Britain (probably in 414–15) there is no suggestion that he is returning to a country given over to abnormal anarchy. 'And again, after a few years, I was in Britain with my kindred, who received me as a son, and in good faith besought me that at all events now, after the great tribulations which I had undergone, I would not depart from them anywhither.' It was there in Britain, about 432, while living with his kinsmen that he heard the voice of the Irishmen crying to him, 'Holy youth, we beseech you to come and walk among us once more'—the call which gave a new purpose to his life. What concerns our present point is that his kinsmen evidently thought that residence with them in Britain would be sufficiently peaceful to compensate him 'after the great tribulations' of his earlier years. Patrick is at pains to defend himself from the charge of shirking his duties by departing from his kinsmen to 'live as an exile among barbarians'. In one place, he says, 'I am born of a father who was a decurion, but I sold my noble rank . . . for the profit of others'. This is a course which needs justification. It is heavily on his conscience. Accordingly at the date when Patrick wrote—probably well into the middle of the fifth century—the imperial system of local government was, it seems, intact in so far as the decurions or *curiales* (the members of the town council) were still the class who were mutually responsible for the load of taxes due to the government. Furthermore, in the eyes of Patrick, Britain is still a land where 'lordly rhetoricians' flourish. He is always expecting these elegant stay-

Department **13** -

ACCT. NO. **9 5 08**

18597- 7

Date _1 - 9_ 19_58_

by _303_   Amount of Sale   Receipt Number

rge to _E. L. Barnard_

et _Lowell D_   Apt. _2_

- State _C_

ARGE	INSTAL. DEFERRED	CASH SEND	CUST. PROP.	C. O. D.	CREDIT	CASH REF.	
				Hist of Anglo Saxon 2 vols		11	20
				air mail sper Del Chang		4	03

DEPARTMENT MANAGER'S O. K.

NET AMOUNT		
NON PAT. REF.		
LUX. TAX		
TOTAL	15	23

THIS SLIP MUST BE RETURNED FOR ANY ADJUSTMENT

at-homes to laugh at his 'rusticity'. He knows he cannot write Latin as if it were his own tongue. This distresses him; but 'I wish my brethren and kinsfolk to know what manner of man I am, that they may be able to understand the desire of my soul'. Britain might have its rhetoricians; but, as we may gather from the *Life of St. Germanus*, it was far behind Gaul as a school of Christianity. Patrick turned for his religious training to Gaul and not to Britain, to Lérins and Auxerre and not to London. Britain was backward, but there was no question of its not being the home of Romans—Romans regarded from an angle different from that of the fourth century—'holy Romans'. Patrick's ideas on the subject come out in his letter to Coroticus, the Briton who had somehow or other obtained rule over the Britons of Strathclyde. The soldiers of Coroticus had made a raid on the north of Ireland; they had 'cruelly butchered with the sword' newly baptized converts of Patrick, 'while the chrism was still fragrant on their foreheads'; they had carried off girls and distributed them; and when Patrick had sent clergy to ask the raiders to return some of the booty and all of the baptized captives, they had laughed at his messengers.

In the shaft of sunlight cast by this letter to Coroticus what is shown to us is once more a topsy-turvy world; not Irish raiding Britons but Britons raiding Irish. Patrick, the Briton, appeals to the soldiers of this chieftain living beyond the old Roman frontier as men who are discrediting the Roman name. 'I have written these words to be sent . . . to the soldiers of Coroticus; I do not say to my fellow-citizens* or to the fellow-citizens of the holy Romans, but to those who are fellow-citizens of demons because of their evil deeds.' He upbraids them for having dealings with 'the most vile and apostate Picts'. The world is still divided into men of civilization and barbarians, but the differentia is changing. To Patrick the name 'Romans' means those who are baptized into the society of Rome. Here, then, in the middle of the fifth century we see in the writings of Patrick a new state

---

* *civibus meis.*

of things. The Roman provinces are not simply beleaguered, as at the end of the fourth century, by barbarians. The Roman world is barbarized; but the barbarian world increasingly reflects sunset tints from the sinking Roman civilization. The Irish are ceasing to be the terror of the western seas because Patrick and his fellow workers are baptizing them by the thousand and are teaching them—not always it must be admitted with complete success—that it is a barbarous thing to live by plunder.

And even 'the vile Picts' had begun to change under the teaching of St. Ninian, a Briton, an elder contemporary of St. Patrick. For some years after 400, Ninian from his new church built of stone, the *Candida Casa*, which gave its name to Whitern, had sown Christianity among the Picts—those of Galloway and, it is sometimes claimed, those also who lived beyond the Forth.

In all the countries bordering on the western seas of Britain we see, not stagnation or mere decline, but activity and the beginnings of new life.

Before we can grope our way any further in this fifth century, we must try to come to an understanding about the date at which the permanent Saxon occupation of British territory began. Three dates have rival claims for acceptance.

(1) A date corresponding to A.D. 428 is one of the suggestions thrown out in the *Historia Brittonum*. But Nennius—or the other writers whose works were incorporated in the *Historia*—weakens the value of his words by offering his readers a confusing choice of dates for the advent of the Saxons.[19] The date 428 also fits in with the story of the Alleluiah battle and possibly with the evidence* of some early Saxon brooches found in the eastern Midlands. When two or three pieces in our jig-saw puzzle can be fitted together in this way, one is loath to say there is a mistake. But looking at the other pieces of the puzzle, we may

* See below, pp. 116–17.

with some confidence add that if there was infiltration of Saxons at this time, it was comparatively unimportant. They were probably raiders rather than settlers. They cannot have been the conquerors of south-eastern Britain who cut the communications between the island and the Continent.

(2) A.D. 441–2. In favour of this date there is a single short sentence in a Gallic chronicle[20] which says: 'The eighteenth year of Theodosius II [A.D. 441–2] the provinces of Britain which up to this time had been on all sides harassed* by various slaughters and disasters, are brought under the dominion of the Saxons.' Some historians[21] think that since the Gallic chronicler was a contemporary, the above statement is sufficient evidence that what the Welshmen later called the *adventus Saxonum* was an accomplished fact by 441–2. If it is objected that the words of the chronicler are vague and that they may describe a temporary submission during a raid like that of 367, a later Gallic chronicler[20] (he wrote about 511) can be produced who says with reference to 441–2: 'The provinces of Britain are lost to the Romans and yield to the rule of the Saxons.' This is indeed more definite; but it is at the best a gross exaggeration.

(3) A.D. 449.† The date which has for so long been current among English historians is derived from Bede. The objections to it are that Bede's statements in his various works are not quite consistent,[22] and, more serious, that Bede, writing some three hundred years after the event, seems to have arrived at his date only by an inference of his own from Gildas. Since Bede's tables showed him that the third consulship of Aëtius was in 446–7, he assumed that the invasion followed within a few years.

Thus when the rival claims of 442 and 449 are compared, we find that we have to balance the words of a chronicler from the south of Gaul, who could only know about events in distant Britain through a fog of rumour, against the words of Gildas, who, though removed by time as well as by place, had none the

---

* *Latae* emended to *late vexatae*.
† Or, owing to Bede's inconsistencies, A.D. 446–57.

less a chance of hearing genuine traditions. If Gildas was right in thinking that when in 446 the Britons appealed to Aëtius for help, their enemies were Picts and Scots, and that the Saxon troops were introduced into the island as friendly auxiliaries, the Gallic annal was misleading. But in truth the words of the chronicler and the words of Gildas cannot fairly be weighed against one another; both are imponderable.

If we are agreed that 'the coming of Hengist and Horsa' occurred within about ten years of 450, that is enough for all practical purposes, and we shall feel that we are not far from the truth if we continue to speak, as in the past, of 'the middle of the fifth century' as the turning-point at which decades, even centuries, of Saxon raiding gave place to decades of Saxon conquest and settlement.

We shall see more fully in the next chapter how the coming of Hengist's band differed from that of previous Saxons who had landed in Britain. They came as federates; they seemed to the British king who employed them unlike the primitive Saxons from the north. And they were unlike. They were trained fighting men, supplied with instruments of warfare such as battering-rams. They could take and sack the towns of sub-Roman Britain. They could penetrate to the western sea. They could conquer and retain a favourite region of the provincials.

At the beginning of this chapter we set out with the purpose of discovering what there was to be learnt about the condition of Britain at the period when the Saxons began their conquest of the country. The time has now arrived to collect the impressions suggested by the few glimpses permitted us as we look back through the almost impenetrable screen of fifteen centuries.

Britain appears before us as a land which for eighty or ninety years, that is ever since 360, had been periodically swept by barbarians and wasted. The villas of the well-to-do had never recovered from the destruction of the years following 360. The imperial officials and the garrison had been the next supports of Romanism to vanish. The towns for a time remained; but if, as is now known, many of them were declining as early as the third and fourth centuries, what chance had they when the peace of Roman rule came to an end? We shall see in later chapters how various were the fates which befell them. No one can say for certain whether their strong walls and their militia were able to preserve them in the sub-Roman period. But if the towns were not sacked many of them were strangled or half-strangled. With pirates on the sea and barbarians molesting the old trade routes on the land, prosperity must have crumbled. In 410 it was the cities which were told to look to their own safety. By the middle of the fifth century it was a 'tyrant', not self-governing towns, who according to Gildas invited the Saxons into the island.

In these ways the three strongholds of Romanism had been largely destroyed by 450. With the well-to-do villas wiped out in the country districts, the Roman garrison dissipated, and the towns in rapid decay, the barely Romanized country folk in the villages were left the chief element in the population. But how far were they indeed left? If the Irish raid which carried off Patrick, and along with him some thousands of other captives, was typical of the anarchy of the fifth century, large tracts of Britain must have been emptied of inhabitants. Patrick's account of his wanderings in a hungry land for twenty-eight days after his escape from Ireland suggests that barbarian devastation in this age could leave a country little better than a desert.

Here, then, we reach a crucial point. If the native villages had been destroyed as the villas before them, the Saxons and Angles might indeed have found Britain, as some archaeologists have believed, a land of great unoccupied spaces which were only waiting for settlers from overseas to come and cultivate them. But does such a picture of Britain fit in with the fragments of our written information?

It is obvious that the available evidence is too defective to permit of any positive assertions; but so far as it goes it tells against the idea that Britain was in any sense derelict. Gildas speaks of the period which followed the appeal to Aëtius—that is, the middle of the fifth century—as a period which saw abundant plenty and the growth of *luxuria*. And putting Gildas aside, we have in the *Life of Germanus*, positively, a statement about the 'great wealth' of the island, and, negatively, an absence of reference to any abnormal dearth of population in sub-Roman Britain. But the evidence of any kind is so meagre that it is needless to labour the question.

If we try to obtain a general view of the Britain which in the middle of the fifth century confronted the incoming Saxons, it is much easier to conceive what things were like in the west than in the east. In the west the folk in the hill-top villages and the rude hill forts were living much the same strenuous life, only slightly tinged with Roman civilization, as had existed in the days of the Empire. We can form our opinions about these Celtic-speaking Britons. We know them from their descendants, the Welsh of later times. We know, too (from our written authorities), how in the west military leaders of different kinds during the fifth century established their power as political rulers—men like Coroticus in Strathclyde, commander of the lawless soldiery who raided St. Patrick's catechumens; or like Cunedda, who with war-bands from beyond the Wall 'drove out the Irish from Wales'. But in the east of the island there is nothing to fill the blank between the imperial rescript of 410 and Vortigern, the Celtic king of about 450.

The period which we have been specially studying in this chapter closes with what Gildas calls 'the groans of the Britons' to Aëtius. *Repellunt barbari ad mare, repellit mare ad barbaros.* It is not so easy, as some critics suggest, to dismiss these words as mere rhetoric. Gildas writes as if he had here some document before him. Rightly or wrongly this cry of the Britons will remain in the ears of posterity like a cry coming through the night from men in a sinking ship.

The ninety years between 360 and 450 seem in retrospect to be filled with little else but raids and destruction and every kind of violence. If we knew more about it we should, of course, see the light as well as the shade. That can be done in the history of the end of Roman Gaul, the nearest, though not a close, analogy to the end of Roman Britain. The letters of Sidonius show how a Gallic aristocrat of the fifth century could enjoy the sociabilities of life and leave the barbarians on one side with little more than a shrug of his shoulders and a contemptuous reference to their greased hair, their gluttony, their harsh and ugly language. None the less the shadow was deep enough in Roman Gaul. To some it seemed that they had reached the end of all things—'*ultima pertulimus*'; '*ultima quaeque vides*'[23]—and in Britain it must have been much the same. There, according to Gildas, pestilence and famine were added in the middle of the fifth century to barbarian invasion and to civil war.

As in all times of great calamity, the troubles affected men in opposite ways. Some were turned to debauchery—'We will eat and drink, for to-morrow we shall die,' quotes Gildas; others turned to religion.

It was in these decades that the British provincials became Christian in more than name. Before this age Christianity had been an official religion; the churches few and small; the Christian emblem, the ☧, used as a charm and stamped like a trade-mark on jewellery or pewter. After this age, i.e. towards the end of the fifth century, we shall come to the development of monastic Christianity. Britons returning from the monasteries of Gaul will teach their countrymen to despise and renounce the world. But in this sub-Roman twilight, the Christianity of Britain was in an intermediate stage. The Britons, deserted by the Empire, divided, beset by barbarians, turned to Christianity as the City of God. The religious temperament, once evident in their cult of Druidism, began in the period 360–450 to reappear in their Christianity. The new-found zeal of the Briton Pelagius and his denial that all men were born evil owing to the sin of Adam

State of the Church

disturbed the whole Roman world. It is true that the other Britons who became notable in this period were, like Pelagius, men who made their name outside Roman Britain; some of them missionaries like Palladius, Patrick, and Ninian; others learned men who attained fame in Gaul, such as Fastidius and Faustus. But the *Life of St. Germanus* indicates that there was Christian agitation also within Britain itself. It was the recrudescence of Pelagianism or semi-Pelagianism in Britain which necessitated the visits of the saint to our island. The fire of heresy had to be extinguished in Britain lest it spread to the Continent. The interest in religious matters or personages was not confined to a select few only. When St. Germanus moved about in Britain the people pressed upon him in their enthusiasm.

The writings[24] of Fastidius, 'bishop of the Britons', composed about 420–30, and the help sent later to St. Patrick from Britain, show that Christianity was now penetrating as a living force. It was the great discovery of the age, and probably occupied the minds of thinking men more than did fear of the Saxons.

In fact, looking at this period, 360–450, it is as fair to fix our eyes on the new life which was stirring among the peoples of Britain as on the decay of the State and the destruction of wealth. If the growth of the spiritual life of man counts for more than changes in political systems or the distribution of material wealth, then it may be held that this period, which witnessed a transition in Britain from the Roman culture of the later Empire through sub-Romanism to a Celtic and a Christian renaissance, was a period of creation rather than of destruction. The Roman Britain which was now to be the prey of the Saxons had passed in ninety years from the age of Julian to the age of Germanus, from an age of toleration to an age when belief was so intense that it was an offence to have mistaken notions about the sin of Adam; from an age when the imperial officials and drafts of imperial troops were guided across the Channel by the light-houses on the cliffs of Boulogne and of Dover to an age when

St. Germanus, an emissary of Gallic bishops, in crossing the Channel was obstructed by demons.

The world had changed. The Romano-Britons who were about to be submerged by a new flood of barbarians had, by the middle of the fifth century, obtained a source of spiritual consolation for the loss of the lands and goods of this transitory world.

Remains of Roman lighthouse at Dover. In Roman times it was probably eight stories and about 80 feet high.

THE CONQUEST OF KENT

THE STORY IN THE WRITTEN AUTHORITIES

WE have now to change our point of view and look back at the fifth century with the eyes of later generations. Through the obscurity of the middle years of that century when the Huns were daring to advance towards the heart of Gaul; when the Franks were consolidating a kingdom round Tournai, in regions not far distant from Britain; when the Empire still lingered as a shadow of its former self in other parts of the West—in this storm-darkened period we have to try to discern what really happened when our Germanic forefathers first effected a permanent lodgement on the shores of Britain.

The event which the Britons in later times remembered as the *adventus Saxonum* is one of the most dramatic stories in the history of our island, and it was in that way that the descendants of the Britons told it. When genuine traditions failed, others were supplied to meet the demand of a later age, and thus came into existence, as we shall see below, the romantic tragedy centring round Vortigern, Hengist, and Rowena.

The critical methods of the nineteenth century shattered most of this picturesque narrative. In the present century experts have been trying to produce from the study of antiquities and of place-names the material out of which a new story may

perhaps some day be built up. How far these new materials can
be fitted together so as to form a safe groundwork for a revised
history is the chief theme of this and the following chapters.
One thing is certain—that for the time being the Germanic conquest of Britain cannot be told as a narrative. How then are
we to treat it? There is no choice. It is a great enigma and
we must treat it as such. The problems which it presents may
interest us in much the same way as a detective story. Using
the jargon of that form of fiction we may call it 'a mystery', the
first and greatest in the history of England. There is no doubt
about the crime itself. But the questions to which we have to
seek an answer are the following. Was the general appropria-
tion of the land of the Britons aggravated by wholesale murder?
Who exactly were the invaders? What were their numbers?
Where exactly did they come from? How did they make their
way into the country?

Thanks to the progress made by modern archaeology we are
now able to set out on our inquiry with a hope of arriving not
at the whole truth—not at as much of it as will be known in,
say, ten or twenty years time—but at more than appeared in
the history books of the last generation. It is unfortunate that the
subject of this chapter, the problem of what happened in the
invasion of Kent—it may be called the problem of the Jutes—is
the most difficult and confusing bit of the whole question.

We must begin by making clear what are the different kinds
of evidence which lie before us, and much in these preliminary
remarks will be an introduction to the subject as a whole.

First we shall follow a well-worn path and trace the growth of
the legend of the Conquest. Later we shall see how far the old
scraps of tradition can be fitted into the new fragments of a
different kind, the inferences which experts in archaeology
and other subjects have been trying to patch into some sort of
history. For the legend we have the following sequence—Gildas,
Bede, Nennius, the Saxon Chronicle, and a few odd sentences
from other authorities. These are the witnesses. They are all

unsatisfactory in various ways; but the first, the familiar statement of what happened, must come from them, and we must now hear the beginnings of their several stories and form a general impression of the credibility of each.

Gildas[1] comes before us, a middle-aged Romano-Briton—really a Briton, it seems, by blood; but enough of a Roman by culture to have a fairly wide knowledge of Latin literature and to write Latin with fluency, though in an over-elaborate style, the fashion for which was spreading from Gaul to Celtic Britain. It is clear that he considers himself and his countrymen as still belonging to the Roman world. They are the *cives*, the citizens, in contrast to the barbarians. He speaks of Latin as 'our language'. Except for the facts that Gildas was born somewhere about 500, that he wrote his book shortly before 547,[1a] that he visited Ireland about 566 and died in 570, there is little else that can be said about his career, since the lives written of him date from the eleventh century or later and are not to be trusted.

His book *De Excidio et Conquestu Britanniae* was written in the form of an Epistle, but was pitched on the high note of a Hebrew prophet. Its purport was to denounce the wickednesses of five British kings and to point out to the Britons in general and especially to the clergy the error of their ways. The History with which he introduces his subject is not a history in the ordinary sense. The author is not trying to inform his readers about events. Hardly any names or dates are mentioned. He is simply a prophet preaching at large against the sins of the Britons; an impressionist seeking to obtain bold effects by massing subjects in the blackest shadows; a patriot, of that melancholy kind which finds most satisfaction in uncovering the faults of his own countrymen.

We see then that while Gildas is our best source of information, since he wrote within about a century of the reputed 'Coming of the Saxons', he is as vague as a man can be. As far as dates are concerned, he may have talked to old men who could remember the first employment of 'Saxons' as mercenaries by a British king—the event which Gildas describes as 'the germ of iniquity and root of bitterness'. But on the other hand, living, as it seems he did, far away in the west of the island (at any rate the five kings whom he denounced lived in those parts), he may give us only hearsay which distorts the truth when he speaks of events in the east.

What he says is this: that all the counsellors, together with a certain 'proud king'* whom he does not name, 'introduced the fierce Saxons, hateful alike to God and man, into the island to repel the northern nations'. He laments this as the most pernicious of all steps ever taken, and he laments the king's hopeless stupidity. He tells how the invaders arrived in what they called three *cyulae*, 'what we call warships'.† He tells how their motherland, finding that the first contingent had prospered, sent a larger body of warriors‡ who joined forces with the others; how they demanded that *annonae* (the allowances or payments in kind which for centuries had been rendered to the 'federates' who fought for the Empire) should be paid to them as if they were troops who were about to undergo great hardships on behalf of their kind host; how for a considerable time the grants which were given them stopped their mouths, but how they then complained that their monthly supplies were not enough and did their best to pick a quarrel, saying that they would break the agreement and plunder the whole island if they were not treated more liberally; finally, how they quickly followed up their threats with actions, 'for the fire of righteous vengeance . . . blazed from sea to sea' until 'having burned nearly the whole island it licked the western ocean with its red and savage tongue'.

Though there are no names or dates attached to this story by Gildas and the number of the ships has a legendary sound, the story in itself is by no means improbable. The Romans had increasingly used barbarians to fight their battles, and nothing could be more natural than that a hard-pressed British king

---

* *superbus tyrannus.*   ‡ *satellitum.*
† *lingua . . . nostra longis navibus. Cyula* is the English word 'keel' latinized.

should follow that example. This story of Gildas does not go far, but it may be accepted as part of the truth.

Some two hundred years later the Northumbrian monk Bede (672–735), in reproducing the story of Gildas, filled in a few details. Somehow Bede knew the name of the 'proud tyrant', Vortigernus, and those of the two brothers who were the first leaders of the immigrants, Hengist and Horsa. He knew that they were Jutes and not Saxons, and that the monument of Horsa, killed in battle, was still to be seen in the east of Kent.

Some historians, strong in criticism, think that Bede's additions make the story less credible. They assert that the names Hengist and Horsa, meaning Stallion and Mare, have a legendary origin. They see in Bede's reference to Horsa's monument an etymological fiction. They think that the location of the incident in Kent scarcely tallies with the story that Hengist's war-band was introduced, as Gildas said, to repel 'the northern peoples', that is presumably the Picts—Kent is a curious base for operations against Caledonian invaders. But too much is often made of these difficulties.[2] Hengist was a well-known name. It was borne by a real war-leader mentioned in *Beowulf*, one who has some resemblance to the conqueror of Britain and was perhaps a Jute. It is also more consistent with the usual custom of the Germanic invaders to suppose that the Horstead near Aylesford in Kent took its name from a real man rather than a legendary hero.[3] It is worth noting that Horstead in Kent has its counterpart, Horsted in Angel (north-east of Husum). Lastly, though it is a far cry from Kent to the land of the Picts, the Picts seem to have been sea-raiders much like the Saxons themselves (they are described as a 'transmarine' enemy by Gildas), and we may suppose that Hengist was introduced to operate against the Picts by sea as well as by land.

Bede is careful to say that the Hengist story is only tradition; it is 'what men say'. But we may suppose that it was the legend believed by intelligent Kentishmen in Bede's own day, since he was the friend and correspondent of such men.

The next additions to the legend of Hengist reflect the new antiquarian and historical interests stimulated by the revival of learning in the Carolingian period. In the early decades of the ninth century Nennius, a Welshman, and in the later decades an anonymous Saxon chronicler each collected what information he could about the first coming of the Saxons. Both works are composite productions. The fragments of information about the past which were tacked together by their compilers were in either case many and various. In either case the date of the compilation and the value of the component parts are still subjects of controversy. In other respects the contrast between the two works is as great as can be.

The doubts about Nennius spring primarily from the fact that his *Historia Brittonum* survives in very different forms, some short, others long, some with a preface, others without. Owing to this, Mommsen, the editor of the book, in the *Monumenta Germaniae Historica*, and other historians before and after him[4] have concluded that the nucleus of the *Historia* was written by some anonymous writer about the end of the seventh century, and that Nennius in the ninth century only added a preface and some trifles of his own to the History which has passed under his name. A different and in some ways a more satisfactory explanation has been suggested by Liebermann. This view regards Nennius as the real compiler (one can hardly call him the author) of the History. All that is known about Nennius himself is that he was a 'disciple' of Elfodd, the chief bishop of Gwynedd and a man of importance, since though he did not die till 809 he had as early as 768 brought the Church of North Wales into closer harmony with the Roman Church. Following Liebermann we may picture Nennius as a learned man according to his lights, one who did his best to write the History which other Britons hitherto had failed to accomplish. He pieced together extracts from Jerome and Isidore; from a *Life of St. Germanus*; from 'annals of the Irish and of the Saxons'; and from what he calls the 'tradition of our elders'. If industry could give his country a History which might rival that of Bede, his industry would do it; so he worked on, patching together his authorities and his 'traditions'. He found himself confused by different stories and by different baffling systems of chronology. But he refused to be daunted. The different versions and the discordant dates were all placed side by side, Saxon and British genealogies, the wonders of Wales, the Lives of saints and heroes, were all brought in, and the centre of all he made the romance of Vortigern, which, with details unimagined by Gildas or Bede, might point the moral of the calamity which had befallen his countrymen.

Now if we are to understand the *Historia Brittonum* what matters is less the editorial functions performed either by Nennius or the hypothetical earlier editor than the nature of the several parts which were somehow incorporated in the History. Each section of the book should be judged by itself; such a judgement, however, is complicated by the interaction of popular tradition and pseudo-historical speculation among the Welsh. Of the sections which bear most directly on the subject of the present chapter, one which enumerates the battles of Arthur has on it some stamp of popular tradition. The chapters about Vortigern, on the other hand, are more suspect. The romantic tales woven round him, his love for the daughter of Hengist, his fatal cession of Kent in return for her hand, the details of victories won over Hengist by Vortimer, the son of Vortigern, the final conference in which the invaders, with the basest treachery, pulling knives from their boots killed three hundred of the British nobles—all this was good entertainment for Welshmen and helped to reconcile them to their defeat and provide a national scapegoat. According to Nennius, the Britons fought magnificently; it was by Saxon treachery that their nobles had been slaughtered. One need not suppose that Nennius himself invented his highly coloured stories, and it is certainly carrying criticism to an extreme to assert, as some have done, that the whole Vortigern romance was a fabrication based on a few words of Bede and without roots in Welsh tradition. None the less, Welsh imagination, whether of antiquaries or bards, ran so wild that the occasional touches in the story which are not in themselves improbable (such as the assertion that Hengist and his band came as exiles to Vortigern to seek his protection) are rightly discredited by the transparent fiction in which they are embedded.

Very different, once more, are the additions made to the story in the Saxon Chronicle. The Chronicle is short and matter-of-fact. Its author resembled Nennius in one respect; he made a show of knowing too much. Nennius supplied five or six different dates for the same event. The chronicler does not hesitate to supply one date for every event. His story for the first twenty-eight years after the landing of Hengist at Ypwines-fleot (? Ebbsfleet in Thanet) is little more than the enumeration of four battles: the first being at Ægelsthrep (probably Aylesford), and the second at Crayford where they 'slew four thousand men; and the Britons then forsook Kent and fled to London in great terror'. Finally, in 473, 'Hengist and Aesc fought against the Britons and captured innumerable spoils, and the Britons fled from the English like fire'.

It is still permissible to give some credence to these entries, since they have a look of being derived from an old saga or poem. 'A look', however, is not a good argument with which to confute a sceptic; and it is most improbable that the dates are anything more than the guesses of a later age.

THE PROBLEM OF THE JUTES

Let us now turn from the stories of Hengist and of Vortigern to the more general problem of the Jutes: who they were and whence they came. Here the foundation from which every argument must start is the statement of Bede that *Angulus*, the home of the Angles, lay 'between the provinces of the Jutes and the Saxons'. This familiar view has for long been questioned on archaeological and philological grounds, but the critics of Bede's statement have generally tried to fortify their argument with one or more *obiter dicta* drawn from continental writings.

The more noteworthy of these *dicta* cannot be ignored. They are:

First, a passage of Procopius, a contemporary of Gildas but a Byzantine. Britain, he states, contains three nations, the Angles, the Frisians, and the Britons. By taking his Angles to mean both Angles and Saxons, and by a simple subtraction sum, it is found that the Frisians of Procopius may be equated with the Jutes.[5] In defence of this statement it is urged that Procopius met certain Angles who accompanied a Frankish embassy to the East and that he may therefore have known what he was talking about. Some hardihood, however, is required by those who maintain that Procopius was well informed about the circumstances of Britain, inasmuch as this author elsewhere says that human life could not be lived in the country beyond the Roman Wall and that Britain itself was a ghostly region to which the souls of the dead were ferried in phantom ships by night.

A second passage is one in which Theudebert, a Frankish king, writing to Justinian about 540, asserts that among the tribes who had voluntarily submitted to him are the 'Saxones Eucii'.* The name *Eucii* can fairly be corrected to *Eutii* and regarded as the equivalent of the *Jutae* of Bede; but it is uncertain whether a hyphen or a comma should be inserted between the two words— that is, whether the Eutii were in American language 'hyphenated' Saxons or whether they were a distinct folk, presumably neighbours of the Saxons and, since they thought it wise to submit to the Franks, not far distant from the Frankish kingdom; possibly therefore within the region loosely described as 'Frisia'.[6]

A third passage from the poet Venantius Fortunatus,[7] who died in 609, mentions a people, the Euthiones, between the Saxons

* *Cum Saxonibus Euciis qui se nobis voluntate propria tradiderunt*; the phrase occurs in a corrupt sentence in which the king claims that in addition to the Visigoths and to northern Italy his *dominatio* extends from the Danube and the borders of Pannonia to the Ocean. *M.G.H.*, Ep. iii, 133.

and the Danes, and for those who are prepared to accept the name as another equivalent for the Jutes, it is a reminder that enough of the tribe must have remained in the Jutish peninsula to pass on the name of Jutland to that region when, probably about the fifth century, it was overrun by the Danes.[8]

The mere enumeration of these passages, slender bases for argument but at times used for the building up of a top-heavy superstructure, is enough to show that the problem of the Jutes can never be settled by reference to our written authorities. If there is an answer it must be obtained from other investigations. Before we diverge on to these other lines which may perhaps be tedious, we may strengthen our resolve with a conviction that the subject is worth pursuit. Since Kentishmen have so often taken the lead in English affairs, we cannot shirk the attempt to discover who they were and whence they came.

The discussions of the philologists about the form of the name which appears in Bede's *History* as Iutae have been prolonged. Their conclusions (anticipated in what has been said above) mostly support the view that the correct equivalent of the Latin Iutae is Iote, which becomes in West Saxon Yte. This rules out the theory which once obtained that the Jutes were to be identi- fied with the 'Geatas', the Götar of south Sweden. It does not in itself decide whence they came; but it assists the argument of those who hold that the Jutes of Kent were related to the Eutii mentioned in Theudebert's letter, that is, to a Saxon tribe thought to be settled in or near Frisia.[9]

In the next stage of our investigation we must ask the archaeo- logists what light they can throw on the problem. We find that there are difficulties, and these must be faced at the outset.

One might suppose that it would be an easy thing to compare the graves of the Jutish and Saxon settlers in Britain with the graves of their kinsmen on the Continent. But the first difficulty arises from the fact that men in the early centuries of our era, and especially in the Migration Age, were liable to change from one mode of burying their dead to another. Their minds were in a state of flux. They were unsettled in their views about what happened after death; and this unsettlement expressed itself in changes in their burial customs. The idea that it was better not to burn but to bury a dead kinsman and to give him ample supplies of everything he might require in the next world was just beginning to affect the tribes of north Germany about the time

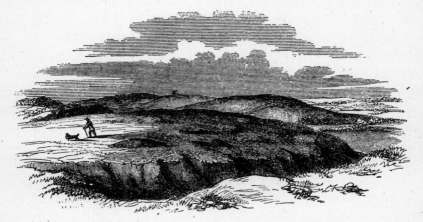

FIG. 23. Barfreston Down, Kent; Jutish Burial Mounds.

that they migrated, as is now shown in the newly discovered cemeteries at Nesse and Galgenberg. Otherwise the almost universal custom of the Anglian and Saxon tribes in Germany had been to cremate their dead. In their cemeteries in Britain the modes of burial adopted by the German immigrants were various. Cremation appears to have been still the prevailing custom among those who came direct from Germany to this island. But cremation is rarely found in the burial-places south of the Thames valley, and it is clear that in the south almost from the first the burning of a corpse was regarded as something primitive, contrary to the new fashions which were spreading in from other Germanic peoples, especially from the Franks.

Thus, while cremation urns are no reliable indication of date, their appearance in any cemetery may justify the opinion that

PLATE 18

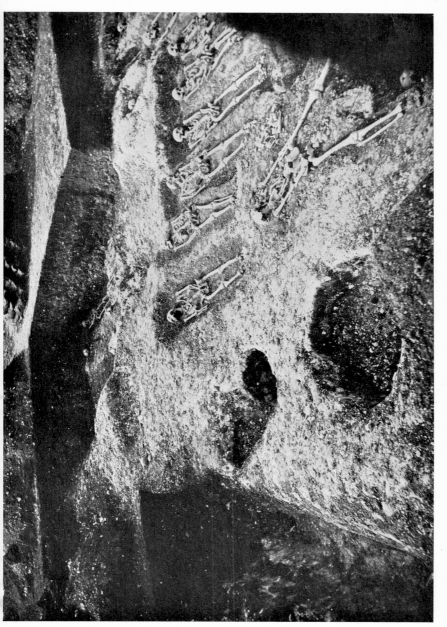

Anglo-Saxon cemetery at Saffron Walden, Essex

PLATE 19

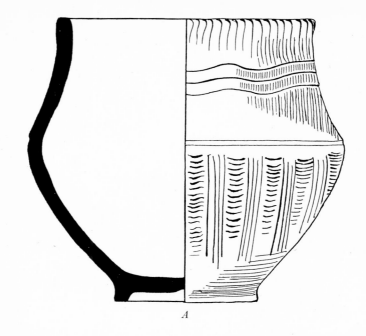

A

B

Kentish vases of Saxon type

A. From Hersden, near Sturry. $\frac{2}{3}$
B. From Sarre, Isle of Thanet. $\frac{2}{3}$

here are traces of some of the original settlers or their children. There were, no doubt, certain groups, especially among the Anglian settlers, who were more conservative than others in their ways. Sometimes in out-of-the-way places the good old custom might be maintained to the end of heathen times.[10] Cremation is thus a positive test of early invaders, but not a negative one. Though we may be sure when we find it that we have to do with invaders who were either newly arrived from Germany or else conservative in their customs, we cannot, on the other hand, assume that cemeteries where it is not found are not early.

So far the change from cremation to burying the dead, while it has made it difficult to trace the migrants with the exactness which might otherwise have been possible, has only presented minor difficulties. At this point, however, we must introduce a further complication; the men of this age had not to choose simply between cremation and burying in the heathen fashion, i.e. with many grave-goods. There was a third choice. They could give up the custom of burning the dead without adopting the new costly custom of burying them with all war-trappings and finery. They could copy the Romano-provincials rather than the Franks; they could bury their dead without anything at all. We shall find that the failure of the archaeologists to reckon with this radical change has falsified not a few of their conclusions.

It must, however, be admitted that an unfurnished grave does not necessarily mean that the Saxons or Angles who made it had been influenced either directly or indirectly by later Roman customs. It may only mean that the kinsmen were too poor to afford the cost of furnishing a grave. It may also mean that the graves are late and reflect the influence of Christianity. In most cases the records of past excavations do not enable us to decide between these possibilities except by conjecture.

The other great difficulty which besets any attempt to reconstruct the early history of the Germanic invaders by archaeological evidence is fundamental; it is the doubt whether the date of a brooch or buckle, still more whether the date of a grave containing such an object, can be determined with sufficient accuracy to be of use for the historian. Now there are one or two burials which have been identified as those of historical persons. There are others, more numerous, which contain a datable coin, often a coin worked up into a brooch or a bracteate. These at any rate give a *terminus post quem*, and by com-

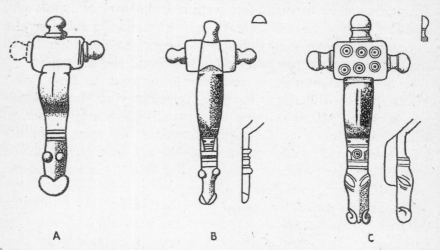

A   B   C

FIG. 24. Typological development of the cruciform brooch. A (Bifrons, Kent) and B (Faversham, Kent) show the second stage—that assigned to the latter half of the 5th century. C (Lyminge, Kent) shows the third stage assigned to the early 6th century. All ⅜.

paring the objects in one grave with those found in another (i.e. reasoning from what the archaeologists call 'the correlation of associated finds') it has been possible to link up the chronology of one kind of grave furniture with that of another. But the line of argument on which archaeologists have chiefly relied in fixing their dates has been that of 'typological development'. Since the validity of their results depends mainly on this method, it will be well at this point to illustrate it from what they have to tell us about the early evolution of the cruciform brooch.

(1) There is no doubt that this kind of brooch, like many others, was ultimately derived from the simple safety-pin type. It has an uncertain relationship with the crossbow brooches common

among the Roman provincials in the fourth century.[11] But the starting-point of the Germanic development is represented by the specimen (Fig. 3) found in the peat at Nydam with the famous boat, and another found in a mysterious grave at Dorchester on the Thames (Pl. 21 E). These are generally assigned to about the end of the fourth century.

(2) The second stage was probably evolved in the latter half of the fifth century. At this time the brooches in use in north Germany and Frisia, as well as among the invaders of Britain, were characterized by a full round knob at the top and a narrow head-plate. To this head-plate side-knobs were attached to hold the cross-bar round which the pin was coiled. As these side-knobs were fitted and not welded to the head-plate, they are often missing in the specimens which have been excavated. Examples of this type have been found chiefly in certain Kentish cemeteries, in East Anglia, and in the Cambridge region.

(3) In the next stage the knob at the top became only half round instead of full round and the lower end of the brooch developed horse-like nostrils which became a special characteristic of the English design. This class is assigned to the first half of the sixth century, and of its fifty-seven examples in England, three or four come from Kent, thirteen from East Anglia, twenty from Cambridgeshire, and eight from Lincolnshire.[12]

We need not here concern ourselves with the later stages, in which the side-knobs were cast all in one piece with the rest of the brooch, and the ornamentation elaborated with a great variety of ever-changing fashions. Our present concern is only with the early forms which help us to trace the course of the first invaders.

Now it is obvious that the room for mistakes in such schemes of typological development is large. The change in one country may be different from that in another. A type which goes out of fashion in one place may remain in fashion elsewhere. At times the genius of an individual craftsman may falsify all ordinary calculations. Inevitably there are disagreements among experts about the dating of any stage and about the normal margin of error on either side. One expert puts this margin at twenty-five years. Others admit that it may be much wider. For the time being, however, our only practicable policy is, while recognizing the element of uncertainty, to accept the chronology worked out by archaeologists in the last decades, and the maps in this volume are based on their results.

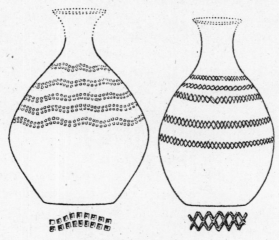

FIG. 25. Kentish bottle vases. $\frac{1}{5}$.

These, then, are the chief difficulties. They are not so discouraging that we need turn from archaeology in complete scepticism; but they are enough to explain why the study is not an exact science, and why we must be cautious in accepting its pronouncements.

The limitations of archaeology are more than usually apparent as soon as we ask about the first conquerors of Kent in the middle of the fifth century, and about their continental home. Any visitor to the Anglo-Saxon room of the British Museum cannot fail to be struck by the beautiful grave furniture found in typical Jutish cemeteries in contrast with the ordinary objects produced by Anglian and Saxon craftsmen. For example, the characteristic

pottery which he will see from Kentish graves is not hand-made
and wide-mouthed urns like those of north Germany, but bottle-
necked vases made on a wheel (Fig. 25). He will also see a pro-
fusion of fine goldsmiths' work, decorated with garnets and
other jewels, some beautiful glass vessels, and curious things
like perforated silver spoons and mounted crystal balls, the
use of which has never been fully explained.

The first systematic attempt to extract the early story of the
Jutish kingdom from its graves was made by E. T. Leeds in his
Archaeology of the Anglo-Saxon Settlements, a book which must be

Fig. 26.   Sarre, Kent; gold bracteate.   ¼.

the starting-point of all subsequent discussions of the subject.[13]
The point which specially impressed Leeds was the resemblance
between these finds from Kent and the finds from Frankish
cemeteries, especially those of the Rhineland between Coblenz
and Düsseldorf. Leeds inferred that these Frankish fashions must
imply that the Jutes were of Frankish origin, or at least that they
had long resided among the Franks before their migration. But
in the cemeteries of east Kent he noted a second distinct culture
'which can only be ascribed to admixture of race'. The lesser
culture, which appeared in cemeteries 'all close to the Thames
or the scene of the earliest landing', was represented by cruciform
brooches such as we have seen both north and west of the lower
Elbe, and by gold bracteates (Fig. 26). Such finds were only
intrusive material among the typical Kentish relics. To Leeds,
therefore, the evidence from archaeology seemed clear. It proved

that the bulk of the Kentish settlers came from the middle Rhine. In a later book[13a] he suggests that this Frankish infusion did not occur till early in the sixth century.

Among subsequent discussions of the subject two constructive theories call for attention. N. Åberg, a Swedish archaeologist, has argued that the grave-goods which seemed to Leeds to be 'intrusive' among the Jutish objects should instead be regarded as those of the earlier settlers. The eight or ten cruciform brooches found in Kent, thanks to the better-established chronology of the type, show 'a development extending over the second half of the fifth century and a little into the sixth century. Then development ceases in Kent, but proceeds with undiminished vigour north of the Thames.' On this kind of evidence Åberg concluded that the peculiarities of Kentish culture did not go so far back as to the time of the invasion. They 'did not exist from the beginning, but developed during the course of the sixth century'.[14]

Thus while Leeds saw in eastern Kent two cultures representing two streams of immigrants, the main one drawn from the Frankish Rhineland, the other from the north, Åberg saw a later and an earlier culture. The earlier was the culture of the original Jutish settlers, the later represented the new fashions which developed in Kent as the Jutes, exploiting their nearness to the Continent, traded with Franks and Frisians, copied their luxuries, and so, growing rich, generated an art and culture of their own superior in many ways to the art and culture of the Franks themselves.

The other contribution comes from T. D. Kendrick.[15] He admits that the evidence is at present insufficient for a trustworthy theory, but he makes a guess which well illustrates the uncertainties now surrounding the whole subject. The way for Kendrick's theory was prepared by Lindqvist, another Swedish archaeologist, who maintained that the Vendel style (which is the Swedish counterpart of the Jutish style in England) was much earlier than had hitherto been thought. Kendrick, following

II. 'KENTISH' JEWELLERY

Ornamented mainly with filigree and with garnets, pearly shells, and blue glass
The buckle is from the Taplow burial. $\frac{1}{1}$

up this clue, examined the gorgeous barbaric jewellery of Kent, and divided it into two main varieties. Style A chiefly used garnets and blue glass, with *cloisonné* (that is, cell-work) setting and with filigree decoration, as in the coloured plate. Style B inlaid its jewels in cast settings, and used chip-carving ornament and niello (a black inlay on metal), but not *cloisonné* or filigree, producing disk brooches and long brooches, both square-headed and radiated, like those in the next plate. Kendrick rejects Åberg's view that the first of these styles was the work of Ethelbert's golden age (the end of the sixth and beginning of the seventh centuries), and thinks that both styles are contemporary and go back to the period of the Jutish invasion and settlement, in other words, that some of the gorgeous jewels of Kent were being worn about A.D. 500. The guess with which Kendrick ends is admittedly daring. He claims that the *cloisonné* jewellery was a British craft, and that 'one of the secrets of Jutish wealth and success was the alacrity with which the newcomers absorbed into their own society the jewellers of the Kent that they had conquered'.[15a]

These rival theories may some day be decided on archaeological grounds either by further excavation or by more intensive study of antiquities in museums here and abroad. The amateur, pending the decision of the experts, can only call attention to some aspects of the problem.

With regard to the original home of the Kentish immigrants, the fact that the graves in Kent only resemble those of the middle Rhine in some respects[16] seems to agree with the view that the similarities were the result of trade between the Rhine and Kent, rather than of a Frankish migration. For instance, if the resemblances between long-necked vases of the two districts did not arise simply from like conditions (in other words, from the survival of a Roman-provincial craft of pottery in either district), they may conceivably be the wine vessels in which Rhenish wine was imported—imported to the only communities in Britain that could afford to pay for such a luxury. One clue which has recently come to light, points us away from the middle Rhine to the settlements of north Germany; urns of a Saxon type have been unearthed at Hersden, between Thanet and Canterbury—a reminder that in the past generations, when archaeology was a hunt for treasure rather than for knowledge, such pots may have been often found but disregarded.*

In the next place it must be admitted that archaeology has failed to support Bede's statement that the Jutes came from Jutland; indeed, it has not yielded any positive support for the view that migrants from Jutland were one among the component elements of the Kentish population. The cemeteries of Kent are certainly unlike those of east Jutland, where, in the Migration Age, the dead were inhumed with an exceedingly generous spread of food and drink, supplied to them in as many as fourteen to sixteen vessels.[17] In west Jutland, on the other hand, the cremation cemeteries seem to come to an end in the second century. A conjecture of Plettke and others that the Jutes migrated from Jutland at that time and reappeared in Kent under Hengist centuries later, can only be accepted if their half-way house is allowed to be some region where they might have remained in touch with folks of Anglo-Frisian speech, a region such as that of the *terpen* on the coast of Frisia.

In the end the chief impression which the archaeological controversies leave on the mind is that the Jutish problem is much more complicated than was at one time supposed. It is not enough to ask whether the settlers of Kent came from Jutland or the Rhineland or from both, or from any one or two districts. The different fashions found in Kentish graves are many. They must be explained not only by heterogeneity among the invaders (important as that is), but also by the variety of experiences enjoyed by the different communities during the two or three centuries in which Kentishmen furnished the graves of their

* To illustrate this point I add in Pl. 19 another vase of Saxon type from Sarre, now in Maidstone museum.

1

2

3

4

Kentish chip-carving jewellery. (Kendrick's 'Style B'. See *Antiquity*, vii, p. 432 and Plate II.) Above, disk brooches. Below, a radiated and a square-headed brooch. About $\frac{2}{5}$

dead. For example, the fact that the chip-carving jewellery (Style B) is found mainly in the Thanet region, and the *cloisonné* jewellery (Style A) mainly on the Dover–Canterbury line may be a result of some change that occurred in the trade route— perhaps owing to the tendency of the Wantsum Channel to silt up. We are all tempted to interpret any peculiarity in terms of race: we must be careful therefore not to overdo that explanation.

Archaeology having up to the present failed, it becomes necessary to point to the other lines of investigation which may supply clues. These are (1) the field system of Kent; (2) the social institutions revealed in Kentish laws; and (3) the evidence of the place-names.

The field system of a people is its signature written on the earth's surface. Once formed, it can scarcely be defaced. Even when incoming races destroy an old system, field survey and air photography are often able to read the old writing on the palimpsest. Being almost unchangeable and indelible, a field system supplies evidence of the highest value.[17a]

Now the system of medieval Kent was unlike the two- or three-field system which prevailed through mid-England from the Channel to the Humber and beyond (see map, p. 174). The holding of a typical Kentish cultivator was not a number of strips scattered in large, open, common fields. It was consolidated. Instead of scattered strips, members of a Kentish family as a rule had fields grouped together much like a modern farm.

Other points of contrast between Kent and the rest of England in the Middle Ages are well known. Gavelkind, that is the ancient custom of dividing a holding among coheirs; the division of the kingdom into *lathes*; the measurement of land by the unit called the *sulung* (or plough-land) and its quarter-share the *jugum* (or yoke)—these are only three out of many peculiarities. Their antiquity is ably demonstrated by Jolliffe.[18] His explanation of their ultimate source is less convincing. He assumes that the field system must be Teutonic and not, as some previous historians[19] have supposed, partly a survival from Romano-

British times. If Teutonic, he maintains that it is necessary to ascend the Rhine to Düsseldorf and beyond to find a district where land was reckoned by jugera and plough-lands, much as in Kent. From this and from other similarities in their institutions he concludes that the Jutes were nothing else than Franks from the middle Rhine.

Here is a theory which, like the middle-Rhine theory of Leeds's *Archaeology*, seems to be contradicted both by the language and by the traditions* of the Jutes of Kent. It asks us to believe that a branch of the Franks ceased to be proud of their descent from that all-conquering race, and forgot their Frankish language so completely that there are not even traces of it in the Kentish dialect.[20]

These aspects of our problem, while they are too involved to be examined in our present survey of the ground, are clearly of great significance.

For the same reason we shall do no more than mention the evidence which may be extracted from the early Kentish laws.† These show that the freemen, the *ceorls*, of Kent were more substantial persons than the ceorls of the neighbouring kingdoms; that their dependent and servile classes were more elaborately classified, and that one of these classes, that of the *læt*, is clearly identical with the *litus*, or *lazzus*, of the Frisian, Frankish, and Old Saxon laws. This evidence seems to strengthen the argument for the connexion of Kent with the neighbouring continental lands rather than with Jutland.

A last line of investigation is that of the place-names of Kent. Here again we can only say that the subject is still waiting for its specialist.[21] In the meantime valuable attempts have been made to differentiate the place-names which contain the element *-ing*, representing the Old English plural *-ingas*.[22] These have the strongest claim to antiquity. They seem to represent a stage

---

* Bede's statements may perhaps have the force of traditions since they were accepted by the Kentish clergy and later by Alfred, a king of Kent.

† See below, p. 205.

in the settlement, perhaps the first stage, when men identified districts by the groups of settlers which were to be found in them rather than by the name of any one farm or village. There are a few of these group-names in the east of the county, especially round Richborough, but the district where they are found most thickly is the Medway valley with its Barming, Binling, Halling, Malling, Yalding, and others.[23]

Our excursion into the Jutish problem has now been long enough to give the reader an idea of the possible lines along which the question must be approached. Much of the evidence is at present incomplete and ill-digested. The problem is not ripe, perhaps it never will be, for solution. It has only been possible to indicate some of the considerations which must in the future be more carefully sifted and weighed. Looking at the problem as a whole, we see that Bede's statement that the home of the Jutes was beyond that of the Angles receives but little support and is in some directions contradicted. In itself, however, it carries weight; Bede's correspondents, the educated clergy in Kent, were presumably in contact with traditions about the early history of their people. Bede's statement needs to be qualified, but it should not be wholly set aside unless the arguments against it become overwhelming.

How is it to be qualified? If we are aiming at safety, we may say that what is needed, the well-constructed theory in which each piece of evidence finds its proper place, cannot be built up until the materials to which we have pointed are better squared by the experts. Let us, however, change the analogy, and revert to that of the detective story. Every reader knows that a stage comes when a working hypothesis is required, one which may help to clear the mind even if it cannot claim to be well ascertained truth. With this justification, let us put together a working hypothesis, basing it frankly on conjecture as well as on evidence.

We begin, as of old, with Hengist and Horsa, since there is no sufficient reason for abandoning these characters of the story. In order to explain Bede's statement, we think of these adventurers and their immediate followers as natives of Jutland who, like other adventurers of the age, as of the Viking age, had been long absent from their original home. When they appear on the scene, since Vortigern thought it worth his while to take them into his pay, they were presumably commanders of a company of some repute. It is possible that they may already have served for a short time as federates or as less formal auxiliaries in Gaul; Aëtius, we know, had 'Saxons' on his side when he defeated the Huns in 451. It is tempting to speculate whether there was any kind of connexion between the appeal to Aëtius and the employment of Hengist's force. There is just a bare possibility that Aëtius, unable to send regular Roman troops, may have recommended the Britons to hire the services of Hengist's war band. But though it is tempting in this period, where we possess only a few fragments of information, to put those few together as cause and effect, it is historically unsound and the temptation should be avoided. All that we can really say is that, if there is truth buried in the story of Gildas, it is probable that the *superbus tyrannus* (that is Vortigern) took Hengist into his pay because more trustworthy reinforcements from Gaul were not to be had. Remembering that the Roman emperors had been for centuries accustomed to employ German barbarians as mercenaries, we must discount the violent abuse which Gildas heaps on the king who admitted the Saxons. It was easy to be wise after the event. When Vortigern handed over Thanet to them, he no doubt imagined that that island with its definite bounds would save the farmers of Kent and their families from molestation. In fact, however, he was giving them the perfect base, that which the Vikings selected four centuries later.

A point which one would like specially to clear up is how long the mercenaries were in the pay of Vortigern before they got out of hand. Gildas says it was 'a long time',* but that might mean, say, ten months or ten years. The Saxon Chronicle implies that it was five or six years; but little reliance can be placed on

* *multo tempore.*

its early dates. In any case, the period was long enough to enable Hengist to bring over large reinforcements. No doubt the barbarian chief had during this interval a good opportunity to form ideas about the military features of the country. Both at this time and possibly during earlier employment on the Continent he and his men had been in close touch with sub-Roman civilization; and the kind of civilization to be assimilated by German mercenaries was the use of engines of war such as battering-rams. Then, when it came to a quarrel and the Germans turned against Vortigern, it was easy for Hengist to obtain his reinforcements. Gildas says that these came from the 'motherland' of the Saxons; but it is more likely that in reality Hengist recruited other roving bands like his own, and drew also from the 'Saxons' who had established themselves in the corner of Gaul immediately opposite the Kentish coast. The supposition that Hengist's forces were composed of adventurers of diverse origin drawn from different folks of the Germanic seaboard—Frisians, Saxons, Angles, even Franks, in addition to the 'Jutes' themselves—may help to explain some of the striking variations in Kentish graves. It may also explain why there are now conflicting theories about the Jutes: why this expert finds in Kent affinities with the Frisian language and another with the Frankish laws. No one theory indeed can yet pass unchallenged. The philologists are not agreed; the jurists without full early codes from the peoples of Jutland and the Saxon-Frisian coast cannot well assess the value of the few resemblances between Frankish and Kentish laws. It may indeed be held that the competing arguments simply cancel one another, and therefore betray no mixing of the races. If so, we may still guess, as a mere probability, that the followers of Hengist, like the Great Army of the Vikings in the ninth century, were a coalition of many bands of different origin.

In any case, it is at least possible that some of Hengist's contingents had been long enough in contact with the Franks to adopt many of their ideas. The early dominance of Hengist and his own *comitatus* of Jutes among the heterogeneous bands of new settlers, and the outstanding qualities of personality and leadership of this Jutish hero himself, may well have set going a tradition which survives in Bede's words.

Lastly and more confidently, we may attribute the sustained development of Kentish culture to the fact that Kentishmen, living on the old trade route and being pre-eminently the trading people of the island, were exposed in a unique way to all kinds of continental influences. Kentish culture was a cross between Frankish and northern cultures, with perhaps some mingling of a British strain in its remoter ancestry; but it was a new type, a native growth.

Three or four other features of this conquest may perhaps be distinguished in the black night of the time. First, some sense of strategy may be detected not only in Hengist's choice of Thanet, but also in the establishment of the group communities —shall we call them in this case detachments from the army of invasion?—in and about the Medway valley. To begin with, Thanet was, as we have said, an ideal base. Later, when the invaders mastered east Kent, it may be inferred from the place-names that they planted their group communities thickly along the Medway valley. By so doing, thanks to the great tract of the desolate Weald to the south, they succeeded in accomplishing what the clever Viking leaders attempted but failed to do in the last war against Alfred; that is, they nipped off a territory which was well defined and easily defensible—a territory almost like an island, one which tended to separate Britain from the Continent.

What happened after the conquest of east Kent is another obscure point. Here we come up against the question whether the invasion of Kent was really the first permanent occupation of British territory by the Germanic peoples. We shall hear in the following pages more about the theory, based on the grave-finds, that the settlement of the eastern Midlands—the country opened by the rivers of the Wash—was begun about the middle of the fifth century. The evidence of the heathen graves, however, is as yet not strong enough to justify us in abandoning the old story that Hengist's seizure of Kent was the turning-point, the event which came to be remembered in Welsh tradition as the *adventus Saxonum*.*

Gildas draws a picture of the first invaders after they had broken faith with the British king, harrying 'the whole island'. It may well be true; and these first bands may indeed have poured down the Roman roads in all directions, plundering and destroying. These raiders, however, have given the archaeologists no clear trace of themselves or of their violence.

The story must end with the establishment of the invaders in east Kent, perhaps a sequel to the return of the bands from raiding up to the western sea. Narratives which introduce other details, such as battles of Vortimer, successor to Vortigern, must be suspect, since they are derived from Nennius.

One point, however, should be noticed before we leave the Jutes, namely, that at some time they made a second settlement in the Isle of Wight and yet another in the country opposite, round Southampton Water.[24] In the Isle of Wight some of the characteristics which we call Jutish can be recognized. For instance, in its graves, as in those of Kent, we see the garnet and square-headed brooches, the crystal balls, and the perforated silver spoons.† This evidence, agreeing with the statement of Bede that the people of the Isle of Wight and of the opposite mainland were sprung, like the people of Kent, from 'the nation of the Jutes', seems at first to drive us back to the idea that the distinction between the Jutes and the other immigrants was a matter of blood and of little else but that. The conjectures to which we have been led in the present chapter point to a somewhat different conclusion. We do not reject Bede's statement as a mere blunder, but for us who, unlike Bede, are seeking for an explanation of the peculiarities of the Kentishmen and their culture, any talk about 'the Jutish nation' is quite inadequate. Our conclusion, our 'working hypothesis', is different: namely,

* Cf. above, p. 67.   † Cf. above, p. 89.

that the peculiarities of Kent were less the result of blood than of time, circumstance, and place.

As for the blood of the Kentishmen, we believe that to have been more than usually mixed, but the ingredients and their proportions to be not yet ascertained.[25] The circumstances of the conquest of Kent were, we have seen, unique and formative: first, the previous experience of Hengist and his men, their discipline as federates, and their consequent knowledge of Frankish and sub-Roman civilization; then, the survival of numbers of the British natives whom the conquerors were sufficiently civilized to employ as their potters and craftsmen and as their serfs on the land—circumstances which combined to produce some parallelism between the conquest of Kent and the regulated occupation of certain parts of Gaul by Goths, Franks, and Burgundians.

Then in point of time, we must remember that the dynasty of Hengist had a start of something like a generation over the other small local monarchies—a generation in which they and their followers were sufficiently cultured to make a good use of their advantages. The decades in the middle of the fifth century when the Teutonic kingdom of Kent was an organized state surrounded, not by the primitive tribesmen of western Britain, but by the more Romanized Britons of the south-east, may have done much in fixing the contrast between the 'Jutes' and the Angles and Saxons.

But, above all, it was the geographical position of the Jutes at the bridge-head between Britain and the Continent which enabled them to generate a culture far above that of the other invaders of the island. The trade of the Jutes was the determining factor in their rise.

This explanation would, it is true, be falsified if it could be shown that the Jutes occupied the Isle of Wight and the opposite coast at the same time as Kent, and that from the first they displayed all the characteristics of Jutish civilization. But there is no evidence that this was what happened. These secondary

Jutish settlements seem to be in the main offshoots, overflowings from Kent. The graves indicate that for a time in the sixth century the Isle of Wight had contact with Kent, presumably political as well as cultural, and that it shared in the Kentish monopoly of trade. These western Jutes were, however, exposed to the influence and enmity of their Saxon neighbours, and this may be the reason why their graves fail to yield objects made in the most magnificent style of the golden age of Kent.

The Jutish problem, therefore, is not decided one way or another by the appearance of Jutish culture in the Isle of Wight and its neighbourhood. 'The Jutish nation' with its peculiar culture was made like the 'English', and so many other hybrid nations, out of different elements, and was made after the conquest. It was to all intents made in Kent.

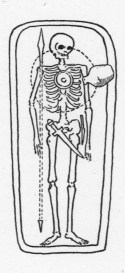

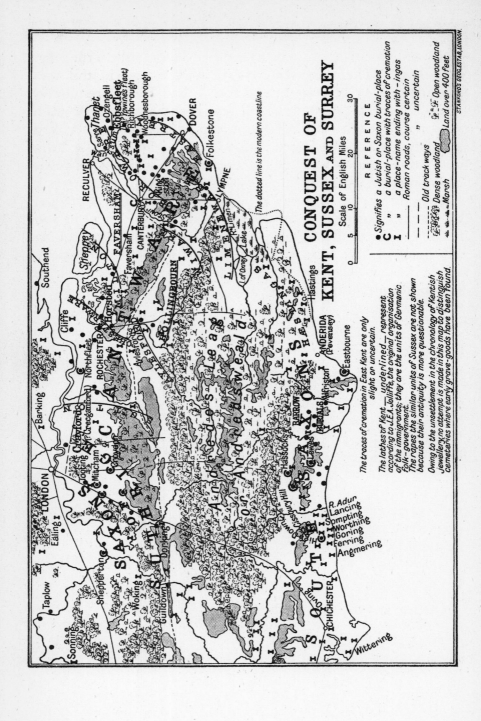

CONQUEST OF KENT, SUSSEX AND SURREY

Scale of English Miles

0 5 10 30

REFERENCE

● Signifies a Jutish or Saxon burial-place
C " a burial-place with traces of cremation
I " a place-name ending with -ingas
━━━ Roman roads, course certain
╌╌╌ " " uncertain
∙∙∙∙∙ Old track ways
Dense woodland   Open woodland
Marsh   Land over 400 feet

The dotted line is the modern coastline

The traces of cremation in East Kent are only
slight or uncertain.

The latches of Kent, underlined, represent
according to J.E.A. Jolliffe, the original organisation
of the immigrants; they are the units of Germanic
Folk-government.
The rapes the similar units of Sussex are not shown
because their antiquity is more questionable.

Owing to the unsettlement in the chronology of Kentish
jewellery, no attempt is made in this map to distinguish
cemeteries where early grave-goods have been found.

STANFORD'S GEOG. ESTAB., LONDON.

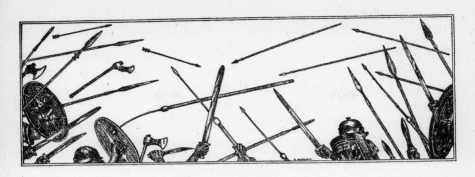

IV

THE FIRST STAGE OF THE SAXON AND ANGLIAN CONQUESTS

THE SAXONS

FOR the conquest of Kent it was reasonable to hear first what legend had to tell us and then to inquire whether the legends were confirmed by evidence from the graves. But for the rest of England the legends are so late or so meagre that we have often to reverse the procedure and to look at the archaeological evidence first, before we pay attention to any written statements made in the Saxon Chronicle. The maps which follow in this chapter attempt to summarize some results of the archaeological evidence. They show two ways by which we may try to trace the presence of early invaders, the distribution first of Saxon cemeteries where the dead were cremated, and secondly of burials containing grave-goods assigned to about the fifth century.

The reasons for caution to which we have drawn attention in previous chapters of course hold good whenever we use the evidence of Anglo-Saxon archaeology as a basis for history. In this even more than in most subjects we must expect to have the conclusions of one generation questioned by another.* But

---

* Indeed, the datings on which these maps are based, those of Baldwin Brown, Reginald Smith (in the volumes of the *Victoria County History*), and of Åberg, are already challenged; and owing to the great unsettlement in the chronology of Kentish jewellery I have given up the attempt to show the distribution of early grave goods in my map of southern Britain.

while our maps are necessarily provisional and give only rough approximations to the truth, they at least illustrate the methods by which we may in time discover the districts where the invaders made early settlements.

Let us first direct our attention to the cemeteries which lie to the west of 'Jutish' Kent. One thing which strikes us when we look at the map of the Surrey and Sussex region is, of course, the great extent of the uninhabited Weald country, and the smallness of the few districts to the north and south of it where there are archaeological traces of pagan settlement. In Sussex there are no cemeteries whatever at the eastern end of the county, in the Hastings district. Towards the west also they almost disappear, and in this direction we have only some barrows on the downs near Arundel to tell us of the presence of heathen Saxons, barrows which, in the phraseology of the archaeologists, were scantily 'furnished', and yielded little more than knives buried with the dead. There is a fairly thick cluster of cemeteries in the chalk country behind and around Brighton. Here in two cases only there were traces, and these slight, of cremation.

To form plausible theories about the conquest of Sussex it is essential at the outset to give special weight to what the place-name experts have to tell us. In no county have their studies been more illuminating.[1] If we accept the axiom that the suffix -*ing* (representing the Old English plural -*ingas*) betokens a colony made by a group in the early days of the settlement, perhaps by a group of the original invaders, we shall be forced to modify the ideas which we had formed from the cemeteries. The name Hastings itself, and a number of -*ing* names round the present town, suggest that the Hæstingas established themselves in these borderlands in an early phase of the migration.* Turning westwards along the coast, we find but few -*ing* names in the downlands around Eastbourne, Lewes, and Brighton,

* Certain Kentish features in the ancient field-system of the district have been taken to mean that these settlers were Jutes, and point at any rate to some connexion with Kent before their absorption into the kingdom of Sussex. Cf. Jolliffe, 73–97.

where the signs of heathen burials are most plentiful. But west
of the Adur they reappear in a long sequence up to and beyond
Chichester: Lancing, Steyning, Sompting, Worthing, Goring,
Angmering, Oving, Wittering, and many others. Thus the burials
and the place-names of Sussex both show marked changes in local
custom as we go from east to west. We therefore infer that the
later kingdom of the South Saxons was a union of at least three
earlier folks, and the inference receives some confirmation from a
record of the eleventh century in which one of these small units,
the Hæstingas, is mentioned as distinct from the South Saxons.
Here, then, we have an example of the process by which the
Heptarchic kingdoms were forged from smaller units.

After these preliminaries we are ready to hear what the
written authorities have to tell us. In the Alfredian Chronicle,*
immediately after the entries about the conquest of Kent, there
come two laconic annals about Sussex.

'477. Ælle landed in Britain and his three sons—Cymen and Wlencing
and Cissa—with three ships, at the place which is called Cymenes ora;
and there they slew many of the Welsh and some in flight they drove
into the wood that is called Andredesleage.'

Then, after another battle:

'491. Ælle and Cissa besieged the stronghold† of Anderida [Pevensey]
and slew all that were therein, nor was one Briton left there afterwards.'

The dates of the Chronicle, here as elsewhere in this early
period, are not to be relied on. But it is noteworthy that in the
opinion of Baldwin Brown[2] 'none of the finds of Teutonic character that have been made in the district suggest a date earlier
than the last quarter of the fifth century, which tradition assigns
for the first entry of the invaders'. Whether 'tradition' is a word
than can rightly be applied to these annals of the Chronicle,
is a question which can be better discussed when we come to the

* The Anglo-Saxon Chronicle is called Alfredian in order to remind the reader of the
period when it was compiled. The term does not necessarily imply that King Alfred
himself was the author. See vol. ii, pp. 624–8.   † *ceaster.*

early history of Wessex. On the face of things, however, it seems
reasonable to infer from all the evidence (such as it is) that the
Saxons who followed Ælle to Sussex had been campaigning so
long either in France or Britain that for the most part they had
given up their old custom of cremation burial; that the nucleus
of the main settlement on the coast was somewhere about the
middle of the modern county; and that the story of the massacre
of Britons who had taken shelter at Anderida behind the walls
of the old fort of the Saxon Shore, must be genuine enough—it
reads much like a passage from an encomium of a Viking hero.

The massacre at Anderida may perhaps be explained by the
old Germanic idea that a wasted land was the safest kind of frontier. Something similar, yet different, may well have happened
also at the western end of Sussex. At any rate the name of the
Roman *Regnum* vanished and the place which succeeded it was
thenceforth known as the 'fort' (*ceaster*) of Ælle's son Cissa,
that is, Chichester.[3]

The only other information about Ælle comes to us from Bede,
and all that he tells us is this: that Ælle was the first king to have
an *imperium* over all the invaders south of the Humber. Now
imperium is an ambiguous word. Later in this passage Bede uses
it as meaning something like our 'empire'; he enumerates kings
who held imperial sway over wide tracts of country south of
the Humber. Since, however, Ælle lived in a very early phase
of the Conquest, it is fair to argue that his *imperium* was military
rather than territorial—a command. No one need doubt that
this mysterious Ælle, founder of the kingdom of the South Saxons,
played a decisive part as a leader of the Germanic invaders of
the second generation. But it must be an open question whether
he was a mere war-leader—a commander-in-chief who at the
end of his life settled down in Sussex—or a petty king, recognized
as the most capable among a number of confederate chiefs who
co-operated in wars against the Britons.

Remembering this uncertainty we will once more refer to the
archaeologists and hear what they have to tell us about the

PLATE 20

Pevensey Castle (Anderida), West Gate

By permission of the Controller of H.M. Stationery Office

PLATE 21

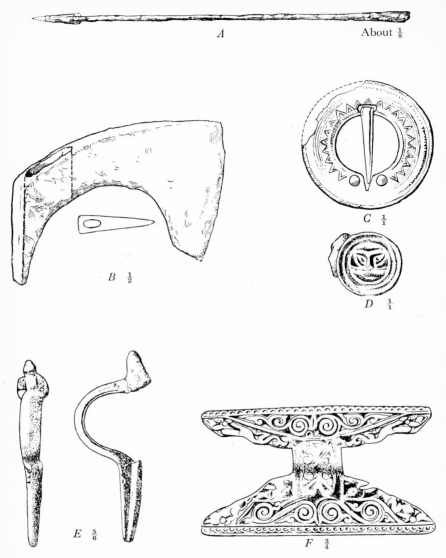

A   About ⅛

B ½

C ⅟₁

D ⅟₁

E ⅚

F ¾

A, B, C, D—Grave finds from Sussex and Surrey

A, An angon, and *B*, a throwing axe or Francisca, illustrate Frankish influence;
C, a ring brooch, and *D*, a button brooch, illustrate Kentish influence

E and *F* are from the Upper Thames Valley

E, Long brooch of primitive type from Dorchester; *F*, Equal-armed brooch from
Sutton Courtenay

conquests of Saxons to the north of Sussex, and especially about the conquest of the Thames valley.

After the first Saxon settlements in west Kent, we next find a large group on good dry soil in the Croydon area, sheltered from London by marshes and woodland. One cemetery of the group, that at Mitcham, with over 300 graves, indicates a place of some importance.

Now the first thing suggested by the cemeteries of Surrey, so widely sundered from those of Sussex, is this: that if the Saxons of the two regions were confederates, if both recognized, as Bede implies, the authority of Ælle, they did not keep much touch with one another by land. There is not a sign of any heathen settlement, late or early, along the Weald section of the Stane Street, the old Roman road which connected Chichester with the Thames valley. The Saxons who ploughed the coastlands and the river valleys of Sussex were almost cut off from their kinsmen in Surrey by the greatest forest of southern Britain. If Ælle's *imperium* was a reality, it probably rested on communications by sea rather than by land. He must have been the leader of a fleet which could operate both along the Sussex coast and in the Thames valley.

Next we find that there are marked resemblances between the cemeteries of Surrey and Sussex. In both areas the practice of burning the dead yielded quickly to the new fashion of burying the dead uncremated. But none the less there are differences: in Surrey cremation seems to have been practised for a generation or two; in Sussex the old custom seems to have been much more exceptional and evanescent. Another characteristic common both to the Saxons of Sussex and those of the lower Thames valley is that when they buried bodies unburnt they laid the bodies east and west. This orientation is no evidence of Christianity, but it is perhaps a sign that these invaders had been in contact with the more advanced Germanic peoples, like the Franks, and had learnt something of Frankish customs. Then, too, much of the gear which was placed with the dead was similar. For example, around Croydon in Surrey and at High Down in Sussex were found, in addition to Kentish fashions such as 'button' and 'ring' brooches and looted glass vases, round brooches with geometric patterns, like those of the Elbe lands, and Frankish imports such as 'angons', long barbed spear-heads which could transfix an enemy's shield and could not be cut by his sword.[4] (Pls. 21 and 22.)

It is possible to claim that the similarities of the graves indicate that somewhere in the past the history of the Saxons of the lower Thames touched that of the South Saxons. Thus it has been said that 'a study of the Saxon relics of the period seems to offer proof that the tradition of Ælle's hegemony contains at least a kernel of truth'. But other explanations are also legitimate. The resemblances between the two may have resulted not from co-operation in war under the command of Ælle, but from a similarity in their circumstances—their nearness to Kent and the fact that they bought their goods from the same or similar traders.

SETTLEMENTS ON THE UPPER THAMES

Having learnt something about early settlements of the Saxons on the Surrey side of the lower Thames, our obvious course is to track the invaders up the river. But at once we are checked. The following map shows us that there is a great gap between the Saxon cemeteries in the Croydon area and those ranging from Reading to Fairford in the valley of the upper Thames, a country which may for the sake of convenience be called after its modern centre, the Oxford region.

We shall discuss in a later section the question of what happened to Roman London. Here we need only remark in passing two things: first, that there is scarcely a trace of a pagan Germanic cemetery within some thirty miles of London on the northern bank of the Thames; and, secondly, that the Alfredian chronicler believed, whether rightly or wrongly, that as late as 571 there were British forces north of the Thames large enough to fight an important battle with Saxons who had, it seems, advanced from the Salisbury region. It is certainly curious that the settlements in the Oxford country, though they are so far from the sea, and though one of them, Fairford, is within eight miles of Cirencester, which, according to the Chronicle, was only conquered in 577, none the less seem from their graves to go back to an early date, that is to a period somewhere about 500. Two graves at Dorchester on the Thames have indeed produced the earliest Germanic objects yet excavated in this country—a brooch anticipating the cruciform type, buckles, and various oddments which were made about 400 or perhaps earlier[5] (Pl. 21 E). The significance of an isolated find such as this may clearly be questioned. The warrior who was buried here may have been a mercenary in the service of the Romano-Britons, or he may have been unusually old-fashioned in his equipment. On other grounds, however, Leeds[6] inferred that 'there must have been not inconsiderable settlements of Saxons in the upper Thames valley by the beginning of the sixth century at latest'; and[7] that 'it is archaeologically certain that the Saxons held the district immediately south and west of Oxford at least three-quarters of a century before . . . A.D. 571'. This point is of such importance that it is incumbent upon us to have some knowledge of the arguments upon which this view is based, even though it is only possible to give here a few samples of the evidence.

To begin with we must notice that in many of these cemeteries of the upper Thames valley there are unmistakable traces of cremation. It is found at Reading and at four or five other burial-grounds, especially in one at Abingdon where part of a Saxon cemetery excavated in 1934–5 revealed 82 cremations to 120 inhumations.[7a] This latest discovery leaves little doubt that the original settlers in this region had come direct from Germany, and were not offshoots from those who had been long established in the east of the island. A stronger argument is constructed from the brooches of these Saxons. Two are 'equal-armed' brooches, a type found in England in a few other places (in settlements on the Ouse and its tributaries), and elsewhere, as we have seen above,* only in the Elbe-Weser region. Now the ornamentation on these unique curiously shaped brooches is of the fifth-century kind, made with 'chip-carving'. One of these equal-armed brooches in the Oxford area was found not in a grave, but buried in earth which had once been the floor of a Saxon hut, near Sutton Courtenay.† True, it is, like the Dorchester burial, an isolated find. But it is a strong reason for thinking that the village here was inhabited by Saxons in very early days of the invasion.‡

The other kind of Saxon brooch, common both in the Elbe-Weser region of Germany and in the upper Thames valley in Britain, is the 'round' brooch made in two varieties, called respectively 'saucer' (or 'cast') and 'applied'. Some of the patterns of the English examples—especially those with spirals (Pl. 22)—resemble so closely the round brooches of north Germany that we are compelled to think that the immigrants brought their first models with them, and that they must have brought them at an early date.[8]

Another, though a fragile, argument can also be constructed from the evidences of continuity between the Romano-British and the Saxon settlements which have been found in quite a number of these upper Thames burial-places: at Long Witten-ham, at Frilford, at East Shefford (up in the Downs), and else-where. Turn up the records of one of these, for example that of Frilford.[9] Here, as elsewhere, the excavators found that the Saxons had buried their dead in a cemetery of the conquered people. They were side by side with Romano-Britons who had sometimes been placed in leaden or wooden coffins, sometimes had been committed to the earth with a coin in their mouth—an obol for Charon—sometimes had been orientated like Christians,

* See map, p. 33, and note 7b.
† See below, p. 223, and Pl. 21 F.
‡ The date assigned to this brooch by Roeder is *c.* 475.

PLATE 22

A

B

C

D

E

F

ROUND BROOCHES FROM GERMANY, SUSSEX, AND SURREY

A, B, C, and *D*—with floreated cross design (*A*, mounted on a square plate, from Wester-Wanna, N. Germany; *B* and *C* from High Down, Sussex; *D* from Mitcham, Surrey). *E* and *F*—with running spiral design (*E* from Wester-Wanna; *F* from Mitcham). $\frac{1}{1}$

with their heads to the west. Again, every stage of transition from
provincial-Roman to Saxon seemed to be represented in this Frilford cemetery. There were a few urns of the first intruders, those
who for a time kept up their old Germanic customs (Fig. 27),
ornamented vessels, or unadorned pots, such as the new-comers
used for their everyday cooking. Then, when the immigrants
began to bury instead of to cremate their dead, their graves

Fig. 27. Frilford, Berks.; urn. Less than ½.

showed evident signs of persistent Romano-British influence.
Sherds of Roman pottery were found thrown into the Saxon
graves just as into those of the natives. Moreover, in addition
to the round brooches of which we have already spoken, there
were Saxon buckles and other goods which showed resemblance
either in shape or in the style of ornamentation to the things
which had been used by the natives before the invasions. Now
it may be said that these signs of continuity do not prove that
the settlement of the Saxons at Frilford was early. This on the
whole must be granted; but it may still be claimed that the
British community which had sufficient influence to pass on its
customs and designs to the new-comers was not removed by
many generations from the times when Romano-British civilization had been vigorous.

The reasons for thinking that the Saxons found their way to the open spaces of the upper Thames at an early stage of the invasion are none of them perfectly strong; but taken together they have a certain cumulative strength—enough to justify us in provisionally marking the upper Thames valley as occupied by Saxon immigrants by the beginning of the sixth century.

And still we have not done with these Saxon graves and the lessons to be learnt from them. We must give due attention to the surprising fact, on which the experts have rightly laid much stress, that 'it is well-nigh impossible to single out any one cemetery as earlier archaeologically speaking than the rest'.[10] Now even if we allow the archaeologists an extra large margin of error, since the dating of these round brooches is admittedly insecure; even if we argue that the burial-grounds of the upper Thames basin, like Fairford, only go back to, say, 525, we still have this result, that for nearly fifty years before the reported capture of Cirencester (according to the annal of the Chronicle for 571) the Saxons at Fairford were settled within eight miles of the Britons who still clung to the old Roman town. And if it is true that the boundary between the two peoples did here remain almost unchanged for a generation or two, this fact is full of significance and must be remembered when we form our opinion about the general character of the Conquest.

In the next place we must direct our attention to important cemeteries in the valley of the Warwickshire Avon. One of these which is typical is at Bidford. The finds showed a community in which Anglian goods and perhaps settlers mingled with Saxon—apparently an offshoot from the Thames valley people. In the opinion of the excavators it was 'established quite early in the sixth century'.[11] The cremation burials were numerous, and plain square-headed brooches were recovered of a type assigned to about 500. Here, then, we seem to have evidence that a strong outpost of Saxons was placed at Bidford not long after the upper Thames valley was occupied. The position of Bidford was one of some strategic importance, since it marks the point

at which Ryknield Street, a branch of the Fosse Way, crosses
the Avon. When the Bidford post was established, Saxons had
penetrated the line of the Fosse Way. The Britons had ceased
to control this road, all-important for the defence of the west.

Another significant cemetery excavated was at Luton, near
the Icknield Way, the track which follows the escarpment of the
Chilterns and which from remote ages had been the chief line

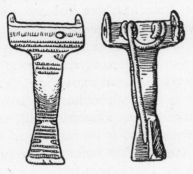

FIG. 28. Luton, Beds.; brooch with
primitive headplate. ⅓. (Roeder's
date, *c*. 400.)

Fig. 29. Kempston, Beds.;
brooch of the 'Luton' type.
⅓. (Roeder's date, *c*. 425.)

of communication between the country south of the Fens and
the region of the upper Thames. The interest of the settlement
is enhanced by the fact that it was placed about three miles from
the Watling Street. Luton, therefore, near the junction of the
two highways, had even more strategic importance than Bidford.
It is said[12] that some of its grave-goods, like the above brooch,
are early—indeed among the earliest of all such finds in
Britain. They, like the finds at Abingdon (p. 109), are claimed
by Leeds to strengthen a notable theory propounded by him,[13]
that the Saxons reached the upper Thames country, not by the
natural route up the river, but by 'a land route from the Wash
along some such line as the Icknield Way'. Leeds, however,
admits that when once the settlement had been made there
would be nothing extraordinary in further bands of immigrants
making their way up the Thames to join the first comers. If we

accept the fact that Saxons entered the Midlands by both routes, the question whether the first Saxons round Oxford came overland rather than by the river loses much of its importance. The dearth of Saxon graves on the middle reaches of the Thames—a dearth somewhat magnified by Leeds—does not mean that the river was not used for traffic. It is easy to see why the early settlers were unwilling to fix their homes on the middle reaches. The Chiltern woods which fringed the northern bank of the river, the poor soil and the heaths of Berkshire on the southern side, held out no attractions comparable with the open corn-lands higher up the valley which had been well-peopled in Roman times. And there were further objections to settling lower down the Thames. Immigrants who took up lands near a river route might expect to have more visits than was pleasant from others who followed in their wake. It has long been recognized that the fear of being molested by travelling war-bands made settlement on the Roman roads—'the army paths'* as the English called them—unpopular in the early days of the Conquest. And a similar fear must have acted as a deterrent to settlement near waterways like the Thames. Disorderly Saxons were more to be dreaded than hostile Britons; and so for safety's sake immigrants stuck together and made for the upper waters of the river. There was nothing abnormal in the neglect of the middle Thames country by the colonists.

Oxford may therefore repudiate the suggestion that the first settlers in its neighbourhood came from Cambridge (what fuel the suggestion would have given the controversialists of the seventeenth century!); but the evidence that Saxons entered the Midlands in some numbers by way of the Cam and of other Fen rivers is so strong that we must now turn our attention in that direction.

SETTLEMENTS IN THE CAMBRIDGE REGION[14]

A glance at the last map shows not only the density of the settlement in this region, but also the reason for it. When the

* *herepaðas.*

Romano-British inhabitants had been somehow or other disposed of, there was no safer channel into the heart of the Midlands than the Ouse and its tributaries. For thirty miles or more the

FIG. 30. Kempston, Beds.; equal-armed brooch. ½. (Roeder's date, *c.* 450.)

FIG. 31. Haslingfield, Camb.; equal-armed brooch. ½. (Roeder's date, *c.* 500.)

shallow boats of the invaders could paddle up through the marshes of the fenlands unobserved and unmolested. Those who turned south-west and west found at last in the valleys of the Cam, the Ouse, the Nene, and the Welland the dry lands which were suitable for habitation. This region in later times was known as the territory of the Middle Angles. The archaeologists mark it as a distinct 'cultural area'. It contains an unusually large number of grave-goods which can be assigned to the fifth century or thereabouts; and Saxon and Anglian things are curiously mixed. Roeder, the German archaeologist to whose careful studies of Saxon grave-goods we have already referred,*[15] dates a brooch of the 'Luton' type, from Kempston, back to about 425. Two equal-armed brooches from the Cambridge area he assigns to about the end of the fifth century (Figs. 30, 31). Equally significant are the unusual urns found both in the Elbe-Weser country and in our eastern Midlands: 'window urns', with pieces of glass fixed into the vessel, sometimes at the side, sometimes at the bottom; 'holed urns', that is, urns in which holes have deliberately been made.† These urns are strange vessels. Their peculiarities need not be explained in terms of religion. The glass was probably fitted into the clay because glass was a rarity, and even a fragment of it was worth framing in a pot.

There can be little doubt that many of these things were treasured belongings brought over by very early immigrants; and if others, like some of the equal-armed brooches, were made in England, then though we may not feel confident about the dates assigned to brooches on the strength of typological develop-ment, we may at least accept Roeder's argument that the in-vaders must have been settled in the Cambridge region for a long time before a craftsman could find an opportunity to pro-duce these elaborate ornaments.

Now the interest of these 'freak' urns and of the 'Luton' and equal-armed brooches is, we repeat, twofold. Besides proving that the Germans were dribbling into the country through the Fens at some very early phase of the invasion they have some-thing else to tell us. They come from definitely Saxon districts of Germany rather than Anglian. Their home is not Schleswig but the district to the west of the Elbe. Moreover, these peculiar grave-goods are not the only things which link up the so-called

---

* Above, p. 10.

† As mentioned above, p. 10, note, the Great Addington urn with a handle per-forated so as to form a spout (Pl. 27D) may now be regarded as evidence for an early Scandinavian contingent in the Midlands.

PLATE 23

A and *B*. Haslingfield, Cambridge; window urn. $\frac{5}{8}$

C. Great Addington, Northants.; spout-handled urn. About $\frac{1}{6}$

D. Kempston, Beds.; holed urn. $\frac{1}{2}$

PECULIAR URNS FROM THE EAST MIDLANDS

'Middle Angles' with the Saxons of Germany. The urns in which they were buried can more nearly be matched with those recovered from the Elbe-Weser cemeteries than from the cemeteries of Schleswig. On the other hand, the Cambridge region has produced unusually large numbers of early cruciform brooches —those with full-round and with half-round detachable knobs. On the strength of these and of other supposed Anglian *differentiae*, and above all, of course, on the strength of their name, the Middle Angles are often included within the boundary-line of the Anglian culture. The confusion of Anglian and Saxon things in the graves of the eastern Midlands points to there having been a mixture of Anglian and Saxon settlers rather than to mere trading intercourse. One may suppose that the Saxons who entered Britain by the back door of the Wash instead of by the front door of the Thames were, perhaps, even from the first intermingled with Anglian migrants, and that they were only transformed into 'Middle Angles' in the seventh century owing to the political conquest of all the Midlands by the Angles of Mercia.

These speculations for the time being can be put aside. What is essential is that we should treat with respect the view that the settlements round Cambridge go back to the fifth century —possibly to the middle of that century—and that others also in the eastern Midlands, such as that at Kempston on the Ouse, may be almost as early.

At this point we finish for the moment with the evidence of the archaeologists. They have said their say, and if their version of what happened is accepted, the new story of the Conquest is something very different from the old story. For their evidence amounts to this: that at an early period of the invasion, probably before the end of the fifth century, there were clusters of Germanic invaders both in the Cambridge region and also, less certainly, on the upper Thames. Between the two in the sixth century, intermediate Germanic settlements were multiplied until they stretched like the string of a bow across the eastern Midlands. The existence of these, and the unearthing of early brooches at Luton, while they show that the Wash rivers and the Icknield Way were early used as an important means of entry into the island, scarcely prove that this was the main, much less the only, route used by the invaders of southern Britain.

THE STORY OF GILDAS

It is time to return to the story of Gildas, the only British writer who was in any sense contemporary with the Conquest. When last we referred to him he was speaking about the 'fire of the invaders' licking 'the western ocean with its red and savage tongue'—rhetorical words which may be interpreted to mean that a mobile force of the first permanent invaders, Hengist's or another's, made destructive marches right across the island before returning to the east to appropriate the best lands available. Now Gildas, in spite of his extravagances, his querulous tone, and his vagueness, is of the greatest value in certain ways. He does give us one side of the story—the British side. Moreover, he brings home to us the truth that the Conquest which we have unavoidably to treat as a tangle of inter-related problems was in fact a series of human tragedies involving as much destruction of life and of civilization as has ever occurred in the history of our island. Gildas was not able to detect, like some modern historians, 'peaceful yeomen farmers' behind the brutal Saxon marauder;. He tells, apparently at first-hand, of what was to be seen in the cities of Roman Britain, after the fury of the invaders had done its worst—of the ruined towns; the tops of towers and stones from high walls tumbled to the ground; the fragments of unburied human bodies lying, covered with clotted blood; the widespread devastation in the countryside, where there was hardly an ear of corn to be seen. He tells how the Britons, sheltering in the hills, were caught and murdered; how some were compelled by hunger to come and give themselves up as slaves to the enemy, so running the risk of being slaughtered at sight; and how others fled, lamenting, over the sea.

This is rhetoric rather than history; it is intended to rouse his countrymen, and not to inform posterity. Gildas is no more attempting to describe all the aspects of the invasion than to weigh his words. But, so far as it goes, we need not question the general truth of the picture. On the contrary, if we admit that it is not the whole truth of what happened, we may accept its lurid details as a part of the truth; and apply it not only to the west of Britain, which was the chief concern of Gildas, but also to the east. Massacres, a flight to the hills, enslavement, migration over sea—these are incidents of the Conquest which undoubtedly occurred. And if Gildas could only have told his story in simple language instead of in the tortured style which he adopted and helped to make fashionable among his countrymen, the miseries and horrors which this generation of Britons endured would have been remembered ever since, as one of the most moving catastrophes in history. As it is, we must not be deterred by his verbiage about the clotted blood and the wolfish, dog-like barbarians, for he tells us just enough of his ideas about the course of the Conquest for it to be possible to extract from it at least a bare sequence of events. What we obtain is the following story.

(1) After the petition of the Britons to Aëtius in 446, there ensued the age of the 'proud king' (Vortigern), who called in the accursed 'Saxons' (Hengist and company) to repel the Picts. It was at this stage, when the Saxon mercenaries turned against the king who was their paymaster, that 'the fire of their rage licked the western ocean with its red tongue'. Thus, apparently during the third quarter of the fifth century—if we accept the chronology of Bede—there occurred the episode of the hopeless collapse when the Britons, too demoralized to put up an effective resistance, endured the horrors of the pitiless raids, which, according to Gildas, left behind them tracks of unburied corpses and ruined towers. In this period we may place the evacuation of Kent. The two graves at Dorchester (above, p. 109) may witness to the bands of marauders who at this time,

when there was little organized opposition, rode across the island. But we have seen in the graves little or no proof of settlement at this stage.

Then (2) 'after a certain interval of time' there followed, according to Gildas, the age of Ambrosius Aurelianus, a man of a distinguished Roman family whose kinsmen, before they were killed in the storm of war, had 'worn the purple' (having presumably been proclaimed emperors by the Britons or by some section of them). Gildas tells us that Ambrosius Aurelianus himself was 'a discreet man';* that he might be considered the only survivor of the Roman nation; and that he became the leader of the remnants of the wretched *cives* (the Romano-Britons) who flocked to him from all sides like bees.

Then (3) from that time there ensued a period of alternate victory and defeat. Sometimes thc Romano-Britons, sometimes the Saxon enemy, had the upper hand. When the chronology is as vague and elastic as it is both in the words of Gildas and in the dating of the grave-gear, there can be no exact adjustment between the two. One can therefore only speculate whether the rally of the Britons under Ambrosius came before or after the Saxons established themselves in the eastern Midlands and in the upper Thames valley. If Ambrosius lived during the time when these regions were inundated by Saxons, then one may guess that the great work of this 'last of the Romans' was to organize resistance along the Fosse Way, in that central part of the line where the Saxon advance had broken most dangerously into the centre of Britain. And if so, the road which had been made to enable the generals of Claudius to consolidate the first Roman attack on the Midlands was now used to prolong the last Romano-British defence. One suspects that the short generalization of Gildas about the alternate victory and defeat of the Britons from the time of Ambrosius conveniently covers up much ignorance and confusion in his mind. For the period of alternating success was prolonged apparently for one or two generations.

* *vir modestus.*

It lasted, says Gildas, 'until the siege of the Badon hill, almost the last and not the least slaughter of the rascals'. And when was that siege or battle? Here we encounter another well-known puzzle. It is one that cannot be avoided; and a glance at it will at any rate serve to show how insecure is our footing throughout this tract. Gildas intended for once in a way to fix the date of this slaughter of the Saxons. The event had a special interest for him as being the year of his own birth. In his original manuscript he said it occurred in the forty-fourth year from something or other; from what he reckoned soon became doubtful owing to mistakes in copying the manuscript. Bede, in reproducing the passage, understood him to mean that it was the forty-fourth year 'after the first coming of the Saxons', i.e. after about 449, so it is evident that Bede assigned the victory to about 493. Was Bede reproducing the original reading? Some think it unlikely that a Briton would wish to set up a national defeat as the beginning of a new era of chronology. Moreover, to Gildas writing about 546, the victory of Mount Badon was 'almost the last slaughter' of the enemy; it was 'in our times' and therefore can scarcely have occurred more than fifty years earlier, in the previous century. Or did Gildas mean to say that the battle was in the forty-fourth year after the time of Ambrosius Aurelianus— the last subject about which he had been writing? That is possible, but since he failed to mention the date of Ambrosius, it is not helpful. Or was he measuring backwards and trying to say that the fight occurred in the forty-fourth year from that in which he wrote? This view has behind it the support of Mommsen, and a conjectural emendation in his edition of Gildas.*

In these uncertainties we can only say that the battle was fought some time between 493 and 516 (or 518), the date found in the *Annales Cambriae*.[16]

---

* C. 26. 'Ex eo tempore nunc cives, nunc hostes, vincebant . . .; usque ad annum obsessionis Badonici montis, novissimaeque ferme de furciferis non minimae stragis, quique quadragesimus quartus ut novi [or, according to Mommsen's emendation, est ab eo qui] orditur annus, mense jam uno emenso, qui et meae nativitatis est.'

One reason for approaching the fringe of this tangled controversy is, as we have said, that it illustrates the chronological uncertainties of the age in which we are groping and of Gildas, our sole contemporary guide. But there is also what we may call a sentimental reason. The British 'traditions' preserved in *Nennius* tell us that the battle of Mount Badon was the twelfth and last battle in which Arthur, the *dux bellorum*, together with the kings of Britain, fought against the Saxons, and that 960 men fell in that one day from the onslaught of Arthur alone. This is one small ray of light which comes from the Dark Ages to show the historian how already, in the ninth century, and doubtless much earlier, the Romano-British commander had caught the glowing colours of heroic tradition.[17]

Arthur evidently lived about a generation after Ambrosius. Collingwood has made a gallant attempt to place his story into an historical setting.

He suggests that Arthur was, in fact, a *Comes Britanniarum*, about the end of the fifth century; a cavalry general whose troopers, wearing heavy armour like that of a late-Roman *eques cataphractarius*, really had some resemblance to the knights of the middle ages; and that as Count of Britain he had a roving commission, and may thus have aided the local kings against the invaders in many parts of the island. This would explain why Arthur's popularity was so widespread that within a hundred years of his death, both a Scottish king of Dal Riata and a British king of Dyfed in South Wales named sons after him. It also explains why though many of the battles mentioned by Nennius are best identified in the north—for instance, one in 'the wood of Celidon' (? Caledonia), and another where Arthur was killed, at Camlann (or 'Camelon', probably Camboglanna, a fort on the Roman Wall)—Mount Badon, which Nennius calls the twelfth battle of Arthur, should be placed in the south, since that was the region which interested Gildas, the only good authority for the battle. Gildas was probably referring to a struggle of the Cirencester and other Britons against the in-

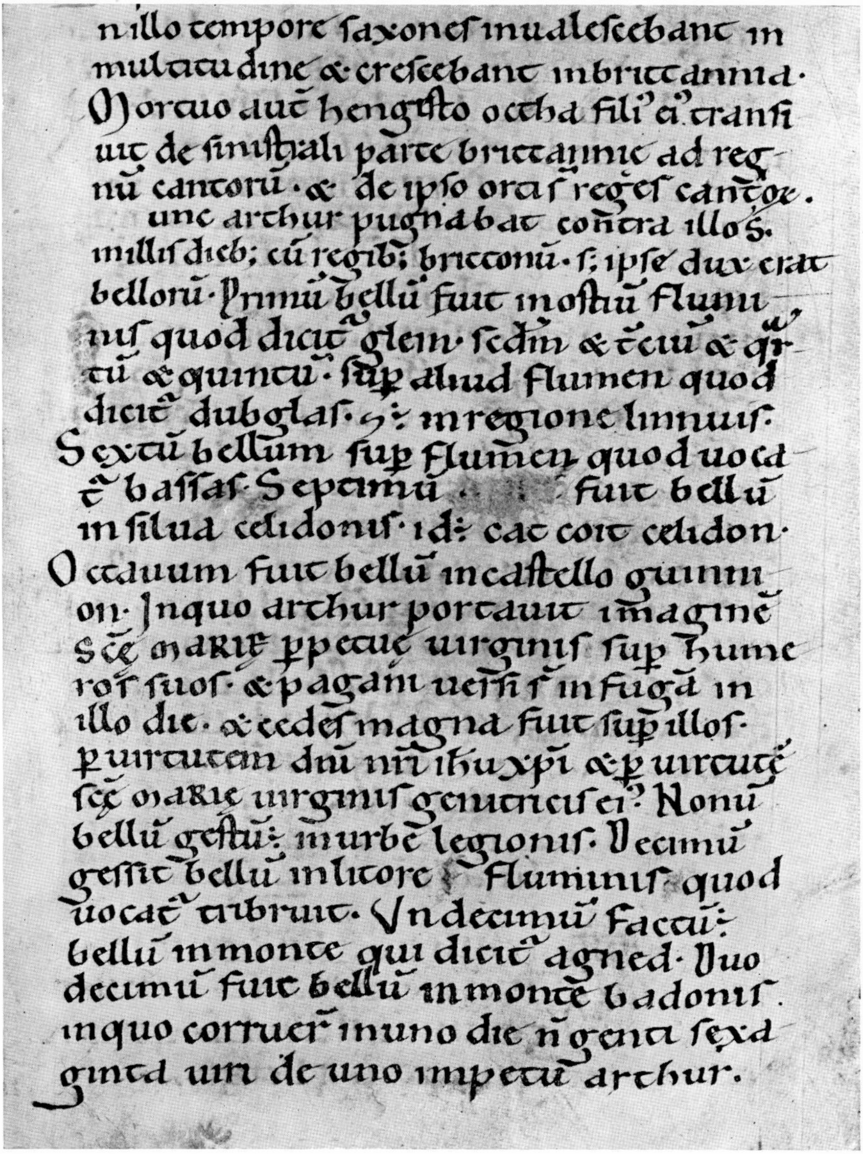

PLATE 24

The earliest mention of Arthur. From Nennius, *Historia Brittonum*, ch. lvi, Harleian MS. 3859. British Museum. About A.D. 1100

(For transcription of this passage see p. xvi. See also p. 122)

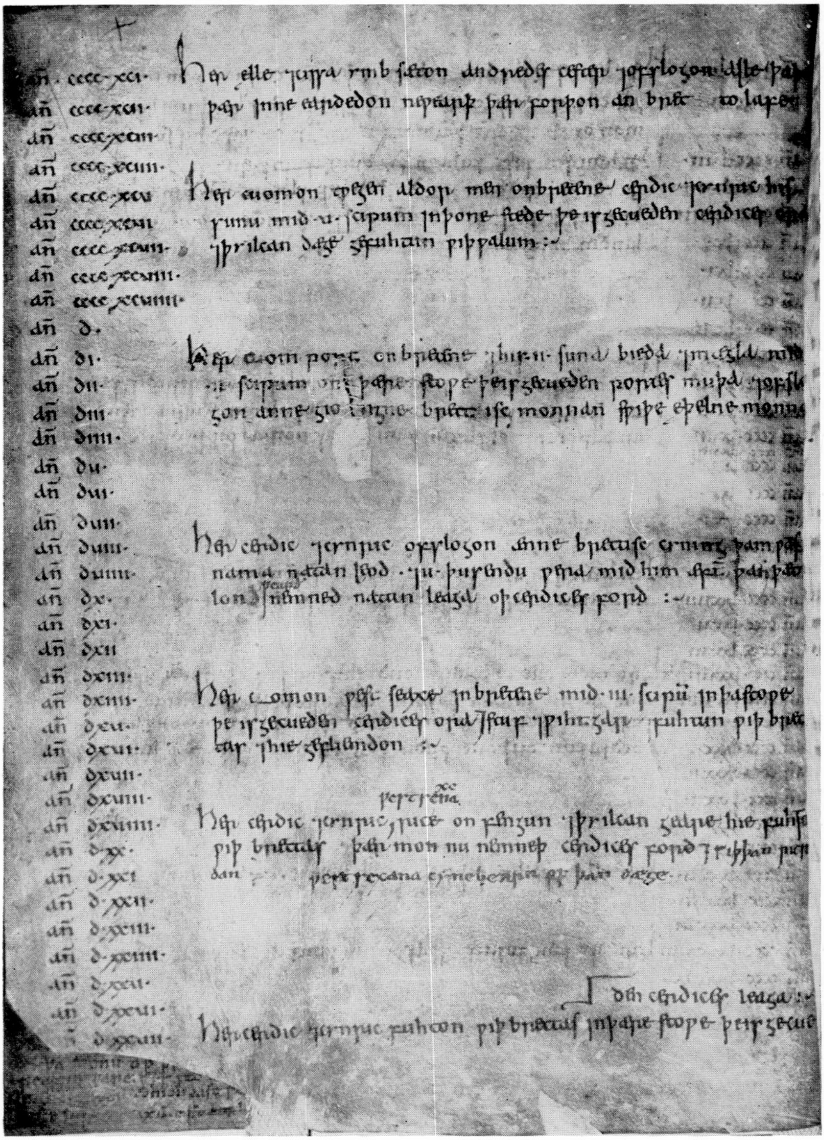

PLATE 25

The Alfredian Chronicle (Parker MS.). Facsimile of entries about Ælle, Cerdic and Cynric, and Port. ½

vaders of the upper Thames. Likely spots for the fight can be
found either at Badbury Hill, near Faringdon, or at the hill
above another Badbury, near Swindon.[19] If this reasoning is
accepted, it leads further. The grave-finds of the upper Thames
region suit a date nearer to 516 than 493 for such a fight. And
Arthur's part in it? This after all may be a fable which has grown
from the two facts, that Badon was the one contest mentioned
in Gildas, and that Arthur was tradition's favourite leader.

(4) After the siege of Mount Badon we come, in the story of
Gildas, to what we distinguish as a fourth period. It was the
beginning of a time in which, though the cities still lay desolate
and though civil wars continued, the foreign wars ceased. This
period of victory, of rest from Saxon aggression, was still continuing when Gildas wrote.

On the whole, the story of Gildas harmonizes well with what
may be inferred from the cemeteries. We see that the invaders
had, early in the sixth century at latest, thrust themselves far
up the valleys on the east side of Britain. It is likely enough that
the years following Mount Badon were a period when the Saxons
were mainly occupied in making good the footing they had
already obtained.

This peaceful period lasted long enough for the generation
which had been eyewitnesses of the earlier desolation to die out.
Looking back at the previous age it seemed to Gildas that, in
the bygone generation, owing to the remembrance of those
troubles, the kings, the public officials, the private men, the
priests and ecclesiastics, had all done their duty.

(5) But in the middle of the sixth century when he wrote, a
new generation had grown up, which knew nothing of the past
storm and had only experienced the existing peace. Accordingly,
in the age in which Gildas flourished, truth and justice were
subverted—or so it seemed to him—by his countrymen, and
there were very few of them who were not gaily rushing down
to hell.

The above five periods of Gildas make up what we may call

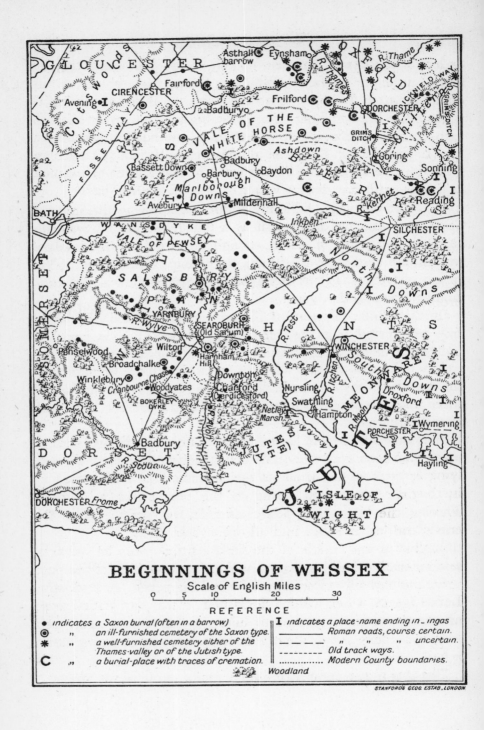

BEGINNINGS OF WESSEX

Scale of English Miles

0   5   10   20   30

REFERENCE

- •   indicates a Saxon burial (often in a barrow)
- ◉   "   an ill-furnished cemetery of the Saxon type.
- ✳   "   a well-furnished cemetery either of the Thames-valley or of the Jutish type.
- **C**   "   a burial-place with traces of cremation.

- **I**   indicates a place-name ending in _ingas_
- ————   Roman roads, course certain.
- ————   "   "   uncertain.
- ---------   Old track ways.
- ....   Modern County boundaries.

🌳 Woodland

STANFORD'S GEOG. ESTAB. LONDON.

'the first stage' of the Saxon Conquest. The beginning is fixed by the appeal to Aëtius, whose third Consulship we know to have fallen in the year 446. The final date is approximately fixed by the fact that Gildas was writing shortly before the death of Mælgwn (Maglocunus), king of Gwynedd—an event which (according to the *Annales Cambriae*) occurred in 547, or 549, when Britain was swept by one of the periodic plagues which visited the island. From 446 to 547 is a century of shifting, dangerous chronology—a great slough to discourage the student of English history at the beginning of his pilgrimage. A slough, however, is not the best simile; though it is better than that of Professor Lot,[20] who calls the age 'a blank page'. Let us rather resume our earlier idea and remember that in the complex of problems before us many are soluble.

THE BEGINNINGS OF THE WEST SAXON MONARCHY

Any one looking at a map in which the heathen cemeteries of the Anglo-Saxons are marked, will at once observe that there are three large areas where the invaders might have been expected to settle, but where in fact there is little or no evidence of their settlement. The first of these areas almost bare of recorded Germanic cemeteries which we propose to investigate is the territory lying between the upper Thames valley and the Channel, that is, roughly speaking, our counties of Hampshire and Wiltshire. The subject is of peculiar interest because we have numerous entries in the Alfredian Chronicle which profess to give something like a story of those settlements, and this story is often said to be at variance with the archaeological evidence.

Our approach to the subject must be through the Chronicle. Let us first read a sentence or two from the genealogy of Alfred's ancestors which was inserted as a preface by Alfred or his helpers.

'In the year when 494 winters had passed from the birth of Christ, Cerdic and Cynric his son landed at Cerdices-ora with five ships. Cerdic was Elesing [the son of Elesa].'

The descent from Woden is then given, the most noteworthy name being that of the great-grandfather of Cerdic, Gewis, the eponymous hero of the Gewisse, the West Saxons.

'And about six years after they landed, they took the kingdom of the West Saxons, and they were the first kings who took the land of the West Saxons from the Britons. And he [Cerdic] had the kingdom for sixteen years, and when he died his son Cynric succeeded and held the kingdom for seventeen winters. . . .'

Turning to the annals we find (cf. Plate 25) these entries:

'495. Two ealdormen [war-leaders] came to Britain, Cerdic and Cynric his son, with five ships, at the place which is called Cerdices-ora, and the same day they fought against the Britons.

'501. Port came to Britain and his two sons, Bieda and Mægla, with two ships, at the place which is called Portsmouth, and they slew a young British man, a man of very noble birth.

'508. Cerdic and Cynric slew a British king, named Natanleod, and five thousand men with him. And afterwards the land was called Natan-leaga up to Cerdicesford.

'514. The West Saxons, Stuf and Wihtgar, came to Britain with three ships, in the place which is called Cerdices-ora; and they fought against the Britons, and put them to flight. . . .

'519. Cerdic and Cynric succeeded to the kingdom, and the same year they fought against the Britons where it is now called Cerdicesford.

'527. Cerdic and Cynric fought against the Britons in the place which is called Cerdices-leaga.

'530. Cerdic and Cynric took the Isle of Wight, and slew a few men in Wihtgaræsburh.

'534. Cerdic died, and his son Cynric continued to reign for twenty-six winters: and they gave the Isle of Wight to their two grandsons [or nephews] Stuf and Wihtgar. . . .

'544. Wihtgar died and was buried at Wihtgaraburh.'

Two subsequent entries about fights of Cynric will come in more appropriately at a later point in the story.

There may well be differences of opinion on the question how far the Alfredian editor had earlier material before him when he wrote the above annals. The forms of some of the names appear to be antique: Wihtgaraburh, for instance, almost certainly contains an archaic genitive singular;[20a] and *leag* is said to be used in the primitive sense of a 'wood' instead of the later sense of a 'field' or 'clearing in a wood'.[21] Again, the fact that the editor conflates two discrepant versions of the story—a landing in 495 and a landing in 514—shows that he is incorporating with honesty, though with little skill, narratives which were already put on record. There is a stronger case for considering the preface to be early, since there are philological reasons for thinking that the names of its genealogy had been written down 'as early as the eighth century, probably before A.D. 750'.[22] This line of argument would carry back the tradition to at least the early eighth century. But even that leaves too long an interval for the handing down of accurate details.

The transparent blunders made by the chronicler have long been notorious. Port, perhaps a genuine Saxon hero, was connected with Portsmouth by some ingenious antiquary who did not realize that the prefix of that place-name was derived from the Latin word *portus*, a harbour. Though Wihtgar may also be a genuine Germanic name, there is a suspicious resemblance between the initial syllable of his name and that of Vectis, the Roman name for the Isle of Wight.[23] Natanleod may be another fictitious personage.

Are we then to give any credence to Cerdic when he is found in this shady company? In recent years historians have regarded the existence of Cerdic with suspicion owing to his Celtic name. This scepticism is a natural rebound from the extreme credulity of the Victorians, and notably of J. R. Green. On the strength of the annals which we have quoted and of the natural features of the country, Green described in a long and vivid narrative exactly what happened in this advance; 'as if he had been present at the landing of the Saxons, and had watched every step of their subsequent progress'.[24] The picturesque imaginings of J. R. Green have been long discredited. At the present day it is more needful to correct the bias to scepticism than that to credulity.

Let us then inquire whether anything of this early story can be saved from the critics.

Professor Lot[25] wishes to sweep aside all the entries of the Chronicle, and insists that tradition cannot survive for so many centuries and that the people remember nothing, even of the greatest events. This cannot, however, be accepted as an axiom; a people's memory may be either short or long. Gildas and the Britons clearly forgot within a century and a half what had happened on the extinction of Roman rule. The Scandinavians, on the other hand, can be proved to have carried certain facts in their memories not for a mere four, but for fourteen centuries.[26]

The Chronicle itself tells us so little about the Saxon Conquest, so little is narrated about the heroes of the invasion, that the English cannot be said to have preserved traditions of their ancestors as carefully as did the Scandinavians. But one thing, it seems, they did try to remember in each of the Heptarchic kingdoms; that was, the succession of their rulers. The lists of kings, and sometimes even the number of the years which they reigned, seem to have been carried in the mind like a kind of chant. They were naturally among the first things to be written down on parchment as soon as the art of writing was introduced.[27] In the West Saxon genealogy, though there are discrepancies in places, there is no confusion about the head of the dynasty. All were agreed that Cerdic was the founder of the fortunes of the family. The Chronicle is most careful to trace the pedigree of one king after another back to Cerdic. Clearly a king was not considered to be in the right line of succession unless it could be said of him that 'his kin goeth back to Cerdic'.

This surprising fact should really be another argument for the view that we are here encountering a genuine tradition. What Germanic invader would go out of his way to invent a despised British name as that of the ancestor of all his kings? One thing, and one thing only, could pass such an idea into

general currency—the existence of such a founder in actual fact.
The modern sceptic says that Cerdic must have been born at
a time (about 450) when 'intimacy with the Britons and the
borrowing of a name from them seems almost incredible'. Such
things are incredible only when this dark period is approached
with preconceived opinions. How exactly it came to pass that
Cerdic was so named we shall never know, but it is easy enough
to imagine a number of ways in which it might have occurred.
For instance, the ancestors of Cerdic—Gewis and his brood—may
have been Saxon chiefs who cruised in the Channel for generations. Cerdic's father may well have been called in to help some
local British leader against his enemies, Irish from the west, Jutes
from the east;[27a] it may be, even against rival Britons. Germans
in the fifth century were in one country after another introduced
in this way. Military service in the Empire had long since been
considered a reputable life for a German chief and his followers
—it was a natural and normal proceeding; nor is there anything
unnatural in intermarriage under such conditions, nor anything
improbable in a British mother giving a Celtic name to the son
of a Saxon chieftain.

Now if Cerdic is accepted as the genuine leader of this invasion, it is reasonable to believe that Cerdices-ora, Cerdicesford and Cerdices-leaga, being well-known places in the ninth
century, had obtained their names on account of some real connexion with the first king of the West Saxon dynasty.[28] Cerdices-ora may indeed have been the place where by a genuine
tradition it was believed that Cerdic had landed. An interesting
attempt has recently been made to fix this place. O. G. S. Crawford[29] revives the old identification of Natan-leaga with the
district Netley, of which a trace is left in the modern name
Netley Marsh; and since Cerdicesford has always† been identified with Charford on the Avon, it is likely enough that Cerdices-
ora was in the neighbourhood of Netley Marsh, at the top of
Southampton Water. It is claimed that even the road by which

† Ever since Ethelweard. Cf. *M.H.B.* 503.

Cerdic advanced can be identified by an air photograph which shows an ancient track leading from Southampton Water to Charford.

Now the fact that the chronicler did find two other place-names formed with the name of the reputed founder of the West Saxon dynasty apparently not far from Charford has definite significance. The bad guesses which he made about Port and Natanleod do not in themselves put this other guess about Cerdic out of court. The author of the Chronicle was in a better position than we are to speculate about the history of Cerdic, since he knew of three place-names embodying Cerdic's name. It does not follow that because we suspect half, or more, of these entries we must needs reject the remainder. The dates, the number of the ships, and many other details are clearly dubious. They may be mere speculations. The entries about the Isle of Wight may be echoes of some rivalry of the seventh century between West Saxons and Jutes. About these things scepticism is justified. But we turn our backs on the truth if we deny the existence of Cerdic and do not see that the place-names go some way to justify the Alfredian theory that Cerdic's invasion occurred in this southern borderland of Hampshire and Wiltshire.

Other objections which have been raised to the story contained in the Chronicle must be considered. One[30] is the assertion that southern Hampshire was, like the Isle of Wight, a Jutish district. There is no doubt that it was so in the time of Bede; but it does not follow that the Jutes were already in possession when Cerdic landed. The Jutes on the mainland may well have been an overflow from the Isle of Wight, coming in at a later period. Even if the assumption is right that the Jutes had occupied southern Hampshire before the war-bands of Cerdic appeared on the scene, even if Southampton Water and the country to the north of it was closed to his Saxons, it is not necessary to regard his invasion as a fiction imagined by a later age. For the Hampshire Avon was a navigable waterway; it led to the region of Charford, and to the good open lands of Salisbury Plain.

But then comes the archaeological argument which is generally said to be fatal to the Chronicle's story—the remarkable dearth of heathen Saxon graves in Hampshire and their rarity in Wiltshire. According to Leeds,[31] 'the absence of pagan cemeteries south of the [Berkshire] Downs suggests that the Saxon occupation of that area did not materialize before the time when pagan burial was gradually going out of practice'. Now it has been suggested above (p. 85) that the principle, 'No heathen settlement where no heathen grave', is unsound. It reduces the whole history of Wessex to an absurdity.[32]

Our contention is that the Saxons of Wiltshire and Hampshire must have conformed to some of the Christian fashions of their neighbours before they actually adopted Christianity. The vital point is, when did they conform? Was it before their arrival in the island when they were unsettled in their religious practices by a long course of piracy, perhaps by living in one of the Saxon colonies in Gaul? Was it in the early days after their arrival, in times when they were perhaps employed by some hard-pressed British chief against his enemies? Or was it on the eve of the Conversion?

Now the fact that the Saxons of Sussex almost ignored the old rite of cremation and began from the earliest times the new custom of disposing of their dead by inhumation is not without significance. If the South Saxons could surrender the burial tradition of centuries so easily, is there anything improbable in the supposition that another group of invaders, giving up cremation, adopted burial customs such as those which they saw practised by the Britons with whom they came into contact, whether in war or friendship? One need only suppose that Cerdic and his chiefs were clever and adaptable men who saw that the depositing of weapons and jewellery with the corpses was an unnecessary extravagance.[32a]

If it is true that Cerdic's people were disinclined to bury with the dead their most precious belongings, we are deprived of the means of estimating their numbers and of following their course.

Most of their graves containing mere bones could no more be identified as Saxon than can those of the provincials be recognized as British. Such Saxons imitating Romano-British customs would disappear from the world and leave no sufficient evidence of their existence. As a matter of fact, Wiltshire can produce one fair-sized Saxon cemetery—at Harnham Hill near Salisbury—a few smaller ones, and many isolated Saxon burials scattered about the district. These last are being steadily revealed by excavation, especially in the uplands to the south-west of Salisbury—often secondary burials in and around old tumuli, sometimes primary mound burials;[33] but no solid argument can at present be built on the evidence either from Harnham Hill or from the other burials of this region. The graves were for the most part poorly furnished. They were only recognized as Saxon owing to the occasional presence of a sword, a spear-head, a knife, a shield boss, a bead, or suchlike.

A clue of a different kind which should be noticed is that an earthen rampart, Bokerly Dyke, was at some time in the fifth century[34] enlarged so as to protect the east of Dorset from raids coming from the direction of Salisbury. There is some excuse for jumping to the conclusion that this dyke, which still in part forms the boundary between Wiltshire and Dorset, was a British defence, and that the enemy in view were Cerdic's war-bands established in the uplands near Salisbury.

It is now time to put together the different lines of our argument. We have first the general probability that a waterway as easily navigable for the light-draught Saxon ships as the Hampshire Avon would not escape the attention of the invaders. Next we have the positive statements of the Chronicle, which in spite of its late date and in spite of some obvious errors cannot be altogether brushed aside; they show that Cerdic and his war-band were located by place-names, probably also by genuine tradition, in the country near Charford on the Avon, that is in the Wiltshire-Hampshire borderland. Lastly, we have found reasons for questioning the common view that the scarcity of

Saxon cemeteries is fatal to the story of the Chronicle; and we observe on the map that this scarcity is in some measure compensated by Saxon burials of a different kind.

We may strengthen the archaeological argument by approaching it from another direction. If we reject the theory of an early occupation of Wiltshire and Hampshire by some Germanic people who quickly ceased to bury their dead according to the ordinary modes of the Germans, the only alternative is to suppose that the Saxons descended at some later date from the north, that is from the Thames valley, as overland migrants. But this migration from the north, if it had ever occurred, should have been marked by a series of cemeteries such as those which we have seen in the Thames valley at Frilford, at Wittenham, and elsewhere. The track of these Saxons across the Marlborough Downs and Salisbury Plain should have been blazed with well-furnished heathen cemeteries. Since we must think that much of Hampshire and Wiltshire was occupied before the coming of Christianity, and since these early Saxon inhabitants left little or no trace of themselves, may we not infer that in their burial customs they resembled the migrants who entered Wessex from the Channel rather than those who came by way of the Thames?

Thus from many angles, but chiefly from the Chronicle, arguments converge to a conclusion very much like the story with which we have been long familiar in the Victorian histories. It is like; but it is not the same. While we accept the main tradition of the Chronicle, we reject many of its details. We no longer believe, as did J. R. Green, that the county boundaries of Hampshire mark the line which the invaders had reached when their advance was arrested for thirty years by the victory of the Britons at Mount Badon. That battle is rightly, as we have already seen, out of the picture. If it was an attempt of the Britons to stem the main advance of the Saxons up the Thames valley, it naturally found no place in the traditions of the small community which had established itself round Salisbury.

Leaving the beginnings of Saxon Hampshire[35] as one of the

pages which are almost blank in our island's history, let us continue to piece together the existing fragments of information about the Saxon community in the valley of the Avon. The two short annals of the Chronicle which profess to give facts from the last years of Cynric's long—indeed, incredibly long[36]— career are the following:

'A.D. 552. Cynric fought against the Britons at the place which is called Searoburh [Old Sarum] and put the Britons to flight.

'A.D. 556. Cynric and Ceawlin fought against the Britons at Beranburh.'

Since Old Sarum is within, or at any rate quite close to, the district which we have taken to be the core of Cerdic's kingdom, it is reasonable to suppose that in the battle of 552 the Saxons were on the defensive. But if the fight of 556 is rightly located at Barbury camp[37] near the highest part of the Marlborough Downs, overlooking the valley of Swindon, we must infer that Cynric in his last years launched out into an ambitious campaign far from his base. Such an advance suggests that the victory at Sarum had been a smashing one; it also suggests that the Saxons had already overrun Salisbury Plain up to its northern edge. The expansion had now begun which was in time to give the dynasty of Cerdic predominance in the Thames valley, and ultimately the rule over all the English.

Before we leave the obscure beginnings of these men who first among Englishmen marched and fought on the soil of England under the command of the founders of our present monarchy, we must take note of evidence which is perhaps the most interesting of any which has been produced in recent years: that is, of the results obtained for the historian by the miracle of modern air photography. Our thanks are due to O. G. S. Crawford, who has put the miracle to good use.[38] The air photographs which he has published reveal to us the roads, villages, and fields of the Celtic inhabitants of southern Britain in the days before the coming of the Saxons (cf. Pl. 8). These photographs demonstrate that the settlements of the Britons round Salisbury were placed almost invariably on the crests or higher slopes of the hills. Their upland villages, set among more or less rectangular fields, are in every way differentiated from the Saxon villages which in time took their place—these villages of ours which are still to be found in the valleys close to the rivers. Crawford claims that in not a single instance did any British village remain inhabited after the Saxon Conquest.

'Their sites were abandoned and may often be seen to-day exactly as they were left, though now of course a maze of grass-covered mounds. We do not know of course what happened during that century and a half of darkness and confusion; but when the dawn broke through once more, we find a totally new system, Teutonic in character and differing in every way from its predecessor. New villages with new Saxon names have sprung up along the valleys; the once populous uplands are deserted; the Celtic fields, now grass-grown, have reverted to grass, thick scrub, or forest. The boundaries of the new "manors" disregard the old field system entirely.'

The change from the hill-villages of Romano-British times to the compact valley settlements of the Saxon period is one of the fundamental facts in our period. But how is it to be explained? Does it necessarily mean that the Saxon intruders into these 'hills of sheep and howes of the silent races', these beautiful chalk uplands of Salisbury Plain, were superlatively ruthless and destructive? That is a possibility; but not the only possibility. When we know little about a period we are always inclined to exaggerate its catastrophic features. The destruction of the Celtic villages need not have been sudden and remorseless. The plantation of Saxon villages in the valleys was certainly a slow process, of which a mere beginning can have been made in the heathen period. Indeed the Saxon practice of burying their dead in or near old tumuli on the hills may mean that there was a phase when they themselves were hill-dwellers before they cleared the land near the rivers and settled down to plough the heavy soils of the valleys. It is conceivable that when a well-watered site for a village came to be preferred to the high and dry uplands, the Celtic inhabitants of the hill-tops may have been induced by fair means as well as foul to come down from their old settlements. The inhabitants who clung to the hills would be a prey for violent men. Even if the Saxon thegn did not reduce the Celts of his neighbourhood to serfdom, the latter might think it desirable to seek his lordship and put themselves under his protection. For whatever reason, the change of fashion became complete.* Since the peasantry of Wiltshire are said to have a high ratio of brunettes (see map, p. 171), it does not seem likely that the Britons of this district were massacred or driven out with any special ruthlessness by the invaders.

One subject remains about which historians who are not prepared to surrender the early Chronicle *in toto* must be ready to meet the arguments of archaeologists. Was the Wansdyke—the massive earthwork which extended from Inkpen near Newbury almost to the Severn—thrown up by the Britons to repel Saxon aggression? (Pl. 26 B.) The existence of a ditch on the northern face of the dyke proves that it was intended as a defence against an enemy from the north. Excavations of the dyke have indicated that the men who made it were using Roman pottery and wearing Roman boots which left a hobnail behind them. It is therefore thought to be either a late provincial-Roman or an early post-Roman work, perhaps the last great effort of the Britons to save the south-west of the island from Saxon barbarism.[39]

Until the early Chronicle is proved to be mere fiction, historians may well continue to place some, though not complete, reliance on its general story. And they must therefore believe that the Wansdyke was either made at different times or that it was constructed, as Sir Charles Oman has argued, to mark the boundary of one British kingdom against another.

Unless some view like this which we have outlined in the present section is accepted, it is impossible to reconcile the

---

* There seems to have been a Celtic drift from the hills to the valleys apart from Saxon compulsion since there are some signs of it even in Wales.

PLATE 26

A. An ancient downland trackway

B. Course of the Wansdyke over the Marlborough Downs (St. Anne's Hill)

PLATE 27

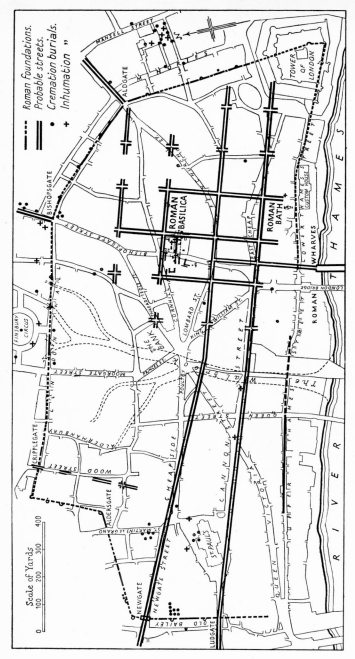

Plan of London, showing lines of Roman streets and walls

evidence of the Chronicle and that of the graves. It is indeed possible to hold that in the period which we have been studying the entries of the Chronicle are mere fiction. But the balance of probabilities is against that view. These early entries cannot be jettisoned without impairing the story of Ceawlin which follows. The misty legends about the origin of the West Saxon dynasty and its first petty conflicts in the borderlands of Hampshire and Wiltshire still deserve a place in our history. The warbands of Cerdic's family were being trained for the great forward movement which, in the second half of the sixth century, was to change the whole situation.

THE FATE OF LONDON AND ITS HINTERLAND

We have now to investigate the dearth of archaeological evidence for early Saxon settlement in the country round London. Here we have not isolated burials instead of cemeteries. The absence of heathen graves is almost complete.

To appreciate this fact let us examine in some detail the few finds which have come to light. In London itself the chief early Saxon relics[39a] cast up have been a buckle outside the Roman walls and a brooch from Thames Street, dropped possibly by a trader or a migrant breaking his journey up the river. Down the Thames on the northern bank no burials have been recorded except some discovered in 1923 near Southend.[40] These show that Jutish influence could be exerted across the Thames towards the end of the heathen period, but they have no bearing on the early history of Essex. Besides this nothing Saxon has been unearthed except some spear-heads found at Witham and some possibly Saxon graves found near Shoeburyness. These were arranged in a circle—an unusual plan for Saxons, but not unique. However an isolated burial of this kind is without clear significance.

To the north-east of London there are only one or two burials of the late sixth or of the seventh century, until round Colchester

we come to cemeteries which seem to mark one of the first settlements of the East Saxons. To the north of London there have
been no pagan Saxon finds either late or early. To the north-
west there has been little or nothing until the country of the
Icknield Way is reached, and though this is within about thirty
miles of London it is really outside the London region; the
cemeteries of the Icknield Way have their own story to tell—a
story which has no relation to London. Circling round to the
west we still find no trace of the earliest invaders; a barrow at
Taplow displayed the remains of a magnificent chieftain—but
a chieftain who lived in the sixth century.

Only at Shepperton do we meet the exception which proves
the rule; for from Shepperton have come cremation urns which
show that here indeed the invaders did occupy a position on the
northern bank. It must be noted, however, that at this point
the Thames makes its farthest bend to the south. The Shepperton cemetery may therefore not unfairly be assigned to the branch
of the invaders who elsewhere, as in the Croydon area, thought
well to keep the Thames between themselves and London.

We see then that with this one exception and the doubtful
burials at Shoeburyness the country round London to the north
of the Thames within a radius varying from thirty miles up to
fifty miles was, according to the archaeological evidence at
present available, free from early Saxon settlements.

This is the London 'gap'—no small one—in the Germanic
occupation of Britain. How are we to explain it?

Shall we say with F. M. Stenton[41] that the discovery of Saxon
cemeteries depends on chance; and that it is therefore not strange
that in Essex few burial-places have been discovered? Chance
of course there is; but the contrast between the grave-finds in
Essex and those in the Cambridge region or in the valley of the
upper Thames is too marked to justify us in putting everything
down to that factor. We must seek for other explanations.

One partial solution may certainly be found in the physical
character of much of this country round London. To E. T. Leeds

the fact that one-third of the surface of modern Essex consists of London clay and that 'areas of clay-land were carefully avoided by the earliest settlers' is the chief explanation for the 'extraordinarily disappointing' results of archaeology in Essex.[42] Moreover, the marshes which to the east stretched down the Thames and up the Lea impeded an enemy advancing from that direction, while dense forest was almost continuous from the Essex marshes to Buckinghamshire and southern Hertfordshire, and only became a patchy and open woodland on the eastern slopes of the Chilterns. The London area was thus screened from the invaders who penetrated Britain from the Ouse and the Cam; and the Essex clay and the woodlands, effective as physical barriers to armies, were even more effective as a discouragement to colonists. But we must not spread our forests and swamps too generously. Even Essex and the north bank of the Thames above London have their patches of gravel; and the forests round London were never such an extensive tract as the famous Andredsweald round Sussex. The great Roman cities of Colchester, London, and Verulam must have had in their neighbourhood some agricultural land to supply their wants. In Roman times the villas and farms in this area, few and poor though they mostly were, might have been expected to tempt barbarians who entered the island by way of the Thames; yet except near Colchester there is no sign that the early invaders squatted on these agricultural lands as, south of the Thames, they settled in the Romanized district round Croydon.

We are driven, therefore, to contemplate the possibility that there was another reason, apart from the clay and woodland, for the distaste felt by the invaders for this region. It looks as if there was something repellent to them in the proximity of London. And what else can this something have been except the survival of a Romano-British population in and around London itself, and if in London, why not also in Verulam or Camulodunum?

This is a question to which Haverfield, writing in 1911 from the

point of view of Roman archaeology, returned an emphatic negative. 'Nothing has been found', he said,[43] 'to suggest that Roman
Britons dwelt in London long after A.D. 400. . . . London doubtless fell in the early fifth century. Then it lay waste a hundred
years and more.' Latterly, however, the views of archaeologists
have been modified.[44] Since the question is of great importance,
it will be well to illustrate here some of the lines on which it may
be argued.

Now, if we examine the grounds for the old view, that London
was destroyed soon after the year 400, we find that it rested in
part on a literal interpretation of the extravagant statements of
Gildas; in part on the fact that the streets of medieval London
did not coincide with the rectangular streets of the Roman city;
but mainly on the fact that when men dig deep into the soil of
London to construct cellars and foundations for city offices, they
find innumerable Romano-British coins, pots, and implements,
but none which are assigned to the fifth or sixth century.

Let us gauge the force of these arguments. Against the theory
that 'London was destroyed soon after the year 400' we may
recall the picture of Britain given in the *Life of St. Germanus*.*

The only other piece of written evidence, apart from Gildas,
is the annal in the Saxon Chronicle under the year 457, which
says that 'the Britons forsook Kent and with great fear fled to
London'. It is one of those entries which perhaps echo faintly
some old poem.[45] If the annal is accepted, Haverfield's view
becomes improbable. It asks us to believe that the Britons fled
to a town which had been 'destroyed soon after 400'.

And the evidence of Gildas? Is this decisive against the survival of a Romano-British London? It is said[46] that the existence
of British principalities in the south-east Midlands in the time
of Gildas is incredible, because this author 'gives us a picture of
Celtic Britain which does not extend anywhere towards the
east coast'. But the preoccupation of Gildas with the politics
and morals of the small British princes of the west is by no means

* Above, pp. 60–62.

inconsistent with a possible survival of British communities in the eastern half of the island, communities screened from the man living in or near Wales by the arch of Germanic invaders which archaeology detects in the Midlands. The Britons, it must be remembered, had not been fused into one solid nation, even though they had been subject for three or four centuries to one external government. There was no all-British nationalism. The patriots of the west had their work cut out in preaching unity and self-control to the Britons of the west. The horizon of Gildas no more included a *Britannia irredenta* in the east than it included the Britons of Strathclyde or those of Elmet.

It is true that certain statements of Gildas, if interpreted literally, contradict the idea of any continuity of society in London from Roman to Saxon times. '*All* the *coloniae* are levelled to the ground by the frequent strokes of the battering-ram.' Yes, and with them the *coloni*, the husbandmen—indiscriminately; and the cities—indiscriminately—are wasted and destroyed. These lamentations of Gildas were written in the spirit of a prophet. In his zeal he clearly does not weigh his words. If we are to take his statements literally, we must argue, not only that London and Verulam and all the cities of the east were levelled to the ground, but no less Gloucester and all the cities of the west. But this is to misinterpret the prophet. His intention was, as we have said, to arouse his countrymen by painting highly-coloured pictures of universal disaster. He does not contrast the east with the west. He speaks of the trade of the Thames in the past tense, but so also does he speak of the trade of the Severn.

On the whole, then, the words of Gildas cannot be pressed to exclude the possibility of a survival of a Romano-British London in this first stage of the Saxon Conquest, and we shall find later on, in the annal for 571 of the Chronicle, a record of a defeat of the Britons at Bedcanford, which points to the survival, even at that late period, of Britons capable of giving fight to a Saxon prince in the eastern Midlands.

The doubtful statements of Gildas have delayed us too long;

for, after all, the views of those who assert that London perished early in the fifth century and lay empty for a hundred years and more, are based mainly on the fact that no remains have been dug up which can be assigned to the fifth and sixth centuries. The words of Haverfield about Bath[47] can fairly be quoted to represent his general line of argument. 'If the Britons held it . . . after their severance from Rome some trace of this period ought to survive. Even savages use pots and pans and live in houses and bury their dead. The Romano-British pottery of the early fifth century would have given way to some newer, perhaps ruder, but certainly distinguishable style.' Here is the crucial point. The archaeologists see no traces of Romano-British life in London from the fifth century onwards, but where do they see traces of Romano-British life? A few grave-stones, especially in Wales;[48] three or four hoards of the debased and minute coins, 'minims'; a pot or two;* possibly some 'Jutish' brooches, and hanging bowls found in the graves of the invaders. Those are all (or more than all) of the goods which can be credited to Britons in this age. Craftsmanship in durable materials had almost ceased throughout the island, and archaeology once more fails us. Since the provincials who undoubtedly survived in the west of Britain left behind them so little evidence of their existence, the absence of evidence from London, where excavation has been conducted for commercial rather than for archaeological purposes, cannot well be taken to prove the annihilation of London.

With regard to Haverfield's argument that London must have long lain waste because its medieval streets did not coincide with those of the Romans (Pl. 27), such a change does indeed prove that the flourishing city fell on evil days, that many of its buildings collapsed through age and neglect, that the old streets were blocked, and that in time new streets were made over or

---

* e.g. the wheel-made pot (Fig. 32), supposed to be of the fifth or sixth century (*Proc. Cambridge A.S.* xxxii (1932), 54–6); and an ill-made urn found in a clay floor at Verulam (R. E. M. and T. V. Wheeler, *Verulamium* (1936), 34 and 199).

round the old ruins to suit the convenience of the inhabitants of a later and more prosperous age. We know that this was what happened in Rome, which certainly was not deserted for more than forty days. Why then should we assume that London lay waste and empty for a century and more?[49]

In recent years there has been more readiness to consider the possibility of some survival in post-Roman London. R. E. M.

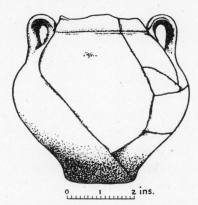

FIG. 32. Bran Ditch, nr. Cambridge. Two-armed post-Roman pot.

Wheeler[50] says: 'It is permissible to imagine their [the Saxons'] small fleets passing up-river beneath the closed gates of a London which may have regarded them with the same wary indifference wherewith, four centuries later, Saxon London often enough regarded the roving long-ships of the Vikings.' Here he is speaking of the decades which immediately followed 410. The London which may have lingered on later was, in his opinion, probably no more than a 'reservation' for the British which 'can have mattered little to any one save to the few decivilized sub-Roman Londoners'.

This view perhaps understates the part played by the remnant of the Londoners. For London was the natural, the traditional port for the Thames valley. It was the natural market for a large though thinly peopled district. Traders from London may have trafficked in such pots and weapons and jewellery as were not home-made. At any rate, among the 320 acres of ruined Londinium some houses may still have remained inhabited, not as the nests of brigands presumed by some, but as the homes of impoverished citizens who, with trade nearly suffocated, struggled on until the city rose in the sixth century from its desolation to be the metropolis of a Teutonic kingdom. If this was in truth what happened, it follows that one reason why the Saxons preferred the Surrey side of the river may have been the existence of London on the north bank.

But the fate of London is not altogether an isolated problem. Its neighbour Verulam was only twenty miles distant; Colchester, a smaller town, was some fifty miles from London; the three had been connected by good roads, and one may suppose that they would have the sense to hold together in the evil days, at any rate for a time, and form a Romano-British triangle. Later they were no doubt sundered by the incoming sea of barbarians. Bede speaks of 'the Londoners'[51] rejecting Christianity as if they acted independently. Saxon grave-goods found in the Roman burial-grounds round Colchester, though they are too late to throw much light on the beginnings of Essex, differentiate the Colchester region from the rest of the province, and suggest that here was a distinct component element which later went to the making of the Heptarchic kingdom. The fortunes of London were presumably linked most closely with those of Verulam, and the systematic excavation of that site should be continued in order to throw the light we need on this dark place of history.[51a]

We have taken note of three reasons which can be put forward to explain the dearth of Saxon graves in the London region: first, chance; secondly, forests and marshes; thirdly, the survival of a Romano-British population in London itself, perhaps also in Verulam and Colchester, and in the forest country which formed the hinterland of these ruined cities.

To these possible reasons we must add a fourth: that the East Saxons, or at any rate the greater number of them, resembled

the followers of Cerdic in Wiltshire in so far as they discontinued
from the first the heathen methods of burial, both the practice
of cremation and that of inhuming a dead body with weapons
and other gear. There are certain considerations which point
to this. One is the fact that Essex possesses quite a large number
of those villages with names ending in -*ing* which are supposed to
be a mark of early settlement (see map at page 109)—Barking,
Epping, Fobbing, Roothing, and a score of others. On the
strength of these place-names it is asserted[52] that Essex, like Kent
and Sussex, was among the counties first colonized. We might be
sceptical if this were the only ground for considering the kingdom
of Essex to be one of the early Teutonic settlements. The chronology extracted from place-names must be even more elastic than
that which we derive from grave-gear. But we find a stronger
and more compelling reason when we turn to Bede. For Bede's
story gives the impression that the kingdom of the East Saxons
(a kingdom which included Middlesex and parts of Hertfordshire) was a well-established state and that London with its
Germanic priests was an important city at the time of the
Conversion, soon after 600. It seems inconceivable that the
East Saxons could have grown sufficiently strong to dominate
London—a city described as 'the emporium of many peoples
who came to it by sea and land',[53] unless they had been well
established in Essex from an early decade of the sixth century;
and it is no less inconceivable that if they were thus established
in the kingdom of Essex and practised burial customs like those
of the Saxons of the upper Thames or like those of the Middle
or East Angles, more traces of their graves should not have been
unearthed by excavators. The conclusion then is almost inevitable that there were East Saxons, as there were West Saxons
of Wiltshire, who from the first did not use the ordinary Teutonic
modes of burial. Whether this was due to the fact that these
East Saxons and West Saxons had in any way a common history
before they landed in Britain, or simply to similar influences
after their arrival in the island, it is vain to speculate.

Historians, both in the Middle Ages and in modern times, have thought that the East Saxon monarchy had its beginning in or about 527.[54] Though the suggestion is not unreasonable in itself, it does not appear to rest on any adequate authority. An interesting point in the genealogy of the kings of Essex is that, unlike the other dynasties, they trace their line back to Seaxneat, a native Saxon god.[54a]

Enough has now been said to show how many pieces of the East-Saxon jig-saw puzzle have been lost, and how impossible it therefore is to obtain any picture of the story of Essex as a whole. Negations are indeed possible. We can deny the necessity for Haverfield's assertion that Roman London 'lay waste a hundred years and more'. We may be equally sceptical about Chadwick's guess[55] that Wessex was an offshoot from Essex and that 'Essex was in early times no doubt the most populous of these kingdoms'. Archaeology makes it clear that there was little in common between the East Saxons and the Saxons of the upper Thames.

Our positive conclusions about the end of Londinium and the beginnings of the East Saxons must be few and insecure. On the strength of the annal for 571 we can believe that the forest lands to the north and west of London remained the refuge of more or less independent Britons until that date. On grounds of probability we can assert almost with confidence that East Saxons, perhaps with little political unity, had been settled on patches of drier soil, especially near the coast and the rivers, from the early decades of the sixth century (perhaps earlier), and that most of them were sufficiently influenced by the modes of Christian civilization to have ceased to bury their dead according to the old Germanic rites. And if we seek for the sites of these early settlements our best guide must be a map showing the villages with names which end in -*ing*. Some, though not necessarily all, of these were no doubt the centres from which the population of Essex subsequently radiated.

And then between the Britons in the Chiltern country and

the Saxon migrants near the coast lay London and Verulam: but whether these cities remained before 571 in touch with the Britons of the woods or with the Saxons of the coastal valleys, and how they dwindled into insignificance, are questions on which more light may be expected from renewed excavation on the site of Verulum.

ANGLIAN SETTLEMENTS—ETHELFRITH

The darkness surrounding the Anglo-Saxon Conquest deepens as we move northwards from Saxon areas into Anglian. Something has already been said (above, pp.114–18) about the 'Middle Angles' (the inhabitants of the patches of open land between the Welland and the Icknield Way), who in spite of the appellation Angle are proved by their grave-gear to have been partly drawn from the Saxon districts of Germany. It would be wearisome to discuss in any detail the evidence of the cemeteries for the other Anglian communities. Those who are interested in the early history of these Anglian districts will find the evidence, such as it is, set out in the volumes of the *Victoria County History*.[55a]

In the following pages only a few suggestions will be noticed; and it must be stated at the outset that we are entering ground which is even more dangerous than that which we have already trodden. The only consolation to be obtained is that, since any theories can be little more than guesses, every man is almost free to construct his own.

If the reader looks at the map at page 9, he may feel disposed to begin his guesswork by conjecturing that the 'keels' which found their way to the Wash and the north-east coast crossed the 130 miles of open sea from Frisia instead of choosing the circuitous route by way of the Rhine mouths and Kent.

In East Anglia (see map at p. 109), while there are some cremation cemeteries near the coast which may mark early settlements, the most notable clusters of fifth-century finds are near the Little Ouse and the Lark. This may be taken to mean that most of the immigrants made their way up those tributaries of the Great Ouse, following the same course as many of the 'Middle Angles', until they turned east instead of west from the swamps of the Fens. The valleys of the Little Ouse and the Lark, and the flats extending as far as Cambridge, seem to have been the chief germinating centre of East Anglia, the next in importance being the district of the extreme north where the map shows many place-names ending in -*ingas* and cremation cemeteries.

Other expeditions of the invaders crossing the Wash made their way for twenty-seven miles up the marshes of the Witham and its tributary, the Slea, to Sleaford. Here the finding of some six hundred graves has indicated that Sleaford was the port where the migrants landed before they set off for the interior. Farther north, the district of Lindsey (taking its name from the Roman Lindum) may have been occupied by Angles advancing down the Roman road from the Humber. In the genealogy of their kings there is one (Cædbæd) whose name, like that of Cerdic of Wessex, indicates some blending with the Britons.[56]

In the valley of the Trent the boats of the invaders were paddled up-stream through long miles of unattractive swamps. Then from Newark up into Derbyshire a series of cremation cemeteries near the river mark out the core of the Mercian* settlement. Farther afield the distribution of the cemeteries points to a gradual occupation of Leicestershire and east Staffordshire, while north of the Trent barrow burials mark a long-drawn-out warfare on the uplands of the Peak.

Beyond the Humber the heathen cemeteries indicate two main routes by which the invaders found their way into the country of the British Dere:[56a] one a river route up the Ouse to York; the other northwards from the Humber by the wolds. These groups of migrants whose immediate provenance is said to be indicated by resemblances between their grave-goods and those of Frisia,[57] were probably independent of other minor settlements on the coast until they were united into a kingdom

---

* Mercians, OE. *Mierce* or *Merce* = Marchmen, i.e. borderers.

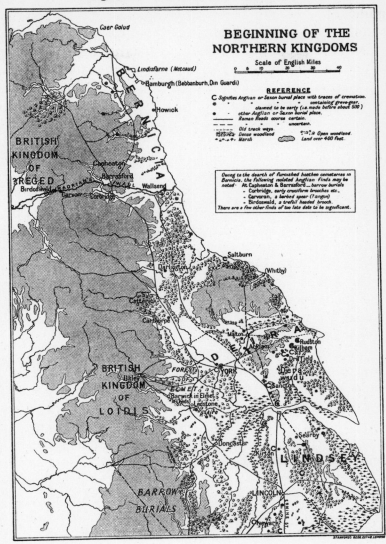

which took its name, Deira, from that of the conquered Britons.
Thus a vigorous seed plot was planted in the East Riding. It was
surrounded on three sides by Celtic populations. Those in the
marshy flats of Holderness were probably few in number and

insignificant. Those to the north, in Blackamore—that is, in the hills to the west of Whitby and Scarborough—also only wanted to be left alone; and since the Angles had no desire for unfertile dales and moorlands, these Britons no doubt had their wish.[58] In the West Riding the kingdom of Elmet, or Loidis (a regional name surviving in Leeds, Ledston, &c.), remained a vigorous British State until its conquest by Edwin of York in the middle of the seventh century.

The beginnings of the kingdom of the Beornice,* generally known as Bernicia, offers a problem which calls for a less summary notice.

According to E. T. Leeds,[58a] 'Perhaps the most inexplicable point in early Anglo-Saxon archaeology is the astounding lack of evidence for the early settlements north of the Tees, which seem to be demanded by the important part played by Bernicia from the first'. The one Anglian cemetery known to Leeds beyond the Tees was only a few miles north of that boundary river near Darlington. It was small and apparently not of an early date; and beyond this little had so far been identified as early Anglian save a few objects found by chance and not in barrows or cemeteries: two brooches of a type assigned to about 500, and a third of a slightly later period, these discovered in excavating Roman sites along the Wall; elsewhere only a sword or *umbo* or other trifle.[59] Since Leeds wrote Anglian cemeteries have been recognized in north Northumberland, for instance, one on a basaltic crag at Howick, not far from the Northumbrian coast. Only a few beads and knives interred with the dead enable modern experts to identify these bodies as Anglian,[60] just enough to show how it is that hitherto the burial-grounds of the Angles, like those of their British predecessors and contemporaries, have failed to be identified.

Thus Bernicia presents an even greater gap in the Anglo-Saxon grave-finds than does the country round London or that

---

* It is noteworthy that these settlers, like the Dere, seem to have taken over the name of a British tribe, the Brigantes of Roman authors. Cf. *Rev. Celt.* li. 10–11.

of Wiltshire and Hampshire. Once more, therefore, we have to decide a question similar to that which has confronted us when dealing with the other two large districts bare of Teutonic burials. What are we to infer from the almost complete absence of urns or brooches buried by the English who first occupied this tract between the Tees and the Forth? About one thing we may feel certain. These invaders did not come direct from those parts of north Germany which had been the homes of the other Angles. If they had done so, it is inconceivable that they should not have cremated or buried their dead like the conquerors of the Midlands and York. If not from Germany, then whence did they come? Leeds and Myres think of them as emigrating northwards from Deira about the middle of the sixth century. One band may have rowed up the Tyne, and another have descended on Bamburgh and Lindisfarne. From then onwards 'the Angles seem to have been in constant conflict with the Britons'. Since the Bernicians were not only next neighbours to the Deirans, but later became united with them in one kingdom, there is undoubtedly on the face of things a presumption that Bernicia was an offshoot from Deira. But as usual there are difficulties. The union of the kingdoms here produced no union of hearts. Friction between Deirans and Bernicians was to be the bane of Northumbria. It may be said that nearest kinsmen can be the bitterest enemies, or that the strife between the two Northumbrian kingdoms was chiefly a feud between two rival dynasties; but this is scarcely sufficient to explain the unhappy relations which existed between Bernicia and Deira. The contrast is great between their hostility and the solidarity which we find elsewhere when a colony was pushed out from a parent kingdom; the Dorsæte, the Sumorsæte, and the Devonsæte, offshoots from the original Wessex, became the most loyal upholders of the West Saxon State.

The only piece of information about Bernicia which can claim much respect is a passage in Bede[62] which asserts that in A.D. 547 'Ida began to reign from whom the regal stock of the

Northumbrians draws its origin'. A seventh-century genealogy carries Ida's ancestors back for nine generations to Woden, but as usual with these genealogies it does not indicate whether the persons named were of kingly rank or where they came from.

Nennius, whose passages about Bernician history have more value than his tales about Vortigern, adds[63] the words that 'Ida . . . joined the fortress of Gua[y]rdi to Berneich [Bernicia]'. It was only about the eleventh century that an interpolation into one version of the Saxon Chronicle[64] amplified the story further with the words, 'Ida reigned twelve years and he built Bebban-burh which was first enclosed with a fence and afterwards with a wall'. We have to go back to Nennius to learn that Bebba, the queen who received the rock fortress of Din Guardi as a gift and after whom it was renamed Bebbanburh or Bamburgh, was the wife of Ida's grandson.*

The year 547 is at any rate a landmark in the rise of the Bernician kingdom, even though there is doubt about what exactly occurred. One recent historian[65] thinks that the real settlement of Bernicia did not take place till a late period, 'when the influence of Christianity had led to a discontinuance of burial in pagan cemeteries'. This view, however, demands miracles—miracles of rapid settlement and propagation—to people the hills and valleys of Bernicia with those Angles who before the middle of the seventh century flocked to be baptized by Paulinus and by the Irish missionaries.

Other historians go to the other extreme and ask us to believe that a settlement in Bernicia was begun near the beginning of the invasion by Octa, son (or grandson) of Hengist, after an expedition against the Orkneys. There could have been no better way than this of doing what Hengist had been called in to do; but the story, since it comes from Nennius, must be con-sidered dubious, though not wholly incredible.

On *a priori* grounds we may suppose that these districts, being farthest from Germany and occupied by Celtic tribes with mili-

---

* Ethelfrith. According to Nennius, he was Ida's *great*-grandson.

tary traditions, would be among the last to be settled by Anglian war-bands and that the invasion therefore took place not long before Ida's kingship. If we attempt to decide what happened in these northern parts our views must be determined by probabilities, and by little else than probabilities. We may picture the pirate bands living for a time, as in the Salisbury Plain region, on plunder and tribute, then reinforced by colonies of fighting farmers, strung out along the coast and up the river valleys. The strips of land occupied by these adventurers were narrow and the Celtic natives up in the hills were not far off. From the first the Anglians of Bernicia were essentially borderers. Whether they were fighting the Celtic tribes or joining as hired troops in the feuds of the Celts, or ruling them as tributaries, the two peoples were in close contact. The Angles, who for safety's sake had established themselves on basaltic crags as at Bamburgh and Howick, must have lived a hard, tempestuous life. But they were being tempered by that life to be the northern spear-point of the invaders, and their proximity to the native hill tribes was preparing them and their race for the part they were to play in Christian times as the leaders in a remarkably vigorous Anglo-Celtic culture.

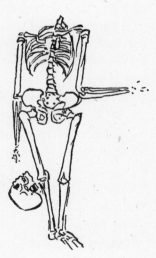

V

GENERAL CHARACTER OF THE SAXON CONQUEST

WE have now seen some of the evidence, chiefly the archaeological evidence, which bears on the opening phases of the Conquest down to the time of Gildas. We have covered what we may call its first stage, the hundred years from about the middle of the fifth century to the middle of the sixth century. On the strength of the grave-finds we may guess that the distribution of the immigrants about 550 was probably similar to that indicated on the following map.⁰ If the so-called 'Conquest' of Britain had really been a conquest, conducted on principles of regular warfare, the positions there shown might be pronounced incredible. But the truth is that the event which we are studying was more a colonization than a conquest. We might as well criticize the positions held, let us say, by early American farmers filtering out into the west of their continent, as apply principles of scientific warfare to the Anglo-Saxon migration to Britain. In saying this, we need not subscribe completely to the theory that the Saxons were 'peace-loving farmers'. The violence which accompanied the first over-running of the country may be grossly exaggerated by Gildas, but it had existed. We see it, for instance, in the cemeteries at Mitcham near Croydon and at Girton near Cambridge, where some of the warriors had been buried with extra heads—presumably the heads of enemies they had slain.[1] Regular fighting no doubt occurred locally in all stages of the Conquest. But the Britons were divided politically and socially. If the sense of common interests was anything like as imperfect among them at the end of the fifth century as it was when Gildas wrote some fifty years later, they must have been incapable of joining in a united campaign.

On the Anglo-Saxon side also there seems to be no firm evidence to support the conjecture[2] that the invaders operated together for any length of time as one conquering host, like the later Great Army of the Vikings. In spite of Bede's reference to an *imperium* of 'Ælle of Sussex', it is inconceivable that the settlements south of the Humber can have been formed by sections of a once-united army. The contrasts between their cultures, the local peculiarities in their burial customs and in the fashions of their ornaments, are too great. Stubbs and Green were surely right in their assumption that the invaders normally operated in small groups. But where they and so many others who have written on this subject have erred, is in speaking of the immigrants coming as 'tribes'. An oversea migration of that kind is most improbable owing to the difficulties of transport. The invaders must have trickled into the island in groups of adventurers rather than have flowed in with a tribal flood-tide. The cemeteries suggest that throughout the fifth century such bands as had obtained a foothold on our shores were small, and that except in Kent it was not until the sixth century that they increased and multiplied and coalesced until they formed some of the petty kingdoms which emerge into history in the chapters of Bede. This word 'coalesced' better than any other gives us the clue to the story of the invasion. The separate bands of the invaders were much scattered and rarely kept in touch with one another. They scored by the number of their aggressions, by their ubiquity, rather than by the shock of massed attack.

But these are generalizations, and generalizations are things of which above all others we must beware. We see now that the story of the Conquest was more complicated than was ever

imagined by the historians who wrote before the evidence of the
graves had been well sifted. It is folly to hunt for one master-
key to all the settlements. In sampling the evidence from the
different regions we have found hints of great diversity: in Kent
a band of mercenary soldiers, who turn against their British
employers; in Sussex an assault on a fort and a massacre; in the
Salisbury district, it seems, a chief whose father had perhaps
married a British woman and had given his son a British name;
near the upper Thames, whole village communities which in-
termingle if they do not intermarry with the natives; and so
on in endless variety from the war-bands of Bernicia to the
colonists who only want land and a quiet life—the furtive immigrants who seek out empty spaces and derelict fields, especially
those who creep stealthily into the Midlands through fen-pro-
tected waterways. When there was such diversity, is it possible
to say that there was any normal pattern?

We may perhaps maintain that the frequency with which
spear-heads appear in the graves testifies to the fact that these
Germans were still for the most part, as in the days of Tacitus,
armed cultivators, farmers who on occasions were prepared to
fight, and soldiers who, when they found fighting unremunera-
tive, were able to get a living from the land. The two activities
could be combined in the same man, but they could also be
separated, and it is possible that even from the first there may
generally have been a division of labour; that the chiefs and their
fighting retainers were the 'storm' troops who opened the way,
and who continued to be the active warriors, protecting the
ordinary folk, the ploughmen and the herdsmen. But it is much
more doubtful whether, as is sometimes said,[3] the two classes
came over in two distinct waves, first the adventurers, the fighting men, and then the farming folk with their wives. Such a
plan might well be dictated by common sense, and it seems to
accord with Bede's statement that the district of *Angul* lay waste
and deserted after the migration. But it is the difficulties of
the voyage which justify our doubt whether any mass movement

across the North Sea was practicable. And once more we must refuse to tie ourselves to a generalization which claims to apply to all these diverse settlements.

ANGLES AND SAXONS

At this point, since we have referred to the question whether the migration can rightly be described as tribal, it will be well to return to a subject about which something has already been said*—the relation of the Saxons to the Angles. In the text-books the two are generally contrasted as if from first to last they had been distinct and well-defined tribes. In recent years there has been a tendency among the experts to insist on the closeness of their affinities. H. M. Chadwick—on this, as on so many subjects, a leader of heresy—has expressed his belief[4] 'that the invaders of Britain belonged not to three but to two distinct nationalities, which we may call Jutish and Anglo-Saxon. . . . The Anglo-Saxons may not originally have been a homogeneous people. . . . But there is no proof that any fundamental difference survived at the time when they invaded Britain.' Chadwick's view of the history of the Angles and Saxons before their migration is different from that suggested in our first chapter. On the strength of a tradition preserved among the Danes he has constructed a theory that the Angles early in the fifth century conquered the Saxons to the west of them, and that the apparent identity of the two peoples in Britain was produced by a union in which the Angles supplied the ruling dynasties (except that of Essex) and the dominant military aristocracy. Now while we need not follow Chadwick in this last speculation, the evidence which supports the idea that there was little or no distinction between Angle and Saxon is impressive. For example, the terms 'Angle' and 'Saxon' were confused both by themselves and by their enemies—they could be interchanged. The word *Angel-cynn*, which was regularly used in Old English literature as the

* Above, pp. 5–6 and 116–17.

equivalent to our 'English people', included equally Saxons and Angles; *Englisc*—English—was the word used to denote the language of the Saxons; both usages seem to be old-established, even if only found in writings of the ninth century. Similarly, the Angles as well as the Saxons were always called 'Saxons' by the Welsh, and *Saxonia* was the Latin word used by Anglian clerks when they described the country which was known in the speech of the natives as *Angelcyn*. Then, too, in Bede's history the recurrence of the phrase *gens Saxonum sive Anglorum* and the application of the name *Angli* to the Saxons of southern Britain contradict the idea of a radical distinction between the peoples; and modify what might otherwise have been inferred from Bede's well-known passage about the names of the three nations.[4a]

Chadwick's views about 'the absence of any fundamental difference' between Angles and Saxons have not passed unchallenged. It has been pointed out that the names of the 'Heptarchic' peoples, the East Angles (*East-Engle*), East Saxons (*East-Seaxe*), &c., and the names of places such as Englefield, the field of the Angles, alike show that the difference between the peoples was recognized by themselves, and that the custom of including Angles under the general term Saxon was a Roman practice easily intelligible in the circumstances of the early raids, and parallel to the later usage which included Norwegians under the term Danes. From the purely linguistic standpoint it must be admitted that the Anglian dialects in England do seem to have some affinities with the old Scandinavian language not shared by West Saxon or Kentish: yet these are mainly in vocabulary and generally confined to the specifically poetical language.[4b] Apart from this still incompletely explored matter of vocabulary, the outstanding differential characteristics of the Old English dialects are mainly to be seen in pronunciation.[5]

The archaeologists on their part are usually clear that, although the differences are slight, there are fairly well-marked boundary-lines between the Anglian culture in England and the Saxon. It is true that they have found it hard to determine

PLATE 28

A. Wrist-clasps, from Malton, Cambridgeshire. $\frac{1}{1}$

B. Florid cruciform brooch, from Icklingham. $\frac{2}{3}$ *C.* Girdle-hangers, from Malton. $\frac{2}{3}$

ANGLIAN FASHIONS

PLATE 29

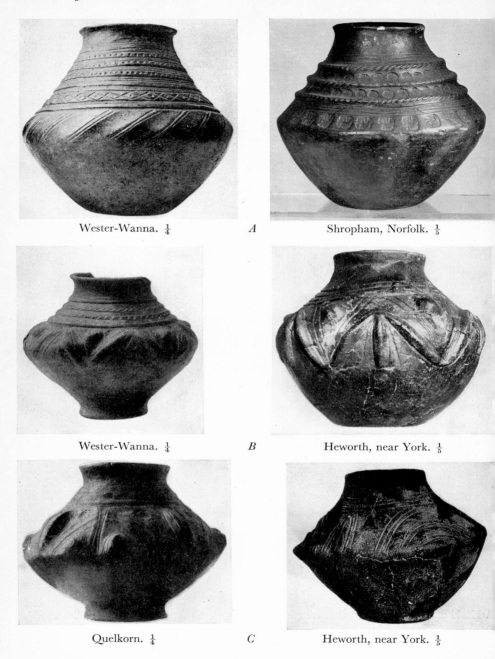

Wester-Wanna. ¼   *A*   Shropham, Norfolk. ⅕

Wester-Wanna. ¼   *B*   Heworth, near York. ⅕

Quelkorn. ¼   *C*   Heworth, near York. ⅕

'SAXON' URNS FROM NORTH GERMANY AND 'ANGLIAN' URNS FROM ENGLAND

The resemblances though clear are not complete. In *A* the shapes correspond but not the markings (English urn has swastikas), in *B* the bosses but not the shapes. In *C* the foot, rim, and ornamentation of the German urn are better developed

what exactly were the *differentiae* between the two.[6] At one time
it was thought that the Angle burned his dead while the Saxon
buried his; but this we have already seen to have been a matter
of time and circumstance rather than of people. Baldwin Brown
tells us that the three main objects found in Anglian graves
which 'do furnish us with very distinct *differentiae* between the
two regions and races' (Pl. 28), are first, cruciform brooches,
both the early types and the late florid; secondly, certain small
clasps which were worn at the wrist, for holding together the
sleeves of the women; and thirdly, certain iron implements called
girdle-hangers. These last were hung from the waists of the
women and were either used like a chatelaine, for the suspension
of small articles, or were made in imitation of the keys habitually
carried by Roman matrons.

These *differentiae* are certainly valuable; but the lines with
which Baldwin Brown and Leeds mark on their maps the
Anglian and Saxon districts really only show this, that in the
sixth century the fashions on one side were different from those
on the other. It is another matter to determine whether these
differences in fashion went back to the age of the migration, and
if so, whether they mean that all the colonists in the 'Anglian'
districts of England had come from the Anglian districts of the
Continent and belonged to a people different from the Saxons
of the lower Elbe valley and of Hanover. Still less do these
varieties of ornaments prove that there was any ethnic distinction
between Angles and Saxons. We have here in fact another
illustration of the insufficiency of archaeology to answer all our
questions.

Such brooches as have been found in the continental cemeteries do, on the whole, confirm the old view that our Saxons
came from the Elbe-Weser lands and that our Angles came from
Schleswig or its neighbourhood; the round brooch ornamented
with running spirals of the former district is lacking in almost
all the Anglian kingdoms of England, while these Anglian kingdoms abound in the cruciform brooch which is characteristic of

Schleswig—that is, they abound in the later varieties of that type of brooch.

When, however, we compare the cremation urns which are so abundant in the cemeteries of the Elbe-Weser Saxons with the urns which have come to light in England, striking resemblances are to be observed between products of 'Saxons' on the Continent and of 'Angles' in our own island[7] (Pl. 29). The subject is one which calls for fuller investigation by experts; but in the meantime it is hard to resist the inference that many of our 'Angles' came in fact from the Saxon districts of Germany. Whether their German homes had been north of the Elbe or south of it, the Saxons were ready to think of themselves as Angles—that is, as English.

If it be asked how this came about, we are not likely to err if we guess that the confusion between Saxon and Angle goes a long way back, that it is older than the Conquest of Britain. In our first chapter we saw Saxons and Angles classed together as *Ingaevones*, and joint members of the religious confederation which worshipped the goddess Nerthus. But was this all? One may observe that there had been ample opportunity for Angles to be mixed with Saxons when, after the time of Tacitus, they turned westwards along the shores of the North Sea. There was a tradition[8] that the Saxons had come by sea to the Elbe-Weser region from the north. Nothing could be more likely than that the region in question should be peopled by oversea migrants voyaging from the Eider mouth, and we have seen that the Eider mouth was 'the window to the west' of the Angles, a window to which Saxons of Holstein as well as Angles of Schleswig could have access. It was thus easy for Angles to be intermingled with Saxons in all the sea-roving and colonizing of the fifth and sixth centuries—not only in the Elbe-Weser country but in Frisia, and again intermingled when they crossed the North Sea and disembarked in Britain, their plans disarranged by all the chances of wind and tide, of uncharted seas, and unmapped land.

If these guesses are near the truth, it follows that the diversities between Angles and Saxons in Britain were largely adventitious. They grew from differences in geographical situation and from different experiences. The 'Saxons' in Britain were among the earlier migrants; their leaders had probably been long in touch with the Empire, sometimes as mercenaries, more often as pirates and raiders. The Saxons were therefore readier than the Angles to give up the old ways of Germany and adopt the habits of the Roman Provincials. The so-called 'Angles' of Britain were more primitive folk, who came to the east coast direct from Germany. Among them were Saxons from west of the Elbe who became submerged by stronger Anglian neighbours. In short, the confusion between Angle and Saxon had many causes: they were originally akin; Saxons could regard themselves as men of Anglian stock, Angles could belong to the Saxon confederation; and lastly, in the course of the migration both folks were often mixed. Hence it was that the differences between the two peoples were only the minute points of apparel, ornament, or dialect, which were doubtless largely developed on British soil.

SURVIVAL OF THE BRITONS

In the next place we must give some attention to the well-worn controversy: how far did the Germanic stock of the invaders come to be mixed with Celtic blood? It is not a subject which need be treated at great length in these pages, since the contributions made to it in recent years have not materially changed the views expressed by the historians of the last generation. There is room for a large measure of agreement as well as for great differences of opinion.

The best way to find the points of agreement is to keep as distinct as may be the three questions: first, was there continuity between the Romano-British and the Anglo-Saxon towns? Secondly, was there continuity in the villages? And lastly, more generally, what proportion of the older population survived?

If we take the first point, we find that here again the problem must be analysed. 'Continuity' may be interpreted in different ways. We may mean continuity (1) of the site of the town, (2) of its name, (3) of habitation by the former occupants, and (4) of culture and institutions. But of these aspects of continuity the only one which as a rule is in serious doubt is that of habitation. Of the others, the discovery of Roman institutions in Saxon Britain is an employment which may be left to those who find amusement in making bricks without straw; the continuity of site is easily proved or disproved by the spade. The question of continuous habitation can in part be decided by excavation, but must be largely determined by inference.

Roughly speaking, three different fates befell these towns. A few, a very few, may have been overwhelmed suddenly. Many more declined—both before and after 410—until they disappeared altogether. But most, and especially the more important cities, seem to have shared the probable fortune of London, that is, they decayed and then revived. Like London, they suffered because the German immigrants, being country-folk, wanted to live in rural huts such as they had had in Germany. They wanted to have their cattle round them, and their fields near-by. The last thing they desired was to shut themselves up in half-ruined houses, constructed largely of stone in an unfamiliar way, ill-adapted for a farmer.

If a town survived, its survival must, as with London, have been due to the fact that its position fitted it to be the centre of what little marketing and trade lingered on. Such places in the eastern half of Britain were Colchester, Winchester, and York; these, being situated on waterways which gave good access into the interior, probably retained some of the characteristics which distinguished them from the surrounding villages, and thanks to an increase in prosperity, they were probably reviving for economic reasons when the Roman Church after the Conversion selected them as the sees for its bishops and restored them to a priority more like that which they had enjoyed under the Roman Empire.

Of the Roman places which degenerated into villages or became mere grass-grown ruins some, like Wroxeter (Viroconium), had failed to make good in the Roman age; many, like the forts of the Saxon Shore, had depended on their garrisons for their existence; or, like Corbridge (Corstopitum) and Caerwent (Venta Silurum), on proximity to a military camp. Some, like Richborough (Rutupiae), suffered owing to natural causes, such as the silting up of a harbour; some, like Silchester (Calleva Atrebatum), lost their *raison d'être* when they ceased to be centres of local government. Others suffered from their position on a Roman road, when the road became the army highway of the invaders, as may be seen from the disappearance of every Roman place-name on the Watling Street, from Verulam to the central water-shed.

With regard to the names of the towns, it is generally easy to understand how most of these came to be changed. We see that, as a rule, the German immigrants could not get their tongues round the whole of the Roman name, but they could catch the first syllable, and then add on to it one of their suffixes in common use. Thus, when referring to Camulodunum, the Britons of the neighbourhood spoke of the *colonia*, the Saxons took the first syllable and added *chester*,* Colchester. Similarly, *Venta* became *Win*chester. In the case of York the change was less obvious; the first two syllables of *Ebura*cum became *Eofer*, the suffix *wic* was added; and the whole, after the coming of the Danes, was contracted to its present form.† In the case of Lincoln the English did better, and managed to connect the *Lin* from Lindum with the *coln* from *colonia*. Altogether there are said to be more than two dozen Roman towns and stations which passed on their names to the German settlers.[9] There is room for controversy about the names of some other Roman towns—those which appeared in what seemed to be new forms in the Saxon period; but now even such a complete change as that of Ratae into Leicester cannot be brought forward as a

---

* OE. *ceaster* from Latin *castra*.   † Through the Old Norse form Jórvik.

conclusive proof that there was a breach in the existence of the town. For it has been argued that the first element in Leicester (Ligeraceaster in the Saxon Chronicle) may represent an alternative British name current at the time of the Saxon invasion of England, in the same way that Legaceaster, 'the camp of the legion', later abbreviated to Chester, took the place of the official name Deva. So too the transformation of the Roman Durovernum Cantiacorum into Cantwaraburh (Canterbury) is not conclusive that the town was deserted; St. Petersburg could be renamed Petrograd and Leningrad without being emptied of its population. The English name for the city supports the theory that the conquerors of Kent were far from being a well-defined homogeneous tribe. They used no tribal name for themselves. They were simply the inhabitants (*ware*) of Cantium, and having seized the old fortress they came to regard it as their own *burh*. The fact that their name for it ousted the old name implies that they were the dominant folk, but not that they in any sense exterminated the Britons.

In the end, when the continuity of the towns has been discussed from every aspect, many may be tempted to agree with Collingwood's view that 'a handful of de-Romanized Britons, squatting among the ruins of a Roman town . . . from the point of view of the social, economic and political historian are discontinuity incarnate'.[10] But the British communities in losing their language and their institutions did not for ever lose their souls; in so far as British blood continued to flow in inhabitants of Britain, the spirit of the older race, though recessive, was not extinguished for ever.

We turn from the towns to the villages of earliest England and we put the same questions.

Was there continuity in the sites of the villages?

To this, at any rate as far as Salisbury Plain is concerned, we have already had a convincing answer. The fields and hut-circles of the British settlements revealed by modern air photo-

graphy were found, it will be remembered, on the top or on the
upper slopes of the chalk hills.* Quite distinct from these were
the settlements which took their place after the Germanic con-

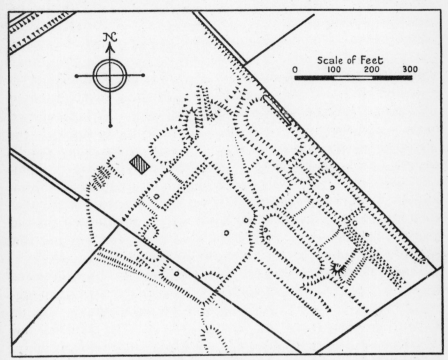

FIG. 33. Plan of Romano-British village at Colne, Hunts., probably inhabited by
fishermen and hunters living as near as possible to the fens.

quest, the villages of the Saxons, placed in the valleys near the
streams and rivers.

Similar changes have been observed in other parts of England,
at any rate in those regions where the surface of the island has
been allowed to retain the imprint of its earlier cultivation.
Celtic lynchetts, or terraced fields of the Celtic type, have been
recognized on the downs of Sussex, on the hills of Wharfedale
in Yorkshire, on the Cheviots, and elsewhere.[11]

* Above, pp. 134–6.

It is not of course to be supposed that the Romano-British villages were only to be found where there were hills. Like those of the prehistoric peoples they were placed on the gravel beds of lower levels and on other gentle rises of well-drained ground, or wherever the land was open enough for the cultivation of corn, and dry enough to escape the discomfort and the rheumatic pains which came from living on damp soil. One of the best-planned British villages yet identified has been found on the flats of Huntingdonshire (Fig. 33); but in general such sites cannot be identified partly because in the valley-soils the plough more quickly removes the traces left by earlier cultivators; and also because the Saxons so often squatted on the same patch of gravel as their predecessors.

In the next place, was there continuity of habitation? This question is for the most part disposed of by evidence now forth-coming which, as we have just seen, proves the discontinuity of site. On the other hand, on gravel beds and at other places well adapted for human habitation, there are a good many cemeteries, like that (noticed above, pp. 110-1) at Frilford near Oxford, where the Saxon dead were placed by the side of the Britons before them. In these cases it is a tempting presumption that the invaders were content to live as well as to lie in death alongside the conquered provincials.[12]

From the measurement of the skulls obtained in one Saxon cemetery, near East Shefford, it has been inferred that a generation of invading warriors intermarried with the conquered natives and that their offspring revealed intermediate characteristics.[13] This village, however, is at present the exception which proves the rule. Some day careful study of the skulls found in Anglo-Saxon cemeteries may possibly show that what is thought to have happened at East Shefford is not wholly exceptional as it now seems;[20a] but in the present state of knowledge nothing can seriously shake the conviction that the Saxon conquerors were not long in the island before they brought over their womenfolk from Germany. Their women are found in

almost all the cemeteries, tall and 'long-headed', decked with
their Teutonic brooches which only occasionally, as in the round
brooches, reveal a liking for some provincial-Roman pattern—
German matrons who were as loath to live in the huts of the
Britons as in the stone-built towns of the Romanized provincials.

Lastly comes the question, what degree of continuity was there
between the names of the British and of the English villages ?

The place-names of our English countryside which have been
such poor guides when we wished to discover the course and
date of the invasions, seem to be our best evidence when we ask
how far the Romano-British population in the villages survived.
They give us statistics, and statistics which at first sight appear
to be almost decisive against the survival of any considerable
proportion of the old population except in Cornwall, Wales,
and their borders. The general result will be seen with sufficient
clearness on the following map.[13a] It is based on the results of those
who worked at the subject in the nineteenth century. The careful revision of the evidence which is now being carried out by
the English Place-Name Society will in time enable new and
more accurate statistics to be compiled, but enough has now
been done to show that this new research will in the main confirm the old results. Among the counties which have now been
investigated by the Society, no place-names clearly Celtic have
been discovered in Bedfordshire, Huntingdonshire, and Sussex.[14]
In Buckinghamshire only Brill and Chetwode and two or three
others; in the North Riding of Yorkshire only about eight, and
some six which possibly contain the old element *wealh* (Briton).
In Worcestershire, a county which must have been mainly settled
in Christian times, the number is inconsiderable. 'Three Celtic
hill-names—*Bredon, Carton,* and *Malvern;* five names containing
British *cruc,* hill, barrow; *Pensax,* containing Welsh *pen,* headland'; Worcester itself, and a few others. In Devonshire 'the
total number of Celtic names in the county, excluding river-
names, is less than 1 %'. The conclusion of an editor of the

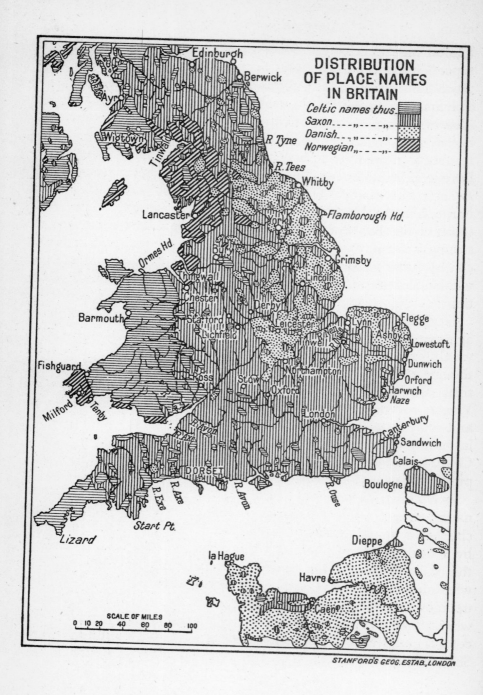

DISTRIBUTION
OF PLACE-NAMES
IN BRITAIN

Celtic names thus
Saxon ___ „ ___ „___
Danish ___ „ ___ „___
Norwegian „ ___ „___

Edinburgh
Berwick
Ayr
Wigtown
Tinwald
R Tyne
R. Tees
Whitby
Lancaster
York
Flamborough Hd.
Ormes Hd
Grimsby
Tintwall
Lincoln
Chester
Derby
Stafford
Leicester
Lynn
Flegge
Lichfield
Ashby
Lowestoft
Barmouth
Dunwich
Ross
Northampton
Orford
Fishguard
Stow
Harwich
Milford
Tenby
Oxford
Naze
London
Canterbury
R.Exe
R Avon
R.Avon
R. Ouse
Sandwich
DORSET
Calais
R. Exe
Boulogne
Start Pt.
Lizard
Dieppe
la Hague
Havre
Caen

SCALE OF MILES
0 10 20   40   60   80   100

STANFORD'S GEOG. ESTAB, LONDON

Place-Name Society in what may be regarded as an interim
report on the work of the Society is unequivocal:[15] 'Taking the
place-name evidence as a whole, it is clear that in these counties
at least, we can build little or nothing upon it in support of the
idea of an extensive survival of a British population after the
Saxon and Anglian conquests. That view may be correct, but
it must be supported, if at all, on other grounds.' Similar results
have been obtained from a study of the river-names of England.[16]
Even in the east there are of course well-known Celtic river-
names like the Thames, the Trent, the Cam, the Derwent, and
some of the British names which meant simply 'water, river,
stream'—Avon, Dover, Esk, Don, Ouse, &c. None the less, in
counties like Essex, Suffolk, and Norfolk, 'the old theory of a
wholesale extermination or displacement of the British population . . . may come near the truth'.

Is then the decision of the philologists so overwhelmingly
against those who champion the theory of Romano-British survival that they have no chance but to yield? No, the Romanist,
though caught in the net of the place-names, can still make a
thrust or two. He may say: Your argument proves too much.
You admit that counties verging on Wales, like Worcestershire,
and counties in the south-west like Devon, conquered only in the
latter half of the sixth or in the seventh century, are very largely
Celtic in blood in spite of the fact that their place-names are
predominantly Germanic.

And one cannot deny that in these counties the change in the
names of the villages and hamlets is much greater than the
change in the blood of the people, when we judge of the latter
by a test such as that of the physical type. Take for instance
the case of Devon. Not only have the river valleys their overwhelming preponderance of Saxon place-names, but even in the
uplands and the outlying parts, even for example on Dartmoor,
where, if anywhere, the Britons must have taken shelter, the new-
comers discarded the old names. The editors of the Place-Name
Society suggest that this may be explained by the fact that 'In

the middle of the seventh century Devon was a sparsely settled
Celtic kingdom, and that when once the resistance of its kings
had been broken down, no considerable native population remained to complicate the life of the new settlers'.[17] But this
view does not tally with the evidence of 'nigrescence', since we
see from the map opposite that the statistics for Devon show
about as many dark people in that county as in north Wales
itself. It is clear that the place-names here are not an exact
gauge of the percentage of British blood, and if they mislead
us in the west why should we trust their evidence about the
east of the island?

The place-name argument is, in fact, two-edged. For consider
how it is that Worcestershire and Devon come to be so largely
filled with English-named farms and villages. Was it not due to a
combination of Anglo-Saxon energy in colonization with Anglo-
Saxon intolerance? When a Saxon thegn or farmer pushed
his way into British land by force or by peaceful enterprise
acquired a new farm, he had little wish to live in the old buildings of his predecessor and he 'had no use for' the unintelligible
names used by the natives. He had no use for their names, but
he had plenty of use for their bodies. He wanted them as boors
to help him in ploughing and as herdsmen for his cattle and
swine. To sum up: it is certain that in many of these western
districts where English place-names have ousted Welsh, there
was no extermination but there was much absorption of the older
population; and what is true of the west may in a lesser degree
be true of the east.

The philologists are ready to supply arguments from the language as well as from the place-names of the English. The
subject is, however, beset by difficulties,[18] and language is admittedly an imperfect test of race. In every direction examples
may be found of subject races who have learnt to speak the
language of their conquerors. Here it is enough to notice that
the one *certain* 'carry-over' in vocabulary from Roman to Anglo-
Saxon Britain is the Latin word *castra* which remained in Old

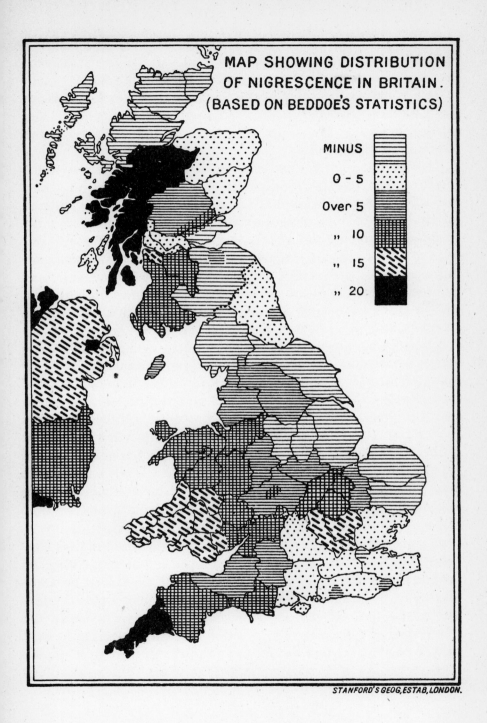

MAP SHOWING DISTRIBUTION
OF NIGRESCENCE IN BRITAIN.
(BASED ON BEDDOE'S STATISTICS)

MINUS

0 - 5

Over 5

" 10

" 15

" 20

STANFORD'S GEOG. ESTAB, LONDON.

English as *ceaster*, and probably owed its survival to its frequent use in the names of towns.

In estimating the value of the evidence from place-names we have already appealed to a map of England showing 'the index of nigrescence'. We must now form an opinion about the credentials of this map.

It was made by the anthropologist J. Beddoe, who wrote a book on *The Races of Britain* in 1885.[19] The statistics on which he based this map were obtained from over 13,000 descriptions of deserters in the army and navy. The plan contrived by Beddoe for making the contrast between the districts stand out, was to count one for every red- and fair-haired man and one for every man with dark hair; but every black-haired man was counted as two 'in order to give its proper value to the greater tendency to melanosity shown thereby'. Men with brown or chestnut hair were regarded as neutral.

Considering how and when these statistics of nigrescence were compiled, we may feel less inclined to put unqualified faith in them.[20] Thirteen or fourteen centuries are a formidable gap between the taking of the statistics and the Saxon Conquest. What migrations large and small, what shiftings of the population, what flights from villeinage and poverty, what industrial movements have in the meantime worked together to change the face of society! And then these nice distinctions between black hair and dark and brown are dependent on the memories of officers about their deserters. Clearly neither the statistics nor the map based on them can claim a high scientific value. And they are further invalidated because our conceptions of heredity have changed since the days of Beddoe. Then the idea of heredity was that characters were 'blended' or halved at each successive generation. But now it is known that they are controlled by discrete factors (Mendelian genes) which can be shuffled about between one generation and the next, independently of all the other factors. Therefore 'the index of nigrescence' of the present population may be very misleading

evidence of the original folk in Saxon times. We must also allow
for the fact that the Celts proper belonged to much the same
fair Nordic type as the Anglo-Saxons, and the darkness of the
British population therefore must have varied in different districts according to the proportion of the pre-Celtic races with
which it had been fused.

It would be possible to supplement the statistics of nigrescence
with similar figures about such things as the stature and head-
form. But for reasons similar to those just considered, these
characters also give no safe ground for conclusions about the
Saxon conquest. The study of the skulls excavated from early
Saxon cemeteries is more fruitful.[21] It has been applied to the
Oxford region. Here, at any rate, the change from the low-
headed type of skull, characteristic in the south of England of
the Romano-Britons, to the high-headed type, characteristic of
the Saxons, seems to have been gradual. After the invasion
there was at first a large survival of the older population, but in
time the Saxon type became dominant.

Unsatisfactory as it is, Beddoe's map is the only thing of its
kind which now lies before us, and we cannot afford to disregard it. What is most significant in it for the first stage of the
Conquest is the large pocket of dark men lying between the
Thames and the Fen country. In so far as this dark patch
corresponds with the wooded districts north-west of London it
in the main supports what we have already learnt from the finds
of Anglo-Saxon grave-goods, and what we are told in the
Chronicle about the second stage of the Conquest. Though the
Oxford zone is fairish, the counties of Buckinghamshire and
Hertfordshire are shown to be as dark as the darkest parts of
Wales.[21a]

The reader must now compare with the two maps to which
he has just been referred, a third map (p. 174), one compiled
by H. L. Gray, to show the distribution of the 'two- and three-
field system' of cultivation in England. Meitzen, the leading
authority on this line of study at the end of the nineteenth

century, believed that large villages co-operating in cultivation on the three-field and similar systems were characteristic of the Germans, in contrast to the separate homesteads—*Einzelhöfe*—of the Celtic or Romano-Celtic system. Gray's map follows up

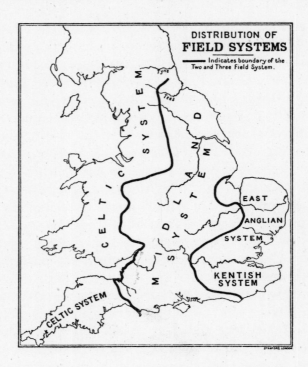

Meitzen's theory and shows the limits of the supposed Germanic system both in the west and in the east of Britain. To the west of his line he naturally finds a Celtic system of cultivation. But what of the south-east? Gray is inclined to class East Anglia —more doubtfully Essex—with Kent* as an 'area within which Roman influence persisted', and to mark Middlesex, Hertfordshire, and the Chilterns as a borderland in which Midland Germanic influences were mixed with Kentish-Roman. If Gray's results could be accepted, they would be decisive in favour of the

* See above, p. 93.

view that a large proportion of the Romano-Britons survived in the district which had once been protected by the forts of the Saxon Shore. The map, however, may be challenged on grounds similar to those which make the previous map (that showing nigrescence) questionable. And though the evidence for the Kentish peculiarities can be carried back to Domesday Book and to pre-Norman charters, as has been done by Jolliffe,* his argument that the system was imported by the conquering Jutes direct from the middle Rhine illustrates the difficulty of interpreting the evidence. As a further illustration, reference may be made to another recent theory, which asserts[22] that the village systems are less a product of race than of geographical conditions; e.g. that in regions where there are hills and the water-supply is abundant men can live on their separate homesteads, but that when the water-supply is concentrated in large streams and rivers, men must collect in village-groups by the side of a stream. This is carrying the reaction against racialism to an extreme. For the present, it is only possible to 'put in' (using the phraseology of the Courts) Gray's map as evidence, and to note its disputed meaning.[22a]

We see now how imperfect and provisional is most of the information at the disposal of those who wish to draw conclusions about the survival of the Romano-British population. Once more the only inference which is safe is a negative one: that it is not and never will be possible to propound any simple solution of a problem which is itself complex.

If we are to generalize about England as a whole, we cannot hope to get beyond truisms. We can say that three fates befell the Romano-Britons. Some were slaughtered; some withdrew; some were absorbed. Extermination, withdrawal, absorption—these were not successive phases of the Conquest. They were almost equally possible from the beginning to the end of the story.

Extermination, the ruthless slaughter of a whole community,

* Above, pp. 93–4.

had long been accepted by the Germans as a practical policy. Before the time of Tacitus[23] the Bructeri had been 'utterly wiped out by neighbouring tribes'. As late as the year 686 a king of Wessex (Cædwalla) 'endeavoured by merciless slaughter to destroy' all the Jutes of the Isle of Wight.[24] Ruthlessness of this kind was specially characteristic of the Germans, but it was not confined to them. It was a British prince (another Cædwalla) who in 632 resolved 'to cut off all the race of the English within the borders of Britain'.[25] Even in Ireland it was possible for an enemy to contemplate making the destruction of a tribe so complete that there should not be a single survivor. Clearly there is no need to rule out extermination, if we mean by this only a local extermination, as one of the ways which helped to change Britain into England. Heathen Saxons, who had the reputation of being the fiercest of the barbarians, were doubtless ready enough to massacre the Britons. None the less, we shall probably be nearer the truth if we guess that the second of the three fates was commoner than the first; in other words, that many more Britons were driven out or had the foresight to flee to the west or to Brittany than were killed. It seems to be in this sense that the Britons are said by Bede to have been *exterminati* by Ethelfrith, king of the Northumbrians.*

A recent writer[26] has pointed out that the colonization of south Pembroke in the eleventh and twelfth centuries by Norman and English adventurers produced results just like those of the sixth-century Conquest. 'Here was a settlement where the colonists drove out the old inhabitants, where they divided the land among themselves and gave places new names from their new owners.'

Absorption, the last of the three fates, is that on which other recent writers have dwelt with special emphasis. Thus, a Swedish philologist has declared:[27] 'The only theory that reconciles all the clashing evidence is that the Britons were not exterminated but absorbed by their Saxon conquerors. Their civilization

* Below, p. 197.

vanished, but the race remained.' This process was in a sense even more prolonged than the others. It has been claimed that there were Welsh-speaking Britons in the heart of Wessex, for instance in Wiltshire, as late as the ninth century.[28] We all know that the Anglicization of the western districts of England was far from complete at the time of the Norman Conquest, and that the Celtic speech, Cornish, was spoken in 'the Duchy' down to the nineteenth century.

We see then that the problem how far the Britons survived in the first stage of the Anglo-Saxon Conquest involves us in the much wider question, how they were absorbed through the subsequent centuries. These are questions which must not be further anticipated. The truth that remains is that if we are to get beyond unsatisfying generalizations, the survival of the Romano-British population must be treated as a separate problem in each area. In this as in other matters each part of the island has its own secret.

Take Kent for example. We have the tradition embodied in the Saxon Chronicle (anno 473) that the Britons 'fled from the invaders like fire'. The index of nigrescence shows that the countries bordering on the Weald have a low ratio of the dark races. We may perhaps infer that the Britons did not flee in very great numbers to the Weald. On the other hand, we have noticed above many small though disputed indications that a number of the older inhabitants survived in Kent: the fact that its potters continued to use a potter's wheel, and perhaps the peculiarities of the Kentish field-system and of the detailed classification of the servile population in the Kentish laws.

Or take Wiltshire; its nigrescence tends to show that many more of the British survived than the place-names of this region would lead us to suspect. The air-photographs of the British villages suggest that the British population in this neighbourhood had been considerable. Here then the inference is that while a large fraction of the population was absorbed, the rest were either massacred or scared into flight.

Take the upper Thames region: here again we carry away a picture constructed on different lines. We see the invaders in touch with the Britons in many directions, living on the same gravel-beds as those on which the Britons had dwelt, and using ornaments which somehow or other reproduce Roman or British motifs. British influence was here inevitable, since within a few miles there existed to the west a British kingdom at Cirencester, and to the east a large pocket of Britons sheltering in the woods of the Chiltern hills; and modern measurements of the skulls from cemeteries round Oxford are thought to prove that Britons and Saxons often dwelt side by side.

Let us agree without more ado that this question about the proportion of British blood in the population of England demands not one but at least a dozen answers.

THE FAILURE OF THE BRITONS

Our last question is this: why did the Britons fail? How came it that they yielded to an enemy lacking in cohesion and long inferior in point of numbers? To this question Gildas supplies the best answer. He supplies it both in the accusations which he scatters broadcast against his fellow countrymen, and also in his own character. He makes specific charges against the Britons as a people and against the princes of the Britons. Let us begin with the latter. Gildas gives the details, or what he believes to be the details, of the scandalous careers of five of the princes who were his contemporaries. The foremost of them was Maelgwn (Maglocunus), 'the Dragon of the Island',* who seems to have ruled north Wales from Anglesey. He was, says Gildas, foremost in evil as well as in power and in military strength. His misdeeds, it is asserted, were known to all men: the violence by which in his early youth he had usurped the crown from an uncle; his short-lived remorse, which led him for a time to atone for his sins by taking monastic vows; his detestable relapse,

* *Insularis draco.*

'like the return of a dog to his vomit'; above all, the double crime of his later years, the murder of his first wife and of his nephew in order that he might take to himself that nephew's wife.

The other British princes denounced by Gildas resembled Maelgwn in wickedness. One, Constantine of Dumnonia, had murdered two 'royal youths' in church before the altar. Another, Aurelius Caninus, whose kingdom was probably in the west Midlands, was a murderer and a maker of civil wars. Both these are also denounced for their adulteries. Yet another, Vortipore, prince of Dyfed, the region round Pembroke, was even more abandoned; and the last of them is accused of putting away his wife to marry her sister, a professed nun.

Gildas is as unsparing in his general as in his particular accusations. According to him it was the feuds as much as the lusts of the British princes which diverted them from the task of expelling the barbarians.[30] He says, 'It has always been a custom with our nation to be impotent in repelling foreign foes but bold and invincible in raising civil war'. Again:[31] 'It has become a proverb that the Britons are neither brave in war nor faithful in time of peace.' What are we to think of these denunciations? How was it that this patriot came to foul his own nest? Are we to give any weight to his unmeasured abuse?

Plainly we may be generous in discounting the words of a moralist who has modelled himself on the Hebrew prophets. Vortipore, for instance, who in the pages of Gildas appears as a deceitful and foolish king, a murderer and adulterer, is described on a memorial stone as 'the protector' (Pl. 30). But there is enough in the specific charges of Gildas to prove that the ruling families of the Britons were in his day profoundly demoralized. He throws on the screen scenes of wild passion and lust which were being enacted in the west of Britain. That is not all. In the *De Excidio* we see clearly the Celtic separatism of which we have already detected signs in the fifth century. We infer that from the first the Romano-Britons had faced the Saxons as a divided and broken race. It is true that, thanks to the tradition left by the centuries in which the Celtic tribes had been under the common rule of Rome, Gildas can think of Britain as a whole. He can speak of his 'country'. To him all Britons are nominally 'citizens': they ought to behave like Romans, but they do not do so. Part of the twist in his outlook is caused by the fact that he, as a Romano-Briton, is hopelessly out of sympathy with the rough country-folk who remained mere Celts in their thoughts and ways, and with those British princes who in his own day were combining the vices of an educated civilization with a barbarism like that of the backward natives, and thus among the hills of the west were now reverting to type. When Gildas for once in a way wishes to praise and not to blame, his praise takes the form of saying that Ambrosius Aurelianus was 'the last of the Romans'.

To understand the failure of the Britons, we must get rid of the idea that the conflict was one between civilization and barbarism. The educated Britons were indeed the *cives*, the heirs of the civilization of Imperial Rome, and the Saxons were, in the old meaning of the word, 'barbarians', that is, peoples outside the pale of Rome. But the verbal distinction rapidly ceased to correspond to the facts. The tendencies which had arisen in the sub-Roman period became fully developed. The remnants of Roman civilization and of Roman tradition died away.

The stages in the destruction of Roman culture among the Britons cannot now be traced. It is evident from Gildas that in the middle of the sixth century the well-to-do classes still retained some knowledge of Latin; it was of course the literary language of the clergy, and Gildas himself knew his Virgil and other classics as well as his Vulgate and the Fathers. Latin names were still in use in the leading families, alternating often with Celtic names, but by the middle of the sixth century we are nearing the boundary-line where the Britons ceased to be, even in their own estimate, Roman provincials, and disappear as Welshmen into the Celtic twilight. The transition of which we are speaking can be seen in the tombstones reproduced on

PLATE 30

A   B

TOMBSTONES OF BRITONS

A. Of Carausius. Penmachno, N. Wales. Assigned to end of fifth century

CARAUSIUS HIC JACIT IN HOC CONGERIES LAPIDUM

B. Of Vortipore. Now in Carmarthen Museum. About A.D. 550

MEMORIA VOTEPORIGIS PROTICTORIS

The stone also bears in the Ogam script the name in its
Goidelic form—Votecorigas

pp. 248, 183, and Pl. 30. Roman thoughts and ways yielded to Celtic. They were choked by new growths, especially by the rise of a monasticism so extreme in its ascetic repudiation of the world that its professors were often reduced in their poverty to the level of primitive men, and in their labour, yoked to the plough, to that of animals.

There is of course no denying that at times, especially in the later stages of the Conquest, the Britons did under good leaders put up a dogged resistance. If the drift of our argument in the previous chapters is correct, the faults on account of which they lost their predominance in the island were many and various: culpable blindness; failure to realize that Kent was the key to the whole island; lack of foresight also in allowing bands of Germans to establish themselves in the basins of the Ouse and the Nene and thus to drive a vast wedge into the heart of Britain; but the root cause of all their troubles was disunion.

It was this which made them prone to take the line of least resistance. When they found by experience that the Saxons were unusually fierce, they too readily consoled themselves with the thought that there was still room in the west of the island, and others—the more adventurous—taking a lesson from the invaders, sailed across the Channel to better themselves in the devastated or vacant tracts of the Armorican peninsula.[32] It seems that this migration began about the same time as the Saxon Conquest; we hear of a British prince in Gaul in 470, and by the beginning of the next century there had been a sufficient transfer of population for western Armorica to be renamed Brittany. Gildas tells us that the Britons as they fled, packed in their boats, 'beneath the sinuous sails raised their voices in loud lamentations, "Thou hast given us as sheep to be slaughtered and among the Gentiles hast Thou dispersed us" '. This may be another touch which Gildas supplied from his own imagination, but even so it is once more symptomatic of the fatalism of the Britons which led to their undoing. The lessons of confidence, unity, and efficiency, which they might have learnt from their Roman masters, were just those which they most ignored.

There was, however, one characteristic in which the Britons, released from the restraint of Rome, did now begin to excel; their powers of imagination were given free play. By the songs of their bards, the 'Histories' of their antiquaries, and the tales of their common folk, they succeeded in weaving a gorgeous web of fiction round the sordid realities of the long struggle and their ultimate defeat, and thus it came about that Artorius, the harassed leader of a rough war-band, living in a low state of civilization, without a currency (except probably that of the contemptible minims) and without the comforts of life, was by the ninth century exalted into a wonder-working national champion who 'in all his battles was the victor',[33] who felled 960 men by his own onslaught at Mount Badon, and whose dog, Cavall, left a magical footprint on a stone in Buelt. Then, in the twelfth century, Geoffrey of Monmouth and the romancers transformed him further into a king whose court was the scene of all magnificence and chivalry.

Fancy can be more efficacious than fact. The Britons were left to themselves in the west of the island, celebrating in their poems their moral victories, creating a national hero whose fame was to obscure that of the unremembered Germans, the conquerors of the richest lands of Britain.

Thus in their virtues as in their vices the Britons were strongly contrasted with their enemies; they alternated between extremes of wild asceticism and self-indulgence, of patriotic endeavour like that of Ambrosius, 'the last of the Romans', and unpatriotic discord born of unrestrained passion. The Saxons aimed lower; they were perfunctory in their religion; they never dreamed of storming the heights of Heaven, but pushed forward their advancement in this world methodically, untiringly, showing at times ferocity to their enemies, but exhibiting also in their dealings with their own race no small sense of the importance of compromise and co-operation. If the Saxons of heathen times are truthfully reflected in the poem *Beowulf*, they set before themselves a high standard of character, of loyalty to the dead no less than to the living, of discretion, of calmness in adversity, and above all, of constant valour.

TAILPIECE.—Llangadwaladr, Anglesey; tombstone of Cadfan, King of North Wales in the early 7th century. The inscription runs—*Catamanus rex sapientisimus opinatisimus omnium regum.*

VI

THE SECOND STAGE OF THE CONQUEST

WESSEX—CEAWLIN

IN the middle of the sixth century, on the eve of the second stage of the Anglo-Saxon Conquest, it was by no means a foregone conclusion that the ultimate domination of the island was to fall to the Teutons rather than to the Celts. The position of the invaders was far from secure. They had fastened their hold, it is true, on many of the richest districts, the corn-producing plains of the east and south, the sheep-walks of the downs, and the navigable river valleys which faced towards the Continent. But the invaders were still, no doubt, a small minority. They had still, it seems, to reckon with numbers of Britons undigested, or only half digested, in their midst. The greater part of the island, all the west and the north, was still in the hands of the natives. Ambrosius Aurelianus and Arthur—and others whose names have not survived—had shown that the Celt, when well led, could still successfully resist the German. If the Romano-Britons could only have organized a united front, the future might have lain with them, and Britain might never have given place to England. But the unity of the Romano-

HEADPIECE.—Old Sarum, from Camden's *Britannia*.

Britons had vanished for ever. The five kings whose morals were denounced by Gildas were only one batch of the petty monarchs who now exercised rule in the west of the island. Two other principalities can be identified in the north in addition to the kingdom of Elmet in west Yorkshire: we can dimly discern a kingdom of Reged centred probably near the Solway, and a kingdom of Strathclyde, peopled by Britons of whom many may have forced their way northwards in order to escape from the pressure of the Angles.

In the Germanic half of the island the welter of small kingdoms and independent groups of settlers was, about 550, even more chaotic than among the Britons in the west. The Germanic kingdoms on the coast were the best defined. The natural features—the forests and the swamps—which did so much to mark their boundaries, prevented them from keeping touch with the invaders who were pushing forward in the centre of Britain, and thus caused them to lose the lead in the conquest of the island. The conquerors of Kent, for instance, were hemmed in by the Andredsweald to the south-west; and when they had absorbed a few Saxon settlers to the north-west beyond the Medway, they found their further expansion westward checked by the heaths and forests of Surrey. The *imperium* of Ælle of Sussex, whatever its real character, was certainly not maintained by his successors. The South Saxons, cut off on land by the Weald and at sea by the more enterprising Jutes to the east and west of them, inevitably lost touch with their fellow Germans, and fell to the rear. The condition of the East Saxons is certain in at least one respect—that landwards they were confined by the forest belt north of London and by what was described in the seventh century as the *deserta Ciltine*, the wastes of the Chilterns.[1] The East Angles were similarly shut in by the great fens and forests on their west; the people of Lindsey by the swamps of the Witham and of the Trent, and by the forests and wastes of Sherwood and Hatfield.

In the interior the groups of settlers were, it seems, small and embryonic. There was as yet nothing to indicate that in the south the followers of the House of Cerdic, or in the Midlands the petty Mercian kingdom of the Trent, ruled by princes sprung from Offa of Angel, were to become the great powers of the future. It is true that the advanced position held by either of these principalities on the western front of the German invasion kept their fighting men well exercised in war; but this advantage, if such it can be called, was enjoyed equally by the settlers on the upper Thames and by the Middle Angles in the country of the Cam, the Ouse, and the Nene. We can only say that the war bands which followed the House of Cerdic, and the Mercians who followed the House of Offa were, like the Bernicians to the north, well situated to lead the further attacks on the Britons. By itself, however, no one of these small principalities could hope to make any spectacular advance. The Germanic communities needed to be banded into larger federations before they could dislodge the Britons in the west of the island.

How these three small kingdoms succeeded in building up the greater kingdoms of Wessex, Mercia, and Northumbria, making these new states so powerful that they could out-distance the older and perhaps richer kingdoms of the south-east, is the chief subject of the present chapter.

We begin with the rise of Wessex. It centres round the career of Ceawlin, the son of Cynric and grandson* of Cerdic, founder of the dynasty. The hypotheses suggested above,† as those best calculated to reconcile the story of the Chronicle with the evidence of the graves—that Cerdic owed his Celtic name to a British mother and that Cerdic's band of invaders plundered and dominated the uplands of southern Wiltshire, expanding from a centre somewhere near the Avon—these guesses must be our starting-point. The early story of this group of settlers is irrecoverable, but it is natural to suppose that their pioneers spread both eastwards in modern Hampshire and northwards towards the Thames valley. These would presumably be the lines of

---

* Or more probably great-grandson. See note 36 on p. 376.   † p. 129.

least resistance. What the Chronicle records is, as we have seen: first, in the year 552, the victory of Cynric over the Britons at Searoburh, Old Sarum, and then four years later the victory of Cynric and of his son Ceawlin at Beranburh (probably Barbury Camp, on the chalk hills between Swindon and Marlborough). With this emergence of Ceawlin we come to a section of the Saxon Chronicle which seems more definitely than anything in the earlier annals to have a substantial basis, perhaps in some lost saga or poem. Though all is still obscure, with the career of Ceawlin we get near enough to the light to justify some conjectures—some may-have-beens which are preferable both to the must-have-beens of J. R. Green and to the 'blank page' of the strictest school of scientific historians.[1a]

Since guesses may help to clear ideas, let us speculate for a while about the outlook of Ceawlin at the beginning of his career.

If the usual identification of Beranburh is correct, we see the war-band which had advanced from the south across Salisbury Plain and the Vale of Pewsey, now established on the Marlborough Downs overlooking the upper reaches of the Thames valley. After holding out for two generations in the most exposed southern salient of the invaders' line, the followers of Ceawlin are at last making permanent contact with their Saxon kinsmen who had penetrated into the heart of Britain by the Thames. Let us guess that Ceawlin, looking northwards from those heights, saw a land of promise and conceived ideas of conquest more grandiose than any which had hitherto contented his people—not schemes of petty ravage or of local thrust and parry with British neighbours; but schemes almost Roman in the scope of their ambition. There is of course another and perhaps a more likely possibility. His career may have been shaped throughout by less exalted motives, and by the circumstances of the moment. Even so, however, it is reasonable to credit him with sufficient intelligence to understand that consolidation in the east and confederation with the Saxons of the

Thames valley were good ways in which to prepare for the
winning of more spoil and more land from the Britons.

We may ask ourselves this question and spin out our guesses,
but all that remain in the end are the short, enigmatic annals
of the Chronicle, sounding from those distant centuries like
minute guns, at intervals which are almost regular.

Let us listen to those which tell of the new forward movements
under Ceawlin and his kinsmen, and let us try to interpret them:

'560. In this year Ceawlin succeeded to the kingdom of the West
Saxons.

'568. In this year Ceawlin and Cutha fought against Ethelbert
[presumably king of Kent], and drove him into Kent and slew two
ealdormen at Wibbandun. . . .'

Nowadays we are told that Wibbandun cannot be identified
with Wimbledon, and that the Ethelbert who was driven into
Kent cannot be the same king who some thirty years later introduced Christianity among the Germanic invaders.[2] These views,
if correct, deprive the entry of 568 of such picturesqueness as
could formerly be found in it; but its significance remains. It is
the first warfare recorded, though surely not the first waged,
between the invaders. It shows us the grandson of Cerdic assert-
ing his superiority over the wealthiest of all the eastern kingdoms.
He is clearing the country to the south of the Thames, prevent-
ing the Kentishmen from spreading westwards, and securing his
own flank before sending Saxon armies into the Chiltern country.

Then we come to three notable annals.

'571. In this year Cuthwulf fought against the Britons [*Bretwalas*] at
Bedcanford and took four towns: Lygeanburh [now identified as
Limbury, near Luton in Bedfordshire],[3] Aylesbury, Bensington [now
spelt Benson], and Eynsham, and the same year he died.'

If our former version of the events which happened to the
north of the Thames in the first stage of the conquest is accepted,
the difficulties found by Sir Charles Oman and others in this
entry disappear. The writer does not, by a blunder, substitute

Britons for Angles; the Britons defeated by Cuthwulf were presumably the remnants of those who had long sheltered in the forest lands of the eastern Midlands, allied perhaps with other British forces from the London-Verulam enclave. The four towns which were taken by the West Saxon leader are rightly given with Germanic and not with Celtic names, because they were Germanic settlements. A glance at the map facing p. 109 suggests that they were the centres of four chief groups of immigrants who had penetrated into the borders of the Chilterns and into the upper Thames valley, probably the people later known as Cilternsæte, whose territory was reckoned to contain 4,000 hides. They form sections of the Germanic arch which spanned the Midlands from Cambridge to Oxford.

We may think that Bedcanford (spelt Bedanford in Ethelweard's version of the Chronicle) was probably our Bedford, though the identification is denied by the experts of the Placename Society.[4] If this is granted and the relationship of Cuthwulf to Ceawlin* is also accepted, the operation may be regarded as part of the general Saxon advance—a move intended to establish dominion over the still British woodlands of the eastern Midlands, with a view to encircling the Germanic Cilternsæte, and thus sweeping them into a West Saxon confederation.

What is important is to understand the historical significance of the annal of 571. The sequence of its statements suggests that the transfer of the four towns was the result of the victory at Bedcanford. The prestige gained by that victory seems to have prepared the way for the absorption of the Cilternsæte by Ceawlin's Saxons, and the fact that the new league of West Saxons was able to advance a few years later against the Britons of the Severn valley points to the adhesion of the Cilternsæte being voluntary rather than enforced after severe fighting. So far as we can see, there were no signs of ill-feeling between these new subjects of the West Saxon monarchy and the original followers of Ceawlin. When Ceawlin was defeated some twenty years

* See genealogy, vol. ii, p. 721.

later, the Cilternsæte did not break away from their connexion with the folk south of the Thames. The name by which the people of the greater Wessex were called was Gewisse. The theory which interprets the name as 'the confederates' is tempting, but not well-proven.[4a] The amalgamation of the four towns in 571 under the dynasty of Ceawlin seems to repeat a characteristic first noticed in the Saxon expansion in Germany before the migration. It recalls the advance of the 'Saxons' in which the remnants of the Chauci and other tribes of north Germany were absorbed into some kind of loose confederation. If this is right, it has significance for the future. It is prophetic of greater political combinations in subsequent ages, unions of Wessex with Kent, of Wessex with Mercia, of England with Scotland, of a Commonwealth of nations under a monarchy which still 'has its descent from Cerdic'. These Saxons of the sixth century, barbarous as they may be in many respects, by their political absorption of the four towns are exhibiting a gift for preserving themselves in the rough and tumble of this world by a readiness to unite and to make friends. Such speculations may be reading more than is warranted into the annal of 571, but this we take to be certain: that here more than in any other entry of the Chronicle we have the key to the history of the formation of Wessex into a great power.

'577. In this year Cuthwine and Ceawlin fought against the Britons and they slew three kings, Coinmael, Condidan, and Farinmael, at the place which is called Deorham [Dyrham, a village a few miles north of Bath], and they took three strongholds, Gloucester and Cirencester and Bathanceaster [Bath].' (Pl. 31.)

This battle at Dyrham is the decisive battle of the second stage of the Conquest. The slaughter of the Britons was evidently great. The territory of the three 'chesters', including the southern Cotswold country and the lower valley of the Severn, was considerable and fertile. We have seen archaeological reasons for supposing that the Britons at Cirencester had been for probably a generation or two near neighbours of the Saxons of the upper

PLATE 31

Dyrham Camp, probable site of the battle of Deorham

End of the Western Towns; the South Gate of Caerwent, built-up for defence. The walls of Roman Gloucester and Bath were also of squared stone; the nature of those at Cirencester is disputed

Thames. Now in 577 the line which had there been held so long
by the Britons was completely broken. The three kings, sons
it may be of the degenerate princes whose crimes and adulteries had drawn the rhetoric of Gildas, brought on themselves
and their subjects the punishment of heaven which he had
threatened. The 'ruddy tongue' of the Saxons' fire again
'licked the western sea', and this time it betokened something
more than a passing raid. Never again were the Saxons to be
ejected from the west of the island. The importance of the battle
has always been recognized and all modern historians have
emphasized the fact that the victory of Dyrham drove a wedge
between the Britons of Wales and the Britons of Dumnonia.
It would be easier to gauge the element of truth in this assertion
if we knew how far the newly conquered country was actually
colonized by Saxons in subsequent years, and how far it was
merely tributary. But at any rate, some thirty years later, when
Augustine held a conference with the British bishops, the Severn
was, it seems, the recognized boundary between the two peoples.

In another way also the battle of Dyrham placed the old
inhabitants in an unfavourable position, for it brought the invading army on to the flank both of the Dumnonians (i.e. the inhabitants of our Somerset, Devon, and Cornwall) and of the
Britons in the Severn valley.

Whatever the reason may have been, Ceawlin apparently
turned his armies to the north rather than to the south. The
development of the campaign is uncertain, because the next
annal—the last of the series claiming West Saxon victories—
introduces us to another battle-field which cannot be located
with certainty.[5]

'584. In this year Ceawlin and Cutha fought against Britons at the
place which men call Fethanleag and Cutha was slain, and Ceawlin
took many places and countless war spoils, and in wrath he turned back
thence to his own home.'

The generally accepted view is that Ceawlin continued his

victorious advance up the Severn. The settlers who percolated into this region, until they were checked in the north of Worcestershire by the forests of Wyre, of Morfe, and of Kinver, came in time to be known as the Hwicce. The later diocese of Worcester is thought to indicate the extent of their kingdom, and Wychwood (i.e. the wood of the Hwicce) in Oxfordshire is said to have been their eastern boundary. The new colony which is found later with its own line of local kings became another outpost of Germanism in the west—an outpost of Germanism, but not for long an outpost of the Saxons; for while the names of its early kings are thought to point to a connexion with the Bernician dynasty,[6] its later land charters, its traditions, and many of its place-names, bear witness to its association from the seventh century onwards with Mercia.

The last years of Ceawlin are left by the fragmentary notes of the Chronicle as a hopeless mystery. Who can say why it was that 'in wrath he turned back to his own home' after capturing 'the many places and countless war spoil' which fell to him as a result of the battle of Fethanleag. The words about returning in wrath sound like a snatch from some oral tradition. They suggest how it came to pass that our information about the first empire-builder of the West Saxons was preserved.

The next annal which tells of his surprising downfall is equally puzzling.

'592. In this year was a great slaughter at Wodnesbeorg and Ceawlin was driven out.'

Since Wodnesbeorg seems to have been in the Marlborough region, seven miles east of Devizes,[7] we see that Ceawlin's career of conquest ended near the place where it had begun. Had he been expelled from some of his new conquests by Britons? Or had he been driven back to the support of his own folk when other Germanic peoples, newly subjected to his rule, revolted? Or were his victories in the north interrupted by troubles among his own kinsmen? Or had he to meet an attack from Ethelbert of Kent, the king whose power was thenceforth to be in the ascendant? The guesses have been endless, but there can be no sure answer. All that is told us is that Ceawlin survived his defeat for only one year; then, if our reconstruction of the genealogy of his family is correct,[8] the crown passed to his eldest surviving son.

The tradition of his conquests lived on among the West Saxons for centuries. While Cerdic, the founder of the dynasty, became little more than a name, men looked back to Ceawlin, his grandson, as the second 'Bretwalda', the second Germanic war-leader who enjoyed south of the Humber an *imperium*— whatever *imperium* may connote. It was Ceawlin who had swept all before him from the Marlborough Downs to Kent, from the lower Thames in the east to the lower Severn in the west. It was Ceawlin who, profiting from the victory of Cuthwulf, had united the scattered Saxon settlements from the Chilterns to the Channel. It was Ceawlin who by the boldness of his schemes of conquest and by his generalship in the field had foreshadowed the ultimate supremacy of the Gewisse.

More than two centuries, however, were to elapse before the glory of the *imperium* was to be claimed once more by a descendant of the House of Cerdic.

MERCIA

The expansion of Wessex under Ceawlin may be supposed to represent roughly what happened also to Mercia and Northumbria, the two kingdoms which showed a corresponding capacity for growth. The Mercians failed to preserve a tradition, even a false one, of their early history; all that has come to us is a list of their kings and a document called the *Tribal Hidage*,* which gives what appears to be a summary of the districts liable for contributions to the armies and to the revenues of the Mercian monarchy in the seventh century. This document can be used to throw light on the political expansion of Mercia in that age,

* See genealogy, vol. ii, p. 719, and vol. ii, p. 389.

that is, in the time of Penda and his sons; but it scarcely helps to elucidate the story of the settlement. For instance, one people enumerated in it which can be clearly identified is the Pecsæte (Peak-dwellers); their territory is reckoned to contain 1,200 hides or households. Who were these Peak-dwellers and whence did they come? The natural inference would be that they sprang from small bands of Anglian settlers who pushed northwards from the older Mercia of the Trent valley and colonized new lands around the Peak. On the other hand, Bede tells us that Northumbrians early in the seventh century carried their conquests up to Chester, and a place-name expert[9] has claimed to find support for the view that south Lancashire was colonized by Northumbrians before it was re-colonized in the time of Penda by Mercians. This is only one example of many obscurities. It is enough to show why, in this second stage of the Conquest as in the first, the early history of Mercia is so dark that it is better to pass it by and admit the impossibility of putting together any trustworthy story.

NORTHUMBRIA—ETHELFRITH

We have seen* that the beginnings of the two Northumbrian States are purely conjectural until about the middle of the sixth century, when a leader called Ælle became king of Deira and one Ida, king of Bernicia. Practically nothing is known of Ælle. But some murmur of wars waged by the House of Ida comes down to us. Four of Ida's sons succeeded him on the throne. Nennius in the ninth century had earlier genealogies and fragments of apparently genuine information about some events of their time. He tells[10] that an alliance of four kings, Urbgen (known in later times as Urien), ruler of Reged,† Riderch, king of Strathclyde, Morcant (or Morgan), and another, fought against the successors of Ida. Then of Theodric, the son of Ida, who reigned about 572–9, he says: 'Theodric with his sons fought bravely against that Urbgen. At that time sometimes

* Above, pp. 148–53.   † Or Rheged.

the enemy, sometimes our countrymen [*cives*] were defeated, and he beleaguered them for three days and nights in the island of Metcaud [Lindisfarne], and while he was on the campaign he was murdered at the instigation of Morcant from jealousy, because he was the most valorous and warlike of all kings.'[11]

Riderch appears also as an historical ruler in the *Life of St. Columba* and in the *Life of St. Kentigern* (based on earlier material, though written about 1175). He is Riderch Hael (the Generous), king of the Strathclyde Britons, and he has at his court a madman endowed with prophetic power. This madman is interesting because Chadwick has produced good reasons for thinking him to be the original (or rather one original) of Merlin of Arthurian romance, and it is interesting to find that Laloecen (as he was then called) was said to have become unbalanced owing to a conviction of blood-guiltiness which came to him in the middle of a battle. Later the same madman, after taking to the woods, 'used to come and sit on a rock over the stream Mellodonor—now called Molendinar—in the north of Glasgow, and interrupt the service of St. Kentigern's clergy by shouting prophecies; but his prophecies were never consistent with one another'.[12] The *Life of St. Kentigern* also relates that Urien, the most warlike king, was the patron of the Saint, and that Morgan the murderer of Urien was a persecutor.

The Welsh poems of Aneurin and Taliessin and of other poets who flourished about the end of the sixth century have something to contribute about the 'Men of the North'—'disintegrated' as these poems are, overlaid with later Bardic additions, and often unintelligible. The outstanding fact about the one fight which can almost be dated (to about 575) and located (at 'Arderydd', either Arthuret, near Longtown, or Airdrie in Lanark)[12a] is this, that it was fought by Riderch against other Britons and not against the Angles. One famous poem, the *Gododdin*, attributed to Aneurin and generally thought to contain some genuine tradition, seems to refer to a raid carried out by a small band of retainers of a prince living near the Forth against the Saxons at Catraeth (? Catterick), a hopeless venture by men 'fed with mead, and drunk'.

> The men went to Catraeth; merry was the host,
> The grey mead was their drink and their poison too.[13]

These side-lights, however flickering, help to illustrate the fatal elements of rivalry, of religious disunity, and of fecklessness, which prevented the Celtic tribes of the north-west from checking the English in Bernicia and Deira while these were still a small minority.

But on the whole it seems to be a fact that in this northern region the fighting was fiercer and more prolonged than in the Severn valley, and that the Britons of the north in the course of the struggle applied to themselves a new name, shared also with the Britons of Wales, but never given to those of Devon or Cornwall; they called themselves *Combrogies* or *Cymry*, meaning 'fellow countrymen', a word still recognizable in the first two syllables of our own Cumberland, the land of the Cymry. The name was evidence, if not of a new patriotism, at least of a new consciousness of Celtic racialism born during these struggles and, however imperfectly, superimposed over the old tribal and regional antagonisms.

It is not till we come to Bede's account of Ida's grandson Ethelfrith (593–617) that at last we have firm ground in the history of the rise of Northumbria. As with the rise of Wessex under Ceawlin, we find two distinct aspects of the process. There is the union of smaller kingdoms or districts, and there is conquest by the armies of the united kingdoms pushed forward till it reaches the western sea. The union of the northern kingdoms was a simpler affair than the union of those in the south and midlands, because in the north there were by the end of the sixth century only two, Deira and Bernicia; and when Ethelfrith of Bernicia married a daughter of Ælle, the old king of Deira, and succeeded in disinheriting Ælle's son Edwin (? 605), all that was required to merge the Northumbrian kingdoms into

PLATE 32

View through the entrance of Dunadd, the rock fortress of the Scots

Alclyde (i.e. the rock of Clyde), also called Dumbarton (i.e. the fortress
of the Britons)

one seemed for the moment to have been accomplished. But even before this union Ethelfrith had apparently carried all before him.[14] 'Throughout his reign,' says Bede, 'Ethelfrith more than all the chiefs of the English, harried the Britons. . . . Like another Saul he conquered more territories from the Britons than any other ealdorman or king of the English, either subduing the inhabitants and making them tributary, or driving them out (*exterminatis*) and planting the English in their places.'

The conflict culminated in 603. In that year Aedan, the Scotto-Irish king of Dal Riata (roughly equivalent to the modern Argyle), marched against Ethelfrith. The battle which ensued is the first recorded between Scots and English. Hitherto the colony of Scots, since they had crossed the seas from Ulster a hundred years earlier, had had enough to do in maintaining their footing against Picts and Britons. Now in 603 King Aedan, an old man of seventy, well known as the patron of St. Columba of Iona, seems to have been inspired by the idea of being a second Arthur (it is significant that his mother was British and that he christened his eldest son Arthur). He made a league with the Britons of Strathclyde and advanced 'with an immense and mighty army'. It is usual to identify Degsastan, the scene of the ensuing battle, with Dawston Rig in Liddesdale, and if we wonder how 'immense armies' could maintain themselves in that desolate spot among the bare hills of the borderland, we may remember that estimates of numbers are usually exaggerated, that the total area of Aedan's rock fortress at Dunadd (Pl. 32) in the Moss of Crinan could not maintain a population of more than some 700 people, and that the head-quarters of his ally, the king of Strathclyde, at Alclyde (Dumbarton) and of his enemy Ethelfrith at Bamburgh[14a](Fig. 34) were similar rock fortresses. The smallness of their 'capitals'—if they may be so described— are a reminder of the diminutive scale on which these early kings of post-Roman Britain conducted their affairs.

But the battle of Degsastan, whatever its true site, and whatever the size of the armies engaged, was at any rate decisive.

FIG. 34. Bamburgh, the rock fortress of King Ethelfrith.

There was no glint of Arthurian romance in the sequel. Almost all the army of the Scots was slain, and the king fled with a few followers. 'From that day', says Bede,[15] 'no king of the Scots in Britain has to this day dared to meet the English nation in battle.' The predominance of the Angles south of the Forth was established in the west as well as in the east.[16]

The crowning mercy came about 616. Ethelfrith raised a great army and advanced boldly for almost a hundred miles from his own borders. In the neighbourhood of Chester, where once had been stationed the Twentieth Legion, he found himself opposed not only by a coalition of British princes but by 1,250 monks who had come from their monastery at Bangor to importune the God of battles. For three days the monks fasted, and then the wild group of holy men took up a position near the battle-field. Bede's well-known story of the massacre of the unarmed crowd illustrates the ruthlessness of this descendant of Ida, and the spirit of the age. The monks were fighting with their prayers; they must be the first to be cut down. The order was carried out, twelve hundred of the holy men were slaughtered. To Bede their fate appeared a punishment not unjustly inflicted on the Britons for their refusal to co-operate in the conversion of the heathen English. To us it helps to explain the loathing with which the Britons shrank back from contact with the Anglo-Saxon invaders.

The career of Ethelfrith like that of Ceawlin—and of so many another early king—ended in defeat and failure. The story of the defeat brings us to the rise of Edwin, the exiled son of Ælle of York, and it will find its place when we come to the history of the Conversion.

The meagreness of the present chapter shows how few are the facts that can be ascertained about the second stage of the Conquest.

We know something about Ceawlin of Wessex and something about Ethelfrith of Northumbria; but the rest is almost a blank. The gap in our written information might in places be filled with conjectures based on the grave-finds, but the reader has no doubt had his fill of the archaeological kind of history in previous chapters, and he may be spared any more of it in these later times when it is less essential. We have learnt enough from the written authorities to perceive that the advance made by the invaders in the latter half of the sixth century and the opening years of the seventh was all-important. It definitely turned the scale against the Britons and drove those who clung to their independence into the hill-country of the west. It also produced some sort of order out of chaos and brought to the front those states whose struggle for existence or for mastery make up so much of the history of the next few centuries.

Among the Germanic kingdoms in the east of the island events had occurred which were to determine the course of history in the seventh century. But in this period as ever, the all-important process in the making of England was more economic than political; it was the unrecorded expansion of Germanic cultivation. In every kingdom, small or great, the enterprising members of the community were farming new lands, and penetrating farther into the woodlands. The south-eastern kingdoms, such as Kent, Sussex, Essex, and East Anglia, were in this way being rounded off and delimited; and the others were stretching out longer tentacles among the Britons of the west.

This second stage has no well-marked termination. The story of the advance fades away. But when in coming chapters we focus our attention on the stories of saints and kings, it must not be forgotten that the process of gradual colonization, of gradual eating by Saxon and Angle into the lands hitherto British, continued unceasingly generation after generation.

VII
HEATHEN SOCIETY °

KING AND PEOPLE

WE wish to know how our Germanic forefathers lived
and governed themselves in Britain during those first
generations which we must necessarily confuse under
the phrase 'the heathen period' of Anglo-Saxon society. What
stands in our way as we approach the subject is once more the
uncertainty about the migration itself. How did the Jutes, the
Saxons, and the Angles, cross the sea? Did they come in masses
much as the Goths had crossed the Danube, and as the Franks
had crossed the Rhine? Is it likely that peoples, the majority
of whom must have lived some way from the coast, could have
mustered a sufficient number of their elaborately made long
keels to ferry more than small parties in any one year? Is it
conceivable that, even in the later stages of the movement, tribes
or even large groups of kindred could have been shipped from the
Elbe to the upper reaches of the Thames, the Ouse, or the Trent?
These questions are fundamental, and must determine our ideas
about the kind of society which was formed by the Germanic
immigrants into Britain.

If we turn to our best guides, we find a certain measure of
agreement. Few could object to the main thesis with which
Stubbs[1] prefaces his account of *The Anglo-Saxon System.* He

HEADPIECE.—Lid of Franks Casket; Ægil defending his home. ½.

points out that the process was not necessarily uniform in the several states.

'In some cases it [the transference of German institutions to Britain] may have been accomplished by unconnected bands of squatters, who took possession of an uninhabited tract, and, reproducing there the local system of their native land, continued practically independent, until the whole surrounding districts were organised by a central state-power. In other cases, the successful leader of a large colony or a victorious host, having conquered and exterminated [here, of course, Stubbs gives an opening to criticism] the natives, must have proceeded to divide their land according to a fixed scheme. The principle of this allotment he would find in the organisation of his host.'

What is objectionable in Stubbs's history is the social system which he builds on this foundation. The victorious host becomes the 'people in arms . . . united by the principle of kindred'; the allotment of the land is 'according to the divisions of the kindred'; the typical village is the community of equal freemen. In Kent, Sussex, and perhaps in Essex and East Anglia, the supreme authority in the State is probably a folk-moot of the freemen, meeting 'in primitive simplicity'. Elsewhere, this primitive simplicity is represented by the shire-moots. Between the shire-moots and the meetings of freemen in their townships or villages are the assemblies of the districts called 'Hundreds', probably introduced by the invaders, arranged in groups of a hundred warriors for the conquest of Britain. Stubbs is cautious in details, but he is clear that what is set up in Britain is a reproduction of the old tribal system of Germany, with little modification—a tribal system in which the old principle of kinship is still the chief force.

Among modern critics of Stubbs the most thorough-going is H. M. Chadwick.[2] He asserts that the Victorian's 'representation of Anglo-Saxon society rests upon a string of hypotheses not one of which is capable of proof', and that there is no evidence for self-government, either central or local, nor for the kindred as a definitely organized body. In his opinion 'it is not of national

assemblies or responsible local bodies that we hear, but of kings
and their officials'. The State is based on allegiance to the king
and to the great men who surround the king; on lordship rather
than on kinship. 'Indeed, it appears that with the exception
of the king himself, every individual in the nation owed obedience
to a lord.'

Now, there is no doubt about the main reason for the difference between these two views of the earliest Anglo-Saxon institutions. They are for the most part derived from different sources.
While Stubbs drew his conclusions from the *Germania* of Tacitus,
from analogy with what were supposed to be the Germanic
institutions of the Continent, from place-names, and, above all,
from the Saxon laws, Chadwick held that the best picture of
early English society was to be found in the literature of the
Anglo-Saxons, in their heroic poetry (especially in *Beowulf*), and
in Bede's *Ecclesiastical History*. We must therefore begin by clearing our own ideas about the relative value of these several
sources of information; and in doing so we find at once that the
main defences of the old position must be almost surrendered.
The *Germania* of Tacitus, eked out with analogies drawn from
other Germanic States on the Continent, may supply us with
ideas about the general principles on which Germanic society
was organized; but it can do no more. The *Germania* must be
out of our picture of Anglo-Saxon society, because it is too
remote; and the institutions found among Franks and Lombards
cannot be trustworthy parallels to those produced by an oversea
migration. The main arguments of those who would emphasize
the element of Germanic self-government or of a tribal system
based on kinship, if they are to be valid, rest on the remaining
sources of information—the Saxon laws, the place-names, and
the village systems. Let us glance at the arguments constructed
along these several lines.

First, with regard to the Saxon laws—it is sufficiently obvious
that the only laws which can be quoted with confidence as evidence of the heathen stage of society are the laws of Ethelbert

[margin note: Tacitus vs. A-S poetry (Beowulf) and Bede]

of Kent, compiled about five years after the Conversion. These can be interpreted, as by Stubbs, so that they tally with the Germanic systems of the Continent. They mention three classes in Kentish society. The *eorls* (a word which through the influence of the cognate Norse *jarl* acquired in time the more exalted force of our 'earl') may be taken as a hereditary nobility of birth. The *ceorls* (a word akin to our 'churl') are freemen— and freemen of substance, since the ceorl's *tun* or farm is protected against a breach of the peace in the same way as the king's or the eorl's, though with a lower fine. In the third class we have the half-free, the *læts*, corresponding to a similar class in the Frisian and Frankish laws. On the whole, it may be said that the social system in Kent is not far removed from those of their nearest neighbours on the opposite mainland. Thus in the law of Ethelbert (c. 2) which inflicts a special penalty 'if the king calls his *leode* to him and evil is done to them there', though the word *leode* may mean only personal dependants it may also mean, as Stubbs believed, the general freemen of the nation, and Jolliffe has recently given a new force and direction to the older views by equating the lathes of Kent with the *gaue*, the old local divisions, of Germany and by claiming that these districts were 'embodied folks'.[3]

Though these Kentish laws may be used as by Stubbs to support the theory which would transfer the tribal system of Germany almost ready-made to all the Germanic settlements in Britain, there are difficulties in the way. In addition to the uncertainty about the real meaning of the terms, there is the question why these laws differ so much from the later laws. Are they peculiar because they are generations earlier—because they describe primitive conditions of English society which later ceased to exist—or are they peculiar because they are Kentish? Now recent studies of Kentish institutions have all tended to stress the fact that the social arrangements of Kent were different from those of the rest of England. Nowhere else in Anglo-Saxon laws do we read of a ceorl's *tun* as if it were a separate estate—what the Germans call an '*Einzelhof*'. Nowhere else does the ceorl occupy such an independent position. In Kent his oath is about as good as that of a cleric, and he has under him dependants (*hlafætan*, 'bread-eaters').[4]

If we go on to the later law-books, those of the kings of Kent in the last quarter of the seventh century,* and that (dated about 690) of Ine of Wessex, we find that the Kentish ceorl is valued at least two and a half times as highly as the West-Saxon ceorl.[5] He seems to be a different kind of man from the normal peasant whom we encounter in the other kingdoms, and to have more independence as well as a more compact property. There is, then, much to be said for the view that since the Kentish men were a peculiar people, their laws cannot be taken to describe a stage of society through which the other kingdoms also passed. Some of the weighty arguments of Stubbs are thus put out of action, and it becomes less necessary to dwell further on the theory of Chadwick, that the *leode* whom Ethelbert specially protected when summoned to his presence were his fighting retainers rather than the members of a tribal folk-moot.

But even if the laws of Kent cannot teach us what had happened in the other kingdoms, there are yet other laws, notably those of Ine of Wessex, which, like outcrops from ancient buried strata, illustrate the nature of Anglo-Saxon society in its early epochs and show certain evidences of a primitive freedom. Thus one of Ine's decrees[6] regulates the fine (*fyrdwite*) which is to be paid by a man of the ceorl class who neglects his service in the *fyrd*, or national army. Another[7] deals with the obligations of ceorls who have 'a common meadow or other—partible—land (*gedalland*) to fence'. It is a mere glimpse of the corporate life of the village community. But it is enough to make it evident that in Wessex something like the later open-field system of cultivation goes back to the earliest centuries of the English occupation. No subject in early English history has received more attention since Seebohm first pointed out the historical significance of the

---

* Hlothere, reigned 673–85; Eadric, *c.* 685–86; Wihtred, 690–725.

typical arrangements of an old English village—its three great arable fields cut up into small strips which were distributed in such a way as to give each villager of substance his hide of land, his virgate (one quarter of a hide), or whatever smaller holding might be his portion, constituting a farm held not in one piece, but in a score or more of scattered strips mixed with those of his neighbours. It is now some decades since Maitland and Vinogradoff seemed to have proved that these features of the English village system were Germanic rather than Roman; that they arose naturally as one piece of waste-land after another was taken into tillage; that they were not maintained to suit the convenience of a lord, whether Roman or Saxon, but sprang from a Germanic sense that men should share and share alike.*

So far in this chapter we have been examining what Chadwick meant when he asserted that the older view of Anglo-Saxon society 'rests upon a string of hypotheses not one of which is capable of proof'. We have seen that the early Kentish laws, the village system, the place-names, the meaning of a term such as *leode*—all are ambiguous. The interpretation put upon them by Stubbs and the nineteenth-century historians is open to criticism. The way is accordingly clear for us to go further, and see if the literary sources used by Chadwick—the *History* of Bede, the *Beowulf* and other poems—make it possible to reconstruct the conditions of early English society on other lines with better probability.

At the outset there is no denying that these sources have obscurities of their own, which render their evidence even harder to assimilate than the epigrams of Tacitus. Bede's aim was to

* One notable modification of the above views has already been mentioned. Gray's map (above, p. 174) has shown us that 'the English village system' was only a Midland system, extended to Wessex and Deira. Even this may have been in a sense pre-Germanic if, as is suggested (cf. below, note 17a on p. 372, and Collingwood and Myres, *Roman Britain*, 210–14), the fields of the Roman villas were cultivated with heavy ploughs like those of the Saxons and were often taken over by the invaders. The half-Celtic system of Bernicia has been well described by Jolliffe, and the peculiarities of the Jutish south-east explained less convincingly.[4a] These problems are by no means solved.

narrate the doings of kings and saints in the age of the Conversion, and his references to institutions are casual and never explicit. The epic of *Beowulf* and the other early poems which seem
to refer to English society in the heathen period are as little concerned as Bede with the institutions of the English, and they
plunge us into baffling cross-currents of modern theories and
counter-theories. The *Beowulf* in particular is beset with difficulties. Modern critics now reject the idea that it is a composite
work.[8] There is some measure of agreement that, while old
myths, old legends, and old lays are of course woven into the
epic, it is the work of a real poet, and not of a compiler; not
a minstrel's casual outpouring, but the studied composition
of a writer who could polish three thousand lines with care;
one conversant both with Christianity and with heathen ideas.
The author knows and loves the tales about the heroes who sailed
the Baltic and the North Sea, who built their halls and fought
out their feuds in that northern world during the fifth and sixth
centuries; but he introduces his heathen heroes to instruct as well
as to beguile the men-at-arms as they ate their bread and drank
their beer in the halls of the great. The epic cannot have been
composed long before the end of the seventh century, since we
must allow for the lapse of some generations before Beowulf, the
nephew of a Scandinavian king (one who appears in history
fighting against the Franks about 525) could be mixed up in
men's minds in adventures with dragons and monsters. On the
other hand, it cannot well be later than the beginning of the
ninth century, since there is no hint in the poem that the Danes,
to save whom Beowulf fought the monsters, have yet become
Vikings, hateful to the English.

But if in point of time the *Beowulf* poem is about as far removed
from heathen England as is Bede's *History*, the pagan spirit
animating the poem, and the setting, seem to take us back to the
ideas and conditions which were to be found in England before
the coming of Christianity. Though coloured, and at times dis-
torted, by the ideas of the later century in which it was actually

composed, the poem can yet be used as a guide to the ways and thoughts of the earliest Englishmen.

From this heroic poetry and from Bede, as well as from the laws and charters, Chadwick has extracted ideas which place the early institutions of the Anglo-Saxons in a new perspective. This is not the place in which to follow in detail his arguments or even his results, but his main contention, to which we have already alluded, is fundamental: namely, that the all-important element in the Anglo-Saxon State was the king himself and those officials and followers bound to the king by a personal tie. We shall, therefore, do well to glance at some of Chadwick's applications of his general theory. There is the idea that the kings themselves could dispose of their kingdoms—for instance on the death of the king who was Beowulf's uncle, his widow is said to have offered Beowulf the throne, because she considered her own son too young to defend the kingdom. There is a theory which cannot well be questioned, that the councillors (*witan*) were little more than the nominees of the Crown—the king's officials and his retainers. The central government, it is argued, was in the hands of the king and his court. 'It is clear from Bede's writings that the court consisted roughly of two classes, which we may describe as the "seniors" and "juniors" (*dugoð* and *geogoð*). The latter were young warriors (*milites, ministri*) in constant attendance on the king, while the former included persons of official position (*eorls*, &c.) as well as *milites emeriti* who had already been rewarded for their services with grants of land.'[9] The local government was administered by 'reeves'—a word which covers both the stewards of the king and those of the landowners under the king. 'There seems not to have been any difference in kind between the two classes. There is no evidence that either was controlled by or responsible to any authority, except their masters.' In this view the units of local government appear, not as natural growths from below, but as arrangements imposed by the monarchy from above: the shires of Wessex represent[10] 'divisions of the kingdom between members of the royal family'; and

the smaller units which preceded the hundreds were administra-
tive divisions grouped round the royal vills. Lastly, the army is
not an assemblage of all the freemen of the nation. It is small and
highly select, and there is no certain indication that normally
any warriors came to the field except the king and his *gesiths*,*
and those freemen who were bound by special personal ties to
follow them.

We have now glanced at some of the older views of Stubbs,
and also at some of the more recent theories put forward by
Chadwick. When we make our choice between the two, we
shall be wise to agree with Chadwick that in Bede's *History* and
in Old English literature generally the kings and their personal
followers fill the picture,[10a] and that little or nothing is to be
seen of the tribalism, the self-government, and the democratic
moots which fascinated Stubbs and his contemporaries. But as
usual the two theories are not wholly irreconcilable. The
question then arises, in what way they are to be combined. One
historian[11] has suggested 'that when some adventurous king and
his *comitatus* had made the first lodgement, free tribesmen were
invited in to strengthen the new community', and that 'they
would stipulate for the perpetuation of their old privileges, in
their new homes, so that the state, when formed, would be much
less autocratic in constitution than might have been expected'.

But this picture of the Conquest will not do—even as an hypothesis. Whatever happened, there can have been no bargain of
this kind about rights. If we are to guess, we must think of the
Germanic settlers introducing old privileges, laws, and customs,
simply because these were all that they knew. The same thing
happens whether Anglo-Saxon migrants are planting colonies in
Britain in the fifth and sixth centuries, or in America and Aus-
tralia in modern times. Most of the laws of the old country
reappear in the new. None the less, profound changes were a
natural consequence of the migration across the North Sea. To
the old aristocracy of birth there was added a new aristocracy of

---

* See below, p. 210, for the general likeness of gesiths to thegns.

Heathen Society CHAP.

service and of wealth. Because the new land was won at the spear's point, the war-leaders, both the kings themselves and the warriors who were round them, stood to gain. But to talk about bargains being struck is as misleading as to assume that there was an importation of a constitution ready-made on the lines of the *Germania* of Tacitus.

All that we can say is that the Anglo-Saxons brought with them three Germanic ways of doing things, three principles on which society was built, principles which were not peculiar to the Germans, since they were found among other primitive peoples, but which stand out in all allusions to the Germanic tribes and are described in classic passages in the *Germania* of Tacitus.

First is the principle of the *comitatus*, which secured for a war-leader, great or small, a troop of devoted followers. We have already noticed the emphasis placed by recent writers on the part played by such war-bands in the conquest of Britain. Here we need do no more than recognize the various forms in which the principle could be embodied. The followers might be, as they were originally, the hearth-companions of their leader, receiving in return for their services board and lodging, supplemented by occasional special rewards, such as bracelets of gold and silver. Later, when fighting had ended in permanent conquest, the rewards of the followers naturally often took the form of land. This, of course, had the result of breaking up the closeness of the connexion between the lord and the follower, and gave rise to new quasi-feudal relationships, from which in time there sprang the tangled feudalistic growths of the later Saxon age.

The word chiefly used to describe the follower of a king in the early Saxon period is *gesith*, and it seems to contain the idea of companionship. It is gradually superseded, though not till the ninth century or thereabouts, by the word *thegn*, which places emphasis on the idea of service, rather than on that of companionship.[12]

comitatus

The principle of the *comitatus* produces also retinues of humbler
fighting-men for the gesiths and thegns themselves. All men,
from the greatest landowners to the humblest peasants, can be
bound to a lord by a devotion which is almost a religion. Since
the groups of lords and of followers branching off from the principle of the *comitatus* were so diversified, it is natural that the
numbers in the bands should be equally variable. In one of the
oldest poems* we hear of a hero being accompanied by sixty
champions. Beowulf sets out with fourteen, but later he offers
to bring a thousand thegns and heroes to help his ally. We need
not speculate here about the question how far a difference in
degree produced a difference in kind. It is enough to see that, in
the consolidation of the settlements, the small war-bands and
the yet smaller informal followings of the local magnates could
by simple addition be aggregated until the army collected by a
wide ruler like the king of Greater Mercia might, according to
one recent guess,[13] amount to 15,000 men.

Secondly, there was the principle of the free nation. The king
could be no autocrat. Of necessity he must always gain the willing co-operation of his warriors. In so far as there was in these
early times anything which could be called a constitutional
theory, it might conceivably be held that the general assent of
the freemen was desirable. In practice the barbarian nations
worried little about theories. All that was really necessary was
that a king should carry with him the leading men of his people.
Having obtained this support, whether formally or informally,
he could have things his own way.

In the nineteenth century much—certainly too much—used
to be written about the functions of the 'Witenagemots', or of
the local courts or 'folk-moots'. Now having acknowledged that
the principle of popular assent existed, we need only recognize
what is sufficiently obvious, that its application varied with time
and circumstances, that is, with the size of the kingdom and
with the character of the king and of his great men.

* The *Finnsburh Fragment*.

Kinship must be reckoned a third basic principle in Anglo-Saxon society. But kinship is a word which may cover much or little; and we must try to make its meaning more precise. Some things may be confidently asserted: that within historic times the unit of Anglo-Saxon society was never a well-defined cohesive kin-group; that it was no clan or sept of the Celtic type; that it was not exclusively patriarchic or agnatic like the Roman *gens*; that Anglo-Saxon armies were not, so far as we know, drawn up by families and clans, as Tacitus believed the German armies to be in his time. On the other hand, kinship brought with it duties greater and more definite than those which fall to the members of a modern family. If a man had the misfortune to kill another of a different kin, his family might sooner or later be called upon to pay a greater part of the money-compensation, the *wergeld*, which would be due to the family of the slain. The same principle would apply if a less serious injury had been inflicted. A man's kinsmen were expected to help him in every way they could—from swearing on his behalf in the local moot to enduring or pursuing a blood-feud if justice broke down. There is no question that this was in a general way the first principle of early English, as of Germanic and of most primitive justice. Moreover, the legal liability of the kindred, often of remote cousins, persisted among many of the north German and Scandinavian peoples throughout the Middle Ages. It was notably so in the regions whence had come the Anglo-Saxon conquerors of Britain. In Schleswig, the fourth cousin of a slain man might claim a few shillings, which were the recognized portion of his *wergeld*, and in the Hamburg district the kinsmen of slayer and slain were making treaties for composition in cases of manslaughter as late as the seventeenth century. There is earlier evidence also which shows that the continental Saxons, like their sometime neighbours, the Lombards, reckoned kinship for the purpose of primitive justice down to the seventh degree.

To what extent were such customs introduced by the conquering Saxons into Britain? Were families directly liable for the crimes of their members? Did the responsibility extend to remote cousins? Here we have a good example of the trend of historical thought in recent times. Scepticism about the 'Germanic' views of the nineteenth-century historians culminated in 1913 in a book entitled *Kindred and Clan*, by Miss B. S. Phillpotts;[14] and this will be our chief guide in glancing at the subject. The code of Ethelbert makes it clear that the primary responsibility for compensation fell, in Kent, on the individual, and only a secondary liability on the kinsmen—they are only called upon to pay if the real culprit has fled. But this was in Kent; and we have learnt that it is not safe to argue from the ways of Kentishmen to those of Englishmen in general.

The laws of the West Saxons (our only other laws) are unfortunately less explicit on this point. A man's *magas* (his kinsmen) have undoubtedly many responsibilities. They may be called in if he defaults and flees the land. They may have to act as guardians and to keep up the home of a dead man. Even the blood-feud is recognized, though the kings attempt to restrict it. A day may come in the life of any Anglo-Saxon when he has to call on the members of his family to take up their spears and defend him in feud or assist him to exact vengeance on another.

But what is this family? Did it include, as on the Continent, distant cousins? No answer to this question comes down to us from the Anglo-Saxon laws; and it is this fact, the complete dearth of regulations in England detailing the rights and liabilities of distant kinsmen, which justifies us in thinking that the Anglo-Saxon *mægth*, or kindred, meant little more than our 'family' in the modern loose sense of the word.

How then shall we explain the comparative insignificance of the kindred on the soil of Britain? Two reasons present themselves. One is the fact that an oversea migration is more upsetting to the old system than a land migration. The ship's crew must be a band of adventurers. It cannot well be a family party. The second cause was not peculiar to England. It was the difficulty of working a cognatic system, like that of the Anglo-Saxon laws, where the mother's relations were recognized as well as the father's. They were, it is true, less important; the relative responsibility was, as amongst many other peoples, two to one—i.e. when owing to the flight of a criminal the kindred had to pay for a murder, the relations on the father's side had to pay two-thirds of the fine, those on the mother's side one-third.* But the fact that there was no fixed kin-group like the agnatic *gens* of the Romans meant that the kin-group of a son was always different from that of his father. The complications arising from such a system were baffling. There was no end to them. Common sense pointed to substituting the family in its narrower sense for the wide and dispersed kindred.

The marvel is that the responsibility of the extended group could be retained for centuries in countries like Schleswig, and not that it disappeared in England.

Now it must not be supposed that there is any fatal antagonism between the older theories of Germanic freedom and the more recent theories which lay stress on the parts played by the kings and the dependants of the kings. The principles of freedom and lordship could exist side by side. For the king could be head of a free nation as well as lord of a war-band. The eorl —and even more eminently, the etheling, the member of a royal family—could be a noble, respected by the ordinary freeman on account of his good birth, and at the same time he could be raised above the common herd by the nobility of his services as a king's gesith. The ceorl might still be liable to perform the old duties once incumbent on all freemen, even when in actual practice those duties were only exacted from those who had bound themselves to follow some particular lord. Similarly in local government, a court might be held by the king's official—his ealdorman or his reeve—and it might assemble in a royal vill and yet be regarded as a popular court. The fighting freemen of the Conquest—such men as we see laid out in the cemeteries,

* See, however, Alfred's Law, c. 27, in Stubbs' *Charters*, p. 70.

sometimes in rows, each with his arms beside him—did not cease to be free because they followed a leader. They did not cease to be free even if the leader and his heirs after him came to be recognized as the lords of a settled community. They did not necessarily cease to be free when, frontier fighting having receded with the frontier, they were no longer practised in war. In fact, however, as these changes came about and the boundaries of the kingdom became enlarged, the ordinary freemen were left behind tending their cattle and ploughing their strips of land, content to leave the burdens of ruling and fighting to the king and to the king's men.

The principles of lordship and freedom could be intertwined in as many different ways as the knotted patterns of an Anglian or Celtic cross. For while on the one hand a free community was a good soil for the growth of lordship, on the other hand the *tun* of a single settler could, in the course of a few generations, so increase its population that to all appearances it became a community much like the settlement of a kindred.

It is sometimes said that 'the Conquest made the king'. This is untrue in so far as, among the Angles at any rate, the monarchy had been strong and the deeds of Offa of Angel by the banks of the Eider were praised, as we have seen,* by Anglian minstrels in Christian England. In other respects the saying is much less than the truth, for the Conquest also made the new aristocracy, and for a time—that is, as long as the war-bands were actually engaged in winning or holding the land of Britain —the Conquest may also have 'made' the freemen; that is, it may have increased the importance of the ordinary spear-wielding ceorls.

To understand the condition of the generality of the English when we first meet them in our literature and laws, it is of primary importance to remember that the freeman had been largely *unmade*, as we have just pointed out, by the extension of the kingdoms. As a state became bigger and the king and his

* Above, pp. 30–1.

men became further removed from contact with the village folk, the gulf between the men who ploughed and the men who fought became greater; and one reason why the ordinary freemen play no part in *Beowulf* and scarcely appear in the pages of Bede is that both these sources represent the conditions at or after the end of the heathen period rather than the conditions of the age of the migration.[14a]

One of the very few ways in which we can track the English village communities back to their beginnings is through the place-names of the villages. These were obviously given not long after the birth of the settlement. If they can be rightly interpreted they may tell us much. We have already tried to use them as material for the history of the Conquest. Now let us see whether they can help us to form any conclusions about the nature of the settlements. Historians of the nineteenth century were almost unanimous in accepting the view that the element *-ing* in our English place-names was patronymic; and that names like Tooting, Nottingham, Kennington all designated settlements made by groups of kinsmen. Nowadays the workers in this field of knowledge are comparing all the early examples of each name and are trying thus to decide whether the *-ing* represents an original plural form (*-ingas*) or a single *-ing* which is a mere possessive. But even in those cases when it becomes possible to assert that the original name was a plural name, we are still a long way from proving that the band of men who had established themselves in that locality were a group of kinsmen. It is said[15] that the plural forms *-ingas* or *-ingaham* often 'have nothing more than some rather indefinite linking force'. They may denote the descendant kin-group of a first settler; but they may also denote his squad of followers, or they 'need mean nothing more than "the people that have to do with" ' the man (or woman) whose name is preserved. All that we can say is that they are 'group names'. The fact is that we are still in the dark, and that if we assert that, say, the Tootings were either the

descendants or the retainers of Tota we are dressing up a speculation in the guise of a dogma. Moreover, in almost all of our
numerous names ending in -*ington* and in a few of those ending
in -*ingham*, the -*ing* seems to be simply a singular possessive.
These names witness it seems to the farms or settlements of individuals. The names containing an -*ing* which represent a
plural -*ingas* are few and exceptional. The character of the
settlement as a whole cannot be decided by them.

THEIR HOMES

In what follows we shall turn our backs on the controversies
about the early institutions of the Anglo-Saxons, and shall collect
what little information there is about their modes of life and
thought; anything which can help us to conceive them, both the
warriors and the workers, as living men. We shall begin by
studying their homes.

In doing this, the first thing to strike our attention is that we
find ourselves in an age of wood. The stone houses built in the
great days of Roman rule are disused and falling into ruin.
There is no new building in stone. The well-to-do, whether
Saxon or British, are lucky if they now inhabit log houses. The
humbler folk we shall find thankful for walls of wattle and daub,
or mud and straw; but with them there is little change from
Roman times. The character of the first habitation in any
particular spot is often revealed by its place-name. Thus, a
name ending in -*wick* (OE. *wic*) should tell us that the place
probably came into existence as a building on the mead, or
hayland, of an earlier settlement. Places ending in *stead* or *fold*
originated in a similar way as outlying buildings; those ending
in *worth* and *cot* had once been the cottages of men who, after the
first colonization of England, were brave enough to live in lonely
surroundings apart from some main community.[16] Since we are
studying the heathen period we are not concerned with these
secondary settlements but with the primary, the original, centres.

Leaving on one side those -*ing* place-names which denote a group of settlers rather than a place, the commonest term for an original settlement is our ending -*ton*.* The word could be applied indiscriminately to a large village containing a group of freemen, to the vill of a king or some other great man (this might equally well be described as a *burh*, a fort), or to the farm of a humble ceorl. It connoted an enclosed agricultural settlement, nothing more definite than that.

It is the existence of the enclosure, giving a fort-like appearance to a tun or burh, which would have seemed strangest to a modern man approaching one of the early settlements. He would see a rampart or stockade, pierced only by a narrow gate which could be held against marauders. But defence was only a secondary consideration; and the peaceful routine of the inhabitants would be clear enough inside the enclosure. There a man would see all the dirt and litter of a farmyard and the miscellaneous buildings of a farm—sheds and byres and barns. The number of these, of course, varied with the prosperity of the settlement. If the village had a lord of some importance, the wooden outhouses would be many, including a small building† for the women and children, a kitchen, and a larder. But the main building, the centre of the settlement where there was a lord, would always be the hall. Some idea about the way these were built can be had from the medieval halls or barns which have survived to our day (Pl. 33).

'Heorot', the hall of the king of the Danes, described in *Beowulf*, is magnificent beyond any ordinary building. It was the poet's ideal, the kind of hall to make men stare and envy. From afar could be seen its gleaming roof, with its stag-horns placed on top of the gables. Outside the hall was a bench on which visitors could wait, and there was a place where they could leave their spears before they entered. Inside the hall the first thing to strike a new-comer would be the smell of wood-smoke, and then through the dim light he would see the open hearth

* OE. *tūn*.   † OE. *būr*, 'bower'.

Fig. 35. A Saxon tun.

running down the centre of the building between the pillars which bore the roof—a hearth with piled-up logs and crackling flames, from which the smoke rose eddying round the draughty room before it could find its way out through holes in the roof. Then the walls would be seen to be hung with arms, and, if it were a royal hall like Heorot, there would be also woven hangings, gold-embroidered.

Round the walls were the benches where the retainers sat through the long evenings, when they feasted and drank and listened to the minstrel, or themselves took their turns at the harp. On these benches they pledged one another, they compared the rings and the arms which had been given them by their lords in return for their services. The veterans,* like petty officers, were separated on the benches from the young soldiers;† but none the less an old warrior could egg on one of the young men to revive an ancient feud and slay a foreign prince, the guest of their lord. The retainers talked of the wonders of their lord's sword, of its magical powers, of the runic lettering on the blade, the gold of its handle, and its ringed pommel. Half-way down one side of the hall was the high-seat of the king or lord. In front of the king sat his spokesman.‡ Along the opposite wall was the place next in honour to the high-seat. The queen or 'lady'§ sat by the side of her husband. The women, who had spent the day in housework or spinning, would come from their bower to attend in the hall during the earlier part of the evening's feast, and the 'lady' and her daughters would bear round the ale.

These feastings in the hall stood out in men's minds among the best things in life: the chink of a byrny when a well-armed warrior strode down the hall, the glint of the spears and swords hanging on the walls, cheered the spirits of the men as they drank at the tables. Their weapons were within easy reach; for who could feel sure that enemies, creeping up outside, might not

* OE. *dugoð.*   † OE. *geogoð.*
‡ OE. *thyle.*   § OE. *hlæfdige,* 'bread-kneeder'.

PLATE 33

Godmersham, Kent. Old barn showing a type of construction used for halls, churches, and barns in the Middle Ages

PLATE 34

Saxon weaver's hut at Bourton. A reconstruction in the British Museum

attempt a surprise attack? Who could tell whether the heavy drinking inside might not end in blows?

So far we have been chiefly concerned with the hall of a great king, as it appears in *Beowulf*. It is the most splendid of its kind; but it may stand for the type, since there was no small similarity in the homes and in the customs of all men of the fighting class. Even a lesser thegn or a substantial ceorl might build himself a log house which reproduced the main features of the larger hall of the great man. As we descend in the social scale, we find the hall becoming smaller, the surrounding outhouses in the *tun* becoming fewer, and the defences dwindling down to the mere hedge which protected the ceorl. Below these, however, in the lowest grades, we find small huts, miserable buildings crowded together in squalid conditions.

Only in the last few years have archaeologists, thanks to the more careful methods of modern excavation, been able to identify any house-sites of the Anglo-Saxons. E. T. Leeds has described[17] vestiges of an early village found in a gravel-bed near the Thames at Sutton Courtenay, south of Oxford. The huts seem to have been arranged in irregular lines (Fig. 36) The men who made them had first dug down for about two feet into the gravel. The construction of the huts above ground was partly revealed by the holes in the gravel, where once had stood the posts which supported the framework of the building. It was inferred that the roof-tree had been stretched from one post to another, perhaps about seven feet above the level of the floor, and that the walls had been formed of mud and straw in alternate layers. Assuredly they were rough-and-ready habitations. The irregularity of their construction can be seen in the inset, which shows the ground-plan of the largest house, one of three rooms. The rooms were separate buildings, but the potsherds found in them indicated that they had belonged to one household. Room no. 3 seemed to have been built as the kitchen for no. 2, and then, when the family increased in size or importance, no. 1 was added as an extra living-room. The floor of the

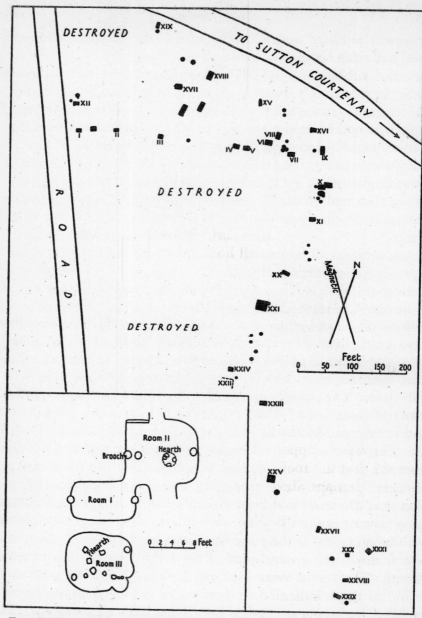

Fig. 36. Plan of Saxon village, near Sutton Courtenay. (The Roman numerals indicate the huts. The rounds in the inset (plan of hut x) indicate the post-holes.)

supposed 'kitchen' during the long period in which it had been used had risen six inches, owing to accumulations of broken pottery and rubbish. Among the things found inside these rooms were: in room no. 1, a bone stiletto, a comb, the pin of a large brooch, and (strange discovery) the skeleton of a middle-aged man, who had been 'buried' on the floor, covered by nothing but a thin blanket of clay, and with him were laid a knife and an ivory comb; in room no. 2, a circular hearth, $2\frac{1}{2}$ feet in diameter, some fragments of grey Roman pottery and Roman glass, and an equal-armed brooch of a fifth-century pattern, a close counterpart of those discovered in the lands between the Elbe and the Weser.*

A somewhat different type of house—perhaps the 'Anglian' type—has been identified on the Car Dyke, in Cambridgeshire.[18] Here there were no hearths, but the floor had been dug out as at Sutton Courtenay, and the shape was irregular. The short lengths of wood found on the site suggest that the walls may have been made of wattle and daub. The thatched roof may have rested on a ridge-pole supported on two posts. In some other respects, also, the hut near Cambridge resembled the Berkshire huts. The inhabitants seem to have been as unpleasant in many of their ways. The floor was a midden of broken bones and potsherds. In one part of the room a dog had been buried. The fragments of the cooking pots were often indistinguishable from the pots in the neighbouring cemeteries in which the ashes of their dead had been placed. These Anglian settlers by the Cam had been so primitive that they threw heated pebbles into their pots to make them boil. And yet they, like the cottagers by the Thames, left behind them traces of some wealth—an ivory armlet and a silver disc—possessions to be compared with the equal-armed brooch of the Berkshire cottage.

These discoveries take us back better than any glass cases in museums to the actual homes and lives of the German peasants who crossed the North Sea to Britain. Here then we see our

---

* See Pl. 21 F, and above, Figs. 8 and 9.

Germanic forefathers in Britain at the bottom of the long ascent to civilization. They are beginning in 'filthy little dens'.[19] A weaver's hut at Bourton-on-the-Water suggests that things were better in the cottages of a later date (Pl. 34). And it is

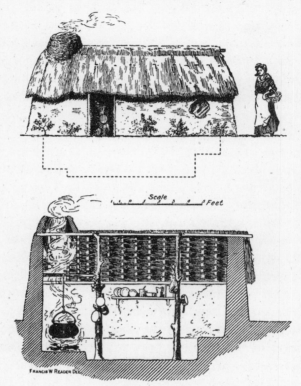

Fig. 37. Primitive type of hut, Athelney.
It survived till *c.* A.D. 1900.

possible to make too much of the squalor even of the Sutton village. Its huts may be small and dark, but in the Fens and in many parts of Somersetshire down to the nineteenth century, English peasants who were decent people lived contentedly in windowless huts of a somewhat similar size and construction (Fig. 37). The six inches of broken sherds and refuse trodden into the gravel of the floor are certainly no good testimonial to the cleanliness of the immigrants.　On the other hand, such things, when meals have to be cooked for generations in one dark narrow chamber, do not necessarily prove an extreme of barbarism.　But what are we to think about bodies buried in the living-rooms?　What were the ideas which led the Berkshire widow to keep the corpse of her man covered with clay by her side, and why did the Anglian cottager leave his dead dog in the hut?　Was it an utter devotion to the physical body, or an incredible slovenliness, curiously out of keeping with the ordered interments of the regular Anglo-Saxon cemeteries? Or are we here in contact with notions about the spirits of the dead?　These are questions to be remembered, even though they cannot be answered.

THEIR DRESS AND ORNAMENTS

We have been able to say something about the best and the worst dwellings of heathen England, about the halls of the great at the end of the heathen period and the huts of the poor made at the beginning of the settlement.　The men and women who lived in these surroundings still escape us.　Is it possible to raise the ghosts of these heathen forefathers of ours, the men who spent their days in hunting, fighting, and ploughing, and the women who spun and wove at home and directed their house-slaves? Can we picture even the clothes they wore?　This must be the first question to which we now direct our attention.　Since there are not English peat-bogs like those of Schleswig, the only pieces of cloth preserved in the heathen graves in England are mere fragments.　They are said[20] to be 'of various qualities, varying from about the texture of a modern flannel shirt to that of Harris tweed'.　The best that we can do is to study the costume por-trayed in the carving of the Franks casket in the British Museum. It must be remembered, however, that this whalebone box is, in all probability, a Northumbrian product, and that while it is the nearest that we can get to a representation of the men of heathen times, it is none the less assigned to a period as late as about 650–750.

On the casket we see that the fighting-men have tunics which hang down to above the knee, much like kilts; garments like sleeved jackets; and cloaks or mantles fastened on the shoulder. Some of the men have clumsy puttees wound round their legs; others have their legs either bare or covered with hose. Altogether it is a costume not unlike that of the Highlander. Close-fitting breeches reaching down to the ankle, like those at Kiel (Pl. 5), and cross-gartered, were also no doubt quite a normal mode of covering the legs throughout the Saxon period. The women shown on the casket, and the men when they are sedentary or men of dignity, wear long tunics reaching to the ankle or nearly to it, and longer mantles also—fine large sweeping garments, with hoods which can be drawn over the head.

With some exercise of imagination we may perhaps obtain a better idea of the appearance of these heathen men and women from their graves.* We can picture the Anglian women with their sleeves caught together at the wrist with the small clasps which are so characteristic a feature of their graves, and their girdle-hangers, like a chatelaine, depending from their tunic-belt and jangling as they move; their men-folk also, long-haired, proud of their cruciform brooches, which become long and flat and increasingly vulgar as the heathen age draws to its close.

The fashions of course changed with the changing decades or generations, if not like ours with the changing years. Even more than ours, in those days of isolation they changed from district to district. Thus, to take a single example, at Sleaford in Lincolnshire there was a large settlement of early immigrants in which the women commonly wore their beads slung in festoons from shoulder to shoulder, both ends of the festoon being fastened to the tunic with a pin.[20a]

Before we turn from the heathen graves of the Saxons, let us pick out one or two of those which are the most richly furnished

---

* e.g. Fig. on p. 101 (the man's shield is indicated by the round dotted line) and Fig. 38.

PLATE 35

A. The Franks casket, Anglian work, about A.D. 650–750
B. The Visit of the Magi, on the front of the casket
C. A scene from the Capture of Jerusalem by Titus, on
the back of the casket

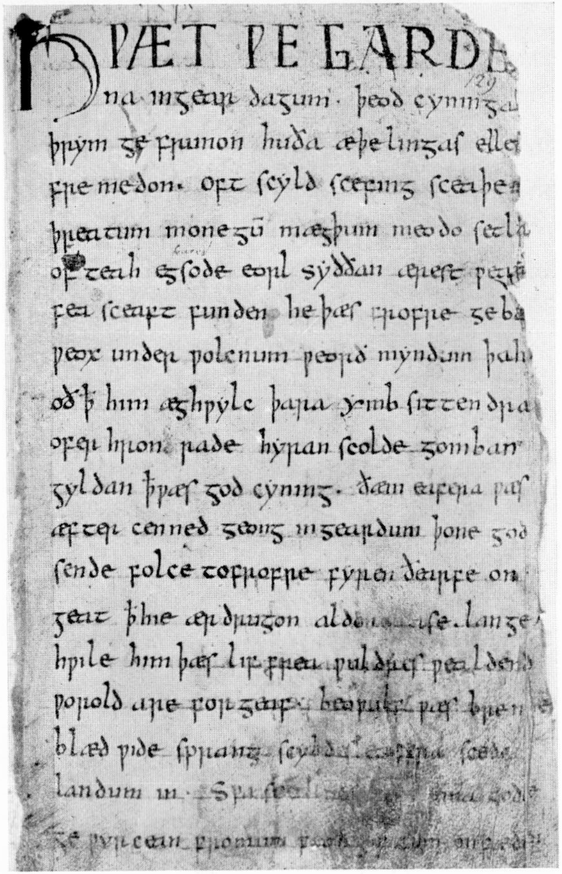

PLATE 36

H WÆT, WE GÁRDEna   in ȝeardaȝum
    þeodcyninȝa   þrym ȝefrunon,
hu ða æþelinȝas   elle[n] fremedon.
Oft Scyld Scefinȝ   sceaþen[a] þreatum,
5 moneȝum mæȝþum   meodoset[a] ofteah,
eȝsode eorl,   syððan ærest wear[ð]
feasceaft funden;   he þæs frofre ȝeba[d,]
weox under wolcnum,   weorðmyndum þah,
oð þæt him æȝhwylc   þara ymbsittendra
10 ofer hronrade   hyran scolde,
ȝomban ȝyldan;   þæt wæs ȝod cyninȝ.
Ðæm eafera wæs   æfter cenned
ȝeonȝ in ȝeardum,   þone ȝod sende
folce to frofre;   fyrenðearfe onȝeat,
15 þæt hie ær druȝon   aldor[le]ase
lanȝe hwile.   Him þæs lilfrea,
wuldres wealdend,   woroldare forȝeaf;
Beowulf wæs breme   —blæd wide spranz—
Scyldes eafera   Scedelandum in.
20 Swa sceal [ȝeonȝ ȝ]uma   ȝode ȝewyrcean,
fromum feohȝiftum,   on fæder

The beginning of the Beowulf MS. (Cotton Vitellius A. xv, reduced) and which show best of all the degree of magnificence to which heathen Anglo-Saxons attained.

As a leading example second only to the Sutton Hoo ship-burial* we may choose the great mound which was made in the sixth century (the period is debated) over the body of a dead chieftain at Taplow. There can be no question that this is the '*hlaw*', the burial-mound, of Tæppa, the unknown warrior from whom the place has borrowed its name.[21]

The site chosen was on a high hill above the Thames with a commanding view over the surrounding country. The mound is a big one, 240 feet round the base, 80 feet in diameter, rising to a height of 15 feet. Tæppa was supplied liberally with precious belongings ornamented for the most part in the Kentish style; and some of them are reproduced in this book (frontispiece to Vol. I, and plate facing page 91).

An interesting comparison with the Taplow tomb may be found in the Asthall barrow which was excavated in 1924.[22] The barrow itself was not so big as that of Taplow, but its position on a spur of the Cotswolds, 440 feet above the sea, made it an even more conspicuous landmark from all the hills round the upper Thames and the Vale of the White Horse. Now while there was possibly no great difference of time separating the burials of the two chieftains, there was a fundamental difference in their religions. The thegns of Tæppa laid his best belongings by his side. They thought of his body continuing in the next world as he had lived in this. The thegns of the nameless hero at Asthall, on the other hand, burnt their lord. They remembered that men had a dual character, and they therefore sent their lord to the other world in the mood of the thegns who buried Beowulf and no doubt with much the same rites. These tumuli, then, reveal to us not a little about the warrior class in the times of heathendom. They show us their magnificence in outward appearance, their gold-embroidered clothing, their gold buckles and their drinking vessels mounted in silver-gilt.[22a] They show us too the

---

* See Appendix, p. 696 *et seq.*

devotion of their thegns and the uncertainty of their heathen beliefs. A great man on the lower Thames, having advanced perhaps from Kent, the kingdom of merchant princes who dressed in cloth of gold, might be buried much like a later Viking. On the other hand, a great man in the upper Thames valley, having perhaps pressed south from Mercia, may have notions about cremation which are deliberately old-fashioned.

These barbaric warrior chiefs, so much alike in spite of variations between cremation and inhumation, are a whole world away from our modern society; it is different if we turn to the homelier articles of the women's graves or consider the craftsmen who made the brooches of the heroes. Here there are points where this oldest England is in touch with modern times. Note for instance the bronze work-box found in an Anglian grave at Burwell, Cambridgeshire (Figs. 38 and 39). Similar though less ornamented work-boxes are not uncommon in women's graves. No doubt they were sold by pedlars. They were of bronze, sometimes gilt. They were neatly made and could be carried, as in this case, in a lady's bag or suspended from her belt. They could contain such sewing things as bronze needles, minute tweezers or knives, and threads of silk or wool. Here then we have a reminder that the gay dresses of the Saxon women about which the clergy will later have much to say were not enjoyed without much labour on the women's part. As formerly in Angel, so again in England, for the women there is an endless round of spinning, weaving, sewing, and dyeing. Of all these activities the work-boxes remain for us the best symbol.

Lastly, the Saxon graves have much to tell us about the skill and the assiduity of the craftsmen, who could make beautiful ornaments like the Kingston brooch and the Sutton Hoo jewellery (Pl. 83),[22b] and those illustrated elsewhere in this volume. Experts agree that some of these Anglo-Saxon jewellers had few, if any, equals in western Europe in their own day and that their work can bear comparison with that of modern craftsmen 'armed with all the appliances of science and machinery'.[23]

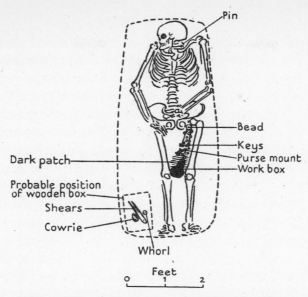

FIG. 38. Burwell, Cambridgeshire. Interment of Anglian woman, perhaps a Christian though buried in the pagan manner (*c.* A.D. 650 or later). The 'dark patch' had probably been a purse.

FIG. 39. Bronze work-box, from above, with repoussé ornamentation. The ends of the box (not here figured) show a man fighting a dragon, in panels.

So far we have picked up a few facts about the well-to-do, who lived in their timbered halls, and about the 'filthy dens' of the poor. What we have learnt is not much, but it is enough to remind us that life in the heathen period had its great contrasts, and that we must suspect historians who dismiss Anglo-Saxon society as if it were all of a piece, picking out a supposed fact about one generation, a surmise about another, and so producing a composite picture which is not true to any one time or place; and labelling it savage or civilized or liberty-loving, according to their varying predilections.

THEIR THOUGHTS

Is there any approach to the minds of the ordinary Englishmen, the ceorls, those whom King Alfred described as the *weorcmen*, 'the workmen'?[24] The nearest that we can get to them is in certain so-called 'Riddles' and gnomic poetry. Both writings come from the Christian period, but both, like *Beowulf*, seem to carry with them ideas from heathen times, mingled with material drawn from Latin literature and the Bible. The Riddle about the Plough, for instance, gives us a picture which, though true for any primitive agricultural society, has about it a characteristic Anglo-Saxon touch.[25] 'My nose is downward; I go deep and dig into the ground; I move as the grey foe of the wood [? man, the wood-cutter] guides me, and my lord who goes stooping as guardian at my tail; he pushes me in the plain, bears and urges me, sows in my track. . . . On one side of me as I go there is green, and on the other side there is black.' These few lines remind us once more of the unceasing labour of the Anglo-Saxon countrymen, which may rightly be mentioned in chapter after chapter since, year in and year out, from early morning to sunset, it was ever bringing wider tracts of forest and waste land under cultivation. Behind the turmoil of the war-bands—slaying and being slain for the honour of their lords, heroically winning (or losing) kingdoms—the ceorls and serfs with bent shoulders were driving their heavy German ploughs, turning the green sods into black furrows, and, as they slowly moved forward, shouting to their team.

The gnomic verses may be called the Book of Proverbs of the Anglo-Saxons, and as is the way with this type of popular literature, they abound with platitudes.[26] But however commonplace, a few quotations may help to bring certain aspects of the Anglo-Saxon world before us. We see, for instance, that these primitive men cling together for support, and pity or suspect those who are not anchored in a village community. 'Hapless is he who must needs live alone.' 'Well should one keep a friend in all ways; often a man passes by the village afar off where he knows he has no certain friend. Unfriended, unblessed, a man takes wolves, for companions, a dangerous beast; full often that companion rends him. There should be terror of the grey wolf. . . .' This and other warnings about fierce beasts like the boar or the bear remind us of the constant apprehension in the minds of the country folk, isolated in clearings reclaimed from the wild nature around them—the fear of creatures of all kinds which lurked in the woods and the wastes. By the side of these passages let us place the early law found in the codes of both Kent and Wessex.[27] 'If a man from far or a stranger quits the road, and neither shouts nor blows a horn, he shall be assumed to be a thief [and as such] may be either slain or put to ransom.'

The thoughts of the seafaring folk are also illustrated in the gnomic poetry. 'Weary shall he be who rows against the wind. Full often one blames the coward with reproaches so that he loses courage, and draws his oar on board.' At the time when these verses were composed, the typical seaman had become a Frisian. But what is true of the Frisian in the eighth or ninth century must have been equally true of the Anglo-Saxon in earlier days.

'Dear is the welcome one to the Frisian wife when the ship comes to rest. His vessel has come, and her husband is at home, her own provider; and she bids him come in, washes his sea-stained garment, and gives him fresh clothes. She gives him on land what love requires. A wife should keep faith with her husband; often she defames a man with her vices; many a one is steadfast in mind, many a one is prying; she loves strange men when the other travels afar.'

Now let us again change our standpoint, and look, not at the 'workmen', but at the chiefs and their war-bands, the inhabitants of the great halls. For these we can turn to *Beowulf*, the only lengthy heroic poem of the Anglo-Saxons which has survived, and we shall be able to see therein much of the workings of the primitive English mind.

Since our last quotation from the gnomic poetry ended with a passage which took the low view of women so often affected by the writers of proverbs, let us make amends by saying at once that, as a rule, women appear in a more favourable light in Old English verse. They mix with the men on terms of equality. They minister to their wants. We recognize the important ladies of the heathen graves whose keys had jangled from their girdles, and whose work-boxes had been neatly supplied with needles and sewing materials. In *Beowulf* they are 'the people's pledge of peace', they 'weave peace' for their men-folk as well as their clothes. They help them with their advice and influence. They are respected, as Germanic women were said to be respected in the times of Tacitus.

In the men who appear in the heroic poetry, it is not mere fancy which inclines us to recognize features of family likeness to modern Englishmen—features both good and bad. Even the monster-fighting of Beowulf foreshadows the restless energy which has characterized men of Anglo-Saxon descent. Beowulf was not happy sitting still. He was said to be 'the strongest of mankind'; but the strongest in body and not in mind. His hunger to win fame, to do something that demanded endurance and heroism, made him seek out his monsters, as the moderns have sought out their conquests over nature in Central Africa, the Polar regions, or the Himalayas.

For those unacquainted with the plot of the *Beowulf* poem, it must suffice to say that the main story turns on three encounters. In the first of them Beowulf, the hero of the Geats (these almost certainly are the Götar, the southern neighbours of the Swedes), hearing that the country of the Danes is vexed by a monster called Grendel, goes with his followers to the court of Hrothgar the Danish king, at Leire in Zealand, and after some talk and feasting in Heorot, the splendid wooden hall recently built by that king, remains to fight the monster single-handed. In the second episode another monster, Grendel's mother, in revenge for Grendel's death, plays havoc in Heorot, and Beowulf seeks her out in her home beneath the waters of a mere in an eerie spot on a lonely heath. The third episode is later. After feats of war in the land of the Frisians and elsewhere, and after ruling well for fifty years as king of his own people, the hero engages in his last encounter. He kills a fire-breathing dragon who is guarding a hoard of gold; but in doing so receives a poisonous and fatal wound.

If we are to interpret the Anglo-Saxons by *Beowulf* we should know what was the intention of the poem. Did it aim rather at amusement or at edification, or was it simply a blend of old stories, a form of history?

The best way to understand what was supplied by the author is to understand what was demanded by his audience. What was it that the retainers in the hall wanted? First and foremost, to be taken out of themselves, and the commonplaceness of every-day life. Tales of monsters could do this, and the creatures of *Beowulf* were prize monsters: Grendel, the dark death-shadow from the misty moors, who entrapped warriors old and young, the creature from whose eyes came a weird light, who could open the door of the hall by touching it, who thirsted for human blood and swallowed men bite by bite, not leaving even their feet and hands. Grendel was frightful and Grendel's mother was equally uncanny—a mere-wife who clutched at men with horrid claws from the depths of a lonely lake. The world was full of monsters —animals of the deep, with tusks; and animals of the moors, like the spotted fire-breathing dragon who gave Beowulf his death-wound, biting his neck with its sharp teeth.

The warriors, returned from chase or war-path, and safe in their hall, when cheered by their ale-cups, liked to hug the thought of the fearful things outside the hall. And so the author of *Beowulf* enlarges on the horrors. For the first time the melancholy note of northern scenery is sounded. We move in a land of haunted moors, of 'wolf-slopes, wind-swept headlands, and dangerous marsh-paths, where the mountain-stream falls down under the darkness of the rocks'. There was the home of the monsters, a blood-stained and turbid lake overhung by gray rocks and mountain trees. The hunted stag would die rather than enter its water. Again those who seek out the lair of the 'twilight foe', that is, the dragon which flies flaming through the night skies, must go to the loneliest barrow of a desolate moor, where in subterranean chambers the enemy of mankind guards a hoard of heathen gold.

The warriors in addition to tales of dragon-killing expected to hear from their minstrels endless variations on the theme of fighting and bloodshed among men. No one could tire of such a subject (was it not at once the business and the sport of eorls?), but these stories also must be rendered in a minor key. Inside the hall revelry, and outside by contrast to it the evil things that beset men—a sobering thought. Even when the Danes are celebrating the double victory of Beowulf over Grendel and his dam, one of the braves 'told a true and *sad* tale'. Beowulf himself, before his last battle with the dragon, is made to dwell, in the characteristic Anglo-Saxon strain, upon the mournful lot of a father who loses a son. 'Unceasingly at every morn he is reminded of the passing of his son. . . . Sorrowful he gazes at his son's room . . . the deserted wine-hall, abandoned, a lodgement for the winds, its merriment all gone. The horsemen sleep, the heroes are in their grave, there is no music of the harp, no merrymaking in the courts as once there was.'

When the warriors were not exalted by battle-fury they

Fig. 40. Vendel, Sweden; helmet of iron with bronze mountings, partly gilded,
showing warriors like those of *Beowulf*.

(Recent excavations show that the face guards were worn further forward than
in the above reconstruction and were large enough to meet over the wearer's chin.
The new reconstruction is illustrated in *Fornvännen* (1950), 5, Fig. 2. A prototype of
this helmet was used in the Roman armies in the fourth century. Cf. Lindqvist in
Acta Archaeologica, iii (1932), 21–38). For a similar helmet of Swedish make found in
Suffolk, see Plate 85 and pp. 707–8.

inclined to melancholy and gloomy regrets. This was something more deeply rooted than a passing fashion. Men's songs were 'true and sad' because death was always round the corner. Any day a feud might spring up which might be their end. If they were merry in the hall they did not forget the stories of how men had been surprised when feasting. The spearmen might wake in the night to find the hall filled with smoke, which did not come from the hearth. The wooden walls could be fired by an enemy. Here, for instance, is the beginning of the fragmentary *Lay of Finnsburh*.[28]

'Then the king, young in war, spoke: "This is neither the dawn from the east, nor does a dragon fly here, nor are the gables [the horns] of this hall here burning, but they are launching a sudden attack; the birds (of battle) are singing; the grey wolf yells; there is din of spears; shield answers to shaft. Now gleams the wandering moon through the clouds; now evil deeds come to pass which will bring destruction to this people. But awake now, my warriors, grasp your shields, think of brave deeds, fight in the front, be resolute." '

Can it be wondered that this fighting aristocracy dwelt almost morbidly on the thought of death? They came back to it, but scarcely pretended to understand it, varying from moment to moment in the explanation they offered about the object of existence. Read, for instance, the speeches on this subject attributed to Beowulf. At one time the end of life is Fame: 'Each of us must expect an end of living in this world; let him who may, win glory before death, for that is best at last for the departed man of war.' Sometimes fame almost crystallizes into the winning of gold. In his dying speech Beowulf is reconciled to death because he has given his own life for the dragon's hoard of gold; the 'countless store of twisted gold' is an end in itself. None the less, the chief does not fight simply for his own gain. He fights for his people. He is the guardian, 'the shepherd of his people', and the warriors in their turn, and especially the hearth-companions of the chief, could find the effective religion of life in the service of their lord. The true thegn would rather die with his lord than desert him

in the fight and carry back his weapons to his home. 'Death',
says the one faithful follower of Beowulf, 'is better for all warriors
than a shameful life.'

And when death comes, the warriors have to send their lord
richly provided and with honour befitting his station to the
realms of the dead. The poem of *Beowulf* opens with lines which
tell how the companions of Scyld Scefing gave to the sea the
eponymous ancestor of the Spear-Danes, equipping the ship with
swords and coats of mail, laying out Scyld upon it with treasures
on his breast and launching this kingly bier into the sea, to let
the ocean carry him where it would (see p. 710). The same note
is struck at the end of the epic, in the lines which describe the
funeral of Beowulf.

'Then the people [*leode*] of the Geats made ready for him on the
ground a splendid pyre, hung round with helmets, battle-targes, bright
corselets, as he had craved; then the sorrowing men laid in the midst
the famous prince, their loved lord. The warriors began to kindle on
the barrow the greatest of funeral-fires; the wood-reek mounted up dark
above the smoking glow, the crackling flame, mingled with the cry of
weeping—the tumult of the winds ceased—until it had consumed the
body, hot to the heart. Sad in spirit, they lamented the sorrow of their
souls, the slaying of their lord; likewise the aged woman [? his widow]
with bound tresses sang a dirge... [words missing in the manuscript] ...
the sky swallowed up the smoke.

'Then the people of the Weders [i.e. the Geats] wrought a mound,
which was lofty and broad, at the edge of the headland, visible far and
wide to seafarers; and in ten days they finished the beacon of the man
mighty in battle; the remnant of the pyre they compassed round with
a wall, as exceeding wise men might most worthily devise it. They laid
in the barrow rings and ornaments, all such adornments as men, eager
for combat, had erstwhile taken from the hoard; they let the earth keep
the treasure of warriors, the gold in the ground. ... Then men bold in
battle, sons of chieftains, twelve in all, rode about the mound; they
were minded to utter their grief, to lament the king, to make a chant
and to speak of the man; they exalted his heroic life and praised his
valorous deed with all their strength.'

Here, at the end of the poem, the intention of the author is put most plainly. He had aimed with all his skill at exalting the heroic life.

When we put *Beowulf* aside and glance at the other evidences of Anglo-Saxon heathendom, we realize at once how specially scanty these are.[29] The scantiness may be explained in two ways. We may, if we like, say that we have here a testimony to the efficiency of the censorship set up by the Christian Church in England. But other explanations cannot be disregarded: that Germanic heathenism had not stood well the crossing of the North Sea; or that it had never recovered its vigour in Britain. In northern Germany, in the first century of our era, the religion of Nerthus as described by Tacitus had been a well-organized cult, with its sacred island and its image of the goddess whose mysteries had drawn the neighbouring tribes together in a bond of common worship. But among the Germanic settlements in Britain we find no trace of religious centralization. There is no one holy place which is a centre for the different kingdoms. Even within the independent states there is little to suggest that religion is highly organized. A king has his own wooden temple within its sacred enclosure, and the wooden effigies of his favourite gods, each image placed on its small altar. But there is no great outcry when his temple is desecrated. There is not in heathen England, as among the continental tribes, an outstanding holy tree or holy pillar which attracts to itself the general devotion of the people. True, we hear of a chief-priest* in Northumbria, but if we may judge from his actions he was not the head of an organized hierarchy. In Norway and later in Iceland the great landowner who erected his temple and placed therein his images took it upon himself to set up, each in his own neighbourhood, as the priest† of the district, with a right of levying contributions for his trouble. If this custom was followed in England, it was not the only arrangement. There are

* *primus pontificum*, also called *pontifex sacrorum*.   † *Goði*.

passages in Bede and elsewhere which indicate a more professional priesthood. Thus the Londoners, when they rejected their
bishop Mellitus (617–18), preferred to be under their priests.
The Northumbrian chief priest was not allowed either to carry
arms or to ride on anything but a mare. The chief priest* of the
South Saxons, who cursed Wilfrid when driven by a storm onto
their coast, and sought to bind him with magic, has the look of
an expert.

Since it is in London and in Sussex that we read of heathen
priests taking a strong line in opposition to Christianity, it is interesting to note (though this may of course be only a coincidence)
that it is also in the south-east of the island that we have the
clearest traces of heathenism in place-names—for example, in
names containing *harrow* (OE. *hearg*, a sacred place), and in
those with an element derived from the Old English word *wig*,
or *weoh* (meaning an idol, or something sacred), such as Weedon
in Buckinghamshire.

As for the gods of the Germanic pantheon, it has been calculated that, out of the thousands of Saxon place-names, only six
were compounded with the name of Woden, and only nine with
Thunor.[30] The other Germanic gods were almost completely
ignored. The settlers were matter-of-fact people in their nomen-
clature. They described their farms or villages by the names of
their owners, or by physical characteristics. Is it probable that
the gods who appear so little in their place-names came much
into their thoughts?

The few glimpses which we catch of Woden in England reveal
him in a variety of characters, but omit many features which in
the past have been fastened on him by borrowing from the Odin
of Scandinavian mythology. He is not the All-Father: he is no
heathen counterpart of the Christian Deity; he has no well-
appointed residence like Valhalla. He is not a one-eyed god who
wanders about the world. He appears to be first and foremost
the god of War. He can give the victory. He can be appealed

---

* *princeps sacerdotum.*

to in stress of battle; he can be appeased by a massacre. He can make an imposing earthwork like Woden's Dyke—'the Wansdyke'.

For the rest, we chiefly hear of Woden in England as a name which in later times could be employed in spells, or to head the genealogy of a royal family, and there, linked with other gods or demi-gods, give the dynasty the stamp of respectability. We have seen that in Germany Woden was a new-fashioned god, introduced late to the northern tribes as the special protector of the kings and the military class. In England the mass of the immigrants had for a time become fighting-men; and it was thus that Woden nearly rivalled Thunor in the number of his place-names, and obtained a lead in other directions.

The English Thunor, so far as our positive information goes, has even less in common with the Norse Thor than has Woden with the Norse Odin, for the fact is that we know Thunor only as the Thunderer.

He and the other gods and goddesses are mere names. The Tiw of our Tuesday, though equated with Mars, had clearly been given a back place among war-gods after the rise of Woden. The Frig of Friday was equated with Venus, and in late chronicles was said to be Woden's wife.

So little is known about these gods and the mythology of English heathenism that there can be no satisfactory comparison between the English and the Scandinavian systems. The similarities in the names and terminology are indeed notable. Thus the Old English word for earth, *middangeard*, carries with it an inference that the earth was the middle-dwelling, the habitation of men, because above or beyond it was the realm of the gods, and below it was hell, the place of spirits. If the gods were no happy family-party and their abode no Valhalla, it had at least a name, the unlovely name *neorxna-wang*.

Of lesser beings we hear of *wælcyrian*, corpse-choosing witches rather than reputable war-maidens like their counterparts the Valkyries of the north; also of *eotenas*, giants, not of the stuff to dream of waging war against the great gods, but mere unpleasant monsters, perhaps man-eaters.

Some knowledge of the ways of our heathen ancestors is derived from a work of Bede called *De Temporum Ratione.*[31] In it he explains the English names of the months and the reasons for them. February was called '*Sol-monath,* because of the cakes which were then offered to the gods'. 'To the gods'—surely to the oldest of all nature deities, the Sun. March was called '*Rhed-monath,* because of sacrifices to the goddess Rheda'. April was *Eostur-monath,* and its sacrifices were made to Eostra, apparently akin to the Greek Ἐώς, the goddess of the dawn. Then after the summer months—the months in which men were fully occupied with their milkings, their harvest, and their weeding— came September, the holy month (*Haleg-monath*),* the month of sacred rites; November (*Blot-monath*), the month of sacrifices, when the cattle which could not be fed through the winter were slaughtered and devoted to the gods; a season when heathenism more than ever spelt bloodshed—bloodshed no doubt accompanied by drinking and revelry. ('Gratia tibi, bone Iesu,' sighs Bede, 'Thou hast converted us from these deceits and hast allowed us to offer Thee sacrifices of praise.') Last (or more strictly first, since the Germanic year began with the winter) came the sixty days of Yule,† covering both December and January. It was only by Roman-Christian influence that this winter season Yule came to be restricted to Christmas. In the mid-winter feast of heathen times sacrifices were probably made for good luck and peace in the coming year, and men dressed themselves up in the skins and masks of animals. Bede calls the octave corresponding to our Christmas and New Year holiday, *Modranect,* Mother-night. In Roman days the pagan soldiers along the Wall erected their altars to the *Matres.* 'The Mothers' —but what Mothers?—were still remembered by their successors.

From glimpses of this oldest England given in passages like the above chapter of Bede, and from the survival of heathen

---

* Better *halig-monath.*   † *Geol* or *Guil.*

fertility rites

customs in Christian times, we see how mixed were the ideas and
how diversified were the practices of Anglo-Saxon heathenism;
and that the cults of Thunor and Woden were but novelties
superimposed on far older and better-rooted beliefs. The king
or rich landowner might build his timbered temple. The teaching of the priests might endow it with a tradition of sanctity. The
slaughtering of the cattle might take place within the holy enclosure of the temple, surrounded by a holy wood. Men might
troop to these sacred spots, and there see the blood flow, be
themselves sprinkled or daubed with blood, gorge themselves on
an unaccustomed superfluity of meat; they might drink and
make merry. But the religious usages which were nearest their
hearts were older, incalculably older, rites which they believed
would appease the spirits of the sun and the corn, bringing
fertility to themselves and their crops and their herds: the offerings of cakes to the Sun (if that is indeed the meaning of *Sol-
monath*); the charming of the plough on Plough Monday (the
first Monday after Twelfth Night), and the May festival. In this
the whole village joined in order to persuade the fertility spirit
to return to their homes and fields, the villagers covering themselves in the greenery and flowers of the new spring life, dancing
round a tree, washing in the dew, or ducking folk in water in
order to mix with the water spirit, lighting 'need-fires' to attract
the spirit of warmth and sunshine, passing their cattle through
the fire, and processing solemnly through the fields, if not with the
image then with the symbol of divinity. The vegetation rites
which accompanied the coming of the spring, and the harvest
rites were everywhere of first importance. But their details varied
in different parts of the country. At any of the village festivals
there might be sacrifices, since it was good to eat the spirit of the
god. At any of them there might be sprinkling with blood, immersions, bonfires, since by such means there could be contact
with the spirits of life, of moisture, of heat. Men danced and sang,
but there was more than merry-making. The rites were necessary to bring good increase in agriculture.

Though the myths of the heathen English were almost entirely obliterated by the subsequent centuries of Christianity, a trace of them remains in the story of Scyld Scefing. The story as told by William of Malmesbury runs as follows:[32] 'Sceaf, as they say, was brought as a child in a ship without oars to Scandza, a certain island in Germany. . . . He was asleep, and a sheaf of corn lay beside his head. He was on this account called Sceaf (in modern spelling Sheaf) and was received as a prodigy by the people of that country and carefully fostered.'

This is not the place to enter into such controversial questions as the original version of the story or the relation of Sceaf to Scyld, to the Nerthus of Tacitus, or to the Vanir gods of the Scandinavians. What is undeniable and significant is that, though the organized Nerthus cult is not reproduced in England, some ideas and usages resembling those of the cult were clearly transferred from the Continent to our island; and that this primitive 'Fertility religion' was so well established that whatever the name of the great god who for the moment was favoured by the rulers of the State, whether Thunor or Woden—or Christ— the old practices could be maintained by the cultivators of the soil, practices essential for prosperity in farming and for good luck in life.

We see then that Woden and Thunor and the great gods introduced into Britain by Saxon conquerors were in some ways less important than the lesser powers like Sceaf and Weland the Smith (who was a living tradition in the times of Alfred) and Wyrd, the irresistible Fate who ruled even the gods; and all the rout of miscellaneous beings and spirits who accompanied the immigrants—elves of all kinds (of the downs, of the woods, of the fields, of the water), giants, nightmares, dragons, sea-monsters (*nicors*), altogether a mixed lot. The number and variety of these supernatural beings is another testimony to the confusion which reigned in the minds of the Anglo-Saxon immigrants. Remembering the diversity of their burial customs, we understand how the small communities of the heathen period were too isolated for their religious notions to be pooled or worked into a coherent system like that of the Icelanders in a later age. The unseen powers which surrounded the Anglo-Saxons filled them with all kinds of confused apprehensions. They had to resort in self-defence to charms and magic and sacrifices. So far as we know, human beings were not sacrificed as among the Scandinavians and the Frisians; but the pits of black greasy earth interspersed with bones of oxen, horses, pigs, and goats, sometimes found in the neighbourhood of Anglo-Saxon cemeteries remind us that their heathen customs were often ugly enough and reeked of blood. The feasts and the less horrid of their rites at the spring and autumn festivals had their hold on the people, but belief in the greater gods was weak. Heathen society was ripe for conversion. The world of Woden was ready to become a world created and ruled by an Almighty Father, dominated by his wonder-working saints, and tended by his bishops and clergy The heavenly powers might change, but the underworld of monsters and evil spirits would remain to be marshalled by Satan into a host of demons (*unholdan*), the enemies of Christian men.

From Franks Casket: Sigurd in his burial mound; his wife and horse standing near.

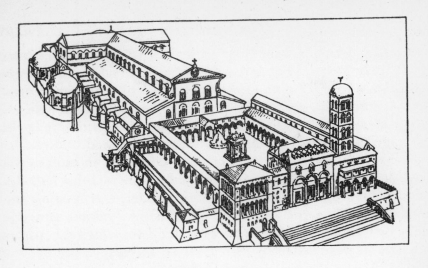

VIII—Part I

THE CONVERSION, TO 633

IT is inevitable that the history of the Conversion of the English should be told on different lines from that of their conquest of Britain. About the conquest so little is known that we have laboriously to fit together the few existing facts or clues. For the Conversion we have the lengthy *Ecclesiastical History* of Bede in addition to many *Lives* of saints. The difficulty is no longer one of accumulating material, but of eliminating it. Though the Conversion is from almost every point of view the most decisive event in the history of the English before the Norman Conquest, it does not call for minute treatment here. The modern reader who is interested in the subject should turn to the pages of Bede, or to classics based on Bede, like *The Early English Church History* of William Bright. All that need be done in this and the following chapter is to tell enough of the story to explain the change which transformed the Anglo-Saxon kingdoms in the seventh century—that century into which were crowded the establishment of the Church in England, the first stirrings of a sense of English unity, the beginnings of English

HEADPIECE.—Exterior of old St. Peter's, Rome.

literature, of architecture, of education, of Christian civilization in all its branches. These are the subjects which most deserve attention, and not the tangled stories of the several petty dynasties. Accordingly, in what follows we shall only give where necessary just enough of the framework of the political history to recall the main facts, well known to most from childhood.

Before we come to the story of Pope Gregory's mission to the English, we must understand how Celtic Christianity had developed new vigour in the west of the island; and, casting our minds back some two centuries, we must observe the progress made by Christianity during the generations in which the Angles and Saxons were fastening their hold on Britain.

THE BRITISH CHURCH

It will be remembered that as the world of Imperial Rome fell into ruins in the fifth century, as the civilized men within the Empire saw their homes destroyed by barbarians, their wives and families carried into slavery, and their best lands appropriated by the invaders, they turned from the disappointments of this world to hopes of redress in a future existence. Incidents which emerged through the obscurity of that age—the mission of St. Patrick to Ireland, and of St. Ninian to the Picts of Galloway; the controversy about the views of Pelagius the Briton; the visits of the Gallo-Roman, St. Germanus, to our island; other visits of Britons to Gaul—all these were illustrations of the new life now infused into British Christianity.

In the sixth century the force of the revival was directed into the monastic movement. This movement had taken its rise in the fourth century in Egypt, where hermits in the desert, refugees from the wickedness of the great cities, joined themselves into communities for common worship and discipline. When monasticism came to the west, it swept, with a current as irresistible as the gulf-stream, up to the remotest islands and headlands of Gaul, of west Britain, of Ireland. To understand how this came about, we must fix our eyes on Lérins, an island of the French Riviera. For in that spot were gathered Gallo-Romans who wished to emulate the holy men of the Egyptian desert, and others who had escaped from the shipwreck of the world. Thither Britons also had found their way; among them it seems Patrick, the runaway slave from Ireland, and Illtud, the reputed teacher of the Welsh saints, Samson, Paul Aurelian, and perhaps Gildas and David. It seemed, as well it might, a blessed and happy island, and there, in its sunshine and among its pine-trees and flowers, seeds of oriental asceticism and oriental lore were transplanted to the congenial soil of the Celtic spirit.

We may speak of such a spirit and of a Celtic Christianity, but we must remember that there was no one Celtic Church. Its two branches which for our present purpose must be distinguished are the Church of the Britons and that of the Irish. Among their common characteristics was the influence received from Lérins, which brought the monastic enthusiasm in both peoples to a white heat. The influence was transmitted to Ireland by St. Patrick, to the Britons by St. Illtud and his pupils.[1] Illtud himself, described in the eighth century as the *magister Britannorum*,[2] the founder of the first recorded British monastery and the first monastic school, that at Llanwyt,* is but a shadowy figure, for the legends which tell of him in youth as a keen hunter and a soldier of Arthur are not trustworthy. Of his reputed pupils David (*c.* 520–88) calls for notice, not only as the patron Saint of Wales, but as an extreme type of the new monastic Christianity of the Britons. We have no first-hand evidence for him as for St. Patrick, but the eleventh-century account of the austerities of his community at Menevia (now St. Davids) probably gives a fair idea of the way in which he encouraged his disciples to abandon themselves to unmitigated asceticism. To avoid idleness, the mother of vices, his monks yoked themselves instead of oxen to their ploughs. To avoid gluttony, they were

* i.e. Llan-Illtud, *Llan* meaning an enclosure, or more definitely a church or monastery.

allowed but one meal a day—a meal of bread and herbs, seasoned with salt. To enforce the monks' vow of poverty, not even one penny was received for the use of the monastery. To exclude the lukewarm in faith, any one who wished to join the community had to remain as a suppliant for ten days, as in Egypt, at the doors of the monastery, and then, whether rich or poor, he was 'received naked, as one escaping from shipwreck'.[3]

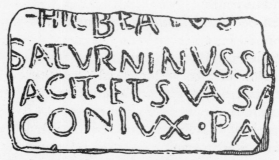

Fig. 41. Tombstone of Beatus Saturninus; from the churchyard of Llansadurn (a name which means the church of Saturn[in]us); inscribed 'Hic Bea[tus] Saturninus se[pultus j]acit et sua sa[ncta] coniux pa[ce]'. (? 6th century.)

The devotions required of the brethren after being admitted to the monastery were, it is said, no less exacting. Whole days and nights were spent without food and without sleep, in watchings and prayers and genuflexions. Thus, in an age of violence and crime, St. David and his disciples attempted to take the Kingdom of Heaven by storm, and in this way to assuage the memory of mundane defeats at the hands of the Saxons. Theirs was the extreme limit of austerity, and though there were among the Britons more moderate men, like Gildas, who criticized the ways of the extremists, David illustrates well enough the revolution which transformed the British Church during the fifth and sixth centuries.

The great number of saints who have left their names in the place-names of Wales and of Cornwall is in itself sufficient to justify the presumption that the tests of sanctity among the Britons were not usually so severe as those exacted at St. Davids. Many of these Celtic saints were, in fact, but well-born clerks in holy orders: men of sufficient wealth to be able to found and endow the small churches and monasteries which have perpetuated their names. Such a one was, for example, Saturninus, whose tombstone (Fig. 41) tells the world that by the side of 'The Blessed Saturninus' there was laid 'his holy consort'.

It has often been a reproach against the British Church that its saints were so fully occupied in saving their own souls that they had neither time nor energy left for the salvation of their neighbours. But this is an over-statement. To give the Britons their due, it must be remembered that in addition to Pelagius, the learned heretic, St. Patrick, and St. Ninian, they produced St. Kentigern (527–612), to whose preachings on the banks of the Clyde, those which were interrupted by a mad prophet, reference has already been made.* Moreover, there are abundant legends which record visits of Gildas, David, and other Britons to encourage the struggling post-Patrician Church in Ireland. Thanks to the enthusiasm with which the Celtic peoples adopted monastic Christianity at this time, there was during the period of the Saxon invasions a coming and going on the western seas of Britain in notable contrast with that on the eastern seas—holy men setting out from Ireland as well as from Britain, seeking both to learn from and to teach their fellow men on the opposite shore of the Channel. If, however, it be objected that the missionaries of British birth worked among their fellow Celts but never among their German enemies, the statement cannot be denied. Though the British clergy wavered for a moment when St. Augustine on his arrival in England asked for their co-operation, their aloofness was a deliberate policy. It was not the result of torpor, for the vitality of the Church is demonstrated by Bede's reference to the monastery of Bangor, near Chester. This community, founded at the end of the sixth century, was soon

* Above, p. 195.

reputed to number more than two thousand monks. It was organized into groups of three hundred and, according to Bede, it produced 'many most learned men'.[4] The Britons gloried in their policy of aloofness. It was a consolation to them to think that the invaders who had stolen their lands and slain their clergy were heading straight for hell-fire and an eternity of punishment.

Whatever the explanation, there is no doubt of the fact that while the British Church was not lifeless, it refused to propagate Christianity among the Anglo-Saxons. Thus the story of St. David, and of the Welsh Church, brings us to a dead end. Between the British Church and the English there was from first to last a complete, or almost complete, barrier. We must therefore turn to the other branch of the Celtic Church, to Ireland and to the followers of St. Patrick; and here it will at once become apparent that exclusiveness was not especially a Celtic characteristic.

ST. COLUMBA

The development of the Irish or 'Scottish'* Church after the death of St. Patrick (461) is obscure. When it reappears into clearer light at the end of the sixth century, the mission stations of St. Patrick and his disciples have blossomed into large monasteries. The period when these monasteries needed to learn from Britons like David and Gildas was passed, and the Irish were already excelling their masters. The monasteries were small towns or forts with inmates numbered by the hundred, and even by the thousand. The site of one of them—the monastery at Nendrum on Strangford Lough—has been recently excavated.[5] The spade revealed three concentric cashels, or dry-built stone walls, nearly circular in form. The church or oratory was the most important building inside the enclosure, and scattered round the

---

* It may be as well again to remind any readers not versed in the history of these times that the name 'Scots' designates until the tenth century, firstly the inhabitants of Ireland, and secondly, small colonies of Irish who had migrated to the west coast of north Britain, i.e. to Argyllshire.

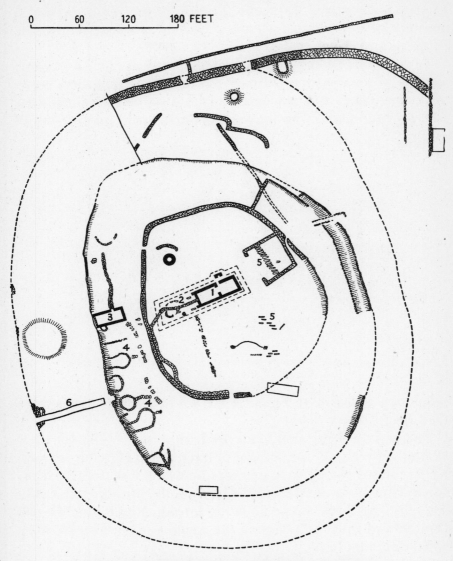

FIG. 42. Plan of Irish Monastery at Nendrum, Co. Down.
1. The Church. 2. Path round inner cashel wall. 3. The school. 4. Cells.
5. Graves. 6. Raised path to the quay.

church were others, no doubt the huts of the brethren, and a number of miscellaneous buildings, such as the refectory, the kitchen, and the guest-house.

In addition to the large tribal monasteries, which became centres of an unexampled enthusiasm for learning and book-making, Ireland also produced unfailing supplies of anchorites, like St. Mac Dara, who lived singly or in small groups, and of

FIG. 43. St. Mac Dara's primitive church on St. Mac Dara's Island off the coast of Galway.

religious wanderers who took to the sea to drift or sail wherever God might direct them.

The best authenticated of all the Irish saints is Columcille, or Columba (521-97),[6] the founder of Iona, a man of heroic temper, whose furious energy gave the impulse which was to carry Scottish or Scottish-trained missionaries from the Moray Firth to the Thames; and there can be no better introduction to the Scottish Church and to its influence on the Anglo-Saxons than the story of St. Columba himself.

The great-great-grandfather of Columba has already appeared in these pages. He was Niall of the Nine Hostages, High King of Ireland, whose raid on the west of Britain (*c.* 400) had helped to shake down the tottering Roman Empire in this island, and

PLATE 37

Early monastic settlement on the rock of Skellig Michael, Kerry, Ireland

PLATE 38

Iona, showing in the foreground the Vallum of the monastery

had probably swept off the boy Patrick into Irish captivity. Columba then, with the hot blood of Irish kings in his veins, was by nature impetuous, masterful, and adventurous. The story goes that when about forty years old he involved his clan in war for the possession of a book. He had surreptitiously copied the codex belonging to his former master, and the High King of Ireland had given judgement against Columba on the principle that 'To every cow belongs her calf and to every book its son book'.[7] Soon after the war, perhaps in expiation, Columba abandoned his native Ulster. 'He sailèd forth resolving to go on pilgrimage for Christ from Ireland into Britain.'[8] He chose the island of Iona as the site of his new monastery because it was close to a colony of his countrymen (called after their Irish motherland Dal Riata). This was placed on the west coast of modern Scotland, near the point where the northern Picts marched with the Britons of Strathclyde. Columba succeeded in giving the Scottish colony a new political importance as well as in reviving their Christianity and in converting also their old enemies the Picts. Columba thus won for Iona an extraordinary supremacy. The Dalriatic Scots, if not also the Picts, regarded it as their mother-church. Columban communities arose even in Skye and the Islands. Many important monasteries in Ireland still obeyed him as their founder. All looked to Iona for direction and rule; and when Columba himself returned to Ireland in later life, he was received at Clonmacnois 'as if he were an angel'. Crowds bowed with their faces to the ground, and 'tying together a canopy [or barrier] of poles, they had it borne by four men around the Saint as he walked', lest he should be thronged by the crowd.[9]

What was it that raised Columba to such pre-eminence? From Adamnan's biography of the Saint (written about 100 years after his death) it is clear that it was his character rather than his royal birth which gave him his dominating influence. It would be hard to find a man more virile and untiring. 'He never could spend the space of even one hour without study, or prayer, or writing, or even some manual labour.' He was a typical Irishman, vehement, irresistible: hear him curse a niggardly rich man or bless the heifers of a poor peasant; see him follow a robber who had plundered a friend, cursing the wretch to his destruction, following him 'to the water's edge, wading up to the knees in the clear green sea-water, with both his hands raised to heaven . . .'[10] In the well-known story of

Fig. 44. St. Columba. From a ninth-century Codex at St. Gall.

his last day, what emerges is the love shown by and to the Saint as he wanders round the farmstead of the community: he gives thanks when he sees the two heaps of winnowed corn; he blesses the old white horse, which comes and puts its head into his bosom; he climbs the hill and blesses the whole monastery.

Here we have a good example of the spirit which will be transfused in the following epoch from the Scots to the Anglo-Saxons and will reappear in the lives and characters of men like Chad and Cuthbert and a host of other Englishmen who came under Celtic influences.

Columba is, in his life and character, an epitome of the Scottish Church. But since for a century or more the history of the English will centre round the interaction between Roman and Scottish Christianity, it will be well at this point to enumerate more systematically the chief features of the latter.

The foremost differences in the eyes of contemporaries were

disputes about the date at which the Easter festival should be celebrated, and about the shape of the tonsure. Of these we shall hear more—indeed, too much—when we come to the Synod of Whitby. Here it is more worth while to recall the fact that Christianity in Ireland, and probably also in Wales, had not adapted itself to the provincial and diocesan system of the Roman Empire. Each Irish king or chieftain had established his own monastery. It was ruled by an abbot who was commonly a member of the founder's family. Its population could grow to the hundreds or thousands sometimes recorded, because the monastery was both a sanctuary in an age of much tribal violence, and also a centre of education at a time when enthusiasm for the new learning was unbounded.

The abbot's power was supreme; it reflected that of the tribal king. The bishop, unless he happened also to be an abbot, was a mere official, whose function was to ordain. The Scottish Church was thus an aggregate of monasteries or of groups of monasteries. In so far as it enjoyed any unity, it was a unity of purpose and enthusiasm. A community like that of Iona might have rights over its off-shoots, but there was no other centralized government.

The monasteries were not only sanctuaries and schools of learning. They were bases for missionary work. The active and the contemplative ideals could be interchanged. Monks might wander abroad either to preach or to become anchorites. They could plant themselves in cells on lonely islands, on headlands, anywhere where they were far removed from their fellow men.

The Irish Church was less marked than the Welsh by extreme asceticism. But the oriental strain was there, and would in time find its way to the English. Mingling with it were other unusual strains of thought; sometimes derived darkly from ideas of magic, from worship of the elements, from Druidism buried deep in the inmost recesses of the Celtic mind; sometimes manifesting themselves in sympathies with the animal world or in ecstatic adoration of the forces of nature.

The best insight into these mysteries of the Celtic soul is to be had from the hymns of the Irish Church. The following are characteristic lines from a translation of the Irish *Lorica* (Coat of Mail) ascribed, perhaps rightly, to St. Patrick.[11]

I arise to-day:
  in the might of Heaven
  brightness of Sun
  whiteness of Snow
  splendour of Fire

. . . .

I arise to-day:
  in the Might of God for my piloting
  Wisdom of God for my guidance
  Eye of God for my foresight
  Ear of God for my hearing

. . . .

I invoke therefore all these forces:
  against every fierce merciless force that may come upon my body
    and my soul;
  against incantations of false prophets;
  against black laws of paganism;
  against false laws of heresy;
  against deceit of idolatry;
  against spells of women and smiths and druids;
  against all knowledge that is forbidden the human soul.

Christ for my guardianship to-day:
  against poison, against burning,
  against drowning, against wounding,
  that there may come to me a multitude of rewards;
Christ with me, Christ before me,
Christ behind me, Christ in me,
Christ under me, Christ over me.

. . . .

Other hymns the recital of which gave defence against the enemies of mankind are ascribed rightly or wrongly to well-known saints of the Celtic Churches. That of Columba, called from its first words the *Altus Prosator*, is probably genuine. It is in Latin, and approaches more nearly to the ordinary thought of the Latin world. None the less it is still far removed. Each stanza begins with a different letter of the alphabet. The fear of the *Dies Irae* sounds through it, but the devil who lies behind all the fear is 'The Dragon, great, most foul, terrible and old'—a monster ready to take the place of the Teutonic dragons which had brought Beowulf and the heathen heroes into action.

The important thing in the history of the English is to understand that while the sons and grandson of Ida were extending Anglian conquests north and west, a detachment of the Irish Church was established at Iona by a man of royal birth who could infect his followers with his own heroic temper, so that they in their turn could win their Teutonic neighbours to a new cult of dragon-slaying. At Iona there existed the enthusiasm which led men into great undertakings. Iona inherited the spirit of self-renunciation which we have seen inculcated by St. David, but it inherited also the devotion to learning somehow transmitted to the Irish Church, perhaps from Lérins through the medium of Illtud, Gildas, and other British saints. And above all it inherited the tradition of propaganda. The community at Iona could supply the evangelistic zeal which had led Columba to convert the Picts as Patrick had converted the Irish.

THE ROMAN MISSION TO THE ENGLISH

A generation elapsed before the Christianity of Iona was passed on to the English in Northumbria. Our attention must therefore now be diverted to Pope Gregory (540–604), a younger contemporary of Columba, one who during the last years of Columba's life was planning a missionary campaign for the conversion of the English with a clearness of purpose and a persistence worthy of his Roman ancestors. In the two centuries which had passed since the Roman armies had been withdrawn from Britain, Rome had seen Visigoths and Ostrogoths lording

St. Gregory

it in the land. She had seen the western Emperors come to an end and the eastern Emperors first establish and then relax their hold on central Italy. There were still in the peninsula imperial officials and generals—*duces, magistri militum, praefecti*—officials by courtesy still Most Illustrious, Glorious, Magnificent, as in the days of Constantine; but even at Rome the old world, like its temples, its aqueducts, and its theatres, was in ruins; the Romans found themselves face to face with the Lombards (those old neighbours of the English in the Elbe lands, who since the year 568 had been pouring a new flood of barbarism over Italy); and the Bishop of the Romans was left the only man with authority and vigour sufficient to save a remnant of the ancient order and uphold in a new ecclesiastical form the ancient traditions of the Imperial City. Gregory in his own life represents the bridge from the old Rome to the new. History has always recognized him as the last great official of secular Rome, the first great Pope of the medieval type. After rising as a Roman noble to be *Praefectus Urbis*, the highest official of the City, he had surrendered his enormous wealth; he had converted the palace of his father, on the Coelian Hill, into a monastery dedicated to St. Andrew, and he himself had entered it as a poor monk.

Thus he comes before us as a man with a conscience. It was conscience which had driven him to sacrifice his worldly position and wealth; it was this which made him miserable when he heard that a man had died of hunger in the City; it was this which made him oppose the traffic in Christian slaves; and once more it was his conscience, working like that of a nineteenth-century philanthropist, which moved him to form new schemes when he saw the Anglian boys with their fair hair, looking like angels in the Roman slave market. Whether or no his punnings are authentic, there must have been some such incident—some encounter with Anglian slaves—to start the oft-repeated story. We may believe that he then asked himself why these boys were vessels of the devil. Could he himself do nothing to rescue their nation from the devil?

The episode marks something more than the birth of an idea in the mind of one of the world's great men. It is a turning-point in the history of Latin Christianity. From that time the Roman Church becomes, as it had not previously been, propagandist, missionary, imperialist. It becomes the Church of the northern barbarians as well as of the Roman world. The sudden conviction of the man with a conscience who was also a man of

FIG. 45. St. Gregory. A modern reconstruction of his portrait based partly on a description of his contemporary portrait and partly on a copy of its copy.

action was equivalent to one of the grand discoveries of history, or one of the great inventions.

Before the idea bore fruit, years later, in the sending of Augustine to Britain, Gregory had made one attempt after another to have Christianity preached to the English. On one occasion he had begged permission from the Pope to go himself to Britain. He had persuaded the Pope by putting before him the thought which had been troubling his own mind—the pity that Hell should have to be filled by such fair vessels.*12 He had set out for Britain. He had travelled three days' journey to the north when the people of Rome made a tumultuous demonstration, and

* *Miserum tam pulchris vasis infernus [infernum] debuisse repleri.*

insisted that he should be brought back to the City. Later, in 595, after his accession to the papal throne, he had instructed his agents in Gaul to devote part of his revenues from Gallic estates to buying up Anglian slave-boys, evidently intending to have them taught Christianity, and sent back to Britain as missionaries.

But Gregory's life was full of more immediate cares—Lombards encircling Rome; quarrels, till 596, with the Franks; pestilence in the City; books to be written for the edification of the Church; immense papal lands to be administered in every province; a world-wide correspondence ever demanding his attention. The wonder is that Gregory, distracted by the pressure of such immediate necessities, and suffering, as he did, from gout and a bad digestion (the result of his monastic fasts), was ever able to drive the English mission through to completion.

There were many advantages in the plan of sending Augustine to Britain, the plan finally adopted in 596 when friendly relations with the Franks opened the road through Gaul. It held out a hope of earlier results than could be expected from the scheme of training heathen slave-boys as missionaries. Gregory could order Augustine and the monks of St. Andrew's to fulfil his wishes because that was his own monastery: he was their founder as well as their Pope. Augustine, the Prior, was well known to him, because at some time or other they had shared a cell. He could be trusted to do his duty. Some of the inmates of St. Andrew's had been trying to escape. The mission to Britain would give to all a new interest, to some a good employment.

In this way, it seems, the plan which was to change the destinies of the Anglo-Saxons grew to maturity.

Before we embark on the main story of the Conversion, it is needful to make clear our course by explaining the situation in Britain in 597, and the outlines of its subsequent political history. Some features of the situation have emerged in what has been already said. We have seen that, by 597, the Anglo-Saxons were almost encircled by Christians, but that while their nearest

neighbours—the Franks across the Channel and the Britons in
the west—were indifferent to the heathenism of the Anglo-
Saxons, the more virile Christianity of the Scots of north Britain
was confronted by Ethelfrith (593–617), king of Northumbria,
who was only now beginning his career of ruthless war against
Britons and Scots. There was little likelihood that he, 'the

destroyer', the slayer of the monks of Bangor, would encourage
any Christian propaganda. Of the other English kingdoms
which were afterwards to play a chief part, the kingdom of
Mercia on the upper Trent had not yet emerged into history; the
kingdom of Wessex since the expulsion of Ceawlin in 591 had
lost its effective unity and power. The small kingdoms south of
the Humber had in general accepted the *imperium* of Ethelbert,*
king of Kent (? 560–616).[13]

We know little about this *imperium* except that it was later

* OE. Æthelberht.

regarded as in some way a succession to that of Ceawlin, that it extended to the Humber and (apparently) to the Severn, and that it was fairly effective over Ethelbert's nephew, Saebert, king of the East Saxons, and in a less degree over Raedwald, king of the East Angles.[14]

To understand how loose was the tie which bound the under-kings to Ethelbert in his vague *imperium*, it is only necessary to remember a fact emphasized by the subsequent story of the Conversion, that the overlord's acceptance of Christianity will not bind his dependants. None of these under-kings, apart from those of Essex and East Anglia, will even pretend to follow their superior's example in changing his faith.

For the rest, we must recall the fact made evident by the Kentish graves, that the kingdom of Kent had long enjoyed a flourishing trade with the Continent: importing the beautiful things which are found in the cemeteries—golden bracteates from Scandinavia, 'Coptic' bronze bowls, shells from the Indian Ocean, glass vases, gold, semi-precious stones, and Frankish brooches; exporting—what was it?—perhaps rich cargoes of human beings, the slave-boys whom Gallic Jews resold in the slave-markets of Rome? Somehow or other, the Jutes became wealthy. These merchants enjoyed the display of having buried with them their costly swords. On occasions, too, one of them would have his purse or his scales placed by his side. This, like the sword, might be useful in the next world. Kent might seem barbarous to the Romans but to the peoples of Britain it was a centre of civilization. These prosperous, almost cosmopolitan Jutes were prepared to receive other things besides jewels and glass bowls from the Christian world.

We can now resume the history of Gregory's mission to England, and at the outset we are confronted by the fact that while Augustine and his companions had (apparently) left Rome in the spring of 596, they did not land in Thanet till shortly before Easter 597.

Augustine 597

Why had they been so long upon the road? In part no doubt it was due to the difficulties of travel in those days; others in the Dark Ages besides Augustine consumed a year over the journey from Rome. But in part also the delay was due to the character of the men themselves. Augustine himself was as unlike the Celtic missionaries—St. Patrick, St. Columba, and the rest—as he could be. Here we are dealing not with a man who acted from passionate convictions and sudden impulses, but with a Roman, well-disciplined, discreet, learned in Holy Scripture, a man who was moved by a strong sense of duty. And the Romans who accompanied their prior were like him. They had been accustomed to the quiet routine of their monastery on the Coelian Hill. They had set out at the bidding of the Pope, little realizing what lay ahead of them. After sailing from Ostia to Gaul, they had spent some time in the island of Lérins, and there no doubt they had heard stories about the savagery of the Saxons, stories which may have originated with those holy men from Britain, such as Patrick, who, coming to Lérins in the fifth century, had doubtless scattered rumours which grew with the lapse of time. At any rate, when the party reached southern Gaul their fears became too much for them. They halted, 'and began to think of returning home rather than proceed to a barbarous, fierce, and unbelieving nation, to whose very language they were strangers'.[15]

Augustine went back to Rome to report their apprehensions, but he returned with papal letters of exhortation and, spurred on by Gregory, they again turned their faces to Britain. When at last they reached its shores, they landed where men said that Hengist and Horsa had landed before them, 'in the Isle of Thanet', within sight of the ruins of Richborough, the port of Roman Britain which, by 597, was suffering as much from the withdrawal of the sea as from that of the Romans. What then happened is a familiar story: how at close quarters the barbarians of Kent proved less terrible to the Italians than they had seemed at a distance; how when King Ethelbert was informed that the forty men who had appeared in his territory 'were come from

Rome and had brought a joyful message, which could undoubtedly assure to those that hearkened to it everlasting joys in heaven, and a kingdom that would never end',[16] he came to Thanet and ordered the men from Rome to be brought to him as he sat in the open air. 'For he had taken precaution that they should not come to him in any house lest . . . if they practised any magical arts they might impose upon him and so get the better of him. . . . But they came with Divine not with magic powers, bearing a silver cross for their banner, and the image of Our Lord and Saviour painted on a board, and chanting litanies.'

The point in the story which most calls for explanation is the facility with which Augustine secured his victory. For Ethelbert at once invited the new-comers to Canterbury, and promised to support them while they preached to his people. He there gave them the old Roman church of St. Martin, and though he refused to allow compulsion to be put upon his people, he himself accepted baptism, and presumably submitted to the rites for those of riper years—the priest blowing in his face to drive away the devil, placing salt in his mouth, and immersing him three times as he stood bare in the cold water. The King's lead was followed with little delay, first by the chiefs and then by the commons of his kingdom. By the end of the year, ten thousand men of Kent had been baptized (so Gregory asserted, no doubt with natural exaggeration), and Augustine had been consecrated in Gaul as 'Archbishop of the English'.

Now there is no difficulty in seeing why the kingdom of Ethelbert offered a good field for the mission from the Roman world. The Jutes, who had derived, or as traders had copied, so much of their material civilization from the Franks, were certainly well prepared to follow Frankish fashions in religion. They had a Christian Frankish queen, and she, with her chaplain Liudhard (Pl. 43, 3) and other Christian attendants, had accustomed the minds of the courtiers at Canterbury to Christianity. The church of St. Martin's had been repaired for her use. Whether Bertha and her retinue had done anything more positive

Bertha

to aid Christianity we cannot say; but Gregory, in one of his letters, written in 601, encourages Bertha by telling her that she should now act so as to make good what had formerly been neglected.[17] Ethelbert, in fact, was so friendly, tolerant, and hospitable to Augustine's party, that there is something to be said for the guess that he or Bertha had beforehand sent some kind of encouragement to the Pope. But what Gregory himself tells us is simply this: that 'the news had reached him that the English people wished to become Christians'.[18] Ethelbert showed statesmanship as well as friendliness by moving with slow deliberation, and by consulting his great men he succeeded in carrying the bulk of his people with him. Though his chiefs might not be greatly moved by the preaching of Augustine, who could only address them through an interpreter, the old Germanic devotion of the *comites* to their lord would weigh heavily in favour of the decision of Ethelbert. If the chiefs could be persuaded the battle was won, for in those times we never hear of the humbler classes in society opposing a lead given them by their superiors. And if it is true* that the great landowners in England as in Scandinavia officiated as priests of the heathen gods, there would be few left to champion the cause of Thunor and Woden when their most powerful priests turned against them. As a further explanation of the rapid victory, we must remember what was said in the last chapter about the failure of Germanic heathenism to appeal either to the reason or to the better instincts of men. There had been no attempt to rationalize the heathenism of the north in the way that the paganism of Greece and Rome had once been doctored for the consumption of the educated. The methods recommended later to English missionaries in Germany show how easily the Christian could use the weapons of reason against the absurdities of the Teutonic gods. Daniel, bishop of Winchester, writing about 723,[19] suggested that Boniface, the English missionary to the Germans, should ask the heathen 'whether they think this

* Cf. above, p. 238.

heathenism not rationalized

universe had a beginning or was always in existence. If it had a beginning, who created it? . . . If they maintain that the universe always existed without a beginning, seek to refute and convince them by many arguments and proofs; if they go on contending, ask them: Who ruled it? How did they reduce beneath their sway and bring under their jurisdiction a universe that existed before them? Whence and by whom and when was the first god or goddess constituted or begotten?' The heathen were to be made to blush for their absurd opinions. They were to be shown that 'the Christians possess the fertile lands . . . and have left the heathen with their gods only the frozen lands in which their gods are wrongly thought to hold sway'.

These considerations help in some measure to explain the sweeping success of the mission. But first and last the credit must be given to Pope Gregory. Augustine and his companions did indeed, when established at Canterbury, show themselves to be both capable and obedient. But the hero of the story continued to be Gregory himself. Till his death he helped and guided the mission which had won such astonishing success in Kent. He sent Augustine reinforcements from Rome—Justus, Mellitus, Paulinus, and others. He sent him relics of the holy Apostles, and he sent him ornaments, vestments, and books. When Augustine propounded problems about liturgical discrepancies, or about the proper division of the offerings of the faithful, when he asked whether a man might marry his stepmother, and asked advice about sundry other questions which were troubling him and his converts, Gregory answered with admirable wisdom.

He told him to choose from the Roman or the Gallican or any other Church whatever custom 'may be more acceptable to Almighty God . . . for things are not to be loved for the sake of places'.[20] He told him that for those who like Augustine himself had taken the monastic vows, there could be no question about the division of church offerings, since they, like their fathers in the primitive Church, should have all things in common.

PLATE 39

Marble throne in St. Gregory's Church, Rome, said
to have been the chair of St. Gregory

Marble table 'of St. Gregory', also in St. Gregory's Church

PLATE 40

Part of the ivory back of the Drogo Sacramentary, written
c. 830 and used in Metz Cathedral. The panels give views
of the Mass in different stages of the ceremony

On the other hand, those in Augustine's mission who were clerics in minor orders were only 'to be kept under ecclesiastical rule that they may live orderly and attend to singing of psalms'. Accordingly, strict monastic rule need not be enforced on all.[21] On the other points, Gregory answered that it was a crime for a man to marry his stepmother. He told him to ordain plenty of bishops—twelve under a metropolitan at London, and twelve more under another metropolitan at York. He sent a special letter to tell Augustine his second thoughts about the treatment of heathen temples and rites. Let the idols be destroyed, but let the temples be converted into churches, sprinkled with holy water, and supplied with altars and relics; 'and because they are used to slaughter many oxen and sacrifice to devils [we have interesting light here on some of the rites of Germanic heathen-dom] some solemnity must be given them in exchange for this'. Therefore on feast days they should build themselves huts of the boughs of trees about those buildings which have been turned from temples into churches and they should 'kill cattle and glorify God in their feasts . . . for there is no doubt that it is impossible to cut off everything at once from their rude natures: because he who endeavours to ascend to the highest place rises by degrees or steps and not by leaps'.[22]

In one point only did the Pope lead Augustine to an unwise policy. Augustine had asked for instruction how he was to deal with the bishops of the Britons. Gregory in reply somewhat rashly committed all the bishops in the island to the care of Augustine, and his scheme for the organization of the Church in Britain was based on the same idea. Partly owing to these in-structions, and partly owing to Augustine's failure to win the sympathy of the Britons in the conferences which he had with them (the first being at St. Augustine's Oak 'on the borders of the Hwicce and West Saxons'),* the Britons refused to co-operate. According to Bede's story, they thought Augustine proud be-cause at the second conference he remained seated instead of

* Usually—but, as the map (p. 261) shows, wrongly—identified as Aust.

rising to greet them on their approach. The chance of a united Church in Britain was lost for centuries. 'It is to this day', said Bede in 731, 'the fashion among the Britons to reckon the faith and religion of Englishmen as naught, and to hold no more conversation with them than with the heathen.'[23]

The quarrel could hardly have been avoided. To have acknowledged the superiority of the metropolitan at Canterbury or London would have been worse for the Britons than a military defeat. It would have undermined their independence. The fault of the Britons was that for a century or more before the coming of St. Augustine they had despised their conquerors as barbarians and heathens. They had lost their opportunity before 597.

Was the Augustinian mission strong enough without the co-operation of the Britons to win over the other English kingdoms? Could it even hold its place in Kent when the personal influence of Augustine and of Ethelbert was withdrawn? The first twenty years of the seventh century brought an answer to these questions.

Ethelbert's *imperium*, at one time recognized up to the Humber, gave an opening for extending the work of the mission beyond Kent, and the last recorded act of Augustine was the consecration of Mellitus as bishop of London for the East Saxons. The deaths of Augustine and Gregory about 604[24] at first produced no obvious retrogression, and Raedwald, the king of East Anglia, when visiting his Kentish overlord, was admitted to the Sacrament. But the years which followed proved, in one kingdom after another, how slight was the hold of the new religion which rested on the patronage of a few great men, and how persistent was the old heathenism, in spite of its nominal defeats.

Thus, in East Anglia, Raedwald, having returned from his Christian overlord to his own heathen family, solved his religious difficulties by setting up in his 'temple' an altar dedicated to Christ by the side of another where victims were offered to 'devils'.

In Essex a Christian king was succeeded by pagan sons; and

when Mellitus, the bishop of London, refused in St. Paul's to give them 'that white bread'[25] which they had seen him give their father, he and his followers were ejected (617). Mellitus, with Justus who had been made bishop of Rochester, then retired to Gaul.

The death of Ethelbert (616) and the accession of his son Eadbald, a heathen, almost put an end to the mission in Kent itself. Laurentius, the successor of Augustine, is said to have agreed with the fugitive bishops 'that it was better for them all to return to their own country, where they might serve God in freedom of mind, than to continue to no purpose among barbarians, who had revolted from the faith'. According to Bede's well-known story, it was only a vision of St. Peter, appearing to Laurentius the night before his departure, which saved the situation. In the morning Laurentius showed King Eadbald his back scarred by stripes inflicted, he said, by St. Peter; and he so frightened the young king that from that time onward he became a supporter of the Church. Kent remained a Christian kingdom; but it was not till 640 that a king arose who eliminated outward heathenism, making Christianity compulsory on all his subjects and destroying the idols throughout the kingdom.

When Mellitus returned after one year's withdrawal, the Londoners, under the influence of their 'idolatrous high priest', refused to receive him. As the preaching of Christianity was not begun again in Essex till 654, the people to the north of the lower Thames continued for almost forty years to worship Woden and Thunor, while those on the southern bank were, at any rate nominally, Christians. During the ten years 617–27, Kent was the only Christian kingdom of all the English States.

Let us avail ourselves of this lull in the Conversion to note such traces of the handiwork of Ethelbert and of Augustine as have come down to us. They are of two kinds, the laws of Ethelbert, and fragments of the churches of Augustine—laws and churches which were to be models for after generations.

The primary motive of Augustine in guiding Ethelbert to formulate written laws is obvious in the first clause of the code. 'These are the decrees which king Ethelbert established in the lifetime of Augustine. (i) Theft of God's property and the Church's shall be compensated twelve-fold; a bishop's property eleven-fold; a priest's property nine-fold; a deacon's property six-fold; a clerk's property three-fold. Breach of the peace shall be compensated doubly when it affects the Church or a meeting-place.' The Roman mission must be protected. Since there were no traditional laws defending clergy, these new rules had to be formulated; and the introduction of parchment and ink made it possible for the barbarian king to imitate Roman methods of legislation.

Most of the ninety articles of the code detail the punishments for injuries to a man's person or property, including his wife and servants. Thus, 'If one man slays another, the ordinary wergeld to be paid as compensation shall be 100 shillings'; 'If a freeman breaks the fence round [another man's] enclosure, he shall pay 6 shillings compensation'; 'If a thumb is struck off, 20 shillings. If a thumbnail is knocked off, 3 shillings. If a man strikes off a forefinger, he shall pay 9 shillings. . . . If a man strikes off a ring-finger he shall pay 6 shillings compensation.'[26] This tariff may be all that the Kentish witan could recall when they were asked to sum up the traditional law of their folk. But something more than memorizing, recording, and adjustment, went to the making of Ethelbert's code. It stands for the Christian ideal which had just been introduced into the land. Order is to be enforced, morality upheld, the agents of the new religion are to be protected.

Of the churches built and repaired in and around Canterbury in this first generation of English Christianity, there exist only a few fragments. But these are now of special interest, because in the last few years they have been re-examined and their character is known to us as it was never known to our fathers.[27]

Two churches at Canterbury, used in the days of Ethelbert,

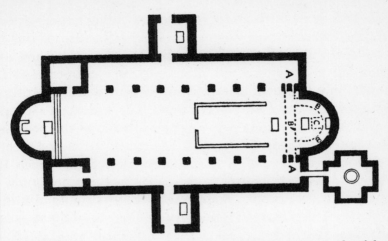

FIG. 46. Canterbury, plan of Saxon Cathedral. The Baptistery on the right was added *c.* 750. The dotted lines and the letters A, B, C, indicate the crypt.

The basilica which in Roman times pointed to the west, was reorientated by Augustine, who added an eastern apse and altar and placed the bishop's throne against the western wall.

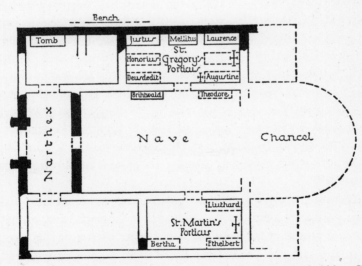

FIG. 47. Canterbury, Church of SS. Peter and Paul (St. Augustine's Abbey Church).

were said to be survivals from Roman times restored by the Jutes for Christian use, the one for Queen Bertha, the other for Augustine. The existing St. Martin's stands on the site of the former, to the east of the city, and its chancel walls (very narrow, only 2 ft. 2 in. thick) are in parts made of Roman brick, probably the work of Ethelbert's time. The other church, handed over to Augustine after Ethelbert's baptism, is now covered by Canterbury Cathedral (Fig. 46).

Most interesting of all are the foundations of the church of the monastery then dedicated to St. Peter and St. Paul but subsequently known as St. Augustine's. Bede says of this:[28] 'He [Augustine] also built a monastery not far from the city to the eastward, in which by his advice Ethelbert erected from its foundations the church of the blessed Apostles Peter and Paul, and enriched it with divers gifts; wherein the bodies of the same Augustine and of all the bishops of Canterbury and of the kings of Kent might be buried.'

In the ground-plans of this and of some other Kentish churches attributed to the period* we seem to see the Augustinian mission working out a type of its own, with the following characteristics: small proportions (the nave of St. Peter and St. Paul is only 39 ft. by 27 ft.); walls narrow but strong, being largely composed of Roman bricks and of good cement like the Roman; floors well constructed, coloured pink by mixing with the mortar the dust of pounded bricks; and lastly, the most distinctive feature of all, side chambers (*porticus*) opening either from the chancel or the nave. The characteristics are thought[29] to point generally 'to an Italian origin, with a strong eastern rather than Roman influence'.

Altogether, what little we know about these Augustinian churches, small and ruined as they are, leaves on the mind an impression of their great ancestry. Though they lack the columned beauty of the regular basilican type, they have inherited a tradition of strength, and they show a sense of proportion. The

* See Fig. 47 and those on p. 281.

evidence of the churches tallies with Bede's information, indicating that the influence of the mission was mostly concentrated at Canterbury. We see, moreover, that even at Canterbury Augustine's efforts were specially directed to the work of building a mausoleum where the souls of the king and queen, with their bodies in proximity to those of the holy men, might be defended alike from heathen spirits and from Christian demons. The foundations of this church, built to hold the tombs of kings and bishops, now that they have been excavated, are a visible reminder that, whatever the intention of Gregory might have been, the mission of Augustine in this first generation was, in fact, a mission to a court rather than to a people.

THE ROMAN MISSION IN NORTHUMBRIA

In 625 the interest of the story shifts from the south to the north. In that year Paulinus, one of the later reinforcements sent by Gregory to Augustine, journeyed from Canterbury to the court of Edwin, king of Northumbria. A Roman is once more seen at York, formerly the station of the Romans' Sixth Legion. His arrival in the wild north is almost as great an event as the coming of Augustine himself.

To understand its significance we must glance at the political developments which followed the year 616. Bede tells us that even before the death of Ethelbert, Raedwald, king of the East Angles, had been acquiring the leadership of the English provinces south of the Humber. The climax of Raedwald's power was reached in 617, when he defeated Ethelfrith, the king who had founded the greatness of Northumbria by overthrowing Celtic rivals at Degsastan (603) and at Chester (? 616). Raedwald's supremacy was, however, a mere flicker. He probably died some ten years after his great victory. The chief power then passed, not to his son, nor to any southern kinglet, but to Edwin, son of Ælle of Deira, who, after twenty-four years of exile, had

Paulinus in Northumbria

been set up by the arms of Raedwald as king of Bernicia as well
as of Deira. From that time till 633 Edwin gradually won his
way to the foremost position in the island.*

These years also witnessed a change of wider significance than
the transference of the supremacy from East Anglia to Northumbria. They saw the leadership among the Anglo-Saxons pass
for ever from the small south-eastern kingdoms. These were
pushed aside by the three states which were still able to expand
by absorbing the Celtic inhabitants of the island. For a time
East Anglia, Essex, Kent, and Sussex, might keep their own
dynasties. But it was the beginning of the end for them when
they all, save Kent, recognized the *imperium* of Edwin. Thenceforth the question which emerges is simply this—to which of
the greater Powers are the small kingdoms of the south-east to
be permanently attracted? If we employ the terms current in
the nineteenth century, we may say that the rise of Edwin
marks the end of the Heptarchy and the beginning of the
Triarchy. However incorrect these terms may be, they have
their uses, and the important thing is to remember that about
this time the Anglo-Saxon world settled down from a confused
strife between a large number of small kingdoms to a more
clearly defined rivalry between Northumbria, Mercia, and
Wessex.

Edwin's reign (617–33) brought Northumbria at one bound
to the height of its power. Deira and Bernicia were strengthened
as well as united. A British kingdom† (in what is now the West
Riding), hitherto protected from the Angles by Elmet forest, was
absorbed. Northwards, though the derivation of Edinburgh as
'Edwin's Burgh' should now be given up,[30] it is likely enough that
his power was established up to the Forth. Edwin put to good use
the knowledge of the affairs of Wales and of the south-Humbrian
states acquired during his exile. His war-bands intimidated or

---

* See map, p. 275, and note, p. 378.

† The centre of this kingdom seems to have been Ledstone (in Bede, Loidis),
where the Roman road crossed the Aire.

forcibly subdued all the British and English kingdoms except
Kent, and his fleet reduced Anglesey and the Isle of Man. Then
the greatness of his success brought about his fall. Cadwallon,
king of North Wales,* a son of the King Cadfan who is said to
have given shelter to Edwin as an exile, formed an alliance in

633 with Penda, king of the Mercians, that is the Angles of
the upper Trent. Britons and English fighting side by side in
their revolt overthrew and killed Edwin in the battle of Heathfield.† It was the beginning of a long feud between Northumbria and Mercia.

With this slight introduction we can now pass to the ecclesiastical history of Edwin's reign.

The conversion of Edwin of Northumbria was in its main outlines similar to that of Ethelbert of Kent. Once more a favour-

* Called by Bede, Caedwalla.
† OE. Hæðfeld (probably Hatfield Chase, east of Doncaster).

able opportunity came from the marriage of a heathen king with a Christian princess (Edwin's queen being Ethelburg, daughter of Ethelbert); once more a king acted with statesmanlike deliberation and referred the question of Christianity to his council of chief men. But there are novel features in the story. Edwin had himself enjoyed some contact with the new religion before his accession. When Deira had been annexed by Ethelfrith, Edwin, according to Welsh authorities, found refuge with Cadfan, a British (and therefore a Christian) king in North Wales. Later he had made his way to the court of Raedwald, and had no doubt seen the East Anglian temple with its altar to Christ alongside of the heathen altar. The other novelty in Edwin's conversion was a mysterious apparition which, like Macbeth's witches, promised him future greatness. But what chiefly distinguishes the story of Edwin is that it is narrated by Bede at such length that it is possible to see something of the workings of the barbarian mind as it turned gradually to the new religion. We see Paulinus, the chaplain who had been sent to the Northumbrian court with the Kentish princess, gaining influence over Edwin by claiming that the king's escape from the poisoned dagger of an assassin, and, on the same night (the night of Easter Sunday, 626), the easy childbirth of his queen, were both due to his prayers to the Christian God. We see Edwin then sitting much alone, brooding over the problem whether he should change his religion. Letters arrive 'from the Pope'; with them are a gold ornament for himself, and for the queen a silver mirror and a gilt ivory comb; then Edwin is victorious in a campaign against the West Saxons—his own mind is consequently made up. The question must, however, be referred to his counsellors, his *witan*. We have their arguments: the worldly wisdom of Coifi, chief of the priests (*he* had not got much good out of his service to the old gods); the more spiritual questionings of the counsellor who spoke of the shortness of man's life ('like the flight of a sparrow through a hall in winter') and of the uncertainty of what was to follow. This debate, and its sequel—the destruction of the heathen

Edwin's conversion

temple at Goodmanham with its idols, the chief priest himself leading the attack and casting a first spear at it—Bede's
familiar story lays bare much of the heart of the barbarian; it
reveals some of the mental processes which induced the fighting-
men of the north to exchange Woden for Christ. But in all probability the proceedings were less spontaneous than is indicated
by Bede. The part taken by Coifi at least must have been pre-
arranged—a clever ruse for carrying the waverers over to the
Christian camp. The leaders of the kingdom were infected by
the enthusiasm of the moment, and quickly found that they had
committed themselves, both by acclamation in the assembly, and
also by the dramatic attack on the temple. Edwin's methods,
like those of Ethelbert, were more skilful and happier than
the arguments of force which in Norway gave Odin his sacrifice of blood before his adherents yielded to the sword of
St. Olaf.

One reason for the calm with which the new religion was
accepted was no doubt the fact that, after it had been officially
adopted by the assembly, each individual was left free to
choose whether or no he would come and ask for baptism.
And as a matter of fact, the mission of Paulinus was evidently
so short-handed—his only helper mentioned by name is James,
the deacon—that the change had to come slowly. We hear of
baptisms or other missionary work, but only at old Roman places
such as York, Catterick, Campodonum,* and Lincoln. And it is
perhaps significant that the place in Bernicia where Paulinus had
remarkable success, being fully occupied in baptizing for thirty-
six days, was Yeavering,† the centre of a district where place-
names and hill-terraces point to a survival of the Celts. No
doubt the people from the neighbouring villages who flocked to
him to be baptized in the river Glen, as well as those who were
baptized in the places which had once been Roman, were largely
of British descent.

Bede[31] makes it clear how it was that information about these

* Perhaps Doncaster.   † Adgefrin.

beginnings of Christianity in the north came to be conveyed to him.

'A certain priest and abbot of the monastery of Partney,* a man of singular veracity, whose name was Deda, told me concerning the faith of this province that an old man had informed him that he himself had been baptized at noon-day, by Bishop Paulinus, in the presence of King Edwin, and with him a great multitude of the people, in the river Trent, near the city, which in the English tongue is called *Tiouulfingacaestir*;† and he was also wont to describe the person of the same Paulinus, saying that he was tall of stature, stooping somewhat, his hair black, his visage thin, his nose slender and aquiline, his aspect both venerable and awe-inspiring. He had also with him in the ministry James, the deacon, a man of zeal and great fame in Christ and in the Church, who lived even to our days.'

Paulinus and James, the deacon, could catechize and baptize in a few places. They could do little more, and it was only a beginning. But the conversion of the Anglo-Saxons came without bloodshed because it came slowly, and with the minimum of compulsion. The Christian Edwin, his queen, and their Christian courtiers, brought some of the merits of the new religion to the notice cf the Northumbrian people, as they made their progresses up and down the land. No ruler before Edwin had been so remarkably successful: before 616 a fugitive, and then after little more than ten years reputed overlord 'of all the parts of Britain that were provinces either of the English or of the Britons'—such an *imperium* as no English king had ever before possessed. When Bede wrote his history a hundred years later, the fame of Edwin and of his magnificence had become proverbial. However well-worn, the passage deserves to be quoted in full since it gives us the first picture of an English king.[32]

'It is told that there was then such perfect peace in Britain, wheresoever the dominion of King Edwin extended, that, as is still proverbially said, a woman with her new-born babe might walk throughout the island, from sea to sea, without receiving any harm. That king took

* In Lincolnshire.   † Not identified.

such care for the good of his nation, that in several places where he
had seen clear springs near the highways, he caused stakes to be fixed,
with copper drinking-vessels hanging on them, for the refreshment of
travellers; nor durst any man touch them for any other purpose than
that for which they were designed, either through the great dread they
had of the king, or for the affection which they bore him. His dignity
was so great throughout his dominions, that not only were his banners
borne before him in battle, but even in time of peace, when he rode
about his cities, townships, or provinces, with his thegns,* the standard-
bearer was always wont to go before him. Also, when he walked
anywhere along the streets, that sort of banner which the Romans call
Tufa and the English *Thuuf,* was in like manner borne before him.'†

There are three points in this passage which should be noted:
the emphasis put on the maintenance of order (the good king is
the king who enforces order); the Germanic custom which made
the king ride round his territory from one royal vill to another;
and lastly, the Roman influence, coming probably through the
court of North Wales, which induced the barbarian to imitate
some of the pomp of a Roman ruler. Edwin's ambitions are
heightened by some traditions of the bygone Empire, and the
dignity of his migrant court is enhanced with some Romano-
British trappings.

For six years (627–33) Edwin ruled as a Christian king. Then,
in October 633, the blow fell. Cadwallon, 'King of the Britons',
with the help of Penda and his Mercians wiped out the Northumbrian army at Heathfield. Edwin's head was carried to York.
For a year, 'the hateful year', Cadwallon 'occupied the provinces of the Northumbrians, not ruling them like a victorious
king, but ravaging them like a furious tyrant'.[33] Roman Christianity for a time died down in Northumbria as it had died in
East Anglia and in Essex. But when Paulinus took ship back to
Kent, his follower James, the deacon, bravely remained at his
post near Catterick, baptizing and teaching. In 634 the tyranny
of the British king was ended by his defeat near Heavenfield,

---

* *Ministris.*   † For the royal standard found at Sutton Hoo, see pp. 698, 712.

and in 635 the whole religious situation was changed by the coming of two new missions to England, that of the Scots to Northumbria, and that of Birinus to Wessex.

Before we pass to this new phase in the Conversion, let us consider what had actually been accomplished by Augustine's followers since 597. Though Kent was still the only kingdom where the Roman Church had securely established itself, real progress had been made elsewhere by breaking the ground in Essex, East Anglia, Lindsey, and Northumbria. In East Anglia, Christianity made two false starts. The first of them, when Raedwald set up an altar to Christ by the side of a heathen altar, has been already mentioned. The second was about 628, when Eorpwald, Raedwald's son, was won over by Edwin's zeal to the new religion, but was soon murdered by a heathen. 'From that time the province was in error for three years.' Then a step-son of Raedwald, by name Sigbert,* gained the throne. Sigbert, 'a good and religious man', had been for some time an exile in Gaul, and had been 'there initiated into the mysteries of the faith, whereof he made it his business to cause all his province to partake as soon as he came to the throne. His exertions were nobly promoted by Bishop Felix, who, coming to Honorius, the archbishop, from the parts of Burgundy where he had been born, . . . was sent by him to preach the word of life to the aforesaid nation of the Angles.' Though the chief fellow-worker of Felix was for a time an Irishman, St. Fursey, the converts in this province looked towards Canterbury. Therefore Bishop Lightfoot's dictum that Augustine was but the 'Apostle of Kent'[34] is not the whole truth though it is near the truth.

There is no denying that the Augustinian missionaries showed eminent discretion in returning to their base when an advanced position became dangerous. There were, however, extenuating circumstances. They were city-bred; their earlier years had been spent within the four walls of a Roman monastery; they were men of southern ways and southern temperaments; and the

---

* OE. Sigeberht.

rough manners and hardly understood speech of the northern aborigines to whom they had been sent must, when combined with the sunless skies and cold and rain of our climate, have made missionary work in England as great an ordeal as the austerities imposed by St. David on the monks of Menevia.

The clergy of Augustine did their duty according to their lights, but, like English missionaries in India, they did not easily mingle with their converts; and it appears that some sixty years after the coming of Augustine, his Italian successors were still not able to speak the English language with any fluency.[35]

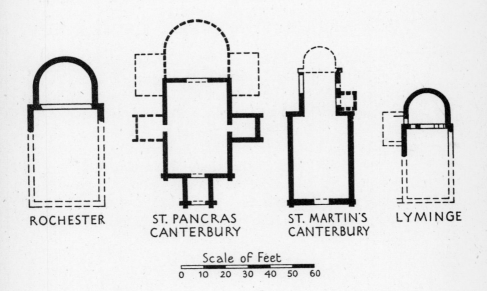

ROCHESTER   ST. PANCRAS   ST. MARTIN'S   LYMINGE
                   CANTERBURY   CANTERBURY

Scale of Feet
0   10   20   30   40   50   60

VIII. Part II

THE CONVERSION: THE SECOND GENERATION

THE outline of political events which has to preface the story of the Scottish Mission is chiefly concerned with the rivalry between Northumbrians and Mercians. Some of the political facts will find a natural place in the narrative of the Conversion which follows, but the reader who is not sure about the main story should now refresh his memory of its outlines by looking at the genealogies of the kings of Northumbria and of Mercia,* at the chronological table,† and at the maps which show the frequent alternations of power in the middle of the seventh century. In the genealogy it should be noticed that, though cousins of Edwin rule in Deira at intervals till eighteen years after his death, the murder of the last of these, Oswin (slain in cold blood by order of Oswy of Bernicia), brings the House of Ælle to an end. For the rest of the century, both Northumbrian kingdoms are ruled by the sons and grandsons of Ethelfrith. Three of these, Oswald (634–42), Oswy ‡ (642–71), Oswy's son Ecgfrith (671–85), are mentioned by Bede as kings who enjoyed the *imperium* (or *ducatus*).

HEADPIECE.—Celtic clergy, from Scottish sculptured stones. Note their book-satchels.

* Vol. ii, pp. 722, 719.   † Vol. ii, p. 729.
‡ OE. *Oswio*.

The Second Generation

But it is only necessary to glance at the maps to see that their supremacy was not as complete as that of Edwin, and that at certain periods the power of the House of Penda was more considerable than that of the House of Ida. On the whole, the Northumbrians were losing ground in this age, and the Mercians

were gaining it. If we summarize the alternations of power, we have some such story as this.

Oswald, the representative of the Bernician dynasty, had defeated Cadwallon and his Britons near Heavenfield; since he came as a deliverer, he had no difficulty in establishing himself in Deira as well as in Bernicia. He also restored Northumbrian influence over some of the southern States, his position being illustrated by the part he took in the baptism of the king of Wessex (*c.* 635). But he did not recover any lasting authority over Mercia proper (that is, the original kingdom round the Trent) or over some of the neighbouring provinces. These remained in the hands of Penda (626–55), who made good use of his position on the flank of Northumbria's road to the south. By 642 Penda was strong enough to defeat and slay Oswald at the battle of Maserfield,* just as nine years earlier he had destroyed Edwin. Then followed a period of Northumbrian eclipse. The two

Northumbrian kingdoms were separated and Penda extended his power, first over Wessex (645), and then over East Anglia (650). By 654 he clearly had won to the south of the Humber an *imperium* approximating to that shown on the map. Penda had, in fact, built up for the first time a Greater Mercia. The king of Mercia had become king of the Midlands. When in 655 Penda vowed to blot out all the nation of the Northumbrians,

* OE. Maserfelð; Plummer (*Bede*, ii. 152) sums up the argument for locating this at Oswestry (Oswald's Tree) in Shropshire. The identification must be considered uncertain. A. Hunt, in *Journal of Arch. Ass.* (N.S.), xxx. 109–17, suggests a site in the Isle of Axholme, but this is improbable.

and Oswy, king of Bernicia, with a small army dared to oppose him, Penda was able to summon thirty 'legions'.[1] 'The engagement began; the pagans were put to flight or killed; the thirty royal commanders . . . who had come to Penda's assistance were almost all of them slain; . . . the battle was fought near the river

Winwaed.* Owing to the great rains the river was then in flood and had overflowed its banks, so that many more were drowned in the flight than were destroyed in battle by the sword.' Penda's legions did not avail to save him from defeat and death at the battle of the Winwaed. Thus, in the middle of Oswy's reign, that is during the years 655–8, Northumbrian authority once more reached the Severn and the Thames. For these three years Oswy was direct ruler of Mercia and appointed his own ealdormen. A revolt followed; and Wulfhere, the successful rebel,

* Apparently located by Bede *in regione Loidis*. See note 1a.

battle of Winwaed

taking up the work of his father Penda, built anew on his foundations the kingdom of the Midlands which we have called Greater Mercia. Accordingly, when the Synod of Whitby was held in 664, the Humber[2] was again the dividing line between Northumbria and Mercia. Wulfhere before his death in 675 had spread Mercian rule over 'all the southern peoples',[3] including Kent and Wessex. His successor, Ethelred, another son of Penda, began his reign with a pitiless devastation of Kent, presumably to punish a revolt. In 679 he fought a great battle with Ecgfrith of Northumbria on the Trent, and was threatening 'a more bloody war',[4] when Archbishop Theodore intervened. A long peace between Northumbria and Mercia ensued. About the same time Mercia also suspended its schemes of aggression south of the Thames.

Thus, looking back on this stormy period, the age wherein the second generation of English converts played their parts, we see that its chief political phenomena were the following: first, the decline of the south-eastern kingdoms into second-class powers; then in the middle of the century the confederation of the Midland States into a Greater Mercia; and thirdly, towards the end of the century, a temporary condition of unstable equilibrium among the three chief kingdoms, Northumbria, Mercia, and Wessex.

THE SCOTTISH MISSION TO THE ENGLISH

We have now to return to the year 633 and to trace the coming of Scottish Christianity to the north of England and to the Midlands, a story which gives us the main theme of the middle period of the seventh century, and to which the wars and the political ambitions of the kings are but a rumbling accompaniment.

If we search back for the very beginning of the new movement, we may find it in the flight of Oswald and Oswy, the sons of Ethelfrith, from Edwin of Deira (617), a flight which brought

them to Iona. This chance incident leading in the second generation of the Conversion to the Scottish mission may be regarded as
a counterpart to the meeting of Gregory with the Anglian boys
in the Roman slave-market, the incident which had led to the
Roman mission of the first generation. A closer parallel offers
itself if we compare the exile of Oswald at Iona with that earlier
exile of Edwin, when fleeing from the father of Oswald. In either
case, the feud between the dynasties of Ælle and Ida was the
determining factor. The banishment of the princes caused them
to mingle with the Christians in the west of the island. Oswald
and Oswy spent some of their seventeen years' exile at Iona;
and there, where Columba was still a living memory, they learnt
to know Celtic Christianity from the inside as no English ruler
had hitherto known it. Oswald's conviction of the truth of the
new religion when he regained his father's kingdom, was to be
a far more potent force than the politic acquiescence of Ethelbert
and of Edwin.

During the 'hateful year' (633–4) which followed the over-
throw of Edwin, men relapsed into heathendom. The kings of
Bernicia and Deira (the two kingdoms being again separated)
acted ingloriously. Eanfrith, the king of Bernicia, the eldest
brother of Oswald and Oswy, coming to sue for peace from the
British conqueror, was struck down by him. The fury which the
Britons had been storing in their hearts for two centuries was let
loose. They took their last revenge.

Oswald returned from the land of the Scots with twelve faithful
thegns[5] who had shared his exile and followed him to baptism.
These, with a small force, withstood and defeated an 'immense'
army of Cadwallon. At Heavenfield, where the Roman Wall
crests a heathery hill before dipping steeply into the valley of
the North Tyne, Oswald made a large cross of rough timber, and
stood it up in a hole in the ground, holding it in both hands while
others filled in the earth—the first cross, says Bede, to be erected
in Bernicia. His army, at his bidding, prayed on their knees
before this cross, Oswald himself invoking St. Columba. Then,

at the first dawn of day, and somewhere[6] in that region of the
Wall, Angle and Briton fought their last great fight; and Cadwallon was slain. This victory was but the first of innumerable
miracles to be worked by Oswald's cross, planted on that same
moor which from one dreary day to another had been scanned
by Roman soldiers, confident in their discipline and asking for
no miracle-working cross.

When Oswald had established himself as king of all Northumbria, it was naturally to Iona that he applied for Christian
teachers; and in one of these, Aidan a Scot, he found (635) the
right man for the work of converting his Northumbrian subjects.
Oswald accordingly gave Aidan and his family of monks Lindisfarne, an island at high tide, situated near his fortress of Bamburgh. On that wind-swept headland, the bleakest spot of
an inhospitable shore, a community of the regular Scoto-Irish
type established itself, raising a collection of huts and an oratory
within a defensive enclosure. From this 'island' members of the
community year after year set out on foot across three miles of
sand to preach, first in the neighbouring villages of Bernicia, and
later in distant centres. Some of these were even hundreds of
miles away in the south.

Bede[7] tells us how Aidan 'was wont to traverse both town and
country on foot, never on horseback, unless compelled by some
urgent necessity; to the end that as he went he might turn aside
to any whomsoever he saw, whether rich or poor, and call upon
them if infidels to receive the mystery of the faith, or, if they
were believers, strengthen them in the faith'. What specially
drew men to him was that he lived as he preached, and that he
refused to accept any riches for himself or his followers. He was
allowed to use the king's vills (which were probably the centres
of local government) as the outposts of his journeys, and so he
was able to cover wide tracts of Northumbria. The Scots were
more successful than the Romans, not only because they perambulated the countryside, but because their mission was recruited by volunteers. Aidan's helpers did not wait to come till

PLATE 41

Lindisfarne, drawing by J. M. W. Turner (1830). The ruins are on the site of the original monastery. Turner gives the spirit of the place, but distorts its details, especially the height of the Castle rock

PLATE 42

Bradwell-on-Sea. Nave of the Church built by St. Cedd within
the Roman Fort Othona (Ythancester)
By permission of the Controller of H.M. Stationery Office

The Roman Road across the Wheeldale Moor, between York
and Whitby

they were bidden.⁸ 'Many came daily into Britain from the country of the Scots, and with great devotion preached the Word. . . . Churches were built in several places; the people joyfully flocked together to hear the Word; lands and other property were given of the King's bounty to found monasteries; English children as well as their elders were instructed by their Scottish teachers in study and the observance of monastic discipline.'

What made these seven years of Oswald's rule seem a golden age to Bede as he looked back at them from a distance of almost a century was the harmonious co-operation of the king and his missionary bishop. Oswald never forgot the lessons which he had learnt at Iona as an exile. When Aidan, who was not skilful in the English tongue, preached the Gospel 'it was a fair sight to see the king himself interpreting the Word of God to his ealdormen and thegns'. The harmony which existed between the king and the missionary saint is echoed in the familiar story about Aidan as he sat at table with the king one Easter Day, blessing the hand of Oswald, the hand which had just presented to the poor a silver dish containing the king's own meal—*Nunquam inveterescet haec manus*. For centuries the uncorrupted flesh of the king's right hand was preserved in the reliquary at Bamburgh, and the uncorrupted spirit of the king was immortalized in Bede's story for ever.

When this golden age was suddenly interrupted in 642 by the battle of Maserfield, and Oswald, like Edwin, became a victim to the enmity of the heathen Penda, the head and arms of Oswald were severed from the trunk. But the dead king was quickly canonized by the people. (It was characteristic of the Anglo-Saxons that their first native saint should be a king.) Miracles were said to be worked by his mutilated corpse; nay more, by the water in which his butchered limbs had been washed, and by a splinter of the stake on which his head had been placed. The corpse of St. Oswald, decapitated and dismembered, helped to propagate the new religion as effectually as Oswald the living king.

The Christianity of Oswy Oswald's successor, was as firm as his brother's, if less effective; and Aidan till his death in 651 continued to receive the support of the monarchy in his work of conversion. The reign of Oswy was in fact the decisive period. Up to his accession, Northumbria had experienced only six years of official Roman Christianity under Edwin, and eight years of Scottish propaganda under Oswald. But Oswy's tenure of the throne (642–71)* was long enough for Christianity to take root and fructify throughout all the Anglian kingdoms, for the conflict between the Roman and Scottish churches to be brought to an issue, and for new personal conflicts, centring round Wilfrid, to be generated. The changing phases of the political situation which we have already noted—the growing power of Penda south of the Humber (642–55), the short supremacy of Oswy (655–8), the re-establishment of Mercian power under Wulfhere, son of Penda (658–75)—these phases in the political history did not greatly affect the progress of the Conversion. The great landmarks in its history at this stage are the sending of Scottish preachers to Mercia and Essex (653–4), the Synod of Whitby (664), and after the Synod the coming of Archbishop Theodore to Canterbury. Little need be said about the first period of Oswy's reign. Aidan continued to preach in Deira as well as in Bernicia, being warmly encouraged by Oswin, a cousin of Edwin, who had re-established the House of Ælle on the throne of York. It was Oswin who gave Aidan a horse, and persuaded him to abandon the Scottish fashion of making his missionary journeys on foot. Then, when Aidan gave the horse to one of the first beggars he met, it was Oswin who, repenting of his first anger, fell down at Aidan's feet begging him for forgiveness. Aidan, as Bishop-Abbot of Lindisfarne, was, except for the theoretical authority of the parent church of Iona, sole ruler of the Northumbrian Church until his death in 651. Under him the monastery of Lindisfarne remained the training-school for preachers, and the centre from which the new learning radiated to distant kingdoms.

* Until 655 he was king of Bernicia only.

The methods of Celtic propaganda were traditional. In Iona St. Columba had trained twelve disciples; legend said that St. Patrick had trained a like number. Aidan accordingly followed the ancient custom and prepared twelve young men to continue and to extend his work. Thus was the idea of the *comitatus* applied to religion, and applied in such a way that the bands of trained followers could increase like a snowball.

The two of Aidan's pupils who were most prominent in extending his work after his death were the brothers Cedd and Chad.* They both took a part in preaching Christianity to the Mercians, but it is Cedd who first comes into the story—in the period before the Synod of Whitby. In the years 653–4 Cedd distinguished himself not only by being one of the first missionaries to the Angles of the Midlands, but also by reviving Christianity in Essex, where, as we have seen, it had died down since 617. Neither of these operations in the Scottish religious campaign need be told in detail. It is sufficient to remember that Christianity came to the Midlands in the same way that it had come to Kent and to Northumbria. When Peada, son of Penda, and under-king over the Middle Angles, wished to marry a daughter of Oswy⁹ 'he could not obtain his desire unless he would receive the faith of Christ and be baptized with the nation which he governed'. Accordingly, Cedd and other disciples of Aidan, headed by Diuma, soon to be made their bishop, were sent to Penda's son-in-law with his Northumbrian bride.

Perhaps the most notable feature in this first step towards the Conversion of Mercia is the fact that the mission was arranged while Penda was still at the height of his power. The attitude of Penda to the new religion is an interesting contrast both to that of kings like Edwin, who came over slowly but surely, and to that of temporizing backsliders like Raedwald of East Anglia. We do not know how far Penda's earlier antagonism to the Christian kings of Northumbria had been dictated by religious motives. What Bede makes clear is simply this, that in his later

* OE. Ceadda.

significance of Winwaed

years he remained a heathen, but no persecutor. 'Nor did king Penda forbid the preaching of the Word among his people the Mercians, if any were willing to hear it. But on the contrary, he hated and despised those whom he perceived not to perform the works of faith, when they had once received the faith of Christ, saying "They were contemptible and wretched who did not obey their God in whom they believed".' Though Penda had come to tolerate the preachers from Northumbria, he was not prepared to accept without challenge the increasing political power of Oswy. When Penda in the third of his great battles against the Northumbrians was killed, Oswy, for the time being all-powerful south as well as north of the Humber, 'converted the Mercians in the adjacent provinces to the grace of the Christian faith'. This battle of the Winwaed marks the final transfer of military and political predominance amongst the Anglo-Saxons from heathens to Christians. Paganism survived in out-of-the-way corners of the island, but never again could it openly challenge the new faith.

MISSIONS TO WESSEX (c. 635) AND ESSEX (653-4*)

Some knowledge of the conversion of Wessex and of the resumed conversion of Essex is needed to understand the situation of affairs in 664. The accounts in Bede of both events are short, and can therefore be given in his own words:[10]

'At that time the West Saxons, formerly called Gewissae, in the reign of Cynegils, received the faith of Christ, through the preaching of Bishop Birinus, who came into Britain by the counsel of Pope Honorius; having promised in his presence that he would sow the seed of the holy faith in the farthest inland regions of the English, where no other teacher had been before him. . . . On his arrival in Britain, he first came to the nation of the Gewissae, and finding all in that place confirmed pagans, he thought it better to preach the Word there, than to proceed further to seek for other hearers of his preaching.

'Now, as he was spreading the Gospel in the aforesaid province, it

---

* Cedd was not consecrated before 654, even if he began to preach in 653.

happened that when the king himself, having received instruction as a catechumen, was being baptized together with his people, Oswald, the most holy and victorious king of the Northumbrians, being present, received him as he came forth from baptism. . . . The two kings gave to the Bishop the city called Dorcic,* there to establish his episcopal see; where, having built and consecrated churches, and by his pious labours called many to the Lord, he departed to the Lord, and was buried in the same city.'

In this way there was established in Wessex a Church in communion with Rome, but at first not wholly under the control of Canterbury. The death of its patron, King Cynegils (641), caused the infant Church some growing pains, but its troubles are of no great importance. Turning to Bede's account of the revival of Christianity among the East Saxons,[11] we have a passage which describes how Oswy, when Sigbert,† the king of the East Saxons,

'came to the province of the Northumbrians to visit him, as he often did, used to endeavour to convince him that those could not be gods that had been made by the hands of men; that a stock or a stone could not be proper matter to form a god. . . . [After baptism] King Sigbert, having now become a citizen of the eternal kingdom, returned to the seat of his temporal kingdom, requesting of King Oswy that he would give him some teachers, to convert his nation to the faith of Christ, and cleanse them in the fountain of salvation. Wherefore, Oswy, sending into the province of the Midland Angles, summoned the man of God, Cedd, and, giving him another priest for his companion, sent them to preach the Word to the East Saxons.'

Cedd built several churches in Essex, notably that which may still be seen among the ruins of the Roman fort of Othona (Pl. 42 A). But even this second mission to the East Saxons was not a complete success. Some of the ground covered was to be again lost.

On the whole, however, it is true to say that some ten years before the Synod of Whitby every English kingdom except Sussex and the Isle of Wight had adhered to Christianity. The stage was set for a new act in the drama.

---

* Dorchester on the Thames.   † OE. Sigeberht.

THE SYNOD OF WHITBY (664)

Success brings its own difficulties, and with the assured victory of the new religion after the middle of the seventh century the interest of the story shifts. The conflict between heathenism and Christianity gave place to a conflict between one type of Christianity and another. Questions which had been of secondary importance now quickly became urgent; was there to be only one Church of the English? Was it to be Roman or Celtic? Or could both types of Christianity continue side by side?

Chaos there undoubtedly was before the Synod of Whitby. In Kent and in parts of East Anglia the Church was Roman and subordinate to Canterbury; in Wessex Roman, but independent of Canterbury; in Northumbria and in Mercia it was Scottish; in Essex the situation was uncertain. And this was not the only trouble. Other evils were threatening: that in each state the bishop and the local Church would be at the mercy of the local monarchy; that Christianity would remain disorganized, undisciplined, separatist; and that it would embitter the old strife between the kingdoms instead of fostering peace and unity. The history of the bishops of Wessex after the death of Birinus (651) is the best illustration of the consequences of a disunited provincial Christianity. The first successor of Birinus was a certain Agilbert, a Frank. The king of Wessex, finding that he could not understand this foreigner, created a new bishopric at Winchester, and gave it to a native bishop, Wini. Wini had at least the merit of speaking English. Agilbert took offence, and withdrew. Wini also quarrelled with the king, and was driven from Winchester. Later on (about 666–7) he succeeded in retrieving his fortunes by an act of simony, and bought the bishopric of London from the king of Mercia.

It was scandals such as these which brought home to some the need for a Church conference and for the appointment of a statesmanlike archbishop to control all the Heptarchic Churches, and to guide their first steps towards unity.

The controversy between Roman and Scot first became acute in Northumbria, when King Oswy's son, Alchfrith, fell under the influence of Agilbert, still nominally bishop of the West Saxons, and of Wilfrid, a handsome Northumbrian noble, newly returned from Rome. But the immediate occasion for the Synod of Whitby was the practical difficulty caused by the observance of Easter at different dates, the king calculating it according to the Scottish method of reckoning, and the queen (a daughter of King Edwin) according to the Roman.[12] In 664 Oswy foresaw that in the following year the difference between the two reckonings would be considerable, and that, while he was celebrating the Easter feast, his queen would be keeping her Lenten fast. No doubt he also realized that the adherence to the Romans of his son Alchfrith, whom he had made under-king in Deira, might revive the old antagonism between the two Northumbrian kingdoms in a dangerous religious form. It seems, however, that it was not so much considerations of policy which moved Oswy and his advisers to summon the conference as an uneasy feeling born of growing intercourse with the continental Church, that those who were following the usages of the Scots might be running in vain; that in spite of all their fastings and good works they might be failing to ensure their entrance to heaven. For these reasons, in 664, nine years after the defeat of Penda and five years after the successful revolt of Penda's son, Wulfhere, Oswy summoned to the place which before the coming of the Danes was called Streanæshalch the conference of leading Northumbrian Christians commonly known as the 'Synod of Whitby'.

This event, which is one of the great turning-points in the history of the race, deserves our special attention. We must think of the monastery where the conference met as one of twelve which had been founded by Oswy, as thank-offerings for his victory over Penda. The monastery was of the 'double' type, that is, it included a community of dedicated women, as well as a separate community of men for the services of the church. Men and women were alike ruled by the Abbess Hilda, who

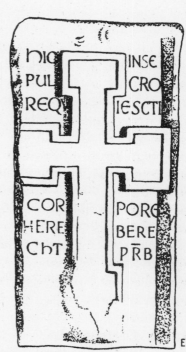

FIG. 48. Northumbrian Recumbent Gravestones.

A and B.—Hartlepool (⅕). A to the memory of (?) HANEGNEUB. B.—ORATE PRO
EDILUINI ORATE PRO UERMUND ET TORHTSUID. C and D.—Lindisfarne. C (less than
⅕) to the memory of AEDBERECHT. D (more than ⅕) to OSGYTH (above in runes,
below in Hiberno-Saxon characters). Since this is a woman's name, Lindisfarne
may at one time have been a double monastery. E.—Monkwearmouth—a much
larger slab (1/12)—probably of seventh century. The lettering is Roman with some
Hiberno-Saxon characteristics.

Hilda

thirty-seven years earlier had been baptized by Paulinus in the first days of Northumbrian Christianity. At Streanæshalch she[13] 'taught the strict observance of justice, piety, chastity, and other virtues, and particularly of peace and charity; so that, after the example of the primitive church, no one there was rich, and none poor, for they had all things common, and none had

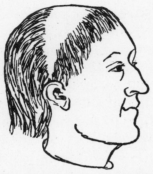

FIG. 49. The Celtic tonsure, probable appearance.

any private property. Her prudence was so great, that not only meaner men in their need, but sometimes even kings and princes sought and received her counsel.' Thus, under her wise discipline, the monastery was becoming the nursery of future bishops.

Thanks to Bede, many of the leading clergy who came to the conference are well known to us. There was Colman, the chief spokesman for the Celtic party, a Scot who had been sent only three years previously from Iona to become bishop-abbot at Lindisfarne; not yet able, it seems, to speak English, and therefore not effective as an advocate; but a prudent man and, like his clergy who accompanied him from Lindisfarne, a lover of simple ways and a despiser of money and wealth:[14] 'For the whole care of those teachers was to serve God, not the world—to feed the soul and not the belly.' There too, inclining to the Scots, was Bishop Cedd, Celtic by training and perhaps by descent, Celtic in his casual pluralism (he was now abbot of Lastingham in Deira as well as bishop of the East Saxons), Celtic also in his demonology: he had recently exorcized the evil spirits of the wilds of Lastingham by continuous prayer and extreme fasting throughout Lent.

Colman and the clergy who adhered to Scottish customs were a strange sight owing to their tonsure. Their heads were shaved from ear to ear: in front, it seemed, a wisp of hair; at the back of the head long flowing locks.[15]

The supporters of Rome were marked out from the Scots by their shaven crowns. The senior in age among them was James, the deacon and expert chanter, who, when Paulinus fled from Northumbria, stayed behind to teach and to baptize. The superior in rank was Bishop Agilbert, who, though a Frank, was no doubt well primed on the Scottish controversy, having himself studied in Ireland. The foremost in energy and ability, the man who had already won over the under-king of Deira, and was giving momentum to the Roman party, was Wilfrid, abbot of Ripon. He was by birth a Northumbrian, one of the fighting aristocracy, an enterprising restless fellow. He had not been happy as a boy at school, nor as a young noble in attendance on the queen at court, nor as an untonsured inmate at Lindisfarne. There, after a few years among the Scots, 'it came into his heart to pay a visit to the see of the Apostle Peter and attempt a road hitherto untrodden by any of our race'.[15a] During the five years (653–8) which he spent on his journey to Rome, he at last found in the cause of St. Peter the ideal for which he could fight with all the pugnacity of his thegnly ancestors. Some three years after his return to Northumbria, his patron Alchfrith, the under-king in Deira, made him abbot of Ripon, having first ejected those members of the community who refused to surrender their Scottish customs. And now in 664 Wilfrid had the great opportunity of his life; for Agilbert, the Frank, on the ground that he himself could not make a speech in English, asked him to plead the Roman cause. Wilfrid's speech was long and eloquent; but one of his sentences will suffice to show the line and the tone of his argument: 'All over the world the Easter which we observe is celebrated, except only by these and their accomplices in obstinacy, I mean the Picts and the Britons, who foolishly in these two remote islands, oppose all the rest of the universe.' Colman, speaking for the Scots, replied that they followed the usage of St. John, the Beloved of the Lord, the usage of Father Columba, and others who had worked many miracles. 'Who are these,' Wilfrid insisted, 'compared with the Apostle Peter, who keeps the door of Heaven?'

A memorable debate for us, if ever there was one! What if Ethelfrith, the heathen, the slayer of the twelve hundred monks of Bangor, could have returned to see his son presiding over these robed and shaven clergy, listening to the involved debate, whether Easter should be celebrated in the Scottish manner, from the fourteenth to the twentieth day of the moon, or in the Roman manner, from the fifteenth to the twenty-first. Oswy no doubt failed to follow the abstruse arguments as closely as he might. His decision at the end was certainly based on the simpler proposition, admitted even by the Scots. 'Peter is the doorkeeper, and he has the keys. Against him I will not contend.' 'The king, having said this, all who were seated there or standing by, both great and small, gave their assent, and, renouncing the less perfect custom, hastened to conform to that which they had found to be better.' The Conference broke up, and those who had taken part in it went their several ways.

'Colman, perceiving that his doctrine was rejected and his party despised, took with him . . . such as would not accept the Catholic Easter and the tonsure in the form of a crown (for there was no small dispute about that also) and went back into Scotland. . . . But Eata, who was abbot of the monastery called Mailros [old Melrose], a man most reverent and gentle, was appointed abbot over the brethren that chose to remain in the church of Lindisfarne when the Scots went away. It is said that Colman upon his departure requested and obtained this of King Oswy, because Eata was one of Aidan's twelve boys of the English nation, whom he received to be instructed in Christ.'

Colman and his followers then wandered from Iona to Ireland. They settled in Innisboffin, an island off Mayo. But those who agreed about the date of Easter found it difficult to agree about other matters. They might keep Easter from the fourteenth to the twentieth day of the moon, and shave their heads from ear to ear, but their ways of life were still discordant, and the thirty Englishmen who had accompanied Colman from Lindisfarne objected that 'the Scots, in the summer season, when the harvest was to be brought in, leaving the monastery, wandered about through places known to them; but returned again the next winter, and desired to use in common what the English had provided'.[16] Finally, a new monastery was established, and the English were transferred to it, to end the bickerings with the Scots.

Of the kings, Alchfrith the son, after securing the promotion of Wilfrid to a bishopric, disappears from history. All we know is that trouble developed between him and his father. At Bewcastle, in Cumberland, we may still see the cross-shaft probably erected to his memory by Wilfrid or some member of Wilfrid's party. It stands where it has stood for some twelve hundred years;* but the fate of this young king, who had taken the initiative in bringing about the discomfiture of the Scots, must remain a mystery.

Oswy survived till 671 and in the end became sufficiently devoted to his adopted Church to wish that Wilfrid should conduct him to Rome itself—a plan interrupted by his death.

Of the champions of Rome, Agilbert returned to France and became bishop of Paris; James, the deacon, lived on into Bede's own time, teaching the Deirans round Catterick how to chant in the Roman manner. Wilfrid at first went from one success to another. A few months after the conference he was, with the consent of King Oswy, made a bishop of the Northumbrians. He crossed to Gaul in great state with a band of clergy, and a troop of twenty fighting men. There he was consecrated by twelve Catholic bishops, who carried him aloft in a golden chair,

* See below, pp. 362 ff.

according to the Gallican rite. But success had come too early, and we shall see in the next chapter how the promise of his youth led to a middle and old age embittered by quarrels both with the rulers of Northumbria and with the archbishops of Canterbury.

The Conference at Whitby settled the question about Easter, but left behind a smouldering feud within the Northumbrian Church. Fifteen years later the Abbess Hilda still headed the opposition to Wilfrid, and laid an accusation against him before the Pope. By that time she had become an old lady of sixty-five, 'whom all that knew her called Mother'.

If we ask, then, what were the results of this so-called Synod, we find that, while in some respects the victory was limited, in the main it was decisive. It was limited because, strictly speaking, it only applied to one kingdom; because it only related to two diversities of custom; because it allowed other Celtic peculiarities to continue; and because it did not put an end to jealousies and ill feelings between the two schools within the Church. On the other hand, it was in fact decisive. Oswy still enjoyed prestige though he had lost supremacy in Britain. The other English kingdoms converted by the Scots quickly came into line. The neighbouring Celtic kingdoms followed more slowly: the northern Irish,* the Dumnonians, the Picts and Scots of Scotland, and the Strathclyde Welsh, changed one or two generations after the Synod of Whitby; but the Welsh of Wales not till 768, and the Cornishmen not till the ninth century. It is no exaggeration to say that the Synod turned the scales and decided that the English should take their religion and their civilization from the Roman world rather than from what Wilfrid called 'One remote corner of the most remote island'. Thenceforth their destiny was to be linked with that of the Continent. The Churches of the Anglo-Saxon kingdoms were to have the advantage of the unity, the organization, and the discipline, which the Roman Church had inherited from the Roman Empire. But while they were thus to escape the dangerous

---

* The southern Irish had changed their Easter some decades before 664.

liberty of Celtic Christianity they were long to retain the spiritual fervour, the originality, the zeal for learning and preaching, which the Scots had brought with them. The next two chapters will help to show how the characteristics of the parent Churches were combined in their English offspring.

TAILPIECE.—The Old Saxon catechism (*Abrenuntiatio diaboli*) in which the German converts of St. Boniface were required to renounce heathenism:

Forsachistu diobolae? ℞. Ec forsacho diabolae.

End allum diobolgeldę? ℞. End ec forsacho allum diobolgeldae.

End allum dioboles uuercum? ℞. End ec forsacho allum dioboles uuercum and uuordum thunaer ende uuoden ende saxnote ende allum them unholdum the hira genotas sint.

[Dost thou forsake the devil? I forsake the devil.

And all the devil's wage? And I forsake all the devil's wage.

And all the devil's works? And I forsake all the devil's works and words, Thunor and Woden and Saxnote, and all the fiends that are their companions.]

MS. Vat. Palat. nro. 577.

IX

THE GOLDEN AGE

THEODORE AND HADRIAN

IN the first generation of the Conversion the Roman mission
had established a base for Christianity in the south. In the
second generation the Scots and their English disciples had
tramped preaching through the North and Midlands, while
another mission from Rome had founded a Church in Wessex.
The third generation was to put an end to the confusion left by
this earlier haphazard growth of Christianity. Its success was in
a sense more remarkable than that of its predecessors; for Christianity was bound to spread to the English either from the south
or from the north or from both; and the chances were all in
favour of the English converts gravitating to the greater Church,
to Rome rather than to Iona. But it was an extraordinary dis-
pensation which sent Theodore of Tarsus to our island after the
Conference of Whitby, just at the moment when it was essential
that order should be organized out of chaos. By a happy chance
the death at Rome of the Englishman who had been sent to Pope
Vitalian to receive the archbishop's pall made it possible for
Vitalian to appoint a successor, and all credit must be given to
the Papacy for its selection of Theodore, who, even more than

HEADPIECE.—Aldhelm, Hildelith, and the Nuns of Barking.

Stephen Langton, that later nominee of Rome, brought the blessing of good government to the English people as well as to their Church. The choice of Vitalian had fallen first on Hadrian, an abbot of African origin, 'excellently skilled both in the Greek and Latin tongues',[1] and it was Hadrian who modestly suggested that the Greek Theodore would be a better man for the post, and offered to go in a subordinate position and accompany his friend to Canterbury. Though Theodore was 66 years old when he was thus chosen in 668, he ruled the Church with vigour until he was 87, and Hadrian, who was made abbot of St. Peter's (St. Augustine's) at Canterbury, survived till about 709. The lasting friendship and co-operation of these two elderly men—the one an Asiatic, the other an African from a monastery near Naples— and the success of their joint work among the newly converted barbarians of the north, is one of the best testimonials to the cosmopolitanism of the medieval Church.

When Theodore, after more than a year's interval, arrived in England in May 669, the situation was critical. Though Oswy had recognized the authority of Rome and of Canterbury in the Conference of 664, for five years there had been no archbishop at Canterbury who could exercise that authority. These five years had moreover been years of plague; and bishops and clergy had been carried off by the disease. Theodore on his arrival found only three bishops in the land: Wini, who had committed simony by buying the see of London; Wilfrid, who had returned from a valid consecration in Gaul, to find that his diocese had during his absence been 'stolen' (that was the word used by his partisans) by Chad,[2] and whose quarrelsome disposition might render him more of a hindrance than a help to his metropolitan; and thirdly Chad, whose position as bishop of the Northumbrians was impaired not only by the charges of Wilfrid's friends but also by the participation of schismatic Britons in his consecration. Such was the situation in 669. Theodore's method of dealing with it, as described by Bede, may be summarized under six heads.

(1) His first business was to see that the bishoprics were filled with men who would co-operate with him. With this object he made a visitation throughout England: he consecrated a new bishop at Rochester, another at Dunwich for East Anglia; at London he allowed Wini to keep his see till his death; at York he removed Chad. Then, seeing the goodness of this humble man, he re-consecrated him according to Catholic rites, and installed him at Lichfield; he ordered him to be sensible and ride a horse in order to get round his diocese, and not to attempt it on foot in the Scottish manner—indeed, it is said that Theodore lifted Chad onto his horse with his own hands. The bishopric of all Northumbria was entrusted to Wilfrid. Thus, in the words of Bede,[3] 'Theodore visited all parts, ordained bishops in proper places, and with their assistance corrected such things as he found faulty'.

(2) His next concern was to enfold in a new unity the existing dioceses which had hitherto kept alive the particularism of the Heptarchic kingdoms. The visitation just mentioned was the beginning of this new policy; it was a visitation of all the island 'wherever the English inhabited'. Everywhere he instructed men in the Roman custom of celebrating Easter, so that, as Bede says, 'this was the first archbishop whom all the English Church obeyed'. Then, in 672,[4] he summoned to Hertford a council of bishops gathered from all the land, a visible symbol of unification; and the nine canons which Theodore persuaded the bishops to adopt were the first laws ever made for all Angles and Saxons. One of the canons provided that a similar synod should be held once a year on August 1st. This was carrying the idea of unity too far to be practicable, and it was not till 679[5] that a second synod was held, this time at Hatfield—a synod which formally declared its adhesion to the Catholic faith.

Thus we see that a united English Church was being consolidated in four different ways. It was acknowledging a common archbishop, it was being visited and reformed by him, leaders were assembling in council under his presidency, and together were formulating legislation to be enforced throughout every Heptarchic kingdom. In all this Theodore was preparing the way for the political union of the kingdoms.

(3) The unity of the Church was a means to an end, and the end was the reform of abuses. Theodore's programme of reform is best seen in the canons promulgated by his Council of Hertford in 672. By these a bishop was forbidden to 'invade' the diocese of another bishop, monks were forbidden to move in the Celtic fashion from monastery to monastery, and clergy were forbidden to wander at will from diocese to diocese. Thus the age of missions, the age of migratory clergy, was coming to an end; but this did not mean that the clergy were thenceforth tied down to small districts like modern parishes. There was an intermediate stage in which a group of clergy served a large district, often corresponding in size to a modern rural deanery. We shall see later that the parish system was to be a growth of centuries. Theodore assisted the growth, but here he was no creator.

(4) One reform discussed at the Council of Hertford was an increase in the number of dioceses. The need for it was obvious. Even after Theodore's division of the Northumbrian diocese, we find Bede still complaining that there were not nearly enough bishops, and that there were still many villages which had never seen a bishop. But vested interests were at stake. The bishops, assembled at Hertford, refused to endorse the proposal of their metropolitan. Theodore was left to act on his own initiative, and in the ensuing period he had to content himself with carrying out his scheme for the division of the dioceses gradually and partially, seizing opportunities as they occurred. On the retirement of a bishop of the East Anglians, Elmham was made a new see for their North Folk. Winfrith, the successor of Chad at Lichfield, was deposed for disobedience about 675; and then or later three new bishoprics were created in the Midlands—for the Middle Angles, for the Hwicce, and for the settlers in the district west of the Severn.* In 678 Theodore, with the consent of the

* Afterwards known as the bishoprics of Leicester, Worcester, and Hereford.

Northumbrian king, but without the consent of Wilfrid the Northumbrian bishop, began to carve out new dioceses, two in Bernicia with sees at Lindisfarne and Hexham, and one in Lindsey, for the time subject to Northumbria. This scheme led

to a long series of conflicts between Wilfrid and those whom he regarded as his persecutors, Theodore and the king of Northumbria. A reckless accusation of corruption was made against the archbishop by Eddius,* Wilfrid's chaplain, who narrated the quarrels at great length. All that need be admitted is that Theodore, though right in wishing to divide the vast bishopric of Northumbria, was irregular and high-handed in his treatment of Wilfrid. On the other hand Wilfrid, however much he might be within his canonical rights, showed in his stubborn resistance

* OE. Æddi.

more the fighting spirit of the thegn than the grace of the Christian. It is no small testimony to Theodore's own vigour that he was able to hold his own against such an opponent. Eddius tells us that the archbishop at the end of his life (686–7) was reconciled with Wilfrid, and puts into his mouth a humiliating and obviously fictitious confession of his past errors.

The result of Theodore's endeavours was that England at his death possessed fifteen dioceses, and though he had failed to apply his policy to Wessex, the omission was remedied by his successors.

(5) Another monument to the enterprise and good sense of Theodore is the Penitential which is known by his name. Though this treatise was written down after Theodore's death, it claims to give his replies to questions put to him about penance. Something will be said in a later chapter of the general attempt of the Church to discipline first its clergy, and later its lay converts, into ways of Christianity, morality, and decency, by requiring confessions from offenders and imposing fastings and other penances as the Church's remedy. Here we need do no more than notice the statesmanship with which Theodore in his Penitential adapts the customs of different branches of the Christian Church to the needs of the English people. The idea of substituting private confession for the public confession in church required in earlier centuries had been developed by the Welsh and Irish. Theodore recognized that the Celtic practice, though novel, was salutary. He revealed his wide experience of the Christian world by comparing the usages of the East and of the West; and he showed his judgement by recommending that which seemed to be the more suitable for his own province. Thus in the chapter on 'The Communion of the Eucharist or the Sacrifice', the Penitential says:[6]

'1. The Greeks, both clergy and laity, communicate every Sunday, as the canons require, and those who do not communicate on three Sundays, are excommunicated.

'2. The Romans similarly communicate, those who wish to do so; and those who do not wish to do so, are not excommunicated.

.   .   .   .

'7. If necessary, confession to God alone is lawful.' [In some manuscripts the clause 'if necessary' is not found.]

Theodore was at times more tolerant than the Papacy. His book allowed an adulterous woman who had been divorced by her husband to re-marry after five years. But the permanent importance of his work is not in its details: it is his acceptance of the usage of private confession which is now recognized as a turning-point in the history of the Western Church.

(6) Last but not least among the services which Theodore and Abbot Hadrian rendered to the Church in England was the establishment of a school at Canterbury, where 'they gathered a crowd of disciples'. There they taught them such art of versification, and such astronomy, arithmetic, and music, as seemed suitable for clerics, giving them not only a sound education in Latin, but also some knowledge of Greek. Both men had come from lands where they had been in direct contact with Byzantine culture, transmitted without a break from the ancient world. Theodore, in particular, had been a student in the schools of Athens and, as a native of Cilicia, had lived in the neighbourhood of Syria, where learning and art had flamed into a wonderful sunset glow before the region was overwhelmed by the Arabs. The indifference of St. Augustine and his followers to learning, an attitude copied from Pope Gregory himself, now gave place to an enthusiasm more disciplined and purposeful than that of the Irish. The influence of the new school overstepped the boundaries of tribe and race. The Irish could not resist the strong attraction of its learning and its library. Aldhelm, a member of the royal House of Wessex, became one of its first students. Benedict Biscop, who had presided over the school in its early days while Hadrian was learning English ways, deliberately transplanted its traditions to Wearmouth and Jarrow in his own Northumbria. It is in the works of Aldhelm, and of

Bede the monk of Jarrow, that the value of the new education can best be illustrated.

It was altogether fortunate that the English converts of the third generation were sufficiently advanced in Christian culture to profit from the learning which Theodore and Hadrian brought them from Mediterranean lands.

When Archbishop Theodore died in 690, the Church of the English, ruled from Canterbury, rose with massive grandeur above the petty kingdoms in which the political energies of the nation were still confined. Under Archbishop Theodore's leadership it had become consolidated, learned, and influential, unmistakably the same Church as that which guided the destinies of the English people in the coming centuries. The miracle wrought by Theodore in uniting, organizing, and educating the Church was not the kind of miracle to win for him the title of Saint. He had not attempted to astonish the world by fastings and mortifications; what he had done was to rule his barbarians in the best spirit of ancient Rome; he had shown clearness of vision; he had formulated definite policies to meet definite needs; he had followed out his policies with skill and caution; he had been energetic and persistent. When the time came to assert the authority of the archiepiscopal church, he had asserted it—perhaps too unflinchingly—even against a prelate like Wilfrid and in the face of papal opposition. The Church canonizes its Saints: it is left for History to crown statesmen; and historians have long acclaimed Theodore as the first recognizable statesman to appear in the story of England. If any one man was the founder of the English Church, it was Theodore.

The main thread of the story of the Conversion in the third generation is to be found in the work of Theodore, which we have now sketched. But this period, after the Synod of 664, is one of many-sided interest. From one point of view its most interesting feature is the interaction of the Roman and Celtic influences; from another it is the characters of the saints, which are as fresh, though not as varied, as those of men in more modern ages of transition such as the Renaissance. From yet another point of view, the wonderful efflorescence of various arts calls for attention. Yet all these aspects are connected, and it is well not to separate them too rigidly. It is the characters of the saints, and the sculptured crosses and illuminated manuscripts, which best illustrate the blending of the Roman and Celtic influences in the new Church.

Our arrangement of the subject must be determined by the fact that, in spite of the union of their Churches, the kingdoms were still so distinct that their contributions to the development of Christianity cannot well be brought into one picture. We must first study the kingdoms separately, and see the fruits of the Conversion produced in each—the saints, the new learning, the new arts. Then, in a later chapter, we shall collect some broader ideas about the general changes which followed the Conversion.

KENT

Our knowledge of the development of Christianity in the kingdom which had been its first home is disappointing. When we have studied the two great men whom Pope Vitalian sent to England, there is little to add. This may in part be attributed to the fact that Bede was too far removed from Kent to be specially interested in the doings of this Church; but, besides this, it seems that the Christianity of the Kentish-men was not of a specially vigorous kind.

On Theodore's death two years elapsed before a successor was appointed, and three more before that successor returned from his consecration at Lyons, to take up his duties. Whatever the cause may have been—whether it was this interregnum, or the disastrous wars of Kent against Mercia and against Wessex, or the characters of the archbishops themselves—it is clear that the successors of Theodore gradually lost the commanding position which Theodore himself had won. In the eighth century they interfered seldom in the ecclesiastical affairs of the other

kingdoms; Northumbria in 735—Mercia also for a time (787–802)
—legalized its emancipation by persuading the Papacy to give
it an archbishopric of its own.

For the rest, we know that Bede had a high opinion of Albinus,
the successor of Abbot Hadrian in the monastery and school at
Canterbury; and further evidence that the monks kept alive its
literary traditions will appear later in this chapter, when we
survey the manuscripts of the age.

The Church in Kent was not lacking in monasteries; it enjoyed
some intercourse with the clergy of the other kingdoms as they
followed the highroad to Gaul; it secured from the Crown good
laws containing clear statements of clerical rights; but we do not
read of any notable zeal for religion in Kent. Its only well-
known saint, Saint Mildred, though descended through her
mother from Hengist, was a native of Mercia and a grand-
daughter of Penda.

WESSEX—INE, ALDHELM, BONIFACE

The West Saxons had to wait till about the end of the seventh
century to produce a saint of their own. Until then their Church
had been much in the hands of foreign-born bishops: St. Birinus
(635–51), who had baptized Cynegils, its first Christian king;
Agilbert the Frank (651–62), who had given offence because he
could not speak English; and later another Frank, a nephew of
Agilbert, Hlothere (670–6). The Church had also suffered from
the weakness of the West-Saxon State and the dearth of able
kings. Wessex, owing to the rise of Mercia, lost control over its
territories north of the Thames—those of the Hwicce about 628
and later those of the Cilternsæte (recovered only for a time in
the age of Ine). Moreover, in what was left of Wessex south of
the Thames there was little unity. Bede tells us that for ten years
(674–84) *subreguli*, under-kings, divided the kingdom between
them, and this was not a state of affairs without precedent.
There is little doubt that the phenomenon of *subreguli*, common
enough elsewhere, was specially a characteristic of Wessex, and

there are traces of their existence in earlier times when the kingdom was nominally under the control of a single king.[7] For
instance, a late version of the Chronicle says that when Edwin
of Northumbria reduced Wessex in 626 he slew five kings. But
the prestige of Wessex evidently reached its lowest point in the
period just before and after the Synod of Whitby, for in 661 we
find a Mercian king (Wulfhere, son of Penda) overrunning Ash-
down, that is, the Berkshire Downs, and then making a present
of the Isle of Wight and the Meonware to a king of Sussex. It was
not till 685 that Cædwalla,* a mysterious descendant of Cerdic,
unbaptized, though called by a Celtic name, and according to
Bede 'a daring young man who had been banished his country',
emerged with his war-band from the forests of the Chilterns and of
Andred, where they had found shelter. Then in a two years' reign
of unchecked success he removed the under-kings, and with much
slaughter established the authority of the house of Cerdic over
Sussex and the Isle of Wight, and even for a time also over Kent.

In the pages of Bede during the period before 685 we read of
humiliations for Wessex; but a different impression can be obtained from the Chronicle and other sources. These give us no
clear story, but they make it almost certain that the West Saxons
were compensating themselves in the west for whatever they lost
in the north and east. During long years of apparent weakness,
turning their backs on their Teutonic neighbours, they were hard
at work making their way westward among the Britons of Somerset, Dorset, and Devon—the 'West Welsh', as they were called—
felling woods, building *tuns*, and reclaiming the heavy lands in
the river valleys. A few stages in the process can be observed—
enough to contradict the view that Wessex did not make much
growth westward between the conquests of Ceawlin and those of
Ine. We might speak of the westward advance being conducted
on two, perhaps on three, fronts, if such a military metaphor
were not unsuited to a process which was as much agricultural
as military, being furthered by the felling axe of the woodman

* West Saxon, Ceadwalla.

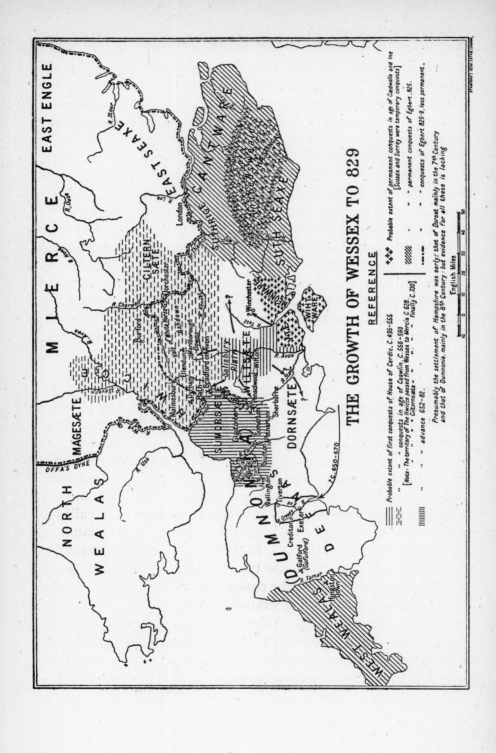

THE GROWTH OF WESSEX TO 829

REFERENCE

Probable extent of first conquests of House of Cerdic. C. 495-555

" conquests in age of Ceawlin. C. 556-593
[Note: The territory of The Hwicce passed from Wessex to Mercia C. 628
finally C. 730]

" advance 652-82.

Probable extent of permanent conquests in age of Cædwalla and Ine
[Sussex and Surrey were temporary conquests]

" permanent conquests of Egbert. 825.

" conquests of Egbert 825-9, less permanent.

Presumably the settlement of Hampshire was early: that of Dorset, mainly in the 7th Century
and that of Dumnonia, mainly in the 8th Century: but evidence for all these is lacking

English Miles

as well as by the spear of the warrior. The most northerly advance was that through the county which we know as Somerset. It was in full swing some twenty-five years after the conversion of Wessex to Christianity. Indeed, it was the fact that the West Saxons were Christians which no doubt accelerated the readiness of the West Welsh to submit. In 652 there was a battle at Bradford-on-Avon. In 658, after a battle fought apparently near Penselwood, King Cenwalch 'drove the Britons in flight as far as the Parrett', and from that time there is evidence in charters that Glastonbury was subject to the Saxons.[8] This was important, not only because south of the Avon it widened the separation between the Britons of Wales and those of the southwest—a separation begun by Ceawlin's victory at Dyrham eighty years earlier—but also because the traditions of Glastonbury made it a holy place. Its ancient wattled church, said to have been built by Joseph of Arimathea, continued to be venerated when it passed into the power of the Saxon king. The subjection to the conqueror and to the Saxon abbot, his nominee, were made tolerable by a tactful gift of lands, and thus,[9] 'Glastonbury never ceased to be a centre of Celtic pilgrimage, and as a temple of reconciliation must have played no small part in blending the two races'.

The next advance recorded in the Chronicle is in 682, when King Centwine 'drove the Britons in flight to the sea'. We shall probably be right[10] in interpreting this to mean a conquest of the country at least as far as the Quantocks, since we find the king enriching Glastonbury with lands near Quantockwood, within a few miles of the site of Taunton.

Of the southern advance through Dorset we know nothing; but the contrast between the place-names of Dorset and those of Somerset shows that the two movements were distinct.[10a]

What is most surprising is a settlement in Devon, which we may perhaps call a third advance. There is good evidence that the valleys of the lower Exe and of the Creedy were at this time occupied by the Saxons, for we are told in a Life of St. Boniface (*c.* 675–754) that this Apostle of Germany (then called Wyn-frith) was educated at Exeter; and a later statement that he was born at Crediton receives some confirmation from a charter dated 739,[11] which speaks of the country round Crediton as if it had long been in the hands of the Saxons. We have there-fore to account for the existence of a Saxon colony in the heart of Dumnonia (Devon) at a time when its British king was still an important, and apparently an independent, monarch. We can only guess what had happened. The situation is not what any one would have imagined were it not for the documentary evidence. An outpost so exposed to attack from Celtic neigh-bours would be unthinkable if we were dealing with warfare of a modern type. But it must be repeated that the expansion of Wessex was the result of gradual settlements rather than of scientific campaigns. The Saxons seem to have spread west much as did the Americans and Canadians in the nineteenth century. They occupied the lands they wanted, often those which they first cleared in the river valleys. The Britons on the higher lands were mostly content to let the new-comers alone; they presumably realized that if it came to open war they were likely to get the worst of it, and they may have consoled them-selves with the thought that the Saxons were for the most part taking land which the Britons had not been in the habit of cultivating. They could live and let live. Even in Exeter there could be a Saxon and a British quarter without continual riots and bloodshed. In further explanation of the surprisingly early origin of the Saxon colony on the Exe and the Creedy, we may guess that the settlers in this region, the hardiest of all the Ger-manic pioneers, must for long have relied on the sea for their communications with the mother kingdom—Exeter was only a short sail from the older ports of the West Saxons. We may also give weight to the theory[12] that Dumnonia had been much emptied of its British inhabitants by the migration to Armorica.

Such was the situation of Wessex when its great men, first Aldhelm and then Ine, grew to manhood—Ine, who as king

(688–725) was to make Wessex again for a short time a powerful state; Aldhelm (*c.* 639–709) who was to be one of its most
renowned saints.

With regard to Ine and his origin, we only know that he was
the son of an under-king (Cenred, probably the ruler of the
Dorsæte);[13] that he was fifth in descent from Ceawlin;* and that
he was the only member of his branch of the House of Cerdic to
be king of all Wessex until Egbert, a descendant of a brother of
Ine, established the line which lasted until the eleventh century.
If it be asked how it was that the succession passed to Ine from
Cædwalla, a distant kinsman, we can only reply with the truism
that authority came as a reward for personal prowess and ability.
Who can say whether Ine won his position as a leader in the war-
band of Cædwalla, or whether as the son of an under-king he
gathered his own retainers round him? It is clear that when Ine
obtained the monarchy he inherited three very different traditions: first, the memory of Ceawlin and of his short-lived West-
Saxon empire, extending in the Midlands well to the north of the
Thames; then, the separatist traditions of the under-kings, who
neglected West-Saxon imperialism and contented themselves
with the rule of small provinces, the later 'shires'; and lastly,
those of Cædwalla, the enemy of separatism and the exponent of
a new and more politic imperialism which found scope for its
ambitions south of the Thames, and sought to plant Saxons in
place of Jutes on the Isle of Wight and to conquer the Jutish
Meonware and the South Saxons. The important point is that
with the reign of Ine we have to all intents a new Wessex and a
new monarchy within Wessex. It is a new Wessex because, while
it has shed many of the districts north of the Thames, it is spreading east and west and beginning to absorb all the south of
England. The process foreshadowed by Cædwalla was carried a
stage further by Ine when, in 694, he defeated the men of Kent
and made them pay compensation for burning a brother of the
late king, 'thirty thousands' (presumably thousands of *sceats*).

* See genealogy, vol. ii, p. 721.

With regard to the westward extension of West-Saxon power, historians used to think that the *tun* of Taunton, built about this time, represented a notable encroachment on Dumnonia. But there is much to be said for the view that Ine's work in the west of England was chiefly that of consolidation. It is not until 710 that we read of open war between Ine and Geraint, king of West Devon. Ine's colonial policy has to be inferred from his Laws; these show how the government regulated the process by which new lands were planted with Saxon settlers. Men of the *gesith-cund* class (in later times they would have been called thegns) were encouraged by a grant of land to become pioneers in the expansion of Wessex. Thus:[14] 'If a *gesithcund* man moves his residence, he may take with him his reeve, his smith, and his children's nurse.' But 'he who has a holding of 20 hides shall show 12 hides of land under cultivation when he means to leave'. 'He who has a holding of 10 hides shall show 6 hides under cultivation', and similarly out of 3 hides, $1\frac{1}{2}$ must be cultivated.

The only reasonable explanation of such regulations is that they relate to a scheme of settlement, state-directed and state-controlled. With the next law we turn from the gentry, who had grants of large estates, to dependent ceorls with their small holdings. 'If a man takes a yard [or virgate] of land or more, at a fixed rent, and ploughs it, [and] if the lord requires work as well as rent* he [the tenant] need not take the land if the lord does not give him a dwelling†: but [in that case] he must forfeit the crops.'

The policy of planting *gesithcund* men and their dependent ceorls in official colonies could clearly give rise to many disputes. What exactly were the obligations of the well-born settlers to the king above them, and to the ceorls who had followed them? Were they to be free to give up the undertaking at will? Might the king on his part evict them? Ine seems to have suggested reasonable compromises on all such points.

Accordingly, when we look at the map of Somerset or Devon

* OE. *gafol*. † OE. *botl*.

and see Saxon *tuns* established in a country which so long remained British—*tuns* such as Somerton, Petherton, Taunton,
Wellington, and the rest—we must remember that a *tun*, like a
burh, was a fensible place, protected by a rampart or stockade.

The making of the Saxon outposts went on unnoticed by any
chronicle. Apart from the Laws of Ine, the only reference to
this all-important piece of history is an annal in the Chronicle
under the year 722, which mentions a step back and not forward.
It says that Taunton, which had formerly been built by Ine, was
destroyed by his queen. The building of the *tun*—though in this
case the work of the king and not of a noble—would have been
too commonplace an incident to be mentioned if it had not been
for its later (and unexplained) demolition.

It is scarcely necessary to point out that in this expansion of
the power of Wessex east and west, the Church was as usual the
ally and patron of the State. The establishment of West-Saxon
authority to the east of Southampton Water and in the Isle of
Wight is best illustrated by the mergence of the bishoprics of
Sussex and of Wight in that of Winchester—facts reported by
Bede; and the policy of westward expansion is equally well
illustrated by the creation in 705 of a new diocese in Wessex
west of Selwood, over which Aldhelm was to rule as first bishop.
The West Saxons as they pushed onward into the lands of the
West Welsh were the champions of Roman Christianity. It was
no doubt the fact that the 'right' (that is the Roman) Easter and
tonsure were identified in the minds of the West Welsh with subjection and dispossession, which made them cling longer than
any other section of the Britons to their Celtic ways.

The alliance of Ine with the Church is also written promi-
nently in his Laws. The first says that the clergy should keep their
'rule'; the second, that all children should be baptized within
thirty days; the third, that Sunday should be observed as a
holiday; and the fourth, that church dues should be paid at
Martinmas.

But it is the Laws themselves, the fact that Ine moved the

West-Saxon *witan* to compile them, which really distinguished his reign from those of all other rulers of Wessex before King Alfred. The idea of issuing a Law Book was, of course, borrowed from the Kentish kings. One of the laws indeed is almost identical with a Kentish law of this same period. It lays down that if a stranger travels through a wood off the highway and neither shouts nor blows a horn, he may be assumed to be a thief, and slain as such—the kind of regulation about which it was well that the rulers of the kingdoms bordering on the Andredsweald should agree.

The note of violence does not recur so persistently in Ine's Law Book as in most of the barbarian codes. On the whole the tone of these West-Saxon laws is that of reason and reconciliation. In addition to the support of the Church and the regulations for the planting of lands by colonies headed by *gesithcund* men, we hear much about the rights of the Welsh, that is, of the subject Britons. It is true that their *wergelds* are only fixed at half the value of those of the Saxons—six hundred shillings for the Welsh holder of five hides of land, a hundred and twenty shillings for a free landowner* owning a hide. But the Welshmen's rights are at least definite;[15] even a Welsh slave cannot be scourged without a formal oath. The king clearly relies on the arms of 'Welshmen', both those who own their five hides and those Welsh horsemen who ride in the king's service.

The Laws of Ine, then, suggest that he deliberately depended on the support of the Church and in some measure on that of the subject Britons; but the main prop of his power was the aristocracy, the big land-owners, the *gesithcund* men. Their privileges and duties appear in sixteen out of the seventy-six decrees.

In these ways Ine's reign, coming a hundred years after Ceawlin and a hundred years before Egbert, shows evident signs of the greatness to which the West Saxons were ultimately to attain. For the moment his work seemed to be as ephemeral as that of Ceawlin. Before his death he had to battle against a

* OE. *gafolgelda*.

Mercian attack. His reign ended in revolts, and was soon followed by renewed anarchy. Provincialism was still to prevail.

None the less, the glimpse of Wessex which we have obtained in Ine's Laws is precious. It enables us to understand something of those processes working beneath the surface of history which were to make Wessex in the end a powerful kingdom, and it provides us with the proper background for the figure of St. Aldhelm.

Of Ine the man we have no information except the fact mentioned by Bede[16] that like his predecessor Cædwalla he resigned his crown and went his way to Rome, 'being desirous to spend some part of his pilgrimage upon earth in the neighbourhood of the holy places, that he might obtain to be more readily received into the fellowship of the saints in heaven'.

What is known about Aldhelm's life can also be stated in a few words. He seems to have been born about 639–40, that is within five years of the Conversion of the West Saxons. Like many other saints of the time, he was nobly born, akin to the royal House of Wessex. He studied first under an Irishman, Maeldubh, at Malmesbury, and then, though he was thirty or even older, at Canterbury under Hadrian and Theodore. Further facts recorded about him are: that after his studies at Canterbury had been cut short by ill health he returned to Malmesbury, where he lived, first as a monk, afterwards as abbot; that he made a journey to Rome about 693;[17] that about 705, when Ine divided the West-Saxon diocese, he chose Aldhelm to be the first bishop of Sherborne; that for four years he administered his new diocese with great energy, being a founder of new monasteries; and lastly, that he died in 709 at Doulting in Somerset.

Now it is easy to read these and a few other traditions about Aldhelm's life without at all comprehending the portent which had appeared in Wessex. Our eyes read the words that Aldhelm drew his learning both from an Irishman and Canterbury, and we give a formal assent to the fact that Aldhelm passed on to the West-Saxon Church a mixed tradition, Roman and Celtic; but

Aldhelm

do we conceive what was really occurring in the minds of Ald-helm and his fellow countrymen? Do we understand how these Saxons as they listened to the Irishman holding forth in his wattled hut were receiving glimpses of unplumbed profundities of knowledge? What mysteries were there half-opened to their astonished minds, what intoxicating draughts at the Hisperic founts of Celtic learning! This is certain, that we cannot begin to understand what was happening unless we make an effort of imagination to see the universe, with its mysteries and profundities, as these men saw it. We must begin by thinking of the scene of Aldhelm's life as a land of forests (those of Selwood and Bredon) so extensive that they were notable barriers. Selwood in particular was spoken of as the feature which divided the old Wessex from the new—that is from the far west where the Saxons were pioneers, scattered settlers among a population still fundamentally British.

The backwoodsmen of Aldhelm's middle west were separated from one another by wide tracts of scrub and forest, and were sundered from the centres of active Christianity—from Canter-bury or Wales or Ireland—by gulfs which were hard to pass. In one of these isolated villages, now known to us as Malmesbury, the Irishman had appeared. He had come to these unknown parts in a spirit of adventure. He was seeking the perfect sanctity of an anchorite, but he was also ready to pass on his stores of the learning of the ancients to such pupils as gathered round him.

In order to gain an idea of Aldhelm's studies, let us glance at one or two of the books to which, as is evident from his writings, he had gained access. One of them was a *Lorica* (Coat of Mail), a poem of words intertwined like the rings of a byrny, the reci-tation of which was potent to protect a man from demons, as a steel coat could protect him from the thrusts of human enemies—to obtain perfect protection it was well to say it three times a day. It is known as the *Lorica* of Gildas, but is also ascribed to Loding, an Irishman who died in 661.[18]

1. Suffragare trinitatis unitas	Help, O oneness of Trinity,
unitatis miserere trinitas	have pity, O threeness of unity,

2. Suffragare quaeso mihi posito

I beseech thee to help me who am placed

maris magni uelut in periculo

in peril as of a mighty sea,

3. Ut non secum trahat me mortalitas

So that neither the pestilence of this year

huius anni neque mundi uanitas

nor the vanity of the world may suck me under.

.   .   .   .   :   .   .   .   .   .

15. Deus inpenetrabili tutella undique me defende potentia

O God, with thy impenetrable defence, protect me round about with power.

The next section of the poem is a prayer that the foul demons may not hurl their darts at the sides of the man who recites the charm, or at his head, his eyes, or any of the vulnerable parts of his body. These are enumerated in the pedantic vocabulary of which other specimens will follow.

Aldhelm knew also the works of Virgilius Maro Grammaticus,[19] who had probably lived at Toulouse earlier in the seventh century and had imposed his pseudo-learning upon a credulous age. Aldhelm therefore had heard of his twelve different kinds of Latin and of the controversy lasting fourteen days between the grammarians Galbungus and Terrentius about the vocative case of *ego*. He had taken to heart the recommendation of Virgilius that new words should be fabricated to replace those commonly used by the vulgar. He knew, it seems, the *Hisperica Famina*, the strange book which, setting out to glorify the schools of rhetoric, had provided Celtic stylists and their imitators with the rich artificial vocabulary admired by those schools in their decline— a new Latin compounded largely of Greek.

Even at Canterbury Aldhelm was in touch with Celtic thought, for Irishmen were among his fellow pupils in that school. Aldhelm caught from them or from Hadrian a thirst for learning which can hardly be appreciated by the modern world where education, universal and compulsory, is thrust upon men. This appears in the legend which tells how he went down to Dover and

did hard bargaining with foreign merchants in his desire to pur-
chase a Bible set out for sale among a number of other books on
the shore. It appears too in a letter of his, in which he refuses an
invitation of his bishop to attend some Christmas festivities on
the ground that his work required all his attention—that work
being the mysteries of Roman Law (a notable study, in a generation which produced Kentish and Saxon law-books), the hundred
different kinds of metre, and the computations of arithmetic and
astrology. To such studies as these, even Christmas festivities
must give place. The Saxon must learn all the secrets in the
wonderful books which were now being brought within his reach.
He set about the work of mastering them in the spirit of the
heroic age. It was a new adventure. With a determination not
to be beaten he would storm the stronghold of knowledge, and
when it was won, what then? What was it that Aldhelm acquired? Chiefly an immense store of curious words: words drawn
from Gildas, from Virgilius the Grammarian, jaw-cracking
words, manufactured from Greek, taken from the Hisperic
vocabulary: words which would have astonished English,
Romans, and Greeks, let alone Aldhelm's Saxon ancestors. And
what was the learned man to do with these words? He might
arrange them in intricate alliterative patterns. A letter[20] to
Eahfrid begins: 'Primitus pantorum procerum praetorumque
pio potissimum paternoque praesertim privilegio panagyricum
poemataque passim prosatori sub polo promulgantes stridula
vocum simphonia, et melodiae cantilenaeque carmine modula-
turi, ymnizemus . . .' Aldhelm here was writing to a Saxon who
had just returned from a six years' course of study in Ireland;
he was showing off. He was having his heavy joke. He was
outdoing Virgilius the Grammarian with his Galbungus. His
P, P, P, P alliteration was a kind of password for savants.

Words were good playthings in other ways. They could be
fitted together in double acrostics and in metrical lines. Aldhelm
liked to expound the mysteries of the pithian metre or hexa-
meter, the caesura penthemimeris, or the caesura trititrochaici.

He could fill parchment equivalent to thirty pages of modern octavo print with discussions about such things, giving illustrations from Virgil, Ovid, Lucan, Juvencus, Sedulius, Venantius Fortunatus, and other Latin poets early and late. It was an achievement, for no Saxon before him had made Latin verses.

In the end all these wonderful words acquired by Aldhelm were something more than playthings. The bent of the Saxon directed him to practical ends. His skill in rhetoric was calculated to impress men. He used it as an advertisement for the new schools of learning springing up in England.[21] 'The fields of Ireland are rich in learners . . . and yet Britain, placed if you like to say so at almost the extreme margin of the western clime of the orb, possesses as it were the flame-bearing sun and the lucid moon; that is to say, Theodore the archbishop . . . and Adrian his companion in the brotherhood of learning.' What need to go to Ireland when there were such teachers of Greek and Latin 'here on the fertile soil of Britain'? Aldhelm used his words also to reprove the Northumbrian clergy for their treatment of Wilfrid, and to better purpose he used them to reason with Geraint,* king of Dumnonia, and so 'persuaded many of those Britons who were subject to the West Saxons to adopt the Catholic Easter'.[22]

Above all, he devoted his rhetoric to the Praise of Monastic Chastity. His work, *De Laudibus Virginitatis*—issued both in a prose and a verse edition—had a practical aim. It was composed for the edification of Hildelith, abbess of Barking, and her nuns (p. 303); for Justina, Cutberga (sister of King Ine), Osburga, Aldgida, Scholastica, and the rest. In the event, it long remained a popular book; and monks and nuns who had taken vows of chastity were for centuries strengthened in their profession by Aldhelm's recitation of the long roll of celibates, male and female, prophets, apostles, bishops, and all the noble army of the religious who had renounced the brass of married life and had been refined to the pure gold of Virginity.

* Geruntius.

Aldhelm can claim our interest not only as the most renowned of the saints of Wessex, but also as a typical West Saxon. For instance, he was an aristocrat who knew how to gain the sympathy and the love of the people. Tradition said that Aldhelm, presumably in his earlier years at Malmesbury, was in the habit of taking up his stand on a bridge by which the country people left or entered the town. There, like a professional minstrel, he used to sing to the people their own Saxon songs till he had collected hearers, and then from his songs he led them on to the serious matters of the Christian faith. This story, and the fact that Aldhelm's chief work in life was the establishment of Christianity in the middle west of Wessex, help to place his half-jocular 'conceits' in their proper proportion. He might be admired by the few for his literary style, but he was revered by the people for his saintly life. He was a man of action as well as a writer. While he made Malmesbury for a time the centre of the new learning, his influence overflowed into the neighbouring forest country. He founded new monasteries at Frome and at Bradford-on-Avon, and during the last four years of his life, as bishop of the new diocese west of Selwood, Aldhelm ruled, Bede says, 'most energetically'.

Another way in which Aldhelm may be said to typify the West Saxons is in his successful blending of Celtic, Roman, and Saxon traditions. His strength lay in his capacity to appeal with effect to the Britons, both those of the newly conquered districts, such as Glastonbury, and those in the neighbouring principalities, such as Dumnonia. He could argue like a Celt in the cause of Latin Christianity. What gave him his influence was his understanding of both points of view. Britons could not ignore a Saxon who spoke with such art. Never before or since has a literary stylist been so enthroned. He could write with authority to a king of Devon or a king of Northumbria; the rhetorician could do as much as the fighting-man to raise the prestige of Wessex.

Aldhelm's prodigies of style did not establish either at Malmesbury or at Sherborne a well-rooted school of learning. There was, however, some fruitfulness in the following generation, when Wessex contributed leaders for the conversion of the Germans of the Continent. Accordingly, to appreciate his influence, we must turn our eyes to Germany and study the career of Wynfrith, the West Saxon who, under the name of Boniface and with the help of a large band of his fellow countrymen, became the Apostle of Germany.[23] No Englishman has ever played so great a part in central Europe. He is the first Devonian of Saxon descent to appear in history, and he displays a spirit of adventure and determination which is not excelled by Gilbert or Drake or Raleigh. His labours form an important part of the history of Germany, France, and the Netherlands in the eighth century; but the greater part of his long life (he lived from about 675 to 754) was spent in our island, and he is a true representative of the school of Aldhelm.

From his biography, written by his follower Willibald, we learn that his father was a man of substance living near Exeter. Boniface—it is less confusing to call him from the first by the name under which he was to acquire his sanctity—was sent, when only six years old, to be in the charge of a friendly abbot at Exeter. He seems to have been some twenty-five years old before he realized that he needed a better education than was to be had in Devon. Then, migrating to the monastery of Nursling, near Winchester, he had the benefit of the full current of learning flowing from Aldhelm. Day and night he studied the liberal arts. He read in his course the acts of the martyrs, and it is significant that some ten years before he set forth on his missionary work, a friend dedicated to him a poem on 'The Pilgrimage beyond the Seas'. In time he became a teacher of repute. Everything pointed to his having a prosperous career before him in the English Church. He had friends at Ine's court; he was chosen to be the emissary of a synodal council and to take a message to the archbishop of Canterbury. Promotion was clearly within his grasp.

At this point, 716 (seven years after the death of Aldhelm), when he was some forty years old, he determined to give up his prospects in England in order to assist a heroic Northumbrian missionary, Willibrord, who had long been struggling against heavy odds to convert heathen Frisia. Boniface, having there acquired some insight into the conditions of missionary work on the Continent, returned for a short while to England; but the year 718 saw him set out on the road to Rome with schemes in his head for better organized work among the Germanic tribes. At Rome his zeal won the confidence of Pope Gregory II, and Boniface, having sworn fidelity to the successor of St. Peter, returned to Germany and Frisia, not as a free-lance like the Irish and English missionaries who had preceded him, but as one under the orders of a papal commander-in-chief. In the great work which he then began Boniface moved from one centre to another—Thuringia, Frisia, Hesse, Bavaria—and used to advantage all the many-sided traditions which he had inherited from the Church in England. Like Augustine, he obtained advice on details as well as general directions from the Papacy. Like Aidan and the Scots, he perambulated heathen villages, baptizing thousands of converts. Like Theodore, he established new sees and formed a disciplined army out of scattered clergy—the Franks and Irishmen who had long been dissipating their energies among the Germans east of the Rhine. The Papacy not only gave him metropolitan powers, but it also delegated to him the work of reforming the Frankish Church in Gaul.

What is the explanation of such extraordinary successes, obtained on the continent of Europe by this Saxon, who had been born in an out-of-the-way corner of Wessex? The explanation may be gathered from what has been already suggested. It was the spirit of enterprise, like that of an Elizabethan exploring new worlds, captivating the minds of his fellow countrymen and winning followers by the greatness of his projects; the persistence of a Saxon who made up for want of genius by the determination and practical sense of a man of affairs—qualities which taught him how to use the great forces of the Papacy and of the Frankish Mayors of the Palace, as well as how to obey them: these and other characteristics—adaptability, tact, and above all, an overflowing sympathy and friendliness, brought Boniface and his English mission to victory. Though raised to be the Metropolitan of Germany, he remained an Englishman, and continued to take an interest in English affairs. However, there was one change: at first he had sought advice from his English correspondents; later he was more inclined to give it.

The correspondence of Boniface and his circle of helpers and friends gives us an understanding of the minds and hearts of English men and women who had dedicated themselves to the service of Christ; an understanding more intimate than that to be found in the *Lives* of the saints or even in Bede's *History*. The letters show also how the mission of Boniface was supplied in many of its small wants by the gifts of friends, as well as supported by their prayers. A king sent a gold bowl; an abbot, knives or finely worked palls; nuns sent offerings of money, books of the Bible written in letters of gold, altar coverings, or clothing made with their own hands. It is the affectionate intercourse between the 'brothers' and 'sisters' in Christ which is the most beautiful flower of this correspondence, a happy sequel to the *De Virginitate* which Aldhelm had written for the nuns of Barking. It reveals a spiritual love which, in all simplicity and without harm, could accompany the spiritual warfare of these English Christians. The missionaries address letters to their 'beloved sisters';* Lul, the right-hand man of Boniface, in writing to an abbess and a nun in England, says:[24] 'I confess to your love; when . . . I departed from the famous kingdoms of Britain, leaving the fruitful soil of my native island whose craggy coasts the dark green waves of the foamy sea hem in on every side, . . . I longed to present myself at the shrine of the Blessed Apostles.' Almost all his kindred were dead, he says, and he was 'left alone and

---

* e.g. 'Venerandis et amandis carissimis sororibus' (ep. 67); 'Delectissimae ancille Christi' (ep. 66).

widowed in sad exile'; but the abbess had cared for him when he
was sick and had shown him as a brother the unwearying affection which springs from the divine love. Boniface[25] tells his
relative Lioba and other nuns of her company about his disappointments in his work. The women in reply pour out their
troubles. Lioba, in her first letter to Boniface,[26] reminds him
that except for her infirm mother she was now left alone in the
world, 'and would that I could deserve to have thee in place of
a brother, for in no one among men do I place such great trust
as in thee. ... I ask thee too, deign to correct the homely style of
this letter, and to send me for a model some words of thine, which
I crave eagerly to hear.' The letter was the beginning of a life-
long friendship. Lioba was one of the many English nuns who
left England to take an active part in the evangelization of Germany; and when she died, abbess of a German nunnery, her
body was laid at her request in the same tomb as that of Boniface.

We have dwelt on the spiritual love which helped to solace the
men and women who, in dedicating themselves to the cloister,
had surrendered the relationships of ordinary life; but this must
not be allowed to lessen our sense of the gallantry displayed in
their spiritual warfare. 'It would be difficult to exaggerate the
praises of these valiant and devoted women, who faced the
dangers of a distant journey, only to bury themselves in wild and
savage regions, exposed to hardships from which even strong
men had shrunk.'[27] It was Boniface himself who from first to
last set the example of boldness. The courage which he required
to hew down before the eyes of the heathen the sacred oak of
Thunor at Geislar was not greater than that needed to speak the
truth to the great personages of Christendom. Even the Pope
had to be told that he ought to suppress the pagan customs still
tolerated at Rome. Then, in 754, in extreme old age, Boniface
won in Frisia what he had long courted—a martyr's death.

For enterprise of the more ordinary kind there is nothing in
this age to surpass the pilgrimage of a kinsman of Boniface
who later was welcomed by him in Germany and installed as

a bishop. This man, a certain Willibald (who must be distinguished from the biographer of Boniface), not content with having travelled from Hampshire to Rome, then set out in 722 to visit the Holy Land.[28] In Sicily he saw Mount Etna. At Ephesus he visited the cave of the Seven Sleepers. Near Damascus he was shown the spot where St. Paul had been blinded; at Cana, one of the vessels in which water had been turned into wine; at Bethlehem, the house in which Christ had been born. The biography of this Hampshire man narrates with much detail the events of his long pilgrimage. It even tells how he smuggled balsam out of the Holy Land in a calabash, disguising its smell by smearing it with paraffin.

Of such stuff were the West Saxons of the eighth century. With enterprise like that of their forefathers, the men who had marched behind Ceawlin, they play the parts which now fall to them as Christians. They are pioneers. They are adventurers. They are fighting as *milites Christi* both in their own Wessex and on the Continent. They are not fighting simply against the sins of the flesh, as ascetics or anchorites. This West-Saxon warfare is well planned and well directed.

But at home, when the generation of Aldhelm's pupils had passed, the West Saxons found it increasingly difficult to understand the Latin writings of this saint who had been so formidable a stylist. When they copied them, they began to gloss them with simpler Latin and then with their own English words. Aldhelm had set his West Saxons too difficult a standard. It was unattainable; and therefore discouraged further growth.[28a]

MERCIA—GUTHLAC

The history of Mercia and of the Mercian Church in this period is little better than a blank. For the purposes of this chapter it will be enough if the reader remembers that the great Midland kingdom built up by Penda in the second quarter of the seventh century continued for the most part to hold together and to increase its power under those of his House who ruled after him; that is successively, two of his sons, then two of his grandsons, and finally a great-nephew. The bearing of the wars of these kings on the struggle for supremacy will be mentioned in a later chapter.

A succession of eminent German scholars[29] have countenanced a theory that the last of these kings, Ethelbald (716–57), is to be identified with a pupil of Aldhelm's who appears under the name of Ethelwald. If this theory could be accepted, we might at this point quote a letter of Ethelwald and some effusions of his in verse as the first extant literary productions of an English king, and as evidence that the new learning was affecting the royal House of Mercia. But the fact that this young man Ethelwald had to be reproved by Aldhelm for his love of wine and women (and at the same time commended for his songs), and the other fact that King Ethelbald forty years later was reprimanded at great length by Boniface and the bishops of Germany in conclave because he conducted himself scandalously instead of settling down in marriage, these are insufficient proofs of identity; for neither was the name Ethelwald uncommon among æthelings, nor unfortunately a life of immorality. It should be acknowledged, however, that the verses of Ethelwald show a royal licence in their disregard of rhythm and grammar.

Mercia in this age cannot produce its learned man but it can claim at least one notable saint; and him we shall treat as the representative of the Midlands.[30]

Guthlac (673–714), was descended from the kingly stock of Mercia, called the Iclingas after Icel an ancestor of Penda. On reaching manhood, after being brought up in his father's hall, he thought of the mighty deeds of the heroes of old. Accordingly he collected a troop of followers and carried on petty wars of his own, devastating towns and villages and forts with fire and sword, and making a great slaughter through the land.[31] After nine years of this, his conversion came suddenly. Returning one night from a raid, he turned things over in his mind. His heart was suddenly filled with spiritual love. He thought of the old kings who forsook this world and its wealth; he thought of how every day brought him nearer to death; then signing himself with the Cross he vowed to become the servant of Christ, and told his war-band they must choose another leader. The first two years after his conversion were spent in the double monastery of Repton, which was ruled by a woman, the Abbess Elfrida. There his refusal to drink anything but water made him unpopular with the other monks. Afterwards, he longed for solitude, and went forth to the fens. The description of the 'immense marshes' formed by the rivers which drain into the Wash helps us to realize the great tracts of dark pools and reed-beds and winding channels which at that time penetrated far into the heart of the Midlands. Crowland, the small island on which he settled, could be approached only by a fishing skiff, and it was so lonely and haunted that no man had yet been able to dwell on it. The rest of the story of Guthlac, telling of his life as a hermit on this island, shows how his fastings and other austerities affected his brain. Devils appeared to him in the form of lions and wolves and bears. They came to him grunting like hogs, howling like wolves, croaking like ravens. One night, at a time when 'the Britons, the troublesome enemy of the Saxon race, were invading and harrying the English', he heard the devils speaking like Britons. The isolation which brought him his devils, brought him also, in true Celtic fashion, friendship with the animals round him. Swallows perched on him. Ravens restored the lost glove of a visitor. Men of all sorts visited him and testified in different ways to their sense of his sanctity. The bishop of Lichfield, it is asserted, begged Guthlac to reconsecrate him to the priesthood. The daughter of the king of East Anglia sent him a present of a leaden coffin and a winding-sheet. Ethelbald of Mercia, as a refugee before his accession, came to the saint to tell him of his troubles, and was comforted by the prophecy that God would destroy his enemies and raise him to the throne.

Many years later, after Guthlac had been long buried in his leaden coffin, Ethelbald (now become the most powerful king of the English), founded on the anchorite's small island the monastery of Crowland.

The story is typical. In similar ways other monasteries, both in Mercia and elsewhere, were springing up, monasteries which were to play a great part in the future of England.

Guthlac's story also reveals how much disorder and local strife, even within one of the greater kingdoms, remains hidden from us beneath the surface history of the Conversion. The devastations of the war-band which followed Guthlac in his youth read as if they were mere private warfare. The Britons who appear in the Fens and harry the English may perhaps be descendants of those who had fled to the forests at the time of the Conquest. Such incidents help to explain why Mercia, the last of the three great kingdoms to accept Christianity, was slow in making up for its bad start. The backwardness of the Mercian Church may be a reality and not merely an illusion produced by Bede's neglect. Guthlac seems to be an inferior imitation of Cuthbert, and his biography is admittedly modelled on that of the Northumbrian saint.

Mercia will make its contributions at a later stage. In the time of Offa and in the time of Alfred, Mercian Christianity will keep the traditions of good work alive when they are becoming moribund elsewhere. But that time is not yet. In the Golden Age the encounters of Guthlac with devils are a poor substitute for the literary feats of Aldhelm and the fine learning and art of the Northumbrians.

NORTHUMBRIA—CUTHBERT, WILFRID, BEDE

When we turn from Wessex and Mercia to Northumbria, we find its Church and the arts of Christianity in a much more highly developed state. Celtic and Roman influences are combining to produce a more abundant vitality. There are more saints, a richer variety of character, and there is a fresh and creative spirit in the works which men are carving in stone and writing on parchment.

The political background to the story is chequered. Seven years after the Synod of Whitby, King Oswy was succeeded by Ecgfrith (671–85), a strenuous king whose efforts to overwhelm the Picts in their fastnesses ended in the disastrous battle of Nectansmere, 685. During the next twenty years Northumbria was ruled by an illegitimate son of Oswy, Aldfrith (685–705), who had studied in Ireland and had become the best educated of all the early English kings, a writer of verse in Gaelic and a learned correspondent of Aldhelm in Latin. During this time Northumbria enjoyed unusual peace. But then, on the death of Aldfrith, it drifted into feuds over the succession to the crown which were to be continued for a century and a half to the undoing of the kingdom. For our purpose we shall do well to disregard this political history, and to concentrate our attention chiefly on the careers of three notable representatives of Northumbrian Christianity, Cuthbert, Wilfrid, and Bede, who represent three different monastic communities. The story of Cuthbert will take us to Melrose and Lindisfarne, where the Celtic tradition remained strong. That of Bede will introduce us to Jarrow and Wearmouth; that of Wilfrid to Ripon and Hexham—four monastic centres of exotic southern civilization. The lives of Cuthbert (*c.* 625–87) and of Wilfrid (634–709) span the period from the early days when Christianity in the north was revived through the teaching of Aidan, to those times when the Northumbrian Church bore its richest fruit after the State had been pruned by the defeat of Nectansmere. The life of Bede (673–735), a man of a younger generation, will bring us down to the period when political anarchy was beginning to exercise an injurious effect on religion.

We begin then with Cuthbert, and we see him first as a shepherd-boy among the rounded hills where the waters of the Tweed and its tributaries take their rise—a country of great lonely tracts of grassland and heather. Though of peasant origin (unlike most of the other saints) he none the less served as a young man in the ranks of some war-band, until he turned in disgust from the old heathen ideal of war service to the new ideal of Christian sacrifice which was being preached by the followers of Saint Aidan. Then we have a picture of Cuthbert riding up to the enclosure which surrounded the monastic huts of old Melrose. He goes as a free warrior, horsed and armed with a spear. He has chosen Melrose because he has heard of the sanctity of Boisil (St. Boswell), its prior. As he rides up, Boisil, looking at him, says to those who stand by: *Ecce servus Dei*. His character is clearly written on his face—men will say of him as of St. Columba, that he has the face of an angel. Thus was Cuthbert enrolled as a *miles Christi*.

The next stage in his life covers the thirteen years (651–64) in which, as monk and then as prior, he had his permanent home at Melrose. In this stage Cuthbert was Celtic in most, if not in all his ways: so Celtic, indeed, that after following his abbot about 661 to a new foundation at Ripon he withdrew before the abbey was handed over to Wilfrid the Romanizer. Until he became an anchorite on Farne Island, Cuthbert conformed to Irish tradition in his migratory habits. He made Melrose a centre for journeys to the most remote and poorest hill villages. The country-folk, in spite of their nominal Christianity, had remained heathen at heart. Cuthbert, we are told, used to wander among them for three or four weeks at a stretch;[32] 'and such was Cuthbert's skill in speaking . . . such a light shone in his angelic face, that no man dared to conceal from him the secrets of his heart'.

Like other representatives of Celtic Christianity, Cuthbert often exhibited a friendship with animals. Once, when passing through a moorland so desolate that there were no human dwellings where food could be had, the boy who was his companion found a fish which had been landed by an 'eagle' from the neighbouring stream, and brought it to Cuthbert. 'But why', said Cuthbert,[33] 'did you not give our hungry fisherman his

share to eat?', and he insisted on the boy throwing half the fish
to the bird. Cuthbert was thoroughly Celtic, too, in his asceticism. When he paid a visit to the abbey of Coldingham near
St. Abb's Head, he spent two or three nights at a time in vigils
on the shore. What was he doing? A curious monk followed him
one night: and the story which he later told the brethren was
that he had seen Cuthbert enter the sea up to his neck; he had
seen him pray on bent knees on the shore; then, as the dawn
began to break, he had seen two marine animals come and
caress his feet and then disappear among the waves.

In 664, a few months after the Synod of Whitby, Cuthbert was
transferred to Lindisfarne as prior. It was a difficult situation in
many ways. The early Northumbrian monasteries could not
cease to be the children of Iona.[34] The calculation of Easter was
only one of many peculiarities; and while Colman, in withdraw-
ing from Lindisfarne after 664, had taken with him those monks
who were definitely opposed to the Roman Easter, many of the
brethren who remained still sympathized with that and other
Celtic ways. They objected to the reformed rule which Cuthbert wished to enforce. With infinite patience he reasoned with
them. At conclaves, with perfect good temper he used the same
arguments day after day until he gradually wore down opposition.

For twelve years (664–76) Cuthbert ruled the monks of Lindisfarne as their prior. He reconciled them to the Roman Easter.
He enforced his new rule of monastic discipline. He persuaded
them to wear simple clothes made of undyed wool. He himself,
in the Celtic manner, still wandered round the shores of the
island at night, or marooned himself on a neighbouring rock.
Then, in 676, he escaped altogether from contact with his fellow
men, and attained the perfect life of a recluse. He shut himself
off from the world on the Inner Farne, seven miles from Lindisfarne, a small island reputed, like that of Guthlac in the Fens,
to be the haunt of evil spirits. With his own hands he excavated
a circular enclosure. He built up the walls with stones and turf
to more than the height of a man. One half of his dwelling was

an oratory, the other half was a living-room, and shut within these walls—where he could only see the heavens and only hear the sea breaking on his rocks—he fought his fight with the evil spirits, chanting his psalms and hymns, and brooding day and night on Divinity.

The victory of Cuthbert over his flesh was a triumph for all Northumbria. His fame was established in his lifetime. When a sister of King Ecgfrith lost the use of her legs and had to crawl on all fours, Cuthbert sent her a linen girdle which cured her in three days. The devout expressed their admiration of his sanctity according to the fashion of the age. An abbess sent him a linen winding-sheet; an abbot sent him a stone tomb; these he hid beneath sods of earth. His renown is best seen in the incidents which for a time put an end to his withdrawal from the world. In 684 Theodore, having deposed a bishop of Hexham, had a conference with Ecgfrith, in which Cuthbert was chosen to fill the vacancy. The following scenes were then enacted. Messengers arrive at the island telling Cuthbert that the archbishop and king have agreed to make him bishop. In vain. He will not leave his cell. King Ecgfrith himself comes to the island, accompanied by a bishop, a crowd of notables, and the brethren from Lindisfarne. They kneel, they weep, they entreat him to leave his oratory. Cuthbert also weeps. At last he yields; and the holy man, some months later, is conducted to the great church at York, and is there consecrated with pomp by Archbishop Theodore. This ceremony, performed on Easter Day, 685, is memorable. It is the climax which precedes the decline of Northumbrian greatness: it is a visible meeting-point of the old and the new, of Scottish and of Mediterranean religion. The cathedral church in which the anchorite is consecrated had been begun by Paulinus. It had been completed by Wilfrid, who had whitewashed its walls, refurnished its altars, covered the ridges of its roof with lead, and glazed the windows to keep out the birds. (That was Wilfrid's way. Cuthbert on his island had made it his custom to talk to the birds; on one occasion to

condemn them: *in nomine Jesu Christi*.) The two men before
the altar are a notable conjunction of the East and the West.
Theodore, the native of Tarsus, once student at Athens, now
emissary of Rome, statesman, successful administrator, maker of
laws, placing his hand on the head of Cuthbert, once shepherd
of Tweeddale, haggard and unkempt as on his lonely rock, an
ascetic who has starved himself on a diet of barley and onions,
and who, for all his Catholic orthodoxy on the Easter question,
still has the soul of a Celtic anchorite. And around these two
and the five other assistant bishops stand King Ecgfrith, his high
reeves and his band of thegns. The minds of these are filled with
thoughts of military glory and of conquests to be won in the
north.

From the consecration in the church at York we must go on
to another scene, two months later. While Ecgfrith and his
army are campaigning against the Picts beyond the Forth, Cuthbert is visiting the queen at Carlisle.* He is being shown the
Roman fountain of that city. Suddenly he stands still; his head
is bent to earth. He raises it again with his eyes turned towards
heaven, and he cries out: 'Oh, Oh, Oh! I think the battle is
finished.' A few days later the news arrived that at that very
hour the battle had been fought in which Ecgfrith and the flower
of his army had been slain. Cuthbert's consciousness of the
distant battle, though sceptics may say it is suspiciously like a
similar story told of St. Columba, is a well-attested case of second-
sight.

There is no need to dwell on the short episcopate of the Saint.
His visitation of his diocese aroused unmeasured enthusiasm;
but he was too much of a recluse to be a good bishop, and, at the
end of two years, he returned to his cell on the Farnes.

A few months afterwards he was a dying man, and from the
long story of his end told to Bede by an eyewitness, one last
incident may remain in our memories. Cuthbert, in spite of his
illness, had forbidden any one to stay with him on the island.

* Caer-luel.

Herefrith, the new abbot of Lindisfarne, after a five days' storm, sailed across to the island and found him in the hut near the landing-place. For five whole days Cuthbert had been unable to move, owing to an ulcerated foot. The only food he had had with him had been five onions; and pulling out these from under his coverlet, he showed the abbot that only half of one had been eaten. A few days later the dying man gave his last admonition: 'Ever keep peace and divine charity amongst you. . . . Have no communion with those who do not celebrate Easter at its right time. . . . Though I have been contemptible to some men during my life, you will see more clearly what manner of man I have been after my death. . . .'

It is evident that Cuthbert knew that his bones would be venerated, but not even he could foresee how his cult, enhanced by the fame of his miracle-working relics (relics carried in a coffin up and down the wilder parts of the north by monks in flight from the Danes), would remain the great binding force in what was left of Northumbria. When the kingdom had been torn to pieces by its feuds and by its Pictish, Scandinavian, and Scottish enemies; when Northumbria, even as an earldom, ceased to be a political entity, the bones of the Saint worked one of the great miracles of history and saved a remnant of independence for the north in the patrimony of St. Cuthbert, the County Palatine of Durham.

In view of the prodigious growth of the cult of St. Cuthbert, it is natural to question whether his fame was deserved. Undoubtedly there was an adventitious element in it; he outshone other saints who 'fought their fight' in the Celtic manner because of his ultimate orthodoxy on the Paschal question. Undoubtedly some of the admiration which he aroused was called forth by feats of mere physical endurance—his escape from the plague, his fastings, his immersions; and it was called forth also by the bodily strength which, for example, enabled him, in making his cell, to lift rocks on to his wall which would have needed four men of ordinary strength—deeds not unworthy

PLATE 43

1. *O.* CARAUSIUS
   R. CONCORDIA MILITUM

2. *O.* MAGNUS MAXIMUS
   R. VICTORIA AUGG.

3. *O.* BISHOP LIUDARD
   R. Double cross on globe

4. *O.* Copy of HONORIUS
   R. SCANOMODV (runic)

5. *R.* PADA (runic)
   ? = PEADA, 655–7

6. *O.* 'Woden' head

7. Four reverses of sceatta to show how the Roman standard
   types were debased; a head becomes a bird

8. *O.* ECGFRITH
   (671–85)
   R. LUXX in angles of a
   cross radiant

9. *O.* ALDFRITH
   (685–705)
   R. Anglian beast

10. *O.* Archbishop Egbert
    (732–66)
    R. EADBERHT

1 and 2. Some coins of usurpers in the later Roman period.

3 and 4. Unique coins of the early Conversion period.

5, 6, 7. Sceatta, probably of the later Conversion period.

8, 9, 10. Northumbrian sceatta of the age of Cuthbert and Bede.

of a Beowulf. Undoubtedly also[35] 'Cuthbert's mind was un-hinged by the austerities which he practised'. But when all is said, the fact remains that his primacy among the Christians of northern England was won by his spiritual gifts—by well-attested powers of second-sight, by complete disregard of self, by a patience which was inexhaustible, by love which overflowed, like that of St. Columba and St. Francis, to his fellow men and to his fellow animals.

Our second representative of Northumbrian Christianity is Wilfrid. When we last heard of him he had been expelled from his see by Archbishop Theodore in 678, presumably owing to his refusal to accept the plans of the archbishop and of King Ecgfrith for the division of his diocese. The years between his victory at Whitby in 664 and his expulsion had been the triumphant period of his life. They had seen him make his second journey to Gaul, attended by a retinue of a hundred and twenty armed followers, be consecrated by twelve Gallic bishops, and raised on their episcopal shoulders according to Gallic custom in a golden chair. They had seen him when driven by a gale on to the Sussex shore repulse the forces of the heathen South Saxons with his armed men, and secure the escape of his whole party through prayers which appeared to control the tides. They had seen him once show unusual moderation, and humbly return to Ripon when he found that during his long absence Chad, the pupil of St. Aidan, had somehow been in-sinuated into the see of York; and they had seen him finally, after the withdrawal of Chad, rule the diocese of all Northumbria —an ecclesiastic of the Wolsey type, living in almost royal state, and building churches in stone in the Roman manner at York, at Ripon, and at Hexham (Pl. 44).

In 678, when the blow fell, Wilfrid was driven from North-umbria, and most of the remaining thirty years of his life he spent in exile, contending for his rights. The authorities are un-satisfactory in their accounts of the quarrel. Bede is reserved:

Eddius, the biographer of Wilfrid, is an unscrupulous partisan. He blames the queen of King Ecgfrith, and says that she egged on her husband by harping on the 'secular glories of St. Wilfrid, his wealth, the number of his monasteries, the greatness of his buildings, his countless army of retainers decked out with royal vestments and arms'.[36] But Eddius discredits his own testimony when he alleges that Theodore's action was due to bribes.

Into the miserable wrangles which from this period until the death of Wilfrid filled up so great a part of Northumbrian history we need not enter. They were a blot upon the Northumbrian Church at the period of its highest vitality, but their permanent significance, either in political or ecclesiastical history, is slight. We need only mark the turning-points in the wearisome story.

Wilfrid, on his way to Rome to appeal against the action of Theodore, spent the winter of 678–9 in Frisia. He improved the occasion by preaching daily to the heathen Frisians, and according to his biographer he baptized almost all the chiefs as well as many thousands of the Frisian people. The winter of 679–80 was spent at Rome. He returned to Northumbria with a papal decree ordering the restoration of his bishopric, with a reliquary full of relics, and with baggage stuffed with ornaments for his churches.

It was something new in the experience of the Anglo-Saxons that the policy of a king and his councillors should be overridden by papal decree. King Ecgfrith had a short way with such opposition. The decree was rejected on the ground that it had been bought for a price, and Wilfrid himself was shut up in solitary confinement. So, for nine months in 681, while Cuthbert was chanting his psalms in his self-chosen island prison, Wilfrid, the champion of Roman customs, the bishop who had appealed to Rome 'as to a fortress and tower of strength', did his chanting in the custody of a king's reeve.

At the end of the nine months the queen 'became possessed with the devil' (she seems to have had a stroke), and since there was a suspicion that her seizure was a punishment for the treat-

PLATE 44

Hexham Abbey. The main chamber of Wilfrid's crypt

ment of Wilfrid, the bishop was released and allowed to depart with his relics and his retinue. There followed a second exile. Ecgfrith's influence was used against the fugitive, who was driven first from Mercia and then from Wessex. In the end he found a refuge in the kingdom of Sussex (681–6); he won the confidence of the South Saxons by teaching them how to catch fish in nets, and so took a leading part in the conversion of that kingdom and the neighbouring Isle of Wight, the two last strongholds of heathendom. (Cf. coin of Ecgfrith, Plate 43, 8.)

In 686 Wilfrid was reconciled to Archbishop Theodore and to King Aldfrith, the learned successor of Ecgfrith. He recovered his monasteries of Hexham and Ripon and a part of the Northumbrian diocese.[37] It was an acknowledgement of defeat, since he had to accept the division of the Northumbrian diocese against which he had so long fought. His administration of Cuthbert's bishopric for a year (687–8) at Cuthbert's death did not lead to a genuine reconciliation. The quarrel smouldered, till in 691–2 it once more blazed up. The old process began anew. Wilfrid departed for his third period of exile (*c.* 692–702). This time he found a home in Mercia, and for eleven years he did good work as bishop of the Middle Angles.

About 702, in a synod at Austerfield attended by most of the bishops of Britain, a new attempt was made to unravel the tangle of Wilfrid's affairs. But the decrees of Archbishop Theodore were again upheld in preference to those of the Pope, and Wilfrid for the second time appealed to Rome. Eddius, his chaplain and companion, says that he made the whole journey to Rome on foot—if true, a remarkable performance for an old man of nearly seventy. Soon after his return in 705 with fresh papal decrees, the death of King Aldfrith made it easier to end the long feud, and at the synod on the Nidd the final compromise was arranged. Wilfrid for the third time was restored—but restored only to his two best monasteries, Hexham and Ripon. All the bishops kissed and embraced, and Wilfrid had four years of peace within his restricted diocese before his death in 709.

Even this short summary of Wilfrid's career makes sufficiently obvious the contrast between him and his Northumbrian contemporary Cuthbert. Though Wilfrid won the devotion of his immediate followers, and kept a party of his own behind him, he stirred up more opposition than love. He had begun his career with every advantage: with great intelligence, unbounded vitality, with good birth, wealth, and friends at court; to these he had added a first-hand knowledge of Gallic and Roman ways, and the prestige acquired by his decisive part at the Synod at Whitby. But in spite of all his advantages he failed to assimilate the inner spirit of Christianity, and became more of a curse than a blessing to the Northumbrian Church. Never a popular saint, he has owed his place in history to the fact that Eddius, his biographer, was as great a fighter as himself. It may be said of Wilfrid that with his pomp, his large retinues, his buildings, his conflicts with the powers of this world, he was the first English ecclesiastic cast in the mould which afterwards produced Becket and Wolsey. He has not, however, the defence that can be set up for these later opponents of the monarchy. The cause for which he fought was primarily personal—his own position, his own rights, both of them obstacles in the way of the general welfare of his diocese. How little the cause of Wilfrid was the cause of Roman Christianity is shown by two facts: that Archbishop Theodore took the lead against him; and that Bede praised Wilfrid's chief opponents and omitted his miracles.

At the present day, as in the past, Wilfrid can well have his admirers. A good case can be made out for him on several counts.

It can be argued that the bitterness which so long pursued him came from those who sympathized with the Scots. Both the kings who persecuted him were in close touch with Scottish Christianity. Ecgfrith aimed at bringing the Picts within his empire; Aldfrith, his successor, had had an Irish education and possibly an Irish mother.

Then, if the actual performances of Wilfrid and Cuthbert are compared, there can be no doubt that Wilfrid accomplished

more both for the Church and for the advancement of civilization. He himself, in making his defence in 702, claimed that he
had been the first to introduce the Benedictine Rule as well as
the first to root out the weeds planted by the Scots, and that he
had also taught the Northumbrian Church to use double choirs,
singing in alternation. And he might have claimed much more:
outside Northumbria, some credit for the conversion of Frisia,
of Sussex, and the Isle of Wight; for the foundation of monasteries,
especially in Mercia; for useful work in administering a number
of dioceses other than his own; above all, for transplanting to the
north the artistic tradition of the Latin Church as well as its
craftsmen, skilled in architecture and in sculpture.

Again, it may be held that Wilfrid, in opposing one king after
another and in upholding the liberty of the Church, was ahead
of his time; that he foresaw, as Theodore did not, the danger of
the Church becoming a mere appendage of monarchy. Wilfrid
may have been the far-sighted man of his age, realizing the evils
which would come if kings and other laymen were allowed to
treat their bishops and clergy like mere dependants. Arguing
along such lines, we may defend Wilfrid's ultra-montanism as
sound policy—a policy neglected by later generations of Anglo-
Saxon churchmen to their own loss.

Or Wilfrid may be compared favourably with Cuthbert simply
as a man. He was more clean, and 'made it his custom to wash
his body during the night hours winter and summer alike, with
blessed and holy water, until Pope John advised him to put an
end to this rigour out of consideration for his age'.[38] The
motives of Wilfrid were religious and not hygienic; but Cuthbert,
acting also from religion, found, it seems, no mean between the
extremes of standing for long periods up to his neck in the sea,
and abstention from washing for months at a time.

There are no doubts about Wilfrid's sanctity in general; and
his quarrels were only occasional eruptions. For long periods he
was patient under rebuffs: from 666 to 669, when he found Chad
in occupation of the see of York; from 681 to 686, when he was

working in Sussex; from 692 to 702, when he was administering his Mercian diocese.

But when all has been said in his defence, can his admitted nobility and the heroic spirit which led him into so many encounters for what he conceived to be the right—or his rights—can these compensate for his glaring defects? The flaws in his character can be detected even in the panegyric of his biographer. Let us illustrate from two scenes Wilfrid's strong possessive instinct. The first scene is the dedication of the church at Ripon. It was celebrated with a feast organized by Wilfrid, lasting three days and nights. Before the feast[39] 'Saint Wilfrid, the bishop, stood in front of the altar and, turning to the people, in the presence of the kings read out clearly a list of the lands which the kings, for the good of their souls, had previously and on that very day as well, presented to him . . . and also a list of the consecrated places in various parts which the British clergy had deserted when fleeing from the hostile sword, wielded by the warriors of our own nation'.

The other scene is the last in his life—the division of his wealth.[40] 'A short time before his death, he ordered his treasurer to open his treasury in the presence of two abbots and some very faithful brethren . . . and to put out in their sight all the gold, silver, and precious stones: he bade the treasurer divide it into four parts.'

The emphasis on the acquisition of lands and treasure attributed to Wilfrid by his chaplain is significant. Cuthbert had gone to one extreme in the repudiation of worldly goods; Wilfrid went to the other. It is a memorable picture, that of Wilfrid, the *miles Christi*, the old warrior, surveying his hoard as did Beowulf before his death. But if, like Beowulf, he gloated over spoil, and like Beowulf, he fought till he was an old man, the treasure and the lands of Wilfrid were amassed with a purpose. The Church could scarcely have survived, and assuredly the monasteries could not have become centres of learning and civilization without endowments. This is true, but not the whole truth. It was the possessive instinct of the Church, even more than the inter-

ference of lay rulers, which was to be its undoing at the end
of the Middle Ages.

Midway between Lindisfarne and Ripon, near the mouths
of the Wear and the Tyne, were the twin monasteries of
Wearmouth and Jarrow. These communities were prominent
among others in England because their founder, Benedict Biscop
(628–90), had concentrated all his energies on making them
models of Roman Christianity according to the pattern of St.
Benedict. For a short time the career of Biscop had coincided
with that of Wilfrid. He had been the companion provided for
Wilfrid when the latter, dissatisfied with Lindisfarne, first wished
to go to Rome. The two men had then much in common. For
Benedict Biscop was like Wilfrid a well-born Northumbrian, another of those young men belonging to the warrior class who had
been disenchanted with the old ideal of bloodshed. Less precocious than Wilfrid, he had waited till he was twenty-five years
old before 'he left his home, his kinsmen, and his country, for the
sake of Christ and the Gospel'.[41] Unlike Wilfrid, Biscop pursued
his pilgrimage to Rome without delaying in Gaul. This journey,
equally decisive in the life of either man, clearly revealed the
contrast in their characters. While Wilfrid, like a knight-errant
of romance, was ever turning aside to make a friend or fight an
enemy, Biscop never allowed himself to be deflected from his
main purpose, that of studying at first-hand the culture and
usages of the Roman Church in order to introduce them to his
countrymen at home. That he might discover the monastic rule
best suited to the English people, he compared the rules of
seventeen of the most ancient of the monasteries in Gaul and
Italy, and, on his second journey, following in the footsteps of
St. Patrick and other Britons to the first great home of western
monasticism, he had himself tonsured in the island of Lérins.

On his third visit to Rome (667–8) he was asked by Pope
Vitalian to escort Theodore and Hadrian back to England.
Then, at the request of Theodore, he presided for two years over

the monastery of St. Peter's (later called St. Augustine's) at
Canterbury, until the time when Hadrian was ready to take over
its charge. Those two years in which Biscop was in contact with
Theodore and Hadrian were all-important for Northumbria, for
when he, with the help of King Ecgfrith, established a monastery
at Wearmouth (674), and then, eleven years later, a sister
foundation at Jarrow, this joint community between the Wear
and the Tyne was almost an offshoot of the Church of Canterbury, and inherited the best traditions of the school of Theodore
and Hadrian. Wearmouth-Jarrow became, as was intended, the
model of what a monastery should be, the embodiment of all
that Benedict had learned in Rome, Gaul, and Canterbury. It
became, in fact, the most flourishing foundation in the island.
Let us see wherein lay its superiority. Firstly in size, we know
of no other monastery in England which could compare with
its six hundred inmates. Then in buildings, if it was surpassed
(as is probable) by the churches of Wilfrid, none the less it was
largely built of stone 'in the Roman manner', with the help of
masons whom Biscop brought with him from Italy. In equipment and ornament, it had the best that industry and money
could procure. The windows were glazed by alien workmen;
'spiritual merchandise' was carried back from Gaul and Italy
on each of his six continental journeys: books, relics, pictures
of biblical history—these last to adorn his churches from wall
to wall, 'so that all who entered the church, even if they
could not read, wherever they turned their eyes might contemplate the lovable countenance of Christ and of His saints'.[42]
Best of all, Biscop introduced teachers of crafts, and a famous
singing-monk, John, arch-chanter of St. Peter's, Rome. Finally
with regard to discipline, nowhere else in the island was the Benedictine Rule so fully realized. The details of this Rule we shall
have to study when we come to the controversies of the tenth
century. For the present it must suffice to remember that St.
Benedict had aimed at stability (his monks were not to wander,
but were to be cloistered from the world); at adaptability

FIG. 50. Monkwearmouth Church. The wall and two-storied porch are probably the work of Benedict Biscop (*c.* 675); the tower, tenth century.

FIG. 51. Plinth of the porch with intertwined animals, surmounted by turned balusters supporting an impost with another animal in relief.

and moderation (instead of extreme asceticism, there was to be a balance in the monks' life between sleep, prayer, and work); and at learning (emphasis was placed by Benedictines on the work of the scriptorium and on teaching). St. Benedict had also provided for self-government; and Biscop, seeing with true instinct the weak spot of northern monasticism, was insistent on this ideal. 'I would rather that this place should be a desert than that my carnal brother . . . should become abbot. . . . Wherefore my brethren beware, and never choose an abbot on account of his birth, but seek out according to the Rule of Abbot Benedict the Great whoever for virtue and wisdom is proved fittest for the office.'[43]

Wearmouth and Jarrow are now remembered, not because of their observance of the Rule, but because of the spirit generated by the founders—a spirit beautifully reflected in the life of Bede and in some well-known stories. There is for example the story of the plague time, when all the inmates of Jarrow were swept away except Abbot Ceolfrid and the small boy (probably Bede himself) who struggled through the responses, so that the services of the church should still be maintained. Let us, however, dwell rather on the long story in which the anonymous monk who wrote the early history of the Abbey describes the grief of the community when Ceolfrid, after ruling as abbot for twenty-seven years, set off for Rome with the intention of spending his last days near the shrines of the Apostles. At the first announcement of his imminent departure, all wept and falling on their faces they clasped his feet and entreated him 'with torrents of tears' not to leave them so suddenly. Later, in the church, when, holding the lighted censer in his hand, he began to give each of the brethren the kiss of peace, he himself and many of his monks were so much overcome with grief that he could not finish the ceremony. Again, when he had seated himself in the boat which was to take him across the river, his deacons by his side —one holding the golden cross, the other, lighted candles—once more 'he could in no wise restrain himself from sobs and tears'.[44]

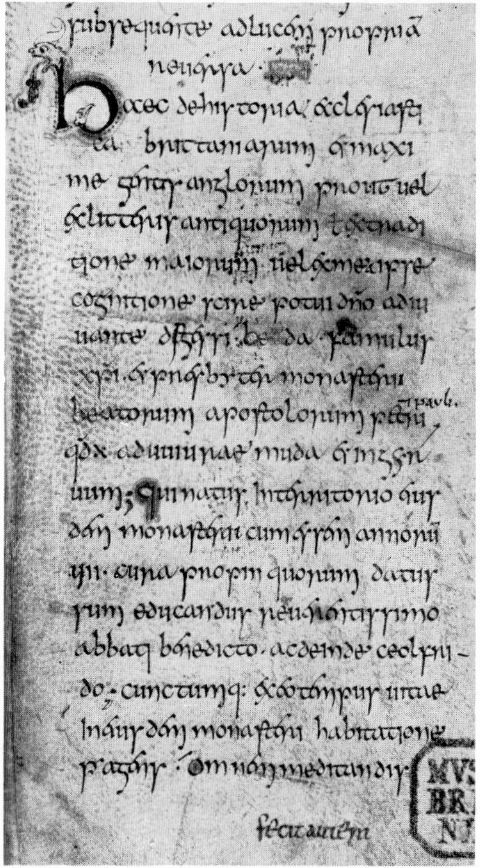

PLATE 45

Haec de historia ecclesiastica brittaniarum, et maxi-
me gentis anglorum, prout uel
ex litteris antiquorum, vel ex tradi-
tione maiorum, uel ex mea ipse
cognitione scire potui, domino adiu-
vante digessi be[a]da famulus
christi, et presbyter monasterii
beatorum apostolorum petri (et pauli,)
quod est ad uuiuraemuda et in gyr-
uum; Qui natus in territorio eiusdem monasterii, cum essem annorum
vii. cura propinquorum datus
sum educandus reuerentissimo
abbati benedicto, ac deinde ceolfri-
do; cunctumque ex eo tempus vitae
in eiusdem monasterii habitatione
peragens omnem meditandis

scripturis operam dedi; atque
inter observantiam disciplinae
regularis, et cotidianam cantandi
in ecclesia curam, semper aut
discere, aut docere, aut scribere
dulce habui.

Bede's record of his own life (Cotton MS. Tiberius C. ii, reduced)

It is in stories such as these that the change produced for the time being in the English character is best perceived. The men of religion (alike the followers of the Scots and those of the Romans) had become a highly emotional people. Many of the old characteristics of the race were turned into new channels. Loyalty, for instance, was still a leading trait. The devotion of the monk to his abbot could take the place of the devotion of the thegn to his lord.

The monastery of Wearmouth-Jarrow was of course pre-eminent above all by reason of Bede himself (673–735), and his writings, world-famous even within his own lifetime. A summary of his life can best be given in his own words, as it is appended to his *Ecclesiastical History*:

'I was born in the territory of the monastery, and at the age of seven years I was given by the care of kinsmen to be educated by the most reverend Abbot Benedict [Biscop], and afterwards by Ceolfrid. From that time I have spent the whole of my life within that monastery. I have wholly applied myself to the study of Scripture; and amid the observance of monastic rule and the daily charge of singing in the church, it has ever been my delight to learn or teach or write. In my nineteenth year I received deacon's orders; in my thirtieth, those of the priesthood. . . .'

Such was Bede's uneventful life at Jarrow—learning, teaching, writing; learning till he had absorbed all the knowledge preserved from the ancient world (including some knowledge of Greek);[43a] teaching till the tradition of classical education was established on a solid foundation; writing so unceasingly that his books fill twelve octavo volumes of modern print. At the end of the *Ecclesiastical History* he gives a list of his works, some thirty-six in number. Most of them survive. In his educational books—presumably among his earliest[45]—we see him teaching others as he himself had been taught. Thus in his *De Natura Rerum* he sums up what was known about natural phenomena. Most of his writings are commentaries on books of the Bible. Since the words of Scripture brought life to the souls of men and were deemed to be full of allegorical meanings, commentaries on them were labours on which a man might well spend a lifetime.

The *Ecclesiastical History*,* on which rests his fame in the modern world, was finished late in life, in 731. If we ask how it came about that Bede alone among the barbarians of northern Europe was moved to write the complete story of the Conversion of his nation, we see that various motives spurred him forward. From one point of view it was a sequel to his other historical works. In his *De Temporum Ratione*[46] he had looked at the history of mankind as a whole. Following Isidore of Spain he had distinguished Six Ages of the world, the Sixth Age beginning with the birth of Christ and continuing till the Day of Judgement. The *Ecclesiastical History* was the detailed study of Christianity in eastern Britain during this Sixth Age. With his co-ordinating and encyclopaedic mind, he was never happier than when he was collecting facts, and putting them into their right places. Just as he had expounded all that was known about 'The Nature of Things', so he determined to expound all that he could discover about the Conversion of the English people. Other monks had written eulogies of their own particular local saint. Bede's idea was to string the saints' lives together. The *Ecclesiastical History* was encyclopaedic hagiography. Consequently its chief aim was to edify. It was to supplement his commentaries on the New Testament. It was to show that the age of miracles was not yet past. It was to strengthen faith, and, as he says in his preface addressed to Ceolwulf, the king of Northumbria, 'If history relates good things of good men, the attentive hearer is excited to imitate that which is good'.

The characteristics of the *Ecclesiastical History* are familiar to all. Here, then, it will suffice to remind the reader of three of the most obvious merits of Bede as a historian.

The first is the high standard of accuracy which he set himself. This can be seen even better in his preface to his *Life of St.*

---

* *Historia Ecclesiastica Gentis Anglorum.*

Cuthbert than in his *History*. The preface of the *Life* is addressed
to 'The father-bishop Eadfrith' of Lindisfarne (of whom we shall
hear again when the wonderfully illuminated Lindisfarne Gospels
come before us), 'and to all the congregation of the brethren'.
He reminds them of the minute investigation which he has given
to the deeds of the saint, and of his *subtilissima examinatio* of the
credible witnesses. He says that in the next stage of the book he
had submitted what he had written to the criticisms of those who
had long been intimate with Cuthbert, and that finally, after
some corrections had been made, the whole had been read aloud
to the senior monks at Lindisfarne, and had been passed by them.
Well might Bede claim that by intent he was a veracious historian,* and his claim cannot be better confirmed than by the
testimony of Mommsen[47] that 'few writers have treated matters
of fact with such laborious accuracy'. If then his stories are not
always credible to us, the age in which Bede lived must obviously
bear the blame.

The thoroughness with which Bede had prepared for the
writing of his *Ecclesiastical History* is explained in his introduction:
the questions which he put to Abbot Albinus the successor of
Hadrian at Canterbury, and to the priest Nothelm about the
south-eastern kingdoms, to Bishop Daniel of Winchester about
Wessex, to the monks of Lastingham about Mercia and Essex;
Nothelm's research, at his request, into the papal archives for
letters of Pope Gregory: all this labour and care to tell the reader
about the sources of his information, give Bede's great work a
place apart from all other histories written in the Dark Ages.

The next characteristic in Bede which has always been singled
out for praise is his 'fair-mindedness'. This, even more than his
skill as a story-teller, is what has raised him above his contemporaries. It is illustrated by his whole narrative of the Conversion.
Though he could be biased against the Britons as a race[48] and
bitter about all error on the Paschal controversy, when he dealt
with the schismatics as men he could be generous. Aidan is

---

* *verax historicus.*

praised as much as Augustine. He has love for Cuthbert, but also admiration for Wilfrid. With deliberate restraint Bede slurs over the quarrels within the Northumbrian Church. His function, like that of his monastery—placed as it was midway between Ripon and Lindisfarne—was to appreciate what was good both in Celtic and Roman traditions, and to help to reconcile those in conflict. Bede was always in close touch with Canterbury. He was devoted to Bishop Acca, Wilfrid's disciple and successor at Hexham. (It is to Acca that his works are often dedicated.) But at the same time he could see the beauty of the simple poverty of Lindisfarne. He visited the community on that island, and his name was inscribed in their *Liber Vitae*. The wealth of Northumbrian Christianity came from its fusion of the Roman and the Celtic traditions, and nowhere were the two more happily blended than in the generous mind of Bede.

And lastly, there is the miracle of Bede's good Latin style. How exactly he managed to escape the 'Hisperic infection' cannot be explained. Aldhelm had caught it, though he had studied under Theodore at Canterbury. The monastery of Wearmouth-Jarrow was not immune. Bede's own superior, the abbot who succeeded Ceolfrid, had succumbed to the fashion. And Bede, like Aldhelm, had read the rhetoric of Gildas and of Virgilius the Grammarian. None the less, thanks to his own good taste, to the sound Roman foundation laid by Biscop or Ceolfrid, to the influence of Pope Gregory's writings and to a northern feeling for simpler Latin, which is also apparent in the anonymous lives of Northumbrian saints, he somehow was able to set a new fashion of lucidity.

The strength and simplicity of his style reflect the character of Bede himself. His letter to Bishop Egbert of York, which will come before us when we deal with the Church of the eighth century, will show that he was not too much of a student to take a strong line on the public questions of his day. None the less, the picture which his own account of himself and of his thirty-six books leaves on the mind, is that of a monk who is for ever at his

desk, writing and copying with his own hand, writing no doubt
in winter (like another, a later, monk of Wearmouth-Jarrow) till
his hand became so numb that he could no longer hold the pen.
It was heroic labour. The story of its end is preserved in a
long letter of his pupil Cuthbert which gives in the original
Northumbrian speech the five lines of verse about 'the inevitable
journey hence' which Bede composed on his death-bed; and describes how he was still at work even on the last day of his life,
translating the Gospel of St. John into English, and making
selections from Isidore. The fear of losing any moments from
his precious writing had become an obsession. 'Write quickly',
'Write quickly', was his repeated entreaty to the scribe. One
incident in the well-known story may be singled out to be placed
in our memories with the picture of Cuthbert waiting for death
on his lonely island, nursing his five onions, unable to move; and
with the picture of Wilfrid dividing his hoard of gold and jewels.
In this incident Bede, like Wilfrid, distributed his possessions.
He said to his pupil, 'I have a few treasures in my casket, that is,
some paper, napkins, and incense; run quickly, call the priests,
that I may distribute to them such gifts as God has given me'. A
few hours later he dictated his last sentence and died on the
floor of his cell, singing the 'Gloria'.

Bede, like Theodore, was never acclaimed as a saint. But he
was 'the master of the Middle Ages'.[49] From the first his writings
were accepted as the standard works on history, natural science,
and grammar; and now, while the earlier heroes of the Anglian
race are mere names, or less than names, Bede's is the first
English mind which speaks to the modern world fully and
lucidly on a wide range of subjects.

THE ARTS

Before we leave the Golden Age of the Conversion, we must
see what remains of its handiwork—some fragments of churches,
some foundations and crypts, some mutilated crosses, bits of a

wooden coffin, a few illuminated books. The list is not impressive, but the objects themselves have supreme interest for those who wish to know what manner of men were these English Christians. They are the best supplement to Bede in that they reflect the Christian mind from different angles.

First, let us look at the churches. There is no building of Theodore of which we can say, as before of Augustine, that here we have the work of Rome's emissary. But at Reculver,[49a] within the ruins of the old Roman fort, there were until 1805 substantial vestiges of a church built during Theodore's pontificate. A sketch made in 1805 while the building was being demolished shows one shaft still in place carrying a triple arcade, constructed of Roman bricks, between the nave and the chancel. This sketch* and the old foundations enable us to realize the continuity of the type of stone church which had become the fashion with Augustine and his followers in Kent. In Wessex recent excavation[50] has proved that Ine's church at Glastonbury was also laid out on the Kentish plan.

Mercia at Brixworth in Northamptonshire offers us something better than mere foundations. There are reasons[51] for thinking that the arches of the nave and the windows of the clerestory may be work of Wilfrid, who is known to have built churches in the Midlands when in exile from Northumbria. The architect certainly knew well the general appearance of a Roman basilica, but he was an amateur and in arch construction could only experiment (Fig. 52c) with bricks from some neighbouring ruin.

In Northumbria the only visible remains of Wilfrid are the crypts at Ripon and Hexham (Pl. 44), constructed with Roman-like solidity to hold the relics of saints. Many, though not all, authorities[52] believe that the west end and the porch of Monkwearmouth and the chancel (once the nave) of Jarrow

---

* Vide Clapham, *Romanesque Architecture I*, Plate 3. This and the other shaft may now be seen in the Close of Canterbury Cathedral. Fragments of the sculptured cross which once stood gaily painted to a height of nine feet at the entering of the choir are reproduced by Sir C. R. Peers in *Arch.* lxxvii (1927), 241 ff.

A

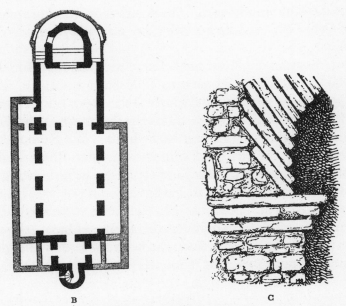

B C

FIG. 52. Brixworth Church. A. The nave and west wall. B. Plan, showing the original aisles, now removed. C. Springing of an arch.

church go back to the days of Benedict Biscop and of Bede. But much imagination is needed if we are to see any of these churches as they appeared to the English men and women who first beheld them. Eddius declares that there were no churches on this side of the Alps built on such a scale as those of Wilfrid. He enlarges on their columns and walls, their winding passages and spiral stairs, the gold and silver and jewels of their ornaments, the purple and silk of their altars.

The large churches have almost vanished, but there is at Escomb in County Durham a minute church of about this period, one with squared chancel and absence of *porticus*, with high walls and narrow doors and windows, which gives a good idea of the type of building now developed in the north on different lines to the Augustinian churches of the south (Fig. 53).

North of the Roman Wall, in the region where Scottish influences predominated, there were at first no more churches built in stone in the Roman manner. The wattled or wood oratories and huts of Cuthbert's monks rotted away and left no trace of their existence.

But the Scotticized Northumbrians produced handiwork more remarkable than stone churches. The most wonderful of all is the Gospel Book which once adorned the altar of the church at Lindisfarne and which is now to be seen in the British Museum. There is general though not unanimous agreement that its colophon tells the truth about its origin.[53] This definitely states that the book was illuminated by the hand of Eadfrith, a monk who became bishop of Lindisfarne eleven years after the death of Cuthbert. Some of his full-page illustrations, those giving pictures of the Evangelists with their symbols, were copied straight from a manuscript brought from the south of Italy by a traveller, perhaps Benedict Biscop (Pl. 46); others contain the initial letters of the Gospels like the *Quoniam quidem* page (Pls. 47, 48; cf. Frontispiece of vol. II), and opposite each initial is a page of pure ornament centring round a cross (Pl. 49). These folios show that Eadfrith loved birds and dogs with something like

FIG. 53. Escomb Church. Interior and exterior. The chancel
arch may have been taken from a building of the Roman period.

the love of which we read in the stories of Cuthbert, and he worked such animals, stylized, but not far removed from nature, into beautiful patterns. Eadfrith's art, when it is not copied from the southern book, is 'Hiberno-Saxon'. It is an Anglian variety—or rather, as some now think,[54] an anticipation—of Irish art.* According to Baldwin Brown, it is 'Anglo-Saxon in its reticence and its instinct for keeping along a path once marked out, which contrasts with the volubility and waywardness of the Celt'.[55] We shall have good authority behind us[56] if we regard these and the other interlaced patterns of the age as no more than patterns, masterpieces of conventional art. But another view is possible if less probable. We may look upon the pages of the Lindisfarne Gospels as manifestations of the thoughts which passed through the minds of those under Irish influence. As Cuthbert and those brought up like him in the traditions of the Irish Church looked out on the world, contemplating interminably the elements of sea and sky around them, their minds were filled with adoration of the Creator and of His works, the earth and its living things. In their illuminations they gave expression to their love for the birds and the hounds whose necks they twisted and whose bodies they elongated into those tortuous designs; and through it all was a sense that living beings also were entangled into strange patterns, that life was twisted like these labyrinthine interlacements which crossed and turned, leading you out into puzzling complications and then bringing you back to the place or almost to the place from which you had set out. Life was like these pictures in the Lindisfarne Gospels. It was a maze; it was full of mazes; but in all there was design. The labour of these artist-monks was prayer—a form of worship. They expressed in colour and pattern, with plait and interwoven bird, the mysteries of this world and wonder of the universe.

As we look at these pages, we think of Eadfrith the monk working away in a hut, dark, draughty, exposed to the storms of wind and rain that sweep up from the North Sea. He works

---

* For 'Irish' or 'Hiberno-Saxon' art see Appendix, pp. 730–3.

PLATE 46

Lindisfarne Gospels, picture of St. Luke and his symbol, copied from a book
brought to Northumbria from S. Italy

Note the Greek legend: Ò ÁCIOS LUCAS

PLATE 47

Lindisfarne Gospels, beginning of St. Luke's Gospel
QUONIAM QUIDEM MULTI CONATI SUNT ORDINARE NARRATIONEM . .

PLATE 48

Enlargement of part of Plate 47

PLATE 49

Lindisfarne Gospels, cruciform page facing the beginning of St. Mark's Gospel

month after month, year after year, completing his one master-
piece, writing his bold half-uncial script, interlacing his birds and

Fig. 54. Ruthwell Cross.

hounds with unfailing accuracy and infinite patience, to the
glory of God; illuminating his folios with colours that cannot be

adequately reproduced by any mechanical process, colours which glow like the stained glass of medieval church windows.

Another form of art was developed by these northern Angles, once more manifesting a harmonious blending of Celtic and Roman influences—the tall stone crosses. These crosses, though in the end sporadic throughout Britain, were raised chiefly and in earliest beauty about the borderlands of Northumbria—in that human eddy caused by the meeting of the two cultures, the one coming from the Celtic West by way of Iona, the other from Rome and the Mediterranean lands.[57]

These tall stone crosses were made continuously from the seventh century until after the Norman Conquest. Then most of them were broken up and many were built into church walls. The reader will find in these pages illustrations both of some of the smaller fragments and also of the two more complete and better-known of the Northumbrian crosses. The shaft of that at Bewcastle still rises to heaven fifteen feet high where it was first set up, within the bounds of a Roman fort six miles north of the Roman Wall and on the edge of some of the wildest moorland of Britain. This shaft remains unchanged except for the weathering of its stone, but the cross-head is lost. The Ruthwell cross, some ten miles from Dumfries, has been partially restored and its general effect has been impaired by its removal from its original site. The two crosses are clearly the work of one period and school.[57a] The figures and the spirit of the two are similar. That spirit is best expressed in the runic inscription which runs round one panel of the Ruthwell shaft, containing lines from a poem on the Holy Cross, better known in its later extended form, the *Vision* (or so-called *Dream*) *of the Rood*.

There is converging evidence for assigning the great development of the stone crosses to about the last quarter of the seventh century,[58] that is to the years following the Synod of Whitby and the coming of Archbishop Theodore. It was probably then that foreign sculptors made the cross for the church within the Roman fort at Reculver. It was about then also that the West Saxons

PLATE 50

BEWCASTLE CROSS, North and West faces

The Runic inscription is below the figure of Christ, treading on the heads of beasts, and above that of a falconer (? St. John the Evangelist with his eagle)

PLATE 51

A   *B*

RUTHWELL CROSS

A. Christ treading on the heads of beasts.   *B.* The Magdalene wiping the feet of
Christ with her hair

erected a cross at Glastonbury. And if these things were done in the south, it argues that the fashion must have been in full flower in Northumbria, the region where the art flourished like a native growth. The stages by which these sculptured crosses, standing three times the height of a man, came to be evolved, cannot now be traced. No doubt the first experiments in carving had been made with wooden crosses. Then Benedict Biscop or Wilfrid or Theodore introduced sculptors who inherited the traditions of later Greco-Roman art (their exact provenance cannot be determined); and soon the Anglian craftsmen became nearly as expert as their teachers.

Returning to the Bewcastle and Ruthwell crosses, we find a strong reason for dating them somewhere about 700 in the fact that high up on the Bewcastle cross there is inscribed in runes the name 'Cyniburug'. There can be little doubt that this stands for Cyniburg, the daughter of Penda, who married Alchfrith, son of Oswy. It seems that the lower half-obliterated inscription is a dedication to the unfortunate Alchfrith, the patron of Wilfrid, who disappeared from history mysteriously soon after the Synod of Whitby. Until the death of Wilfrid, there was good reason why Alchfrith should be commemorated in the region not far from Wilfrid's own Hexham.

Those who believe in the native authorship of the Ruthwell and Bewcastle crosses call attention to the crude carving of the Magdalene's hand in one panel (Pl. 51A), to the traces of a Teutonic moustache on the face of Christ (Pl. 51B), and to the characteristically English delight in birds and beasts. But whatever be decided about particular specimens, when we regard the Northumbrian crosses as a whole, there can be no doubt that the Anglian stone carvers did at this period quickly attain to a skill and artistry which lifted their works above all other sculpture of the age either in Europe or the Near East.

The Anglian is eclectic, but once more he is no mere imitator. In his crosses, as in his illuminated manuscripts, whatever he borrows he makes his own. From the Celts he takes the idea that a tall cross is the best kind of monument, a good memorial to a departed friend or an emblem round which country-folk may gather for worship; from the Byzantines or Romans he takes the pose of the figures and the vine-scroll, from them or others the interlace. He takes Roman letters, but they are written in an Irish style. He takes runes from his Teutonic ancestors, on one border he inscribes a verse from the Vulgate, on another a stanza composed by a new Anglian poet. All these are fused harmoniously, and the 'Victory Beacon' (*sigbecn*) raises its shaft and cross-head aloft, every panel and almost every border on it enriched with ornament or lettering intended either to teach men about the new Judge and Saviour of the world, or to proclaim His triumph. At the top of the Ruthwell Cross is inscribed i.h.s.; xps. On the Bewcastle shaft, above the figure of Christ is *Gessus Christus*. On either cross Christ is shown trampling on the snouts of animals—the *Bestiae et Dracones*.

That the victory was the victory of Love is shown by the panel wherein the repentant Magdalene weeps at the feet of Christ. But that the Christian triumph was regarded from the regular Anglo-Saxon standpoint as a victory of the old fighting instincts of the race is told in the verse which is given a central position at Ruthwell, the lines from the so-called *Dream of the Rood*:[59] 'Then the young Hero that was God Almighty, stripped Himself, strong and steadfast. Bold in the sight of many, He mounted the high cross when He would redeem mankind. I trembled when He clasped me, yet I durst not bow to the ground.'

The quotation must serve as a reminder that in our survey of the growth produced by Christianity from the soil of the English people we have said nothing about the efflorescence of Anglo-Saxon poetry. Every one knows Bede's story of how the first inspiration to compose verse came to Cædmon (*c*. 670–80), the diffident herdsman attached to the monastery at Streanæshalch; 'I cannot sing, and for this cause I left the banquet and retired hither, because I could not sing.' 'Nevertheless, thou must needs sing to me. . . . Sing the beginning of Creation.'

The present chapter has been devoted to the achievements of saints and others who can be conveniently assigned to the Golden Age of the Anglo-Saxon Church, from about 665 to 735. When we come to Old English poetry, except for the few lines assigned to Cædmon all else is treacherous ground, offering no certainty in its chronology. It is therefore safer to use the Christian poetry to describe the general changes in society produced by Christianity, rather than to illustrate the features of any one period. We shall therefore return to the poetry in later pages.

The present chapter has already led us on a far cry, from the coming of Archbishop Theodore. We have wandered by way of Aldhelm and of Guthlac to the Northumbrian saints and the vigorous life which both to the south and the north of the old Roman frontier wall was producing masterpieces in literature and the arts. Wherever we have gone we have seen foreign influences, if not foreign teachers, working on the raw material of Anglo-Saxon humanity. Whether it was produced by the stimulus of Celtic infusion coinciding with the Roman influence, or whether there is some other explanation, enough has now been told to show that this period was not only the most remarkable in the history of our pre-Norman ancestors, but that it can claim comparison with the ages of greatest vitality in medieval and modern England.

This period of the Conversion, more truly than the age of the Renaissance, gave Englishmen a new heaven and a new earth. It offered them also a new language, a new writing. It offered them books and an education based on books. It opened to them the literature of Rome, and a civilization gathered from all the Mediterranean world. It introduced them to all kinds of new ideas and new arts. What was impossible to a Christian people when old and young had their visions, and when signs and wonders were reported from every quarter? Even the relics of native saints were, it seemed, as efficacious as those imported from Rome. And the other miracles—the stone churches, Aldhelm's Latin style, Bede's *Ecclesiastical History*, the art of the

Lindisfarne Gospels, and of the sculptured crosses—are not these enough to demonstrate that the Anglo-Saxons, or at least a few of them, were as much alive and as gifted as the Elizabethans? It is true that there can be no comparison of progress where two generations start from quite different points. One thing, however, may be asserted, that while the Elizabethans were fascinated by plunder and the lure of Spanish gold, and were too often moved by new hatreds—hatred of Rome, hatred of Spain —the heroes of the Conversion were inspired by a great love for their fellow men. Their rivalry was to excel one another in good works.

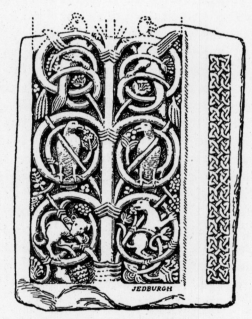

Jedburgh. Fragment of Cross-shaft. About the end of the seventh century.

NOTES

[*For the Abbreviations used in the Notes see vol. ii, pp. 711–17*]

I. THE ANGLES AND SAXONS IN GERMANY

Frontispiece. For the Taplow burial see below, p. 227, and note 21 on p. 382 *b* for references to discussions about the style and date of the Taplow grave-goods.

[1] Bede, i, c. 15. Here and in other passages of Bede I have made use of Miss A. M. Sellar's *Bede's Ecclesiastical History of England, A Revised Translation* (Messrs. G. Bell & Sons, 1907).

[2] Wadstein, 29.

[3] For this controversy and further references see Chadwick, *Origin*, c. viii; Schmidt, ii. 22–33; Wadstein, 15 ff.; Siebs, 56 ff. Siebs, writing in 1931, concludes that the evidence of Tacitus and Ptolemy makes it 'certain' that the Cimbrian peninsula was not the home of the Angles; that 'Bede knew nothing about the continental peoples'; and that the home of the Angles cannot be fixed with any certainty.

[4] Chambers, *Widsith*, 194; La Cour, 131, 149, 188–9.

[4a] The Map of the Saxon Migration represents the supposed conditions of the first centuries of our era; by the fifth century the sea had, no doubt, gained on the land. The sources used in making the map were stated in the first edition and need not be repeated. Dr. H. Schütte, the chief authority on the history of the coast-line of North Germany, has published his results in *Abhandlungen Naturwissensch. Verein Bremen*, Band xxx (1937). Cf. pp. 197–237 and bibliography, pp. 207–8. For a list of heathen Saxon cemeteries see H. Schütte and O. Rink, in *Oldenburger Jahrbuch* (1934), 162–3. For the *terpen* see J. H. Holwerda, *Nederlands Vroegste Geschiedenis* (1925), Kaart III; Collingwood and Myres, *Roman Britain*, 334.

[5] For references to this controversy see Pauly-Wissowa, *s.v.* 'Saxones'; Collingwood and Myres, *Roman Britain*, 338–41; L. Schmidt, *Die Westgermanen*, i (1938), 33 f. The question is still and may long remain *sub judice*. As is to be expected, the evidence of the urns is disputed. K. Waller (in *Mannus' Zeitschrift für Vorgeschichte*, xxv (1933), 40–59) identifies the urns of Plettke's types A1 and A2 as those of Chauci and not of Saxons. If he is right there was some continuity at least in the cemeteries of the Chauci and Saxons. He infers from the development of these types of urns in low-lying cemeteries that the Chauci gave way before the invading Saxons and fled to the marshes. Cf. Schütte, ii. 234.

[6] P. Zylmann, *Ostfriesische Urgeschichte*, 133 ff.

[7] For references to Roeder's writings see below, p. 371, note 15.

[8] Cf. H. Müller-Brauel, 'Sächsische Friedhöfe bei Stade' in *Praehist. Zeitsch.* xvii. 134–5.

9 At Nesse near Wesermunde and at Galgenberg to the south-west of Cuxhaven. See F. Roeder's *Neue Funde* (Sonderdruck aus *Anglia*, lvii). Roeder thinks that the fashion of inhuming the dead was probably introduced into the Elbe-Weser lands by Saxon soldiers returning from north-east Gaul, 350–400. For archaeological evidence that Saxon soldiers served under the Empire in north-east Gaul see *Neue Funde*, 17–18, and references there given.

10 Liber xvi (1), 1. Pliny's description is for the most part applicable to the *terpen* of Frisia, though he applies it to a territory of the Chauci. See D. J. H. Nyessen, *The Passing of the Frisians* (1927), 268; P. C. J. A. Boeles, *Friesland tot de Elfde Eeuw* (1927), 123 ff.; P. Zylmann, *Ostfriesische Urgeschichte*, 142.

11 e.g. J. H. Holwerda, in *R.G.K. XVI Bericht*, 135 ff.

12 *Waldbäume und Kulturpflanzen im germanischen Altertum* (1905), c. 14. Hoops is here following Kluge in Paul's *Grundriss*, i. 336 and 349.

13 F. Lot, *Rev. Hist.* cxix. 28 f.

14 Bibliography in Pauly-Wissowa, *s.v.* 'Saxones'; also F. Lot, *ut supra*.

15 Some historians believe that the settlements round Boulogne go back to the time of Carausius in the third century: G. Kurth, *Clovis* (1901), i. 73 and 180; G. des Marez, *Le Problème de la colonisation franque* (1926), 36.

16 See J. B. Bury, *Hist. of Later Roman Empire* (1923), 292.

17 See T. Hodgkin, *Italy and Her Invaders* (1892), ii. 366–7; O. M. Dalton, *Letters of Sidonius* (1915), ii. 150.

18 C. Blümel in *Germania*, xvii (1933), 29. Cf. P. Bienkowski, *De Simulacris Barbararum Gentium apud Romanos* (1900), 90; H. Koethe, 'Beiträge zur Darstellung von Germanen', in *Germania*, xxi (1937), 250–3.

18a Shetelig, *Scandinavian Archaeology* (1937), 312, suggests that the long trousers found at Thorsberg had belonged to a man of some tribe which had migrated from the south. Trousers were well known to the south Germans. H. Jankuhn, in *Forschungen und Fortschritte* (Berlin, 1936), xii. Jahrgang, 202, points out that the finds at Thorsberg seem to have been deposited during three or four centuries, and to have been offerings, but not victory offerings, to a god. He thinks that the place where the deposit was made was in the heart of Angeln, and that the Thor's hill which gave it its name was probably a moot hill. He concludes that it may have been at Thorsberg that the assembled Angles took their decision to migrate to Britain. Cf. Shetelig, op. cit. 204–5; J. de Vries, *Altgermanische Religionsgeschichte* (1935), 182–6.

19 H. Shetelig in *Acta Archaeologica*, i (1930), 1–30; ibid. *Scandin. Archaeology*, 353–9.   20 J. J. A. Worsaae, quoted in Engelhardt, 28.

21 S. Müller, ii. 132 f.; Hastings, *E.R.E.* xi. 755.

22 e.g. Schütte, i. 223–4; Philippson, 128–9.

23 K. Malone, *Widsith* (1936), 32. The quotations are from R. W. Chambers, *Widsith* (1912).

²⁴ Especially R. W. Chambers.

²⁴ᵃ For runes, and the various controversies about them, see Shetelig, *Scandinavian Archaeology*, c. xiii.

²⁵ E. Foord, *The Last Age of Roman Britain* (1925), 176–9, 190.

²⁶ i. 15.   ²⁷ Wadstein, *Norden*, 3f.

II. THE END OF ROMAN BRITAIN

P. 37, *Map of Roman Britain: corrigenda*, Uxellodunum, for Uxellodurium; Margidunum should be east, not west, of the Trent.

¹ For a fuller treatment of this subject, and an account of Britain under Roman rule, see Collingwood and Myres, *Roman Britain*, Books III and IV; and for bibliography, ibid. 462 ff., esp. 467–8. New excavations and finds are reported annually in the *Journal of Roman Studies*.

² D. Atkinson, *Romano-British Site at Lowbury Hill*, 25.

³ Cf. D. Atkinson in *Essays . . . James Tait*, 6–11.

³ᵃ Cf. Collingwood and Myres, *Roman Britain*, 279.

⁴ J. Bushe-Fox, *Richborough Castle, Official Guide* (1930).

⁵ Wheeler, *Wales*, 261–8, 291–2, and *Trans. Soc. Cymmrod.* (1920–1), 83.

⁶ Haverfield, *Roman Occupation*, 263.

⁷ Statement of Dr. R. E. M. Wheeler.

⁸ *Antiquity*, iii. 271–2. This view of Collingwood has been modified in Collingwood and Myres, *Roman Britain*, 302–3.

⁹ Cf. Kendrick and Hawkes, 294.

¹⁰ *J.R.S.* xviii (1928), 204 ff.; xix. 202–3; R. E. M. and T. V. Wheeler, *Report on the Excavation of the . . . Site in Lydney Park* (1932).

¹¹ Claudian, *De Consulatu Stilichonis*, i. 253–5.

¹¹ᵃ See *J.R.S.* xxvi (1936), 71–3; C. H. V. Sutherland, *Coinage and Currency in Roman Britain* (1937), 121.

¹² *M.G.H. Auct. Ant.* ix. 652–4 as emended by the editor, T. Mommsen.

¹³ *Historia Nova*, vi, §§ 6–10, in *M.H.B.*, p. lxviii.

¹⁴ J. B. Bury, in *J.R.S.* x (1920), 130 ff. In support of Bury—E. Stein, in *R.G.K.*, xviii *Bericht* (1928), 92, note 2; H. S. Schultz, in *J.R.S.* xxiii (1933), 36–54; Collingwood and Myres, *Roman Britain* (1936), 295–301; C. H. V. Sutherland, *Coinage and Currency in Roman Britain* (1937), 93–6. In opposition to Bury—R. G. Collingwood, in *J.R.S.* xii (1922), 74 ff.; F. S. Salisbury, in ibid. xvii (1927), 102–6, and xxiii (1933), 217–20; and *Num. Chron.* vii (1927), 108 ff. Cf. also MacDonald, *Roman Britain 1914–1928*, 67–73.

¹⁵ Schultz, art. cit., and *Antiquity*, vii (1933), 381.

¹⁵ᵃ The study of minims and sub-Roman coinage has advanced since 1934. Cf. C. H. V. Sutherland, *Num. Chron.* xv (1935), 284–6; id. *Coinage and Currency in Roman Britain* (1937), 98–105, 122–5.

15b An alternative expansion is: *Felicium Temporum Reparatio.* Cf. *Num. Chron.* xiii (1933), 182.

15c E. T. Leeds, *Early A.S. Art and Archaeology,* 2 ff.; id., *Celtic Ornament* (1933), 144–64; T. D. Kendrick, in *Antiquity,* vi (1932), 161 ff.; id., *A.S. Art* (1938), 40–60; Françoise Henry, in *Journal of Royal Society of Antiquaries in Ireland,* lxvi (1936), 209–39.

16 c. 62, ed. Mommsen, 205–6. Cf. Welsh genealogies in *Cymmrodorion,* ix. 170; Lloyd, in *R. Irish Acad.* xxxvii (1926), 132; Chadwick, *G. of L.,* 309–11. In Collingwood and Myres, *Roman Britain,* 288–90, it is suggested that Cunedda and his tribesmen were transplanted as *foederati* from one frontier to another by Stilicho.

17 Bibliography for St. Germanus in Kenney, i. 163.

18 Text and trans. of N. J. D. White, in *P.R.I.A.* (1905), 260 ff.; id., *St. Patrick, His Writings and Life* (1920). For general bibliography for St. Patrick see Kenney, i. 165–70. For a theory that Patrick's home in Britain was at Bewcastle see G. H. Wheeler in *E.H.R.* l (1935), 109–13; *Analecta Bollandiana,* liii (1935), 185 f. On the other hand, for evidence from excavation that Bewcastle was not occupied after 367, see *J.R.S.* xxviii (1938), 176.

19 The authority of the *Annales Cambriae* is sometimes quoted in support of 428; but (1) the *Computus* which, in Harleian MS. 3859, gives this date may be really the end of the *Historia Brittonum* and not the beginning of the *Annales*; and (2) in any case it is probably only an echo of the *Historia.*

20 *M.G.H. Auct. Ant.* ix (ed. Mommsen), 660, and 661.

21 e.g. R. Thurneysen, in *Englische Studien,* xxii (1895), 174; F. Lot, 'Bretons et Anglais', *P.B.A.* xvi (1930), 327–45, and *La Fin du Monde Antique* (1927), 236. For a criticism of this view see R. V. Lennard, in *History,* xviii (1933), 204–15; and for an eccentric interpretation A. Anscombe, in *Brit. Num. Journ.,* 2nd ser., ix (1927–8), 20–1.

22 See passages collected in E. K. Chambers, *Arthur,* 237–8. Also Plummer, *Bede,* ii. 27; Thurneysen, *ut supra,* and E. W. B. Nicholson in *Zeitschrift für Celtische Philologie,* vi (1907), 439 ff.

23 Migne, *P.L.* li, col. 618, *Carmen de Providentia Divina,* line 38; col. 612, *Poema Coniugis,* line 30.

24 At least the *De Vita Christiana.* Cf. R. Morris, in *Trans. Soc. Cymmrod.* (1914–15), 43–6.

III. THE CONQUEST OF KENT

1 Bibliography for Gildas, in Kenney, i. 150–2, note specially F. Lot in *Medieval Studies in Memory of G. S. Loomis* (1927), 229–64.

1a 547 or 549. Cf. E. K. Chambers, *Arthur,* 13–15, on the *Annales Cambriae.*

2 e.g. by F. Lot, in *Mélanges,* 1 ff.

³ Some writers think that the Hengest of *Beowulf* and Hengist the Conqueror of Kent have more than the name in common. M. G. Clarke, *Sidelights on Teutonic History during the Migration Period*, c. v, esp. 186–7; cf. Chadwick, *Origin*, 53; R. W. Chambers, *Beowulf* (1932), 443 ff. With reference to p. 78, line 12, note that the name Horsa is derived from the O.E. word for 'horse', not for mare. Ekwall, *Oxford Dictionary of E.P.N.*, 240, explains the name Horstead as 'Place where horses were kept, horse-farm'.

⁴ The history of the *Historia Brittonum*, and the relations of the various versions and manuscripts to one another and to Nennius remain tangled problems in a long controversy. Bibliography in Kenney, i. 152–5. Note especially—H. Zimmer, *Nennius Vindicatus* (1893); *D.N.B. sub* 'Nennius' (1895); T. Mommsen, *M.G.H., Chronica Minora*, vol. iii (1896), 111 ff.; E. Faral, *La légende arthurienne* (1929); J. Loth, in *Rev. Celt.* xlix (1932), 150–65, li (1933), 1–31; A. G. von Hamel, *Lebor Bretnach, The Irish Version of the Historia Brittonum ascribed to Nennius* (1932); H. M. Chadwick, *Growth of Literature*, i (1932), 153–8, 297, and *passim*; R. Thurneysen in *Zeitschrift f. Celtische Philologie*, xx (1933), 97–138; F. Lot, *Nennius et l'Historia Brittonum* (1934); I. Williams in *Bulletin of Board of Celtic Studies*, vii (1935), 380–9; A. W. Wade-Evans, *Nennius's 'History of the Britons'* (1938),—a translation, with notes marred by peculiar theories.

⁵ Wadstein, 36.

⁶ Chadwick, *Origin*, 97–107; Schmidt, ii. 26, and 510; J. Hoops, *Waldbäume*, 585–6; F. Lot, in *Rev. Hist.* cxix. 23–34. Cf. also Schütte, ii. 297–312.

⁷ *M.G.H. Auct. Ant.*, vol. iv, *pars prior* (ed. F. Leo), Carminum liber IX, i, line 73 f.

⁸ Collingwood and Myres, *Roman Britain*, 345, may well be right in suggesting that the order of the peoples mentioned by the poet 'is determined by the necessity of getting the names into a hexameter and has no geographical significance whatever'. Inferences are made from a fourth, and even more unsatisfactory, passage—this time from the anonymous geographer of Ravenna (*c.* A.D. 650)—by Oman, 209; Chadwick, *Origin*, 47; and others.

⁹ Cf. R. W. Chambers, *Beowulf* (1932), 8–10, 260 ff., 272 ff., 333–45, 401–9, 417–18; id., *Widsith*, 237–41. Siebs (p. 61) suggests that the Eutii or Euthiones may be localized in the Ems-Weser region by a phonological connexion which he traces with the modern name Iade, a river of that region.

¹⁰ e.g. in the territory of the Gyrwe, between Norfolk and Peterborough (*V.C.H. Northants.* i. 250) and at Girton near Cambridge (E. J. Hollingworth and M. M. O'Reilly, *Anglo-Saxon Cemetery at Girton College, Cambridge*, 13); E. T. Leeds, in *Ant. Journ.* xiii (1933), 234 ff.; *V.C.H. Cambridgeshire*, i. 306.

¹¹ Cf. R. G. Collingwood, *Archaeology of Roman Britain* (1930), c. 15; Schetelig, *Cruciform Brooches*; B.B. iii. 248–64; Åberg, 28 f.; *B.M. Guide*, 23 ff.

[12] Cf. E. T. Leeds, in *Ant. Journ.* xiii. 240. Note that part of Cambridge-shire is reckoned as East Anglian.

[13] Leeds, *Archaeology of the A.S. Settlements*, cc. 6 and 7. For what follows, see also B.B. iv. 690–6, 742–4; Åberg, *passim*; Brenner, 342–6.

[13a] E. T. Leeds, in *Early A.S. Art and Archaeology* (1936), cc. 3 and 4, re-examined the problem. He admitted (p. 45) that he had formerly 'under-estimated the existence and amount of early material which Kent has to show in common with other invaded districts. It is only after the Jutes were firmly established in Kent that a change takes place.' 'This change', he says (p. 53), 'falls into line with the gradual westwardly shift of a large part of the Franks, and may indeed be due to the settlement of them in this country. I do not for a moment believe that it is possible that the Jutes should have undergone such a complete transformation simply as the result of mere commercial imports.' Cf. J. N. L. Myres, in *History*, xxi (1937), 323–5. See, for further references to this important controversy, below, p. 382 *b*, note 21.

[14] Åberg, 30–1, and 2.

[15] *Antiquity*, vii (1933), 429–52. Cf. T. D. Kendrick, *A.S. Art* (1938), 62–73.

[15a] Ibid. 73.

[16] E. Brenner, in *R.G.K.*, vii *Bericht*, 344.

[17] Cf. H. Kjaer, *Ligbraendingen i Danmark i Oldtiden* (1931), 73 ff.; H. Schetelig, in *Praehist. Zeitsch.* iv (1912), 351 ff. Cf. id., *Scandin. Archaeology*, 236.

[17a] For 'The Present Position of Studies in English Field-Systems' see an article by E. Barger in *E.H.R.* liii (1938), 385–411. The notes of this article give a bibliography of recent work on the subject down to 1938. Barger argues that the contrasts between Celtic, Roman, and Germanic field-systems are less clear than has often been assumed. He suggests 'that the two systems of agriculture, one based on the plot [like the Kentish] and the other on the strip, existed, both in the Roman Province of Germany and in the Germanic North, at least a century or two before the appearance of the heavy plough was chronicled by Pliny'. The plot is the product of the light plough, the strip is that of the heavy plough. Otherwise the causes and mean-ing of the distribution of the two systems cannot at present be explained. In Britain, strip cultivation existed some centuries before the Saxon invasion. Barger (mainly following Collingwood and Myres, *Roman Britain*, 210–11) suggests that in Roman Britain the villas 'were cultivated by the heavy plough with its concomitants of open fields and strip agriculture'; also, even more speculatively, 'that the Roman villa is the *Einzelhof* out of which a communal agriculture grew up'. Many of his suggestions are admittedly not firmly grounded; but at least they serve to illustrate the uncertainty of much which has in the past been written about field-systems.

[18] J. E. A. Jolliffe, in *Pre-Feudal England, The Jutes* (1933).

[19] H. L. Gray, *English Field Systems* (1915), c. vii, esp. 415; and G. Slater, in *V.C.H. Kent*, iii. 323 ff.

[21] Note, however, J. K. Wallenberg, *Kentish Place-Names* (1931), and *The Place-Names of Kent* (1934).

[22] Ekwall, *E.P.N.I.* 34, 107; Karlström (1927); Ordnance Survey, *Map of Britain in the Dark Ages* (1935); J. N. L. Myres, in *Antiquity*, ix (1935), 458–64, discusses the relationship between '-ingas' names and cemeteries.

[23] Ekwall, *E.P.N.I.* 107.

[24] See Leeds, 116–20; B.B. iv. 744–51.

[25] Cf. above, note 13a; Schütte, ii. 238.

IV. THE FIRST STAGE OF THE SAXON AND ANGLIAN CONQUESTS

P. 103, *Map, Conquest of Kent, &c.*—In this map single burials are in general not shown owing to the number of heathen cemeteries. They are shown in the Ordnance Survey *Map of Britain in the Dark Ages*. Some of the *-ingas* shown, especially in east Kent, are doubtful, and are not accepted by Ekwall, the O.S. map, and J. N. L. Myres. I have refrained from deleting them since suggestions made by J. K. Wallenberg give some ground, even if hypothetical, for them. I have added other *-ingas* and cemeteries omitted in the first edition, following Map VI in *Roman Britain* by Collingwood and Myres. Cymenes Ora (cf. p. 105) is sometimes located near Wittering in west Sussex, but the evidence for this is not very good.

[1] *E.P.N.S.* vi. and vii (1929–30), esp. xxiv; Ekwall, *E.P.N.I.* 109; A. Mawer, *Problems*, 15–19.

[2] B.B. iv. 674.

[3] See in *E.P.N.S.* vi. xiv, some arguments of H. M. Stenton for accepting Cissa as a son of Aelle.

[4] *V.C.H. Surrey*, i. 260–2; *V.C.H. Sussex*, i. 345; Leeds, 45–9; B.B. iv. 688–90; *Arch.*, 2nd ser., liv. 369–82; lv. 203–14. Cf. Leeds, in *Ant. Journ.* xiii (1933), 229 ff.

P. 109, *Map, Conquest of Mid-Britain.*—Since for technical reasons coloured maps cannot be corrected or brought up to date, readers may be referred to the Ordnance Survey *Map of Britain in the Dark Ages*, to maps vi and vii in Collingwood and Myres, *Roman Britain*, and to the map in *V.C.H. Cambridgeshire*, i. facing p. 305.

The following are some of the additions which should be made in the map: 3 cemeteries on the Surrey hills; 7 in the Thames valley (near Cliffe; Horton Kirby on the river Darent (cf. *The Times*, Sept. 16, 1938); Shepperton; Wallingford (E. T. Leeds, in *Berks. Arch. Journ.* xlii (1938), 98–101); and 3 in the Fairford region); 5 west of the Fosse Way, including one near

Stratford-on-Avon; east of the Fosse Way, Baginton, near Coventry (*Ant. Journ.* xv (1935), 109–12); several in the Lincolnshire region (see map, p. 149 and *Arch. Journ.* xci (1934), 137–54).

In East Anglia, 4 -*ingas* place-names should be added near the coast, besides a sprinkling of others inland and another early cemetery near Caister by Norwich.

The names of the early *regiones* are best shown on the maps of Collingwood and Myres. The annual volumes of the English Place-Name Society often identify new early divisions; for example (in vol. xiii, 1936, p. xvii, the *Stoppingas*, in south Warwickshire, and the *Tomsetan*, the settlers of the Tame valley).

[5] Leeds, 56; B.B. iii. 261; Åberg, 13.

[6] *Archaeology*, 60.

[7] *History*, x. 105.

[7a] E. T. Leeds and D. B. Harden, *The Anglo-Saxon Cemetery at Abingdon, Berkshire* (1936); Leeds, *Early A.S. Art and Archaeology*, 38.

[7b] T. C. Lethbridge, in *V.C.H. Cambridgeshire*, i. 314, questions the argument based on the equal-armed brooches. He says: 'The ornaments are provincial Roman in character, and before we can say that the Saxons brought them over we must know where they were made. It is possible that they really took them back.' If he means that the Saxons carried them back from Britain to the Elbe lands, the suggestion is sufficiently refuted by the distribution map on p. 33.

[8] Leeds, 58–9; also *Arch.* lxiii (1912), 159–202; Åberg, 16–24; B.B. iii. 274–8; R. Smith, in *B.M. Guide*, 33–6.

[9] *P.S.A.*, 2nd ser., iii. 136; *Arch.* xlii (1869), 417–85, and xlv. 405–10; *Ant. Journ.* i (1921), 87–97. Later excavations (to be reported in *Oxoniensia*, vol. iv) confirm the earlier evidence.

[10] Leeds, in *Arch.* lxiii. 173; B.B. iii. 52; iv. 645, 662 ff.

[11] *Arch.* lxxiii (1923), 86–116, lxxiv. 271–88. Cf. E. T. Leeds, in *History*, x (195), 101; Collingwood and Myres, *Roman Britain*, 408–9. The important cemetery at Stratford-on-Avon has not yet been fully described.

[12] *Ant. Journ.* viii (1928), 177 ff.; F. Roeder, *Typol.-Chronol. Studien*, 54.

[13] *History*, x (1925), 97 ff.; and in *Ant. Journ.* xiii (1933), 229–51. Cf. Leeds, 54–5.

[14] For what follows see Leeds, *Archaeology*, 78–82; *Ant. Journ.* xiii. 229–51; B.B. iv. 621–2; Fox, 237–96, esp. 276 ff.; E. J. Hollingworth and M. M. O'Reilly, *Anglo-Saxon Cemetery at Girton College, Cambridge* (1925); Lethbridge, *Recent Excavations*, 76–7; id. in *V.C.H. Cambridgeshire*, i. 305 ff.; J. N. L. Myres, in *History*, xxi (1937), 326.

The labours of the Fenland Research Committee have demonstrated that the Fenlands were largely settled in Roman times, and were submerged only about the fifth century. Cf. Myres and Collingwood, *Roman Britain*, 383–5; H. C. Darby, in *Antiquity*, viii (1934), 185 ff.

¹⁵ F. Roeder, *Die sächsische Schalenfibel der Völkerwanderungszeit* (1927); 'Die sächsischen Fenstergefässe', in *R.G.K.*, xviii *Bericht* (1928), 149 ff.; 'Die Henkelgussurnen', in *Mannus, Zeitschrift für Vorgeschichte*, Ergänzungsband, vi (1928), 190–201; *Typologisch-chronologische Studien zu Metallsachen der Völkerwanderungszeit* (1930).

¹⁶ See G. H. Wheeler, *E.H.R.* xli. 497–503; R. W. Chambers, 94–6; Sir E. K. Chambers, *Arthur*, 197–201; de la Borderie, in *Rev. Celt.* vi (1883), 1 ff.; Collingwood and Myres, *Roman Britain*, 460 f.; P. K. Johnstone, in *Antiquity*, xiii (1939), 92–5.

¹⁷ Sir E. K. Chambers, *Arthur*, esp. cc. i and vi; Collingwood and Myres, *Roman Britain*, 320–4, 477; O. G. S. Crawford, in *Antiquity*, ix (1935), 277–91. An attempt to identify Arthur with a Roman officer of the second century (see K. Malone, in *Modern Philology*, xxii (1924), 367–74) has found little favour.

¹⁹ T. C. Lethbridge, in *Man*, xxxi (1931), 247; E. K. Chambers, *Arthur*, 197–204.

²⁰ Lot, in *Mélanges*, 19.

²⁰ᵃ For another explanation cf. K. Malone, in *Anglia, Beiblatt*, xlvii (1936), 220.

²¹ W. H. Stevenson, in *E.H.R.* xiv (1899), 32–46.

²² A. S. Napier, in *Modern Language Notes*, xii (1897), 110–11.

²³ Cf. Plummer, ii. 14; W. H. Stevenson, art. cit.; and O. G. S. Crawford, in *Antiquity*, v (1931), 457.

²⁴ Plummer, *Bede*, ii. 28.

²⁵ *Bretons et Anglais au Vᵉ et VIᵉ siècles* (P.B.A. (1930)), p. 6.

²⁶ Cf. R. W. Chambers, *Beowulf* (1932), 411–17.

²⁷ See H. Sweet, *Oldest English Texts* (E.E.T.S. lxxxiii (1885), 169–71). For Wessex cf. G. H. Wheeler, in *E.H.R.* xxxvi. 161 ff.; H. M. Chadwick, *Origin*, 23–5.

²⁷ᵃ Cf. O. G. S. Crawford, in *Antiquity*, v (1931), 444.

²⁸ To these may be added Cerdices-beorg (Cerdic's barrow) mentioned in Kemble, *C.D.*, no. 1077. P. K. Johnstone, in *Antiquity*, xiii (1939), 92–6, suggests that this barrow at Stoke, near Hurstborne in north-west Hampshire was the actual burial place of Cerdic, and that he was buried by his followers retreating after the defeat at Mount Badon, *c.* 517.

²⁹ In *Antiquity*, v (1931), 441 ff.

³⁰ Oman, 225.

³¹ *History*, x (1925), 108.

³² To see that heathen cemeteries are not a reliable test of heathen settlements, first look at a map of the Saxon cemeteries (e.g. that of *Britain in*

the Dark Ages, published by the Ordnance Survey). Then note (1) that the Severn valley was apparently conquered in the years following 577, about two generations before the Conversion of Wessex; (?) that the West Saxon conquest had advanced so far into the south-west of Britain that by 658 they pretty certainly had overrun most of Somerset and, according to the learned editors of the English Place-Name Society, even the Vale of Taunton; (3) that sometime before 663 Winchester was made the see of the bishop of the West Saxons, and that the district must presumably have been settled by the Saxons for some generations before that event. (Cf. *E.H.R.* vii. 438, for evidence from church dedications.) It seems, therefore, that in all these three directions there must have been large tracts of territory settled by heathen Saxons who left no trace of themselves in heathen burials. It is not enough to say that grave-furnishing went out of fashion shortly before the Conversion. The fashion could just as well have changed at an earlier date.

[32a] See Preface to Second Edition for a criticism of this statement.

[33] See Mrs. M. E. Cunnington, 'Wiltshire in Pagan Saxon Times', in *Wilts. Arch. and Natural Hist. Mag.* xlvi (1933), 147–75, esp. 152–7, and references there given to recent excavations; id. *Catalogue of Antiquities in the Museum at Devizes*, Part II, 2nd edition (1934), 239–56. On Harnham Hill, cf. Collingwood and Myres, *Roman Britain*, 400.

[34] Coins of Honorius (A.D. 395–423) have been found under the dyke. For references see Kendrick and Hawkes, 295.

[35] For the settlement of Hampshire and a theory that the Gewissae should be specially located in Hampshire see Collingwood and Myres, *Roman Britain*, 400–5.

[36] In order to avoid confusing the reader, I have in these and in subsequent pages accepted the statement of the Alfredian Chronicle as it has come down to us that Cynric was the son of Cerdic. The probabilities are, however, that the name of Creoda has dropped out, and that Cynric was really Cerdic's grandson and not his son. See Stevenson, 159; Chadwick, *Origin*, 24; P. K. Johnstone, in *Antiquity*, xiii (1939), 94.

[37] E. Ekblom, *Place-Names of Wiltshire*, 19; Grundy, in *Arch. Journ.* lxxv (1919), 187–8.

[38] O. G. S. Crawford, *Air Survey and Archaeology* (1928), esp. 7–8; and *Wessex from the Air* (1928). On the 'Celtic fields', cf. above, p. 372, note 17a.

[39] E. T. Leeds, in *History*, x (1925), 107 ff.; O. G. S. Crawford, in *Antiquity*, i. 251. Cf. also A. Major and E. J. Burrow, *Mystery of Wansdyke* (1926), esp. 138 ff. and bibliography; O. S. Taylor, in *Trans. Bristol & Glos. Arch. Soc.* xxvii. 131–55. Sir C. Oman, in *Quarterly Review*, ccliii (1929), esp. 297–8.

[39a] Cf. R. E. M. Wheeler, in *Antiquity*, viii (1934), 290 ff., and 443 ff.; id. *London and the Saxons*, 139. An addition to the Saxon finds in London was made in 1937—a small Saxon vessel found buried near the corner of

Drury Lane and Great Queen Street. Cf. J. N. L. Myres, in *Ant. Journ.* xvii (1937), 432–3.

⁴⁰ *Ant. Journ.* x (1930), 387–8.

⁴¹ In *E.P.N.S.* i. i. 52.

⁴² Leeds, 43; S. W. Wooldridge, in Darby, *Historical Geography* (1936), 91 ff.

⁴³ *J.R.S.* i. 170.

⁴⁴ R. E. M. Wheeler, in *Roman London* (R.C.H.M.), 64–6; id., *London and the Saxons* (1935). Opposed to Wheeler, J. N. L. Myres, in *Antiquity,* viii (1934), 437–42, and ix (1935), 458–64; id., *J.R.S.* xxvi (1936), 87–92; Collingwood and Myres, *Roman Britain,* 437–8.

⁴⁵ Sweet, in *Englische Studien,* ii. 310; W. H. Stevenson, *E.H.R.* xiv (1899), 38, n. 29.

⁴⁶ e.g. Oman, 230.

⁴⁷ *The Roman Occupation of Britain,* 278.

⁴⁸ See Hübner, *Inscriptiones Britanniae Christianae, passim.*

⁴⁹ See Gordon Home, *Roman London,* 150–2.

⁵⁰ R.C.H.M., *Roman London,* 65.

⁵¹ Bede, ii, c. 7.

⁵¹ᵃ For preliminary excavations in 1930–4 see R. E. M. and T. V. Wheeler, *Verulamium* (1936), esp. 31–4.

⁵² Ekwall, *E.P.N.I.* 114–15.   ⁵³ Bede, ii, c. 3.

⁵⁴ References in *V.C.H. Essex,* i. 316; Chadwick, *Institutions,* 276, and *Origin,* 59.

⁵⁴ᵃ On Seaxneat, or Saxnot, see J. de Vries, *Altgermanische Religionsgeschichte,* i (1935), 237–8.

⁵⁵ *Origin,* 87–8.

⁵⁵ᵃ Admirably summarized and revised in Collingwood and Myres, *Roman Britain,* cc. xxii and xxiii. For J. N. L. Myres's theories about the Humbrenses see also his article in *History,* xx (1935), 250–62. Cf. P. H. Blair, in *E.H.R.* lii (1937), 687; and Preface to Second Edition.

⁵⁶ F. M. Stenton, in *Essays presented to R. L. Poole* (1927), 139.

⁵⁶ᵃ Cf. A. H. Smith, in *E.P.N.S.* xiv (1937), xviii.

⁵⁷ Collingwood and Myres, *Roman Britain,* 412.

⁵⁸ So F. Elgee, *Early Man in North-East Yorkshire* (1931), 219–20.

⁵⁸ᵃ Leeds, 71.

⁵⁹ For the beginnings of Bernicia see Leeds, 71–2; B.B. iv. 752–61 and 810–13; Oman, 188–92; *Northumberland County History,* x, 12–13; Watson, *Celtic Place-Names of Scotland,* 127 ff.; Collingwood and Myres, *Roman Britain,* 420–2.

⁶⁰ Information supplied by Mr. R. C. Bosanquet. An article on the Howick cemetery by G. S. Keeney is to appear in *Archaeologia Æliana,* xvi.

[61] Leeds, 72.

[62] Bede, v, c. 24.

[63] *Nennius*, c. 61, 201.

[64] Into Chronicle A (the Parker MS). Thence copied into E (Peterborough MS.).

[65] B.B. iv. 760.

V. GENERAL CHARACTER OF THE SAXON CONQUEST

Head-piece. Detail from the Utrecht Psalter.—This and other details from the Psalter have been taken from *The Illustrations of the Utrecht Psalter*, edited by E. T. Dewald (Princeton University Press, 1932). A complete facsimile of the Psalter was published privately. It is necessary to caution readers of this History against the idea which has often existed in the past that the Utrecht Psalter illustrates the fashions of the Anglo-Saxons. It seems to have been brought to England some time before A.D. 1000, but, as was shown by P. Durrieu in *Mélanges Julien Havet*, 646 f., it was produced in or near Rheims about the second quarter of the ninth century. It would therefore be much better to call it the Rheims Psalter than the Utrecht Psalter, since this last name only indicates the place where it has been for the last two centuries. It has been long obvious that the book derives from a Greek or Greco-Latin archetype of the fourth or fifth century.

A good modern account of the Psalter, with notes on previous discussions about it, will be found in articles by Mrs. G. R. Benson and Mr. D. T. Tselos in the *Art Bulletin*, xiii (1931), 11–79. These authors hold that the archetype must have been copied and certain western features introduced into the copy about the seventh or eighth century. 'The fusion of the Greek and Latin elements whether at one or two points certainly must have been done in the West', probably by a Greek artist. This artist was, it seems, the master who gave life to his figures and well-balanced proportions to each crowded scene. The Utrecht Psalter itself was a copy in line technique of this intermediate work, and at least three, perhaps more, persons had a hand in it.

Several features in the drawings appear to be later than the fifth century, and there is at least one, 'The Globe-Mandorla', in which the Christ-logos is surrounded, which must be a Carolingian addition. As a whole, however, the fashions and objects depicted are those of the fifth century or earlier. This being so, I am better justified in using the Psalter to illustrate my early than my later chapters.

It may be asked why drawings deriving from a Greek original should have any place whatever in a book about Saxon England. To this I can only reply that they are better than nothing, and for my purpose far better than the illustrations of the other manuscripts produced during these centuries in the West. Though they do not portray the fashions of Anglo-Saxon society, they do give vivid sketches drawn from men of the Dark Ages. They render them as living and moving beings; and a group of spearmen like that on p. 154 or a hunting scene like that on p. 539 gives the reader some idea of what was to be seen, whether in Britain or Gaul or the Eastern Empire.

Moreover, the Utrecht Psalter has a connexion with Anglo-Saxon England, even if it is only adventitious. From the influence of the Utrecht Psalter on another book of the Psalms (Harley MS. 603), made at Canterbury early in the eleventh century, it is commonly inferred that the Utrecht volume was brought to Canterbury during the Reform movement of the tenth century. The reason for placing its arrival so late is that Harley MS. 603 is the earliest English manuscript to reveal its influence. The argument is by no means conclusive. Few English illustrated manuscripts of any kind survive from the previous period, and it may be that the Utrecht book had been long in England before men were ambitious enough to try to copy its skilful drawings. The occasion of its arrival can only be conjectured, but to my mind the intercourse between the province of Rheims and England which occurred in the ninth century gave likely opportunities for the book to be brought to our island. When Ethelwulf visited the court of Charles the Bald and was married to his daughter by Hincmar, archbishop of Rheims, the Utrecht Psalter was nearly a new book. It is quite possible that Hincmar gave the book either to Judith or to Ethelwulf (we know of other books which he gave away). Or it may have been brought to England later on, when Grimbald became an intermediary between the churches of Rheims and England. In either case its pictures may have been seen and admired by Alfred. But however it came to England, my excuse for reproducing so many drawings from it is that they, though wrong in their details, give the best general idea of what men looked like in the Dark Ages.

P. 155, *Map, Britain* c. *550.*—There is probably too much red (indicating Germanic settlements) both in the regions of Wiltshire and of Northumberland. Both these regions may have been occupied by raiding bands; it is less probable that they were occupied by agricultural settlers. The existence, or, at any rate, the importance, of the 'Picts of Galloway' is questionable. Cf. Watson, *Celtic Place-Names of Scotland*, 174–80; *Map of Britain in the Dark Ages, North Sheet* (Ordnance Survey), p. 17.

1 D. C. Whimster, *Archaeology of Surrey* (1931), 177; Hollingworth and O'Reilly, *Girton*, 15–17.

2 Oman, 213–14; cf. R. V. Lennard, in *History*, xviii. 204–15.

3 e.g. E. T. Leeds, 17; G. Sheldon, *The Transition from Roman Britain to Christian England*, 54.

4 *Origin*, 88–9, see also 296–302. Cf. Hoops, i. 89–90.

[4a] Cf. Kemp Malone, in *Review of English Studies*, v. 174. He shows that Bede followed Pope Gregory the Great in using *Angli* in the sense 'the English' rather than 'the Angles'.

[4b] The links now established by archaeological evidence between East Anglia and Sweden at the aristocratic level (see Appendix on the Sutton Hoo ship-burial) may be noted in this connexion.

[5] I owe these remarks to Mr. C. L. Wrenn.

[6] Leeds, 73 ff.; B.B. iv. 597 ff., 617, 626; Fox, 284–95.

[7] On the decoration of Anglo-Saxon pottery and its relation to the pottery of the Anglian and Saxon homelands cf. B.B. iv. 570, 581; J. N. L. Myres, in *Ant. Journ.* xvii (1937), 424–37, id. in *Antiquity*, xi (1937), 389–99. Myres points out that ornamentation by stamps occurred in the fourth century sparingly in the Saxon homelands, but not in the Anglian; that in Britain 'perhaps in the first half of the sixth century, it came to dominate all other forms of ornament', and that the 'focus was in the Midlands in the lands radiating from the Wash and the Fens'.

[8] Quoted from Widukind (i. 1) by Chadwick, *Origin*, 92.

[9] Zachrisson, 76 ff.   [10] *J.R.S.* xviii (1928), 118.

[11] e.g. E. C. Curwen, in *Antiquity*, i (1927), 261 ff.; ii (1928), 168–72; A. M. Raistrick and S. E. Chapman, in *Antiquity*, iii (1929), 165 ff.; R. Eckford, in *P.S.A. Scot.* (1928–9), 110–18; H. E. K. Jones and M. E. C. Mitchell, in ibid. (1932–3), 70–81. Cf. E. Barger, in *E.H.R.* liii (1938), 386 ff.

[12] See B.B. iii. 51–2; 130 ff.; iv. 643, 683, 695, 732, 741, 802, &c.; *V.C.H. Essex*, i. 319–27; Rolleston, in *Arch.* xlv. 4. For a good example of continuity in Yorkshire, see *J.R.S.* xxviii (1938), 179, on excavations at Elmswell.

[13] *J.R.A.I.* xlv (1915), 107.

[13a] Isaac Taylor's map, showing 'Distribution of Place-Names in Britain', gives a general picture which is approximately correct. Any one will see how wrong are many of its details if he compares with the map some of the statistics which I quote from the volumes of the Place-Name Society. Unsatisfactory as it is, the map is the only one of its kind now available.

[14] See Mawer, *Problems*, 2–5.

[15] Ibid. 3–4. See also the prefaces of the *E.P.N.S.* volumes, *passim*; also Zachrisson, 47 ff.; E. Ekwall, *Oxford Dictionary of E.P.N.*, *passim*; R. E. Zachrisson, in *Englische Studien*, lxxii (1938), 257–70, arguing that Ekwall exaggerates the Celtic element; F. M. Stenton, in *T.R.H.S.* xxi (1939), 1–20.

[16] See E. Ekwall, *English River-Names* (1928), esp. xlvii and lxxxix.

[17] *E.P.N.S.* viii. xx.   [18] M. Förster, in *Texte und Forschungen* ... 119–243.

[19] For what follows see J. Beddoe, *The Races of Britain* (1885); W. Z. Ripley, *Races of Europe* (1899), 319 ff.; W. Bradbrooke and F. G. Parsons, article in *J.R.A.I.* lii (1920), 113–26 (in part confirming Beddoe's results); H. J. Fleure, *Races of England and Wales* (1923), 98 ff.

[20] In the first edition I added, as a long Supplementary Note, a criticism

of Beddoe's conclusions by Dr. G. R. de Beer, now Reader in Embryology at University College, London. In this edition I have, as far as was practicable, embodied these criticisms in my text, often repeating the words used by de Beer. The whole note will be found on pp. 382 *d–e* of the first edition. It ends as follows: 'To establish the persistence of any racial type, it would be necessary to take into consideration not one but all the characters. This is unfortunately impossible, owing to the very complex mode of action of Mendelian factors in the human race, and to the extraordinarily mixed and "heterozygous" nature of almost all populations. . . . There have not been wanting occasions since the Saxon Conquest on which persons carrying the factors for dark hair could have "inoculated" these factors into the British population. Libertine Spanish seamen or prolific Jewish women may well be expected to have produced "evidence of nigrescence" during fourteen centuries.'

None the less, the great contrast between the nigrescence in the west of England and the fairness in the east remains a fact; and though the pocket of nigrescence in the south-eastern Midlands is more open to dispute, it is sufficiently attested to justify the speculation that it is due to other causes than Spanish seamen or Jewish women.

[21] For the study of Romano-British, Saxon, and later skulls, especially in the Oxford district, we are indebted to L. H. D. Buxton. See his articles in *J.R.S.* xxvi (1935), 35–50; *Custom is King* (1936), 203–13.

[21a] The Place-Name Society volume on Hertfordshire supplies one piece of evidence for the late survival of a British-speaking population in that region. Cf. *E.P.N.S.* xv. xv.

[22] G. des Marez, *Le Problème de la colonisation franque* (1926), 82 ff.

[22a] Cf. p. 372, note 17a, for an article by E. Barger on 'The present Position of Studies in English Field-Systems'.

[23] *Germania*, c. 33.   [24] Bede, iv, c. 16.

[25] Ibid. ii, c. 20.

[26] H. J. Randall, in *Edinburgh Review*, ccxlii (1925), 355.

[27] Zachrisson, 64; referring to Fox, 282, 320, &c.

[28] Stevenson, 241.   [30] Gildas, c. 21.   [31] Id., c. 6.

[32] See Cabrol, xi. 960 ff., for theories and bibliography of this migration.

[33] Nennius, c. 56.

VI. THE SECOND STAGE OF THE CONQUEST

[1] Eddius, c. xlii.

[1a] For another attempt to reconstruct the early history of the West-Saxon kingdom see pamphlet by G. M. Young, summarized in *Wilts. Arch. and Nat. Hist. Mag.* xlvii (1935), 146–8.

² *E.P.N.S.* III (1926), xiv; G. H. Wheeler, in *E.H.R.* xli (1926), 501–2.

³ *E.P.N.S.* iii. 155–6. Cf. article on this campaign by W. M. Hughes, in *Antiquity*, 1 (1931), 291–314.

⁴ Op. cit. xiv and ii. The reasons for questioning the judgement of the editors in this case are (1) the spelling of the name by Ethelweard, *M.H.B.* 504, a point which I owe to Mr. Lethbridge, and (2) the opinion of W. H. Stevenson. Even if the opinion of the editors of the *E.P.N.S.* is accepted, the argument in the text is scarcely affected, since they suppose the battle to have been fought 'in the district east of the Middle Thames'.

⁴ᵃ Cf. Oman, 228; Collingwood and Myres, *Roman Britain*, 403–4.

⁵ *E.P.N.S.* IV. xiv, note; cf. Chadwick, *Origin*, 5–6.

⁶ Oman, 286.

⁷ Grundy, in *Arch. Journ.*, 2nd ser., xxv (1918), 175–8.

⁸ See vol. ii, p. 721; and cf. G. H. Wheeler, in *E.H.R.* xxvi (1921), 161 ff., and xli (1926), 497 ff.

⁹ E. Ekwall, *Place-Names of Lancashire* (1922), 231. Cf. the same author's *Scandinavians and Celts in the North-West of England* (1918), 6.

¹⁰ c. 63.

¹¹ Cf. A. P. Forbes, *Lives of St. Ninian and St. Kentigern* (1874), lxxv, lxxvii, 212 ff.; H. Zimmer, *Nennius Vindicatus* (1893), 78 ff.; Chadwick, *H.A.* (1912), 105–9; *G. of L.* i. 151, 156; &c.

¹² Chadwick, *G. of L.* i. 109, 102 ff.

¹²ᵃ Cf. *Trans. Cumberland and Westmorland Antiq. and Arch. Soc.* viii (1908), 236–46.

¹³ Lloyd, 162–71; Chadwick, *G. of L.* i. 527; Skene, *Four Ancient Books of Wales*, i. 374–409, esp. 376–7; I. Williams, in *P.B.A.* xviii (1932), 270–1; K. Jackson, in *Antiquity*, xiii (1939), 25–34, a summary of the important edition of the *Gododdin*, with introduction in Welsh, by I. Williams, 1938.

¹⁴ The authorities differ about the date of Ælle's death. I have followed Bede, *De temporum ratione*, in *M.G.H. Chron. Minora*, iii (ed. T. Mommsen), 309, as against the *Saxon Chronicle*, which assigns it to 588.

¹⁴ᵃ *Sketch of Bamburgh.*—The small hill in the left foreground is one of two unexcavated pre-Anglian *tumuli* marked on the Ordnance Map (about 400 yards south of the main gateway). I am confident that the sea penetrated in the eighth century to near this spot. Its meanderings are a contribution of the artist.

¹⁵ i, c. 34.

¹⁶ E. Ekwall, *Scandinavians and Celts in the North-West of England*, p. 2, thinks that the northern part of Cumberland was probably conquered by Ethelfrith but that 'the southern part perhaps remained British till the time of Ecgfrith (671–85)'.

VII. HEATHEN SOCIETY

Headpiece. The name Aegili is carved in runes above the archer defending a crenellated house. This incident in the career of Egil, the brother of Wayland, is otherwise unknown. Cf. P. W. Souers, 'The Top of the Franks Casket', in *Harvard Studies and Notes in Philology and Literature*, xvii (1934), 163–80.

o. For a general bibliography of subjects covered in this chapter see F. B. Gummere, *The Founders of England* (edited by F. P. Magoun, 1930), esp. 485–99.

1 i. 76.

2 *Origin*, 154–8.

3 J. E. A. Jolliffe, *Pre-Feudal England, the Jutes*, 71. Cf. below note 14; also Chadwick, *Institutions*, 167, 347; Brünner, ii. 14 n.

4 *Laws of Wihtred*, c. 21; *Ethelbert*, c. 25. Here and in other quotations from the Laws, I generally follow, with permission, the translation of Mr. F. L. Attenborough, *The Laws of the Earliest English Kings* (Cambridge University Press, 1922).

4a J. E. A. Jolliffe in *E.H.R.* xli (1926), 1–42; id., *Pre-Feudal England, The Jutes* (1933). C. S. and C. S. Orwin, *The Open Fields* (1938), 1–48, approach the subject from the standpoint of the practical agriculturist.

5 Chadwick, *Origin*, 78; *Institutions*, 105–14 and 156.

6 c. 51.   7 c. 42.

8 For short summaries about the *Beowulf* see W. Lawrence, *Beowulf and Epic Tradition* (1928); R. Girvan, *Beowulf and the Seventh Century* (1935); J. R. R. Tolkien, 'Beowulf, the Monsters and the Critics', in *P.B.A.* xxii (1936), 245–96. For fuller treatment of the controversies surrounding the poem see R. W. Chambers, *Beowulf* (2nd edition, 1932), with bibliography to 1930, on 538 ff.; subsequent bibliographies annually in *The Year's Work in English Studies*.

9 Chadwick, *Origin*, 157.   10 Chadwick, *Institutions*, 288.

10a A similar impression is derived from the Sutton Hoo ship-burial, which illustrates the great gap in material culture between court circles and all other classes of the population.   11 Oman, pp. 357–8.

12 See Liebermann, ii. 424–30, for references; also Brünner, i. 186–95; A. G. Little, in *E.H.R.* iv (1889), 23–9; M. Larsen, *The King's Household* (1904), 76–88; Beck, in *E.H.R.* xxvi (1911), 555.

13 Chadwick, *Origin*, 160.

14 *Kindred and Clan* (1913), esp. cc. 7 and 8; cf. Pollock and Maitland, ii. 240 ff.; Chadwick, *H.A.* c. xvi. For the Germanic views of the nineteenth century see Kemble, i, c. ii; Stubbs, *C.H.* i. 87 f. See also P. Vinogradoff, *G. of M.* 135–40, 241–2; Seebohm, *T.C.* esp. cc. 3 and 15; Liebermann, ii,

s.v. 'Sippe'; Brünner, i (1906), 110 ff. J. E. A. Jolliffe in *Constitutional History* (1937) emphasizes—in my opinion over-emphasizes—the part played by ideas of kinship in the formation of the early English nations. He even speaks (p. 4) of 'the common maegth of the Mercians or Kentings'. See also his 'Era of the Folk', in *Oxford Essays in Medieval History presented to H. E. Salter* (1934), 2 ff. J. Goebel, in *Felony and Misdemeanour*, i (1937), 399 ff., discusses 'Anglo-Saxon private jurisdiction'. Though he deals chiefly with the later Anglo-Saxon period, his views about the strong powers of the early monarchies are a useful corrective to those of Jolliffe. Cf. also F. E. Harmer, *Anglo-Saxon Charters and the Historian* (1938), 30–1.

¹⁴ᵃ Something should have been said in this chapter about the differences between the institutions of the chief kingdoms. This subject is well brought out by J. E. A. Jolliffe in *Constitutional History*, 32–41.

¹⁵ Mawer, *Problems*, 115–16.   ¹⁶ See *E.P.N.S.* i, Part ii (1924); G. B. Grundy, *Saxon Charters of Worcestershire* (1931), iii–viii.

¹⁷ *Archaeologia*, lxxiii (1923), 147; lxxvi (1926); 59–80; *Early A.S. Art and Archaeology* (1936), 21–8. For other house-sites cf. Kendrick and Hawkes, 323–4; T. C. Lethbridge and C. F. Tebbutt, in *Proc. Cambridge Ant. Soc.* xxxiii (1933), 133–51; *V.C.H. Cambridgeshire*, i. (1938), 299–300.

¹⁸ *Ant. Journ.* vii (1927), 141; Lethbridge, 84.   ¹⁹ So Lethbridge, 84.
²⁰ Id. 80. For English dress in the heathen period see B.B. iii. 372 ff. Cf. also Hoops, iii. 58–64; iv. 345–6.

²⁰ᵃ For changes of fashion in the later heathen and early Christian periods see E. T. Leeds, *Art and Archaeology*, 79–114; T. C. Lethbridge *V.C.H. Cambs.* 318–20; id., *A Cemetery at Shudy Camps, Cambs.* (1936), esp. 27–9.

²¹ *V.C.H. Bucks.* i. 199–204; *B.M. Guide*, 63–5; Åberg, 10–11; E. T. Leeds, *A.S. Art and Archaeology*, 59–78. Also Lindqvist, 130–3, and T. D. Kendrick in *Antiquity*, vii (1933), 437; in *I.P.E.K.* (*Jahrbuch für prähistorische und ethnographische Kunst*), ix (1934), 66–76; in *Ant. Journ.* xvii (1937) 283–93; *A.S. Art* (1938), 75 ff.—these last pointing to an early date in the sixth century.

²² E. T. Leeds, in *Ant. Journ.* iv (1924), 113–25.

²²ᵃ For the greater material wealth of pagan Saxon courts see, however, Appendix, p. 696 *et seq*, on the Sutton Hoo burial, esp. p. 727.

²²ᵇ For illustrations of the Kingston Brooch see R. F. Jessup, *Anglo-Saxon Jewellery*; T. D. Kendrick, *Anglo-Saxon Art*; and 'Polychrome Jewellery in Kent', *Antiquity*, vii (1933). This brooch is amongst the finest specimens of Germanic jewellery known.   ²³ B.B. iv. 517.   ²⁴ *Boethius*, 40.

²⁵ 'The foe' may be the ox. Tupper, *Riddles of Exeter Book*, 115; Gordon, 327.

²⁶ Grein-Wülker, i. 338–52; Gordon, 341–7. Here and in other quotations from OE. poetry, I generally follow, with permission, the translation of R. K. Gordon, *Anglo-Saxon Poetry* (Everyman's Library, Messrs. J. M. Dent & Sons).

27 Wihtred, c. 28; Ine, c. 20.

28 A. J. Wyatt and R. W. Chambers, *Beowulf*, 158–9.

29 On Anglo-Saxon heathenism, see A. E. Philippson, *Germanisches Heiden-tum bei den Angelsachsen* (1929), with bibliography; J. de Vries, *Altgermanische Religionsgeschichte* (1935), i. 244–50. The English reader may be recommended P. D. C. de la Saussaye, *The Religion of the Teutons* (1902); E. K. Chambers, *The Medieval Stage* (1903), cc. v and xi; Chadwick, *Origin*, cc. x and xi; and the older classics, Kemble, c. xii, and J. Grimm, *Teutonic Mythology*, 4 vols., ed. J. E. Stallybrass (1880–8); Bruce Dickins, 'English Names and Old English Heathenism', in *Essays and Studies*, xix (1933), 148–60. Interesting evidence that the worship of Tig, the oldest of the great gods, was carried to the western midlands is found in the place-name Tysoe (i.e. the hill, *hoh*, of *Tig*, genitive Tiwes) in Warwickshire. 'At Tysoe was a cut figure of a horse after which the Vale of the Red Horse was named.' Cf. E. Ekwall, *Oxford Dictionary of E.P.N.* 462; *E.P.N.S.* xiii (1926), xviii, and 284.

30 Mawer, *Problems*, 59–61.

31 *Opera* (ed. Giles), vi. 139–342, c. 14.

32 Quoted from Chadwick, *Origin*, c. 11, where the subject is fully discussed. See also R. W. Chambers, *Beowulf* (1932), 68–86, 314–22.

VIII. PART I. THE CONVERSION, TO 633

1 For general bibliographies of Celtic Christianity see *C.M.H.* ii. 791–2; Gougaud, xviii–lv; Kenney, i, *passim*.

2 *Vita S. Samsoni*, c. 7.

3 Rhygyfarch's 'Vita Davidis', in *Y Cymmrodor*, xxiv (1913), §§ 22 f., trans. by A. W. Wade-Evans, *Life of St. David*, 15; J. Vendryes in *Rev. Celt.* xlv (1928), 140–4.

5 H. C. Lawlor, *Monastery of St. Mochaoi* (1925). Cf. the Celtic monastery at Tintagel, Cornwall, revealed by excavations reported by C. A. R. Radford in *Ant. Journ.* xv (1935), 401–19.

6 See preface of J. T. Fowler in his *Adamnani, Vita S. Columbae* (1920).

7 See reasons for identifying this book with that in the Museum at Dublin in *P.R.I.A.* xxxiii. 241–436.

8 Adamnan, *Secunda Praefatio*.

9 Ibid. i, c. 3.

10 Ibid. ii, c. 22.

11 *Irish Liber Hymnorum*, ed. J. H. Bernard and R. Atkinson, ii. 49–51 and 208–12. Translation by N. J. D. White in his *St. Patrick* (1929), 61–71; L. Gougaud in *Bulletin d'ancienne littérature et d'archéologie chrétiennes*, i. 271–2; ii. 38–41, 101–7; Kenney, 272–4.

11a P. Grosjean, in *Analecta Bollandiana*, liv (1936), 200, suggests that the real turning-point in the history of Latin Christianity was the missions of Palladius and Patrick c. 430. Patrick made a conquest beyond the frontiers of the Roman Empire.

¹² *Life of Gregory* by a Monk of Whitby, extract in Plummer, *Bede*, ii. 390. Emendation of P. Ewald in *Historische Aufsätze . . . G. Waitz gewidmet*, 48.

¹³ It is still reasonable to follow Bede rather than Gregory of Tours in the chronology of Ethelbert's reign. For other views see G. H. Wheeler, in *E.H.R.* xli (1926), 501–2, and H. H. Howorth, *Augustine the Missionary*, 39–40.

¹⁴ Note on the maps showing Supremacies. It will be convenient to notice here some unsatisfactory features of the map on p. 261 and of similar maps on later pages. To illustrate the element of guesswork in these maps, it should be understood that the only reasons for showing the territory of the Hwicce as part of the *imperium* of Ethelbert are the inferences that Ethelbert's safe-conduct protected Augustine when he travelled west to confer with the Welsh, in Wessex, and that the Hwicce were a dependency of Wessex.

Bede's patriotism or his admiration for the first Christian kings of Northumbria leads him into some exaggeration when he speaks of the empires of Edwin and Oswald. In Book ii, c. 5, he says that Edwin had 'the overlordship over all the peoples who inhabit Britain, alike English and British, except only the people of Kent'. If this is taken literally it means that all the princes of Wales and the other Celtic princes from Cornwall to the Clyde bowed to him—a claim which can scarcely have corresponded to the facts. His statements about Oswald are less clear and less probable. He says that Oswald was the sixth who held *imperium*—'et ipse Nordanhymbrorum rex Christianissimus hisdem finibus regnum tenuit'. Since, as Plummer rightly points out (ii. 86), Bede carefully distinguishes between *regnum* and *imperium*, this passage tells us nothing about Oswald's *imperium*. But in Book iii, c. 6, Bede says of Oswald 'Denique omnes nationes et provincias Brittaniae, quae in iv linguas, id est Brettonum, Pictorum, Scottorum, et Anglorum, divisae sunt, in dicione accepit'. This statement accords ill with what little we know of Wulfhere's power in the Midlands and of the power of the Welsh princes both before and after Oswald. It also seems at variance with the statement in Book ii, c. 5, which implies that Oswy was the first to reduce the Picts and Scots and make them tributary. However, some support for Bede comes from Adamnan, who says (i, c. 1), 'Postea totius Britanniae imperator a deo ordinatus est'.

Again, Bede's information is incomplete. For instance, he makes no mention of the kings of the Lindisware (i.e. of Lindsey). I have, with some hesitation, followed F. M. Stenton's view in *Essays in History presented to R. L. Poole* (1927), 136–50, that the list of these kings preserved by 'Florence' of Worcester indicates that Lindsey was, till the extinction of its monarchy in the eighth century, probably part of the *imperium* and not of the *regnum* of one or other of its two neighbours.

The existence of a local dynasty is a good but not a sufficient test for distinguishing *imperium* from *regnum*. Thus there were kings in Kent and Essex throughout the reign of Offa; but the Kentish charters of the period and the inscriptions on the coins suggest that the effective power in Kent was exercised by Offa himself; and if this was true of Kent, it was also in all probability true of Essex and of the other south-eastern kingdoms. When a king delegated power in a sub-kingdom to a son or near kinsman (e.g. Penda to Peada or Egbert to Ethelwulf) I have generally assumed that the effective authority remained with the overlord.

In most Anglo-Saxon institutions there was little that was well defined, and one may therefore infer that there was also an absence of logical distinction between *regnum* and *imperium*.

Names of lesser principalities (e.g. of the Gyrwe in the Fen district), and especially those in Wales, are omitted from the maps so as not to crowd them.

The political conditions existing in the west of the island from the Mersey to the Clyde are especially obscure.

To conclude, though my maps correct those of Green in many particulars, I cannot pretend that they are satisfactory. Here as elsewhere it is better to make mistakes than to leave complete blanks.

[15] Bede, i, c. 23. Cf. A. S. Cook, 'Augustine's journey from Rome to Richborough', in *Speculum*, i (1926), 375–97.

[16] Bede, i, c. 25.

[17] *Greg. Ep.* ii. 304.

[18] Ibid. i. 431.

[19] *Bon., Ep.* 3, 271–2; Kylie, 52–4.

[20] Bede, i, c. 27.

[21] Cf. vol. ii. 427–9.

[22] Bede, i, c. 30.

[23] Id. ii, c. 20.

[24] The date of Augustine's death may be 605. Cf. Plummer, *Bede*, ii. 81.

[25] Bede, ii, c. 5.

[26] *Laws of Ethelbert*, cc. 21, 27, 54.

[27] See Sir C. R. Peers in *Antiquity*, iii (1929), 65–74, and in *Arch.* lxxvii (1927), 201–17; B.B. ii, 2nd ed. (1925), c. 4; Clapham, 16 ff., 85–6.

[28] Bede, i, c. 33.

[29] Clapham, 33.

[30] Watson, 340–1.

[31] Bede, ii, c. 16.

[32] Id.

[33] Id. iii, c. 1.

[34] J. B. Lightfoot, *Leaders in the Northern Church* (1890), 11.

[35] Cf. Bede, *Hist. Abb.*, c. 3, in Plummer, i. 366.

VIII. PART II. THE CONVERSION (*contd.*)

1 Bede, iii, c. 24.

1a Mr. J. W. Walker, Secretary of the Yorkshire Archaeological Society, has pointed out to me that there is now no river Winwaed, but a Win moor, five miles NE. of Leeds, a boggy place with a small beck.

2 Or perhaps the lower Trent. It is doubtful whether Lindsey passed to Mercia in 658 or later. *V.C.H. Lincoln,* ii. 247.

3 Eddius, c. 20.

4 Bede, iv, c. 21.

5 So Adamnan (i, c. 1). Bede says 'with a large band'.

6 Bede, iii, c. i, implies that the battle was fought and Cadwallon killed at Denisesburna. The burn later known by that name, some three miles south of Hexham, is strangely far from the traditional site of Heavenfield.

7 Id. iii, c. 5.

8 Id. iii, c. 3.

9 Id. iii, c. 21.

10 Id. iii, c. 7.

11 Id. iii, c. 22.

12 The complicated points at issue are well summarized in Plummer, *Bede,* ii. 348–52; and in Gougaud, 185–201.

13 Bede, iii, c. 23.

14 For the Conference of 664 see Bede, iii, cc. 25 and 26; and Eddius, c. 10.

15 Authorities differ on this point. For a summary see L. Gougaud, 201–6.

16 Bede, iv, c. 4.

IX. THE GOLDEN AGE

1 Bede, ii, c. 1.

2 Eddius, c. 15. For different views about the positions of Chad and of Wilfrid see G. F. Browne, *Theodore and Wilfrid,* 34–50, 94–9; R. L. Poole in *E.H.R.* xxxiv (1929), 8–10; J. L. G. Meissner, *The Celtic Church in England* (1929), c. ii. The reasons why it is impossible now to discover the rights and wrongs of the situation are (1) that Bede and Eddius do not agree, and while Bede was the more truthful, Eddius, having long been in close contact with Wilfrid, may have been more fully informed; and (2) that there was, no doubt, genuine confusion at the time, owing partly to quarrels between Oswy and his under-king Alchfrith, the special patron of Wilfrid, and partly to the fact that the Northumbrians as yet were more accustomed to Celtic than Roman ideas of episcopacy. Oswy, in having Chad consecrated bishop as well as Wilfrid, probably did not realize that according to Roman ideas each should have a clearly defined diocese.

3 Bede, iv, c. 2.

[4] The date is usually given as 673. For its correction see R. L. Poole in *J.T.S.* xx (1918), 22.

[5] Usually given as 680. Ibid. 33.

[6] I, c. xii in *H. and S.* iii. 173–203. For bibliography on the Penitentials see Kenney, i. 228–9, 239. Note also P. Fournier and G. le Bras, *Hist. des collections canoniques en occident* (1931), 50–65.

[7] See Chadwick, *Institutions*, 282–90.

[8] J. A. Robinson, *Somersetshire Essays*, 28–9.

[9] Ibid. 35.

[10] Ibid. 30; cf. *E.P.N.S.* viii. xvi.

[10a] The grave of a Saxon warrior of the seventh century, buried in the heathen fashion with his knife and scramasax, was found by Dr. R. E. M. Wheeler in excavating Maiden Castle, near Dorchester, Dorset. Mr. T. Dagren-Reed writes to me as follows: 'The idea that Dorset was settled late from the north-east does not square with the evidence. This points to early settlement by small groups, arriving early, and working inland up the estuaries of the Stour, Piddle, and Frome.'

[11] *Crawford Charters*, pp. 1 and 44; W. Levison, *Vitae Sancti Bonifatii* (1905), xxix.

[12] *E.P.N.S.* viii. xix–xx.

[13] Chadwick, *Institutions*, 286.

[14] Ine's Laws, cc. 63–8.

[15] cc. 23, 24, 32, 54.

[16] Bede, v, c. 7.

[17] Some of these statements rest on post-Conquest biographies and have been questioned. For the life and works of Aldhelm see bibliography in Schubert, 280–1; and Manitius, i. 134–42. The best Life in English is G. F. Browne's *St. Aldhelm* (1903).

[18] C. Singer, *From Magic to Science* (1928), 123 and 115. See also L. Gougaud in *Bulletin d'ancienne littérature et d'archéologie chrétiennes*, i. 268. The true reading of the author's name in the oldest manuscript is Laidcend, not Loding.

[19] References in Manitius, i. 119–26.

[20] Ehwald, 488. Cf. Kenney, i. 227.

[21] Ehwald, 492; trans. of G. F. Browne, in *St. Aldhelm*, 263.

[22] Bede, v, c. 18.

[23] For bibliographies see Manitius, i. 142–52; Schubert, 281. The English reader will find a good biography in G. F. Browne's *Boniface of Crediton and his Companions* (1910).

[24] Ep. 98; translation of E. Kylie, *The English Correspondence of St. Boniface*, 99–100.

[25] Ep. 67; Kylie, 149–50.

[26] Ep. 29; Kylie, 110–11.

[27] E. Bishop, in *Transactions of the Devonshire Association for the Advancement of Science, Literature, and Art*, viii (1876), 512.

[28] *Vita Willibaldi*, in T. Tobler, *Descriptiones Terrae Sanctae ex saeculo VIII*, &c., p. 76; C. R. Beazley, *Dawn of Modern Geography*, i. 140–57.

[28a] An article on 'St. Frideswide and her Times', by F. M. Stenton, in *Oxoniensia*, i (1936), 103–12, throws light on political and ecclesiastical conditions in the region of the middle Thames in the seventh and eighth centuries.

[29] E. Dümmler in *Ep. Bon.* 238, note 2; Manitius, i. 141; R. Ehwald, *M.G.H. Auct. Antiq.* xv. (1919), 522. Cf. L. Traube, *Carolingische Dichtungen* (1888), 132; H. Bradley in *E.H.R.* xv (1900), 291–2.

[30] See *Vita S. Guthlaci*, by Felix (composed 716–49), edited together with the early OE. rendering in P. Gonser's *Das angelsächsische Prosa-Leben des Hl. Guthlac* (1909). Earlier editions by C. W. Goodwin (1848) and W. de G. Birch (1881).

[31] A versified version of the *Life* (Grein-Wülker, iii. 98 ff.) makes the young Guthlac a mere plunder-seeking outlaw.

[32] Bede, iv, c. 27.

[33] *Auct. Anon.* § 18.

[34] J. L. G. Meissner, *The Celtic Church in England* (1929), c. x, argues that 'Lindisfarne remained outside the Northumbrian Church and under Celtic discipline' till 721. Cf. J. A. Duke, *The Columban Church* (1932), 103–5.

[35] Plummer, *Bede*, i. xxx.

[36] Eddius, c. 24.

[37] With his see either at Ripon or at York. Cf. R. L. Poole in *E.H.R.* xxxiv (1919), 13–16, and J. L. G. Meissner, *The Celtic Church in England*, 70–5.

[38] Eddius, c. 21.

[39] Id., c. 17.

[40] Id., c. 63.

[41] Bede, *Hist. Abb.*, § 1, in Plummer, i. 365.

[42] Ibid., § 6, in Plummer, i. 369.

[43] Ibid., § 11, in Plummer, i. 375.

[44] Plummer, *Bede*, i. 396–8.

[45] For the Life and Works of Bede see Plummer's excellent introduction *passim*; also, *Bede, His Life, Times and Writings*, ed. by A. Hamilton Thompson (1935); esp. pp. 111–51, an essay on 'Bede as Historian', by W. Levison; R. W. Chambers, in *P.B.A.* xxii (1936), 129–56. Bibliographies in Kenney, i. 230; Hoops, i. 189; Manitius, i. 70–87.

[46] Edited by T. Mommsen in *M.G.H. Chronica Minora*, iii. 247.

[47] Quoted by R. L. Poole in *E.H.R.* xxxiv. 2.

[48] Bede (ii, c. 2) speaks of the Britons as *gens perfida*. Cf. Faral, i. 513.

[49] Quoted from Wattenbach by C. J. B. Gaskoin, *Alcuin* (1904), p. 32.

⁴⁹ᵃ On Reculver see, in addition to the works mentioned in the notes on p. 356, R. F. Jessup, in *Antiquity*, x (1936), 179–93; T. D. Kendrick, *A.S. Art*, 115–18. Kendrick thinks it possible that the cross may have been produced as early as the time of St. Augustine.

⁵⁰ Sir C. Peers in *Ant. Journ.* x (1930), 24–9.

⁵¹ B.B. ii. 105; Howorth, *G.D.* ii. 187–96. Cf. Clapham, i. 32–5.

⁵² B.B. ii. 128–32; Clapham, i. 38. Sir C. Peers, in *Bede, His Life, etc.*, ed. by A. H. Thompson, 106 ff.

⁵³ B.B. v, cc. 15, 16. See refs. there given to those who hold different views; also Bronsted, 92–3; F. Henry, *La Sculpture irlandaise*, i (1933), 62 ff.

⁵⁴ A. W. Clapham in *Antiquity*, viii (1934), 43–57. Cf. T. D. Kendrick, *A.S. Art*, 97–106—opposing the view that Lindisfarne art anticipated Irish.

⁵⁵ B.B. v. 375–6.

⁵⁶ e.g. R. H. S. Macalister, *Archaeology of Ireland*. Cf. F. Henry, *La Sculpture irlandaise* (1933), *passim*.

⁵⁷ References to the literature on the subject will be found in B.B. v, cc. 1–12; W. G. Collingwood, *Northern Crosses of the Pre-Norman Age* (1927); see also Bronsted, 16–86; Sir C. Peers in *P.B.A.* xii and in *Arch.* lxxiv (1923), 253–70; Clapham, i, c. 3; R. G. Collingwood on 'The Bewcastle Cross' in *Trans. of Cumberland and Westmorland Arch. Soc.* xxxv (1935), 3–19; E. Kitzinger on 'Anglo-Saxon Vinescroll Ornament' in *Antiquity*, x (1936), 61–71; T. D. Kendrick, *A.S. Art*, 115–16 and cc. vii–xiii.

⁵⁷ᵃ T. D. Kendrick, op. cit. 126–34, thinks that the Ruthwell Cross is earlier and more Romanesque than that at Bewcastle. This last he dates *c.* 700 on stylistic grounds.

⁵⁸ Clapham, i. 61–9. Cf. W. G. Collingwood in *Antiquity*, vi (1932), 35–54. T. D. Kendrick, in a review of this book (in *Ant. Journ.* xv (1935), 485), pointed out that the renaissance of art represented by the crosses should have been more emphasized. 'They are an incomparable achievement and we must not have it counted as a little thing that the Anglo-Saxons anticipated in time the continental Carolingian renaissance, and, alone in western Europe, at this early date, avowed themselves the inheritors of the antique classical tradition, and by reanimating it became the harbingers of the future Romanesque style. The point surely is the precocious medieval quality of the Golden Age sculptures.'

⁵⁹ Following mainly the translation in B.B. v. 219–20.